"working through the negativity"

Serenity rose

the personal journals
of a local witch

..as told to aaron a.

VOLUME ONE:

"working through
the negativity"

COLLECTING
ISSUES 1–5 OF
THE SLG SERIES
"SERENITY
ROSE"

PUBLISHED BY SLG PUBLISHING

PRESIDENT AND PUBLISHER
DAN VADO

SLG PUBLISHING
P. O. BOX 26427
SAN JOSE, CA 95159

ISBN: 1-593620-11-X

INTRODUCTION BY
SERENITY ELIZABETH ROSE,
LOCAL WITCH.

WELL, IT'S A BIT **DENSE**, ISN'T IT?

AND THE WORD BALLOONS ARE **WAY** TOO SMALL. TOO MUCH STUFF IN THERE. THE LINEWORK GETS SORT OF (VERY) MUDDY IN PLACES, ESPECIALLY TOWARD THE BEGINNING (NICE WORK WITH THAT MECHANICAL PENCIL, BUD). THE STORYLINE IS KIND OF, WELL... HAPHAZARD. BIG IDEAS ARE BROUGHT UP AND FORGOTTEN, IMPORTANT INFORMATION IS LEFT UNSTATED, AND MAJOR CHARACTERS BEHAVE INCONSISTENTLY OR WITH ILL-DEFINED MOTIVATION. THE PACING IS LUGUBRIOUS, THE TONE IS INORDINATELY PISSY, AND I APPEAR TO BE WEARING SHORT PANTS THROUGHOUT THE MAJORITY OF ISSUE THREE. WORST OF ALL, IT'S A... (WAIT FOR IT...) **GOTH COMIC**. (HOO BOY).

BUT STILL...

I MET AARON A. ABOUT FOUR YEARS AGO, BACK WHEN HE WAS STILL A "DEAD-EYED PEON" FOR THE TV ANIMATION INDUSTRY. SEEMED NICE ENOUGH (KEEPS QUIET, WEARS GLASSES). HE TOLD ME HE HAD THIS "BURNING NEED" TO TELL MY LIFE STORY IN COMIC BOOK FORM, THIS DESPITE HAVING NEVER, Y'KNOW, ACTUALLY **MADE** A COMIC BOOK IN HIS LIFE.

SAYS HE: "I JUST WANT TO MAKE SOMETHING THAT FEELS LIKE **LIFE**, Y'KNOW? SOMETHING TOTALLY CHARACTER BASED, PLOTLESS, THAT FOLLOWS ALL THE MEANDERING LITTLE LEFT TURNS AND DEAD ENDS OF A PERSON'S **REAL** LIFE. NO FILTERING. BUT NOT JUST **ANY** PERSON; A **REMARKABLE** PERSON. IT'S LIKE... PEOPLE ARE ALWAYS TALKING ABOUT 'EVERYDAY PEOPLE IN EXTRAORDINARY CIRCUMSTANCES,' RIGHT, BUT ME, I'M MORE INTERESTED IN 'EXTRAORDINARY PEOPLE IN EVERYDAY CIRCUMSTANCES'. CALL ME A REBEL."

WHATEVER YOU SAY, PAL. I GAVE THE GUY LIKE EIGHT PAGES FROM MY JOURNAL AND BID HIM "GOOD LUCK," FIGURING I'D NEVER SEE HIM AGAIN.

FOUR YEARS LATER HERE WE ARE.

LOOK: THIS WHOLE THING IS KINDA WEIRD. I'M NOT REALLY SURE WHAT I'M DOING HERE, TO BE HONEST. I MEAN, WHY DO BOOKS LIKE THIS EVEN HAVE "INTRODUCTIONS," ANYWAY? I GUESS IT'S SOME KIND OF MARKETING THING, RIGHT, BUT SERIOUSLY, WHAT KIND OF SLACK-JAWED MOUTH BREATHER BUYS A COMIC BOOK BECAUSE OF THE INTRODUCTION? "HMMM... THIS BOOK DOESN'T **LOOK** LIKE SOMETHING I'D NORMALLY READ, BUT... BOY HOWDY, YOU JUST CAN'T ARGUE WITH A SWEET-ASS PATRICK STEWART INTRODUCTION."

"THAT GUY WAS PICARD."

BUT I DIGRESS.

THE POINT IS, A LOT OF PEOPLE LIKED THIS STORY, SO MAYBE YOU WILL, TOO. I REMEMBER QUENTIN TARANTINO SAYING ONCE, ON SOME COMMENTARY TRACK SOMEWHERE, THAT IF YOU'RE NOT AT LEAST A LITTLE BIT EMBARRASSED BY YOUR ART, THEN YOU HAVEN'T DONE IT RIGHT.

WELL, THERE'S PLENTY TO BE EMBARRASSED ABOUT HERE, SO I GUESS IT MUST BE PRETTY GOOD.

SERENITY ROSE
CRESTFALLEN, 2005

...ISSUE ONE

Serenity Rose

the personal journals
of a local witch

..as told to aaron a.
with assists by rikki s.

issue number one:

"warts and all"

here is a drawing
of a happy flower →

hi there!

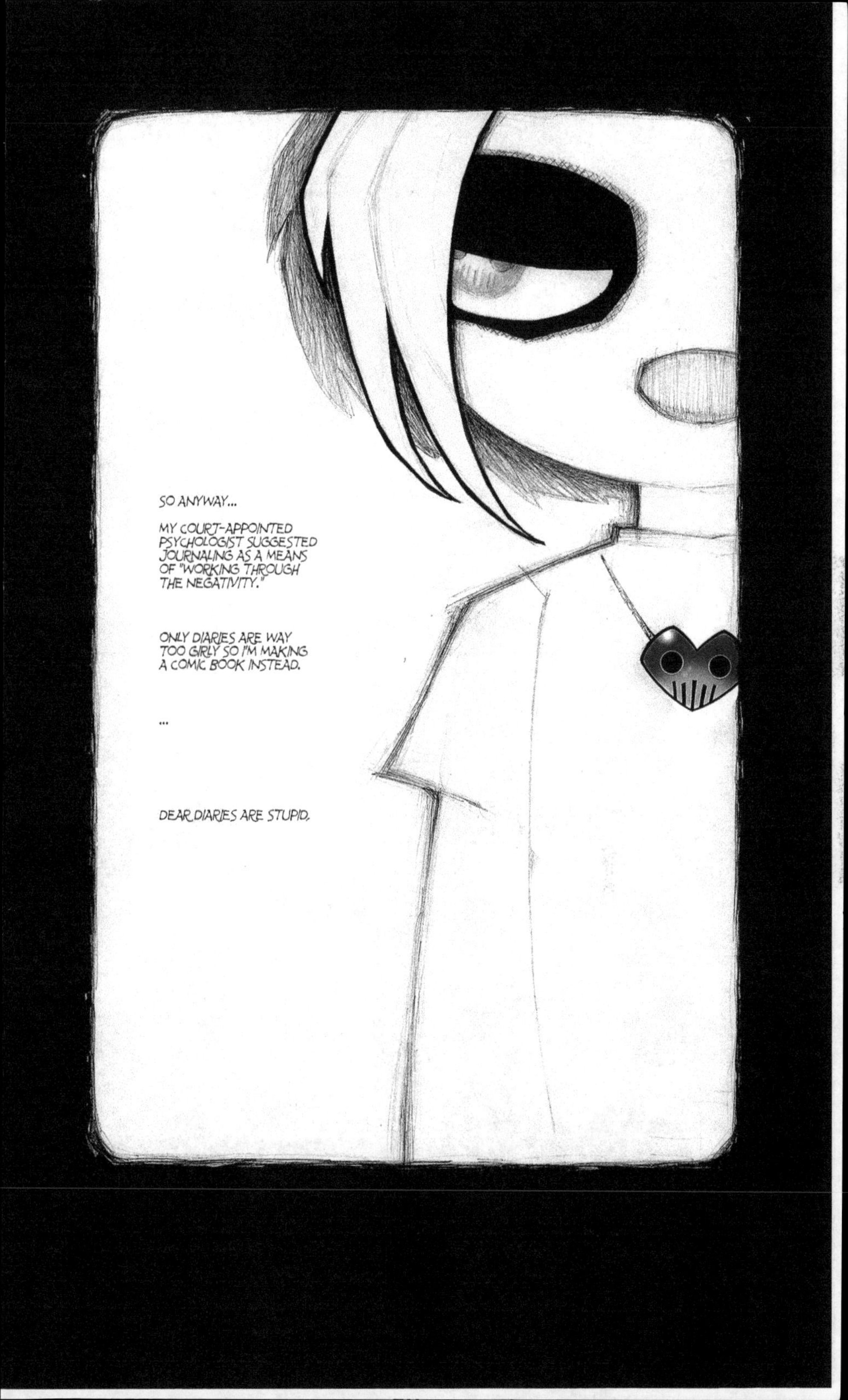
SO ANYWAY...
MY COURT-APPOINTED PSYCHOLOGIST SUGGESTED JOURNALING AS A MEANS OF "WORKING THROUGH THE NEGATIVITY."
ONLY DIARIES ARE WAY TOO GIRLY SO I'M MAKING A COMIC BOOK INSTEAD.
...
DEAR DIARIES ARE STUPID.

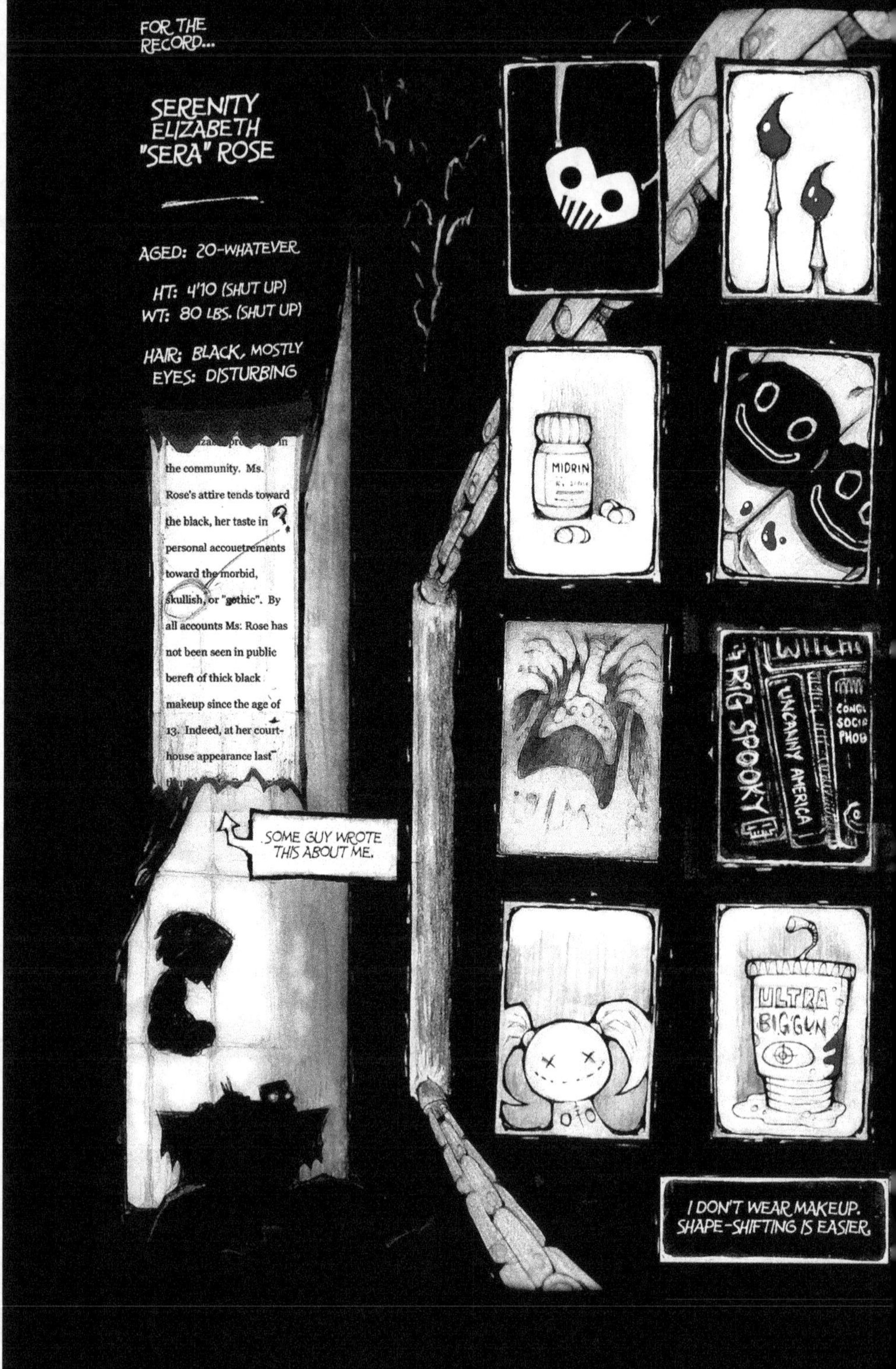
FOR THE RECORD...
SERENITY ELIZABETH "SERA" ROSE
AGED: 20-WHATEVER
HT: 4'10 (SHUT UP)
WT: 80 LBS. (SHUT UP)
HAIR: BLACK, MOSTLY
EYES: DISTURBING
the community. Ms. Rose's attire tends toward the black, her taste in personal accouetrements toward the morbid, skullish, or "gothic". By all accounts Ms: Rose has not been seen in public bereft of thick black makeup since the age of 13. Indeed, at her court-house appearance last
SOME GUY WROTE THIS ABOUT ME.
MIDRIN
BIG SPOOKY
UNCANNY AMERICA
ULTRA BIG'GUN
I DON'T WEAR MAKEUP. SHAPE-SHIFTING IS EASIER.

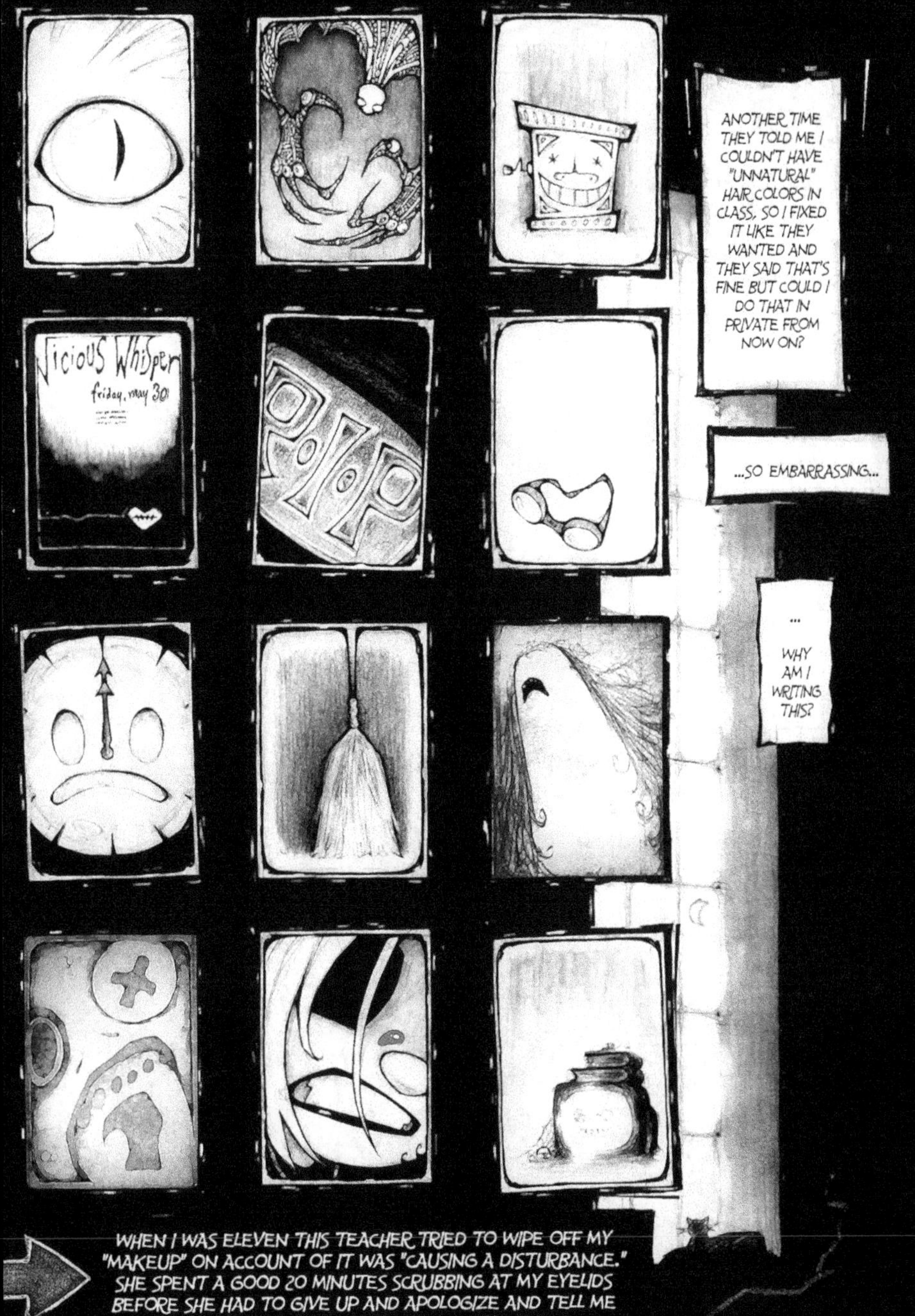

ANOTHER TIME THEY TOLD ME I COULDN'T HAVE "UNNATURAL" HAIR COLORS IN CLASS, SO I FIXED IT LIKE THEY WANTED AND THEY SAID THAT'S FINE BUT COULD I DO THAT IN PRIVATE FROM NOW ON?
...SO EMBARRASSING...
...
WHY AM I WRITING THIS?
Vicious Whisper
friday, may 30!
WHEN I WAS ELEVEN THIS TEACHER TRIED TO WIPE OFF MY "MAKEUP" ON ACCOUNT OF IT WAS "CAUSING A DISTURBANCE." SHE SPENT A GOOD 20 MINUTES SCRUBBING AT MY EYELIDS BEFORE SHE HAD TO GIVE UP AND APOLOGIZE AND TELL ME NOT TO TELL ANYONE ABOUT THE WHOLE THING.

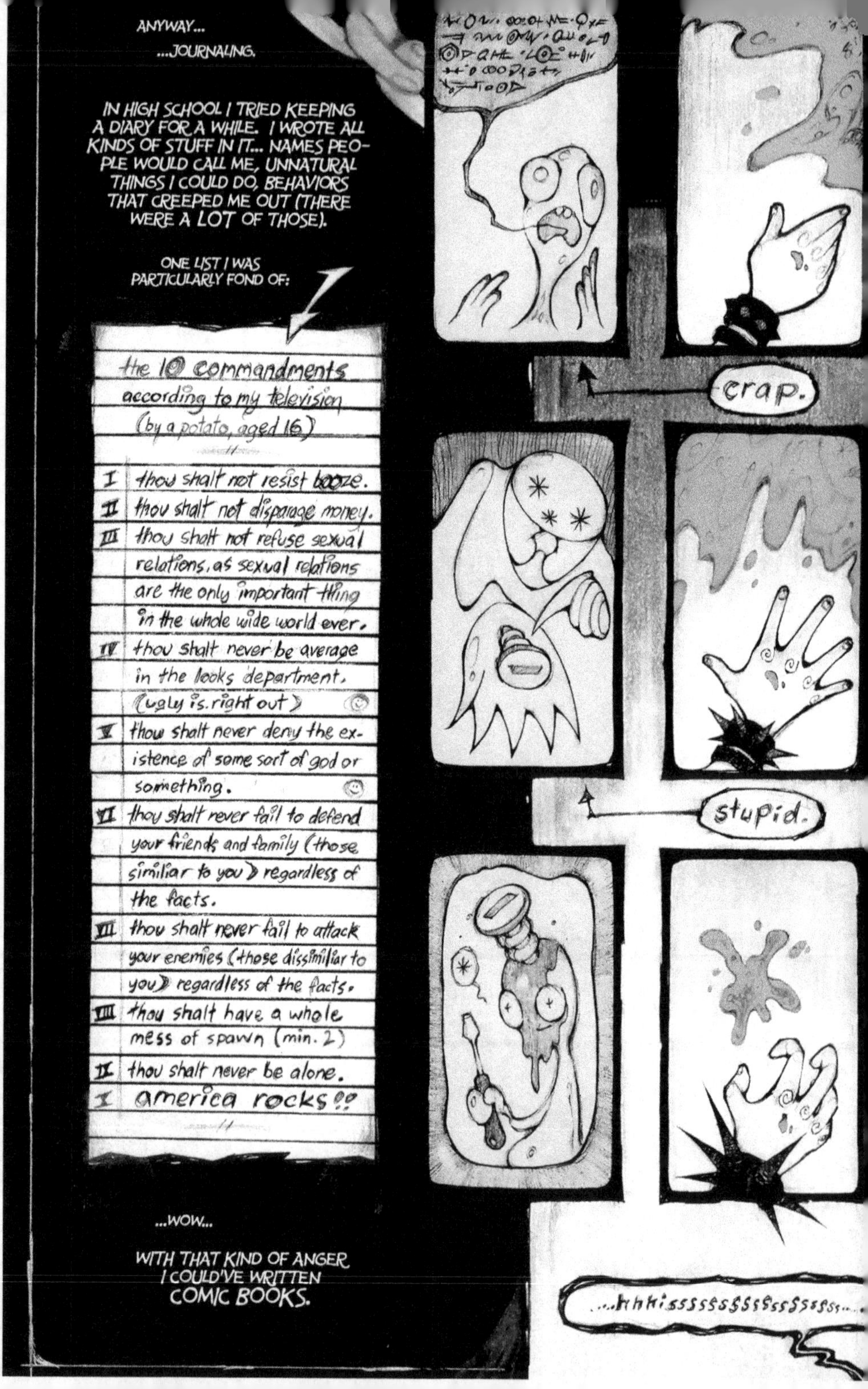

ANYWAY...

...JOURNALING.

IN HIGH SCHOOL I TRIED KEEPING A DIARY FOR A WHILE. I WROTE ALL KINDS OF STUFF IN IT... NAMES PEOPLE WOULD CALL ME, UNNATURAL THINGS I COULD DO, BEHAVIORS THAT CREEPED ME OUT (THERE WERE A LOT OF THOSE).

ONE LIST I WAS PARTICULARLY FOND OF:

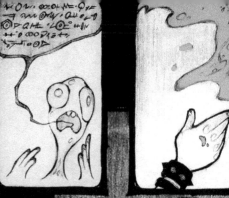

crap.

the 10 commandments according to my television (by a potato, aged 16)

I   thou shalt not resist booze.

II thou shalt not disparage money.

III thou shalt not refuse sexual relations, as sexual relations are the only important thing in the whole wide world ever.

IV thou shalt never be average in the looks department. (ugly is right out)

V   thou shalt never deny the existence of some sort of god or something.

VI thou shalt never fail to defend your friends and family (those similiar to you) regardless of the facts.

VII thou shalt never fail to attack your enemies (those dissimiliar to you) regardless of the facts.

VIII thou shalt have a whole mess of spawn (min. 2)

IX thou shalt never be alone.

X   america rocks!!

stupid.

...WOW...

WITH THAT KIND OF ANGER, I COULD'VE WRITTEN COMIC BOOKS.

...hhkissssssssssssssssss...

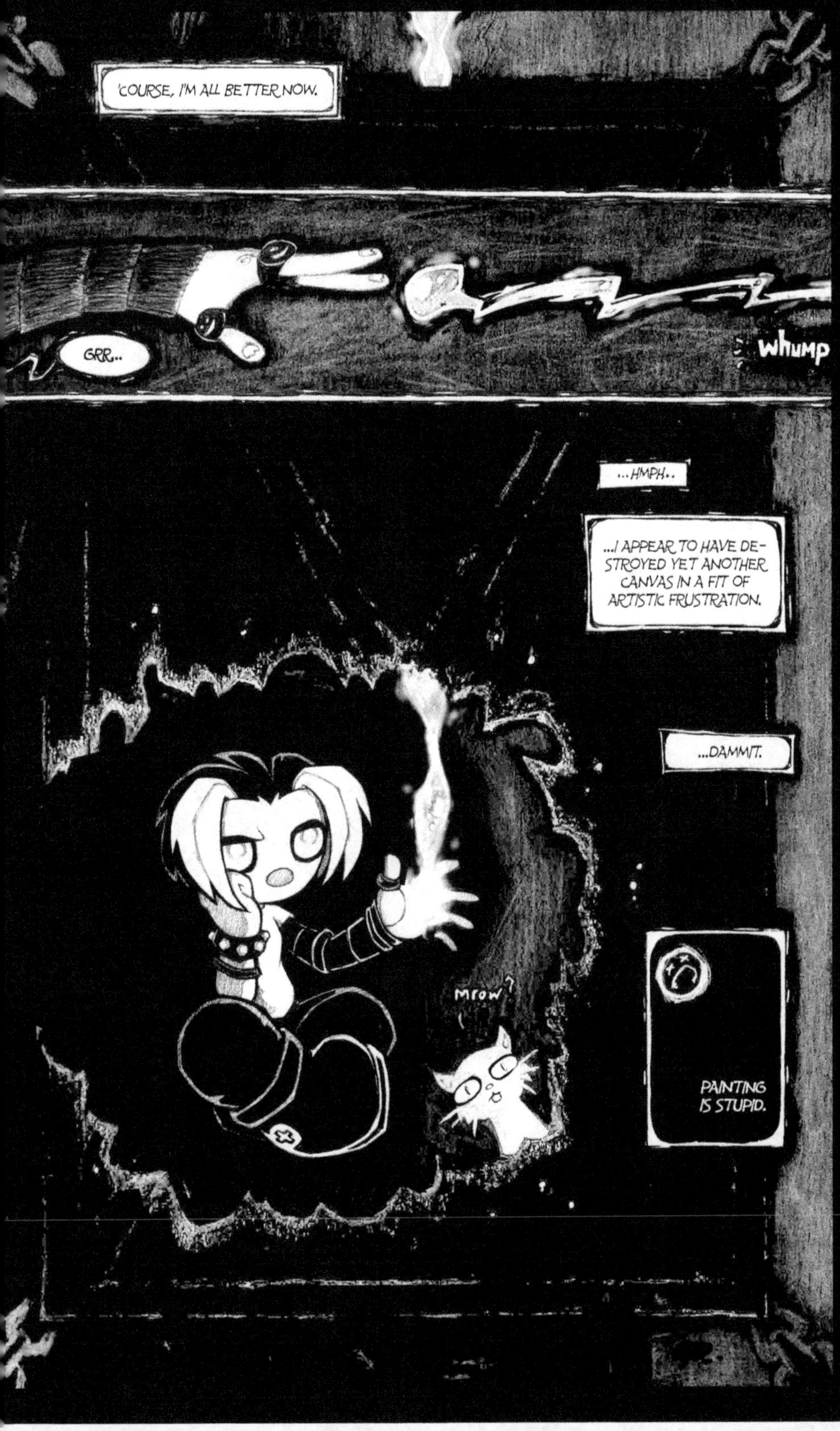
'COURSE, I'M ALL BETTER NOW.
GRR..
whump
...HMPH..
...I APPEAR TO HAVE DE-STROYED YET ANOTHER CANVAS IN A FIT OF ARTISTIC FRUSTRATION.
...DAMMIT.
Mrow?
PAINTING IS STUPID.

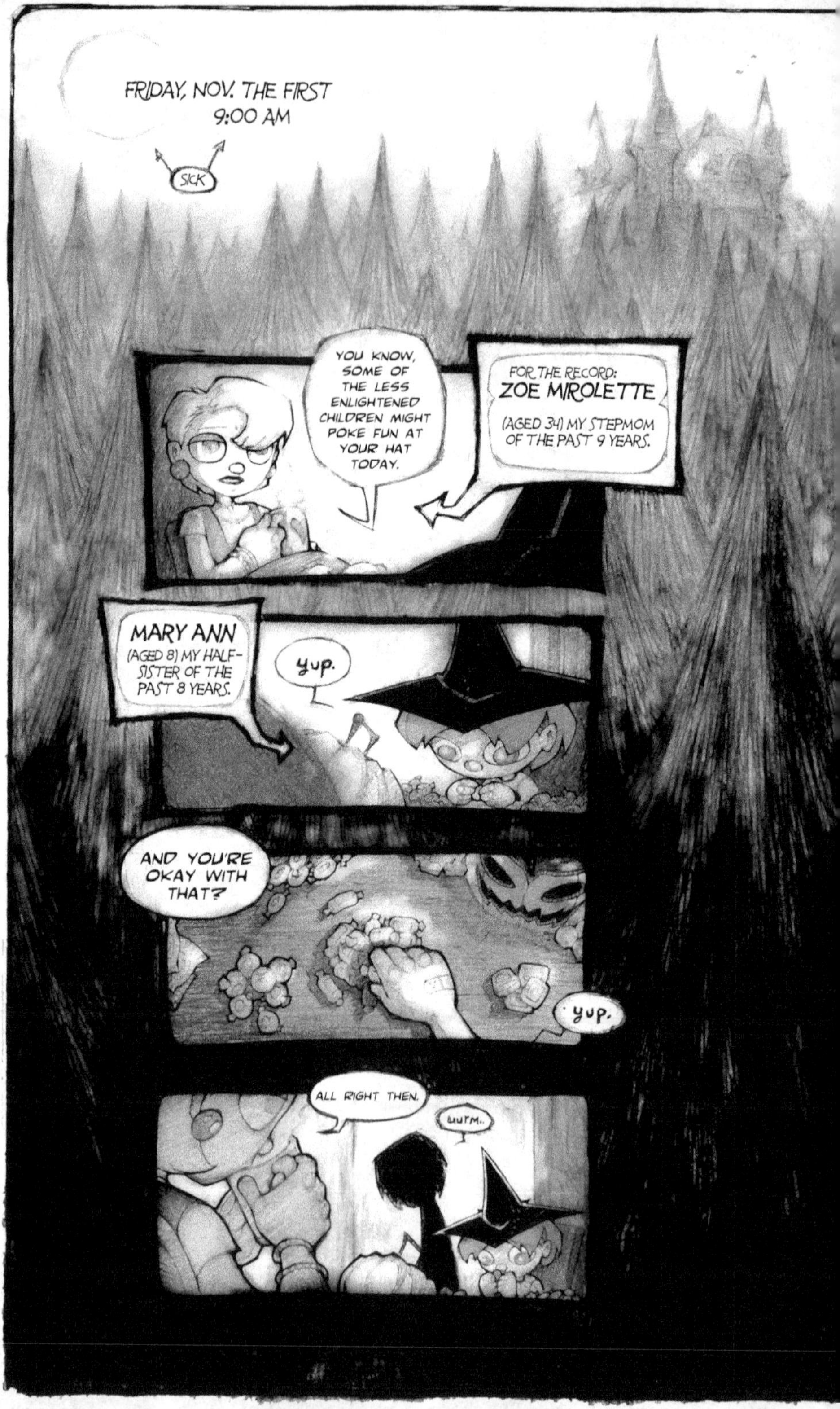
FRIDAY, NOV. THE FIRST
9:00 AM
SICK
YOU KNOW, SOME OF THE LESS ENLIGHTENED CHILDREN MIGHT POKE FUN AT YOUR HAT TODAY.
FOR THE RECORD: ZOE MIROLETTE
(AGED 34) MY STEPMOM OF THE PAST 9 YEARS.
MARY ANN
(AGED 8) MY HALF-SISTER OF THE PAST 8 YEARS.
yup.
AND YOU'RE OKAY WITH THAT?
yup.
ALL RIGHT THEN.
uurm.

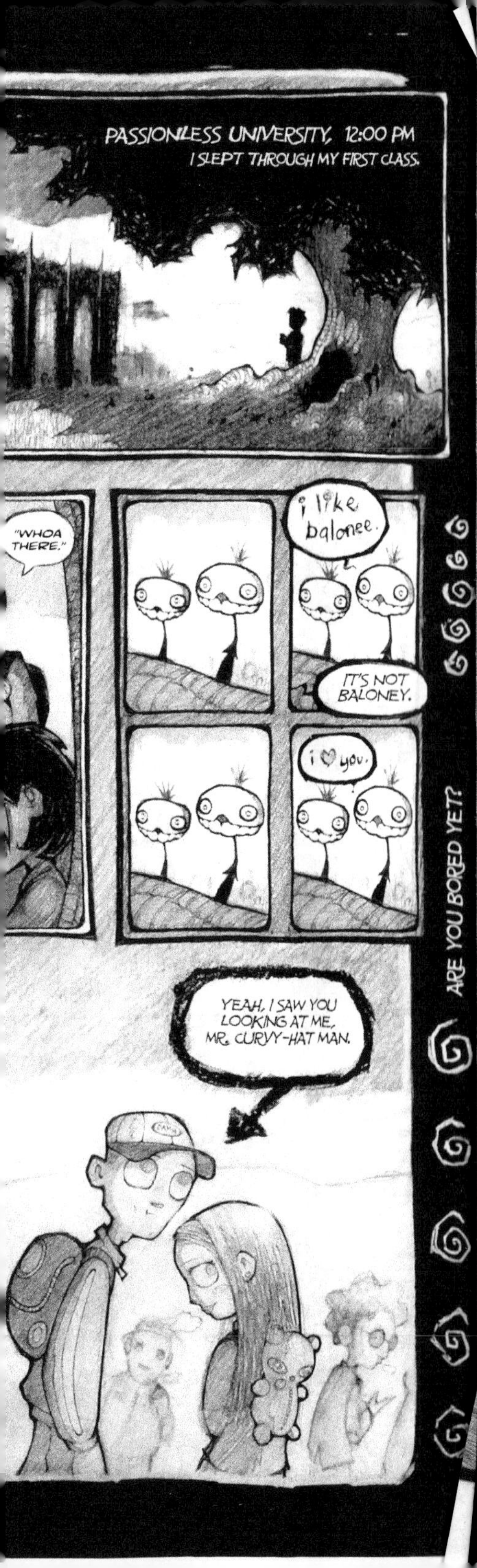
PASSIONLESS UNIVERSITY, 12:00 PM
I SLEPT THROUGH MY FIRST CLASS.
"WHOA THERE."
i like balonee.
IT'S NOT BALONEY.
i ♥ you.
ARE YOU BORED YET?
YEAH, I SAW YOU LOOKING AT ME, MR. CURVY-HAT MAN.

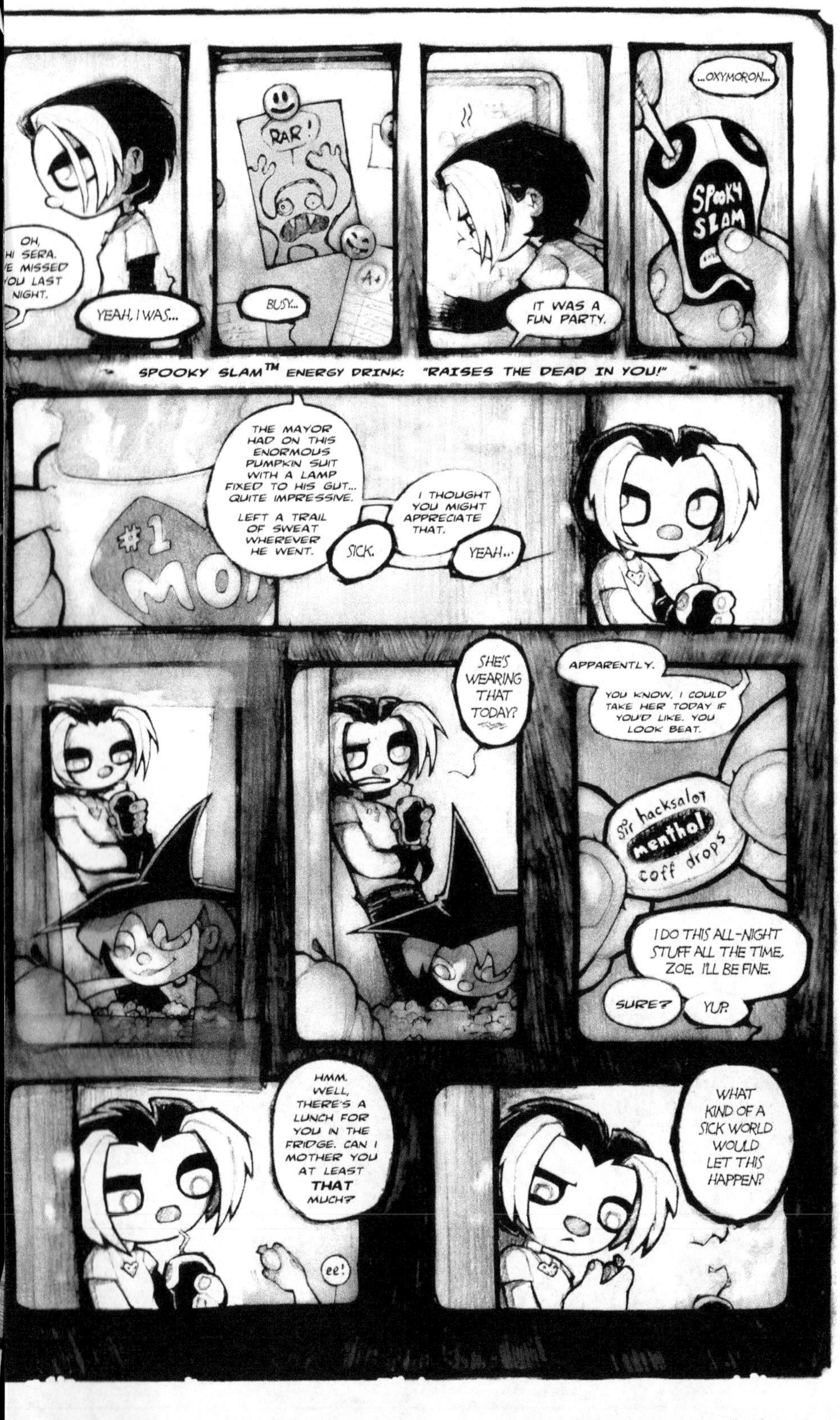
OH, HI SERA. MISSED YOU LAST NIGHT.
YEAH, I WAS...
RAR!
BUSY...
IT WAS A FUN PARTY.
...OXYMORON...
SPOOKY SLAM
SPOOKY SLAM™ ENERGY DRINK: "RAISES THE DEAD IN YOU!"
THE MAYOR HAD ON THIS ENORMOUS PUMPKIN SUIT WITH A LAMP FIXED TO HIS GUT... QUITE IMPRESSIVE.
LEFT A TRAIL OF SWEAT WHEREVER HE WENT.
SICK.
I THOUGHT YOU MIGHT APPRECIATE THAT.
YEAH...
SHE'S WEARING THAT TODAY?
APPARENTLY.
YOU KNOW, I COULD TAKE HER TODAY IF YOU'D LIKE. YOU LOOK BEAT.
Sir hacksalot menthol coff drops
I DO THIS ALL-NIGHT STUFF ALL THE TIME, ZOE. I'LL BE FINE.
SURE?
YUP.
HMM. WELL, THERE'S A LUNCH FOR YOU IN THE FRIDGE. CAN I MOTHER YOU AT LEAST THAT MUCH?
ee!
WHAT KIND OF A SICK WORLD WOULD LET THIS HAPPEN?

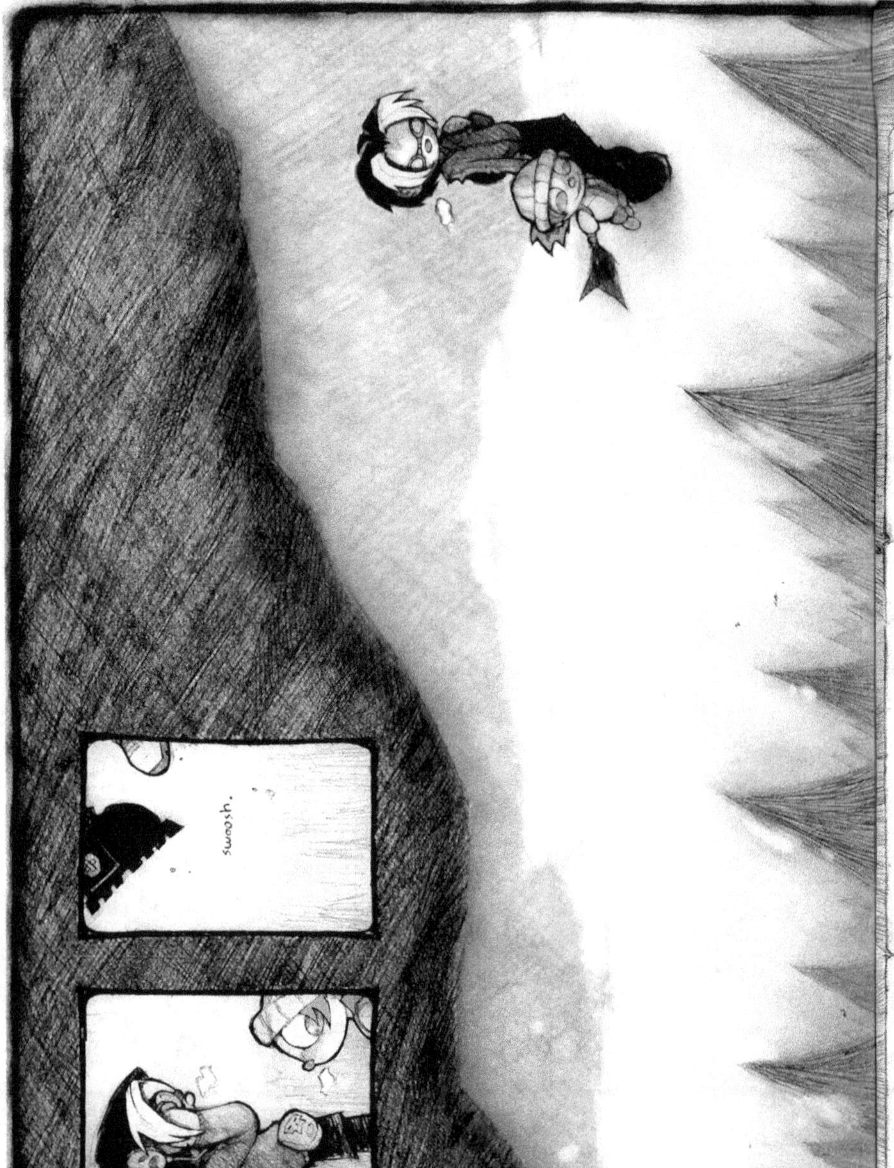

DID YOU BRING YOUR BROOM?
swoosh.

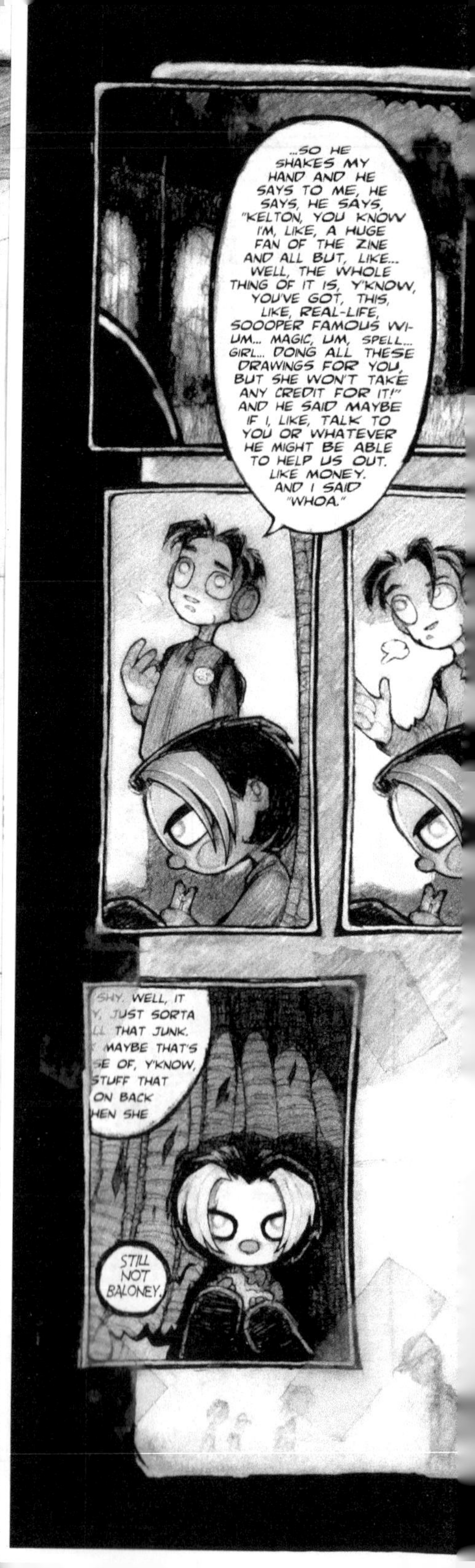

...SO HE SHAKES MY HAND AND HE SAYS TO ME, HE SAYS, HE SAYS, "KELTON, YOU KNOW I'M, LIKE, A HUGE FAN OF THE ZINE AND ALL BUT, LIKE... WELL, THE WHOLE THING OF IT IS, Y'KNOW, YOU'VE GOT, THIS, LIKE, REAL-LIFE, SOOOPER FAMOUS WI- UM... MAGIC, UM, SPELL... GIRL... DOING ALL THESE DRAWINGS FOR YOU, BUT SHE WON'T TAKE ANY CREDIT FOR IT!" AND HE SAID MAYBE IF I, LIKE, TALK TO YOU OR WHATEVER HE MIGHT BE ABLE TO HELP US OUT. LIKE MONEY. AND I SAID "WHOA."
SHY. WELL, IT Y, JUST SORTA LL THAT JUNK. MAYBE THAT'S SE OF, Y'KNOW, STUFF THAT ON BACK HEN SHE
STILL NOT BALONEY.

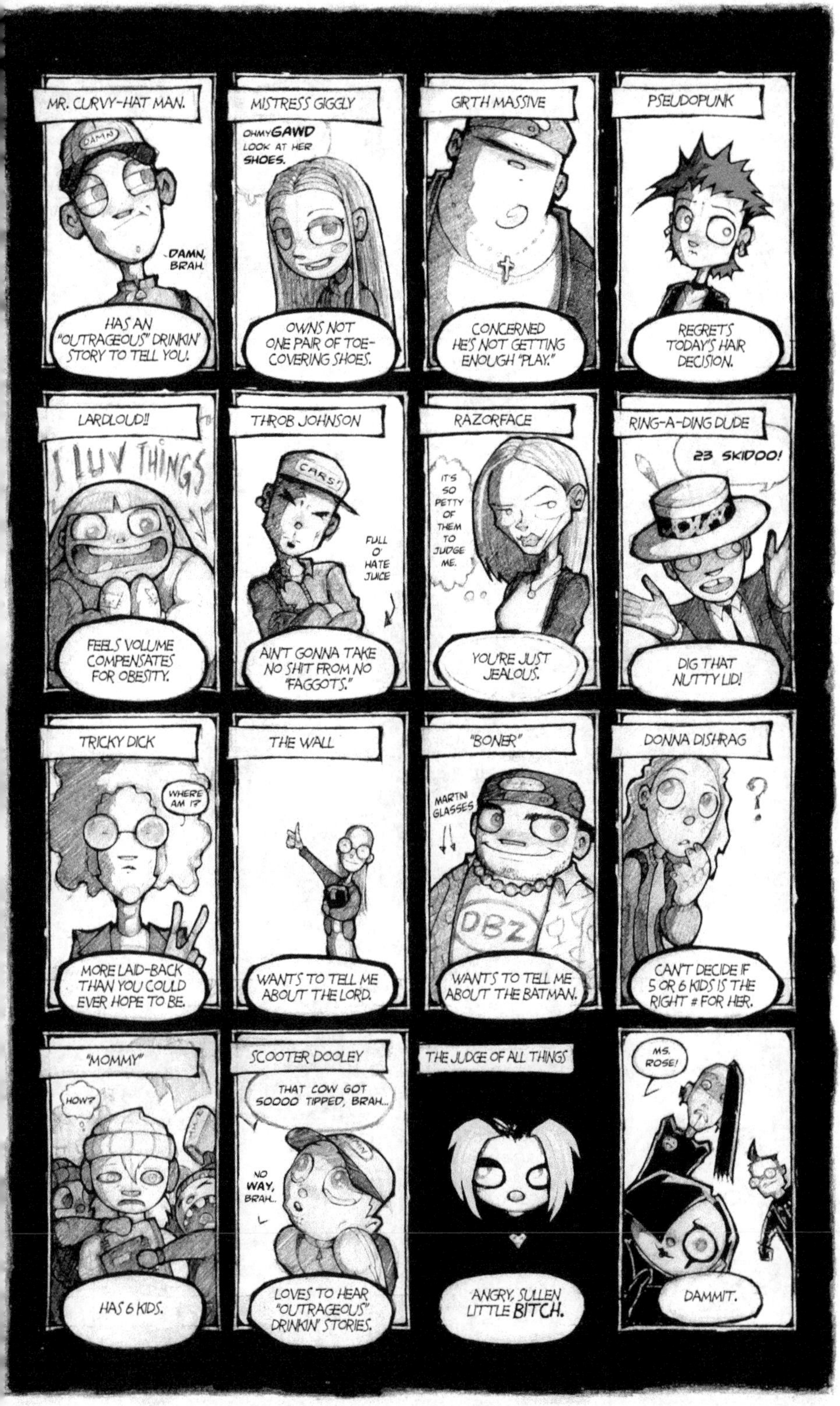
MR. CURVY-HAT MAN.
DAMN
DAMN, BRAH.
HAS AN "OUTRAGEOUS" DRINKIN' STORY TO TELL YOU.
MISTRESS GIGGLY
OHMYGAWD LOOK AT HER SHOES.
OWNS NOT ONE PAIR OF TOE-COVERING SHOES.
GIRTH MASSIVE
CONCERNED HE'S NOT GETTING ENOUGH "PLAY."
PSEUDOPUNK
REGRETS TODAY'S HAIR DECISION.
LARDLOUD!!
I LUV THINGS
FEELS VOLUME COMPENSATES FOR OBESITY.
THROB JOHNSON
CARS!
FULL O' HATE JUICE
AIN'T GONNA TAKE NO SHIT FROM NO "FAGGOTS."
RAZORFACE
IT'S SO PETTY OF THEM TO JUDGE ME.
YOU'RE JUST JEALOUS.
RING-A-DING DUDE
23 SKIDOO!
DIG THAT NUTTY LID!
TRICKY DICK
WHERE AM I?
MORE LAID-BACK THAN YOU COULD EVER HOPE TO BE.
THE WALL
WANTS TO TELL ME ABOUT THE LORD.
"BONER"
MARTINI GLASSES
DBZ
WANTS TO TELL ME ABOUT THE BATMAN.
DONNA DISHRAG
?
CAN'T DECIDE IF 5 OR 6 KIDS IS THE RIGHT # FOR HER.
"MOMMY"
HOW?
HAS 6 KIDS.
SCOOTER DOOLEY
THAT COW GOT SOOOO TIPPED, BRAH...
NO WAY, BRAH...
LOVES TO HEAR "OUTRAGEOUS" DRINKIN' STORIES.
THE JUDGE OF ALL THINGS
ANGRY, SULLEN LITTLE BITCH.
MS. ROSE!
DAMMIT.

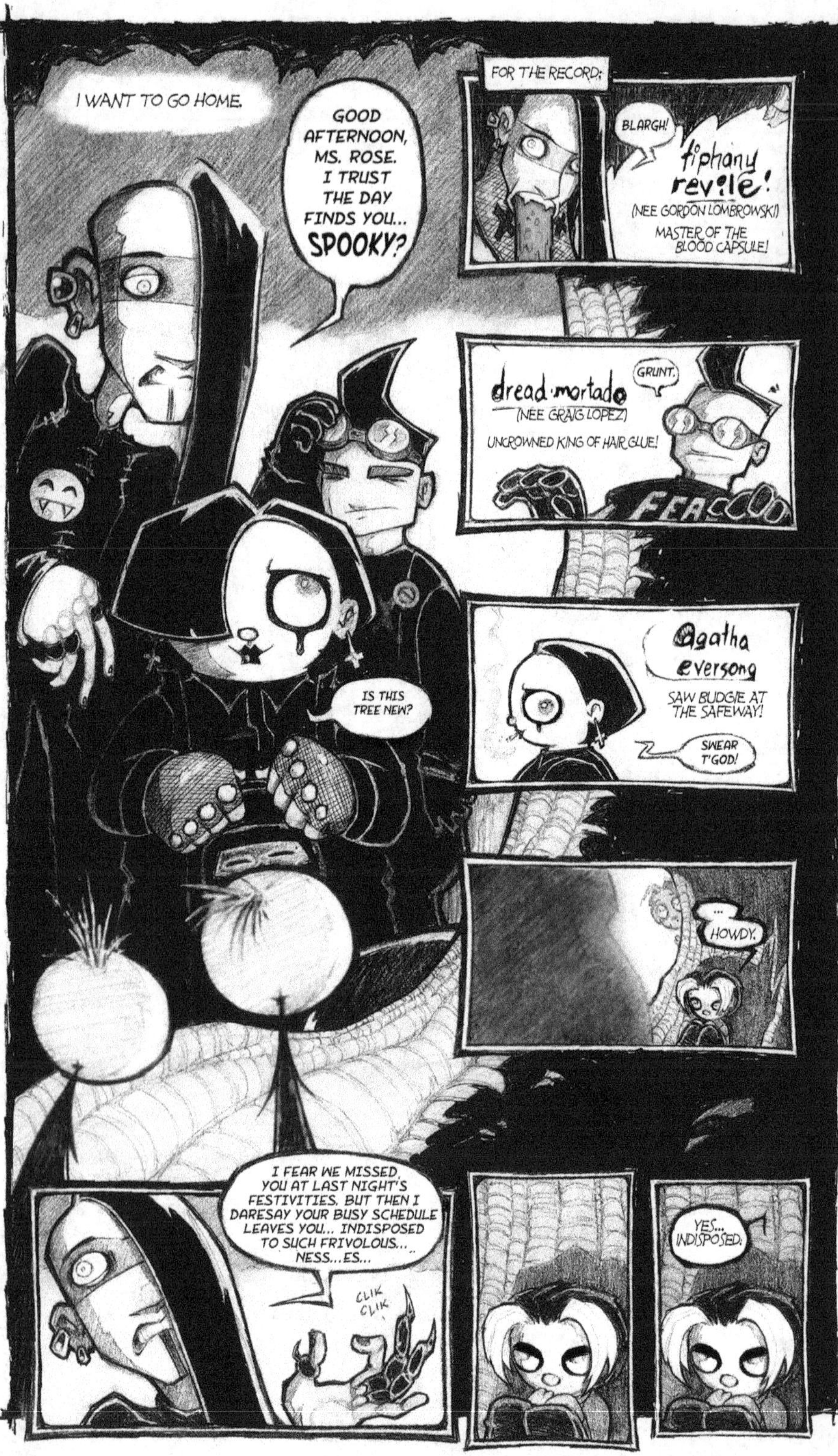

I WANT TO GO HOME.
GOOD AFTERNOON, MS. ROSE. I TRUST THE DAY FINDS YOU... SPOOKY?
FOR THE RECORD:
BLARGH!
tiphany revile!
(NEE GORDON LOMBROWSKI)
MASTER OF THE BLOOD CAPSULE!
GRUNT.
dread mortado
(NEE GRAIG LOPEZ)
UNCROWNED KING OF HAIR GLUE!
agatha eversong
SAW BUDGIE AT THE SAFEWAY!
SWEAR T'GOD!
IS THIS TREE NEW?
... HOWDY.
I FEAR WE MISSED YOU AT LAST NIGHT'S FESTIVITIES. BUT THEN I DARESAY YOUR BUSY SCHEDULE LEAVES YOU... INDISPOSED TO SUCH FRIVOLOUS... NESS...ES...
CLIK CLIK
YES... INDISPOSED.

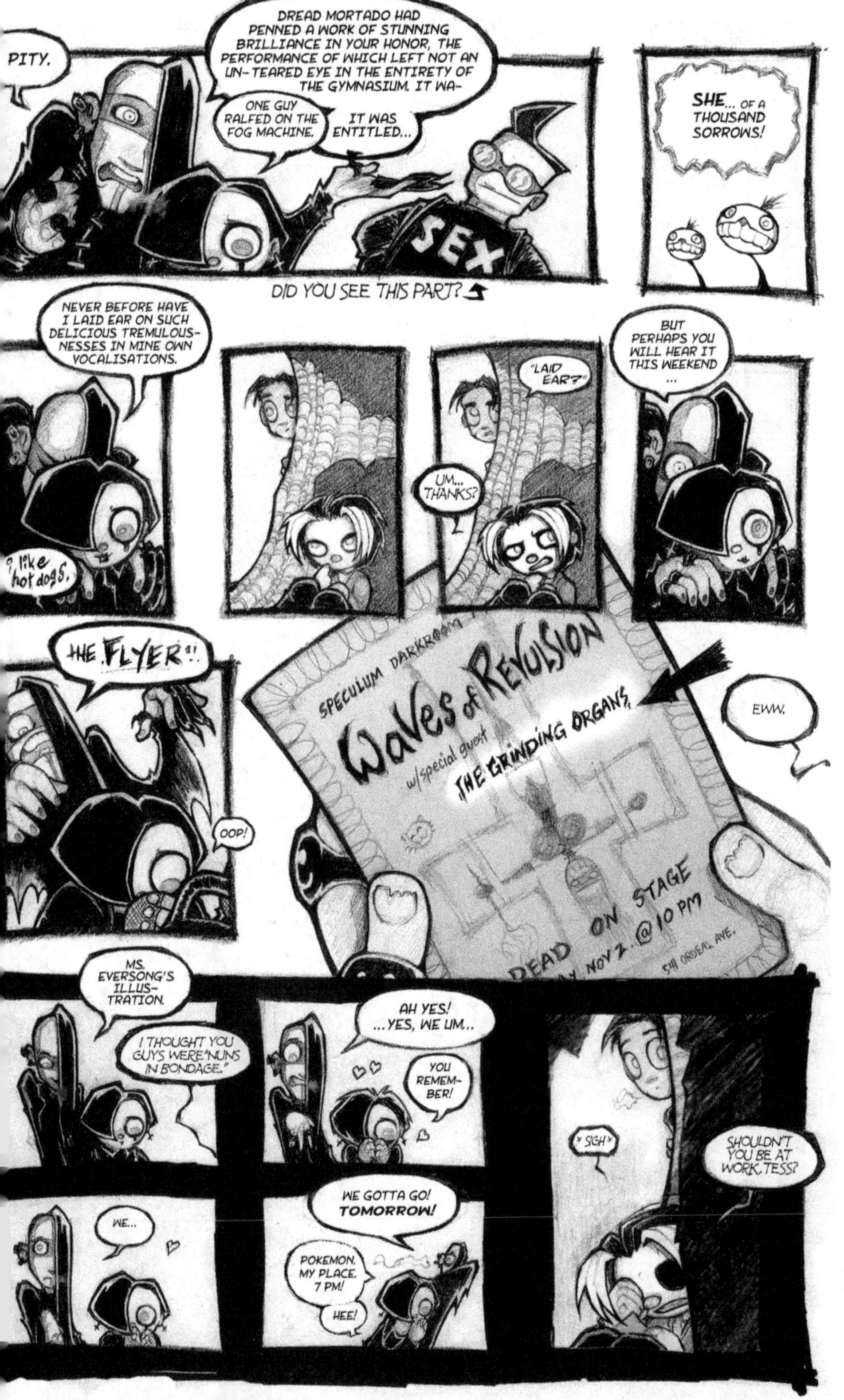

PITY.
DREAD MORTADO HAD PENNED A WORK OF STUNNING BRILLIANCE IN YOUR HONOR, THE PERFORMANCE OF WHICH LEFT NOT AN UN-TEARED EYE IN THE ENTIRETY OF THE GYMNASIUM. IT WA-
ONE GUY RALFED ON THE FOG MACHINE.
IT WAS ENTITLED...
SEX
SHE... OF A THOUSAND SORROWS!
DID YOU SEE THIS PART?
NEVER BEFORE HAVE I LAID EAR ON SUCH DELICIOUS TREMULOUSNESSES IN MINE OWN VOCALISATIONS.
I like hot dogs.
UM... THANKS?
"LAID EAR?"
BUT PERHAPS YOU WILL HEAR IT THIS WEEKEND ...
THE FLYER!!
OOP!
SPECULUM DARKROOM
Waves of Revulsion
w/special guest
THE GRINDING ORGANS
DEAD ON STAGE
NOV 2 @ 10 PM
541 ORDEAL AVE.
EWW.
MS. EVERSONG'S ILLUSTRATION.
I THOUGHT YOU GUYS WERE "NUNS IN BONDAGE."
AH YES! ...YES, WE UM...
YOU REMEMBER!
SIGH
SHOULDN'T YOU BE AT WORK, TESS?
WE...
WE GOTTA GO! TOMORROW!
POKEMON. MY PLACE. 7 PM!
HEE!

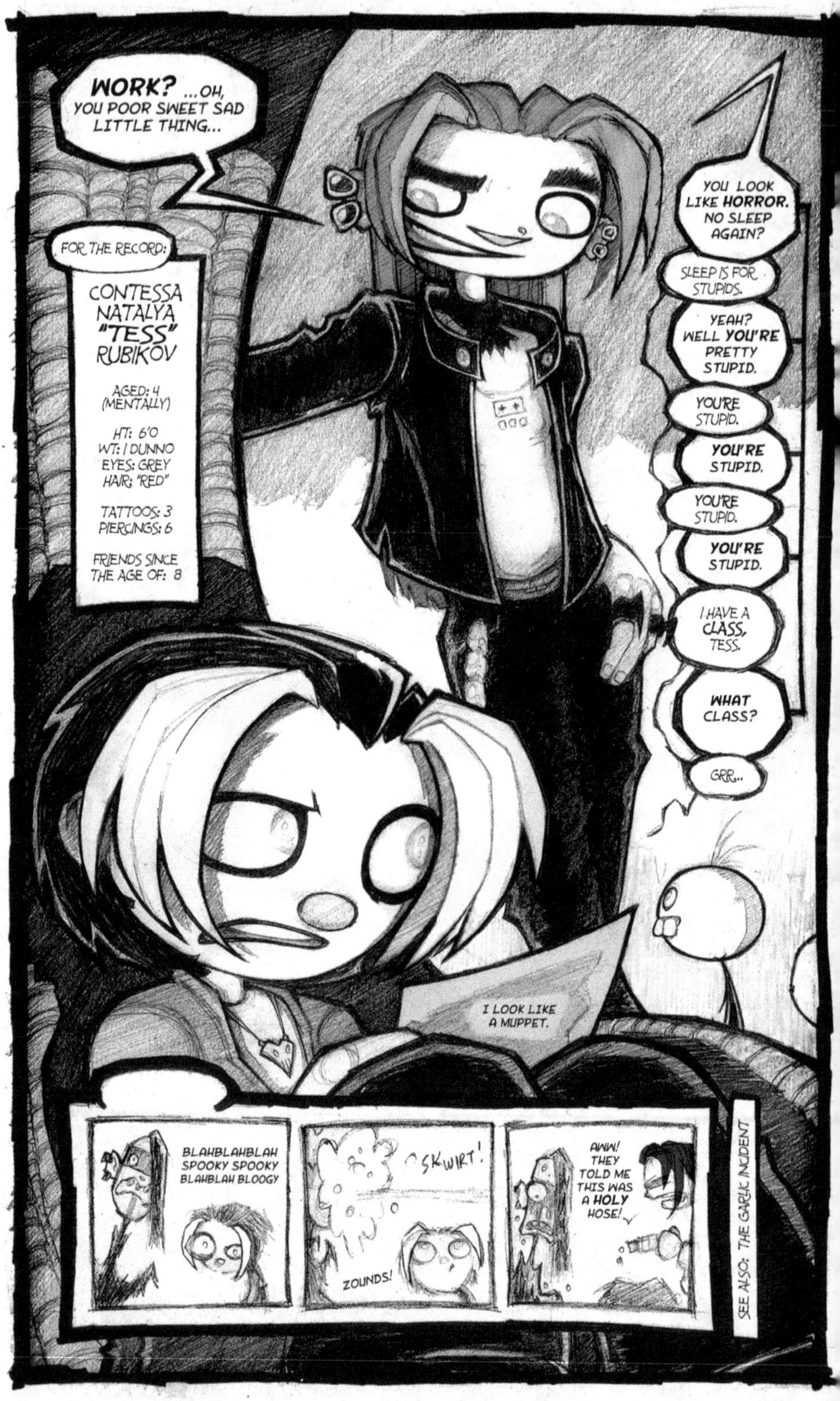
WORK? ...OH, YOU POOR SWEET SAD LITTLE THING...
FOR THE RECORD:
CONTESSA NATALYA "TESS" RUBIKOV
AGED: 4 (MENTALLY)
HT: 6'0
WT: I DUNNO
EYES: GREY
HAIR: "RED"
TATTOOS: 3
PIERCINGS: 6
FRIENDS SINCE THE AGE OF: 8
YOU LOOK LIKE HORROR. NO SLEEP AGAIN?
SLEEP IS FOR STUPIDS.
YEAH? WELL YOU'RE PRETTY STUPID.
YOU'RE STUPID.
YOU'RE STUPID.
YOU'RE STUPID.
YOU'RE STUPID.
I HAVE A CLASS, TESS.
WHAT CLASS?
GRR...
I LOOK LIKE A MUPPET.
BLAHBLAHBLAH SPOOKY SPOOKY BLAHBLAH BLOOGY
SKWIRT!
ZOUNDS!
AWW! THEY TOLD ME THIS WAS A HOLY HOSE!
SEE ALSO: THE GARLIC INCIDENT

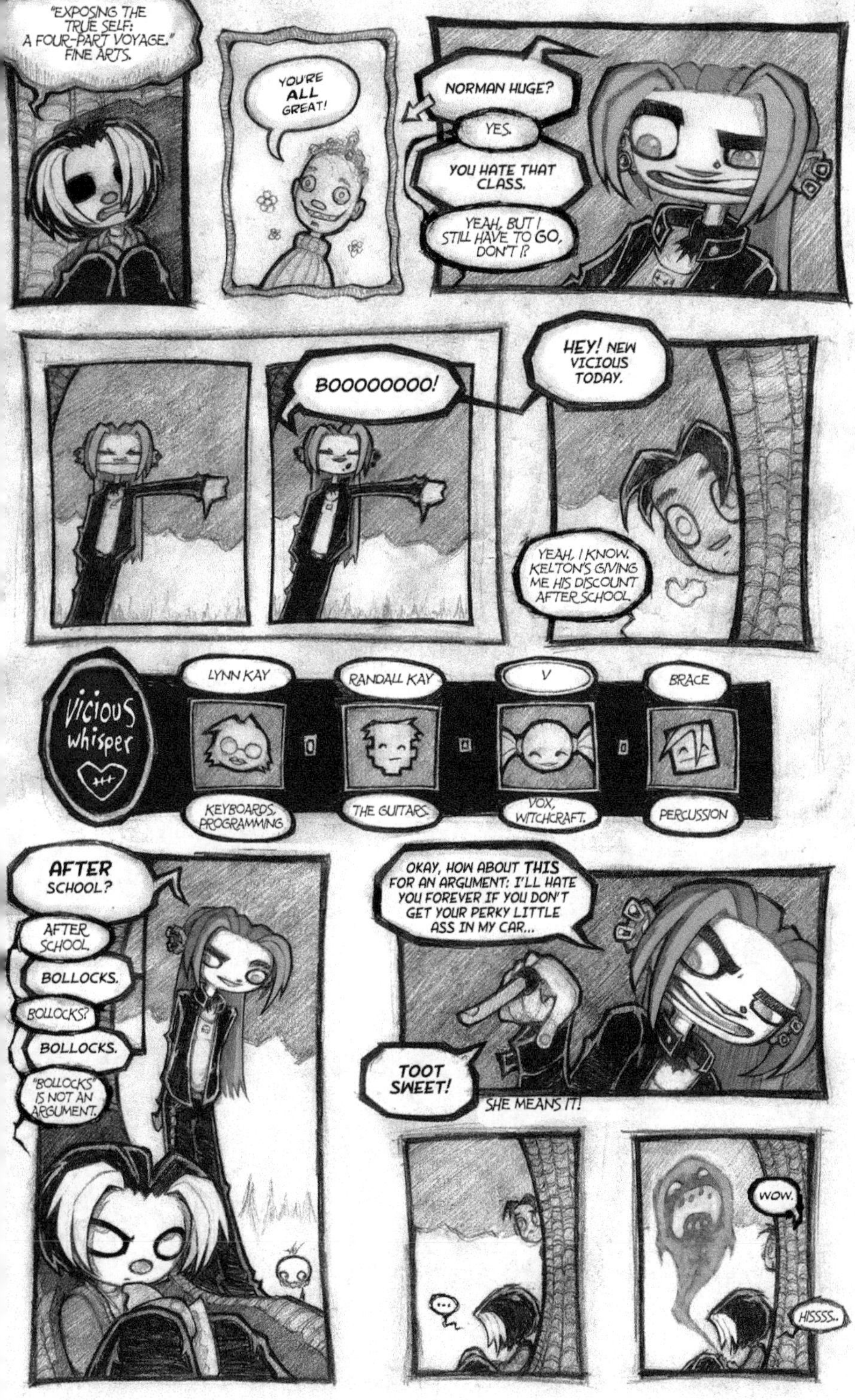
"EXPOSING THE TRUE SELF: A FOUR-PART VOYAGE." FINE ARTS.
YOU'RE ALL GREAT!
NORMAN HUGE?
YES.
YOU HATE THAT CLASS.
YEAH, BUT I STILL HAVE TO GO, DON'T I?
BOOOOOOOO!
HEY! NEW VICIOUS TODAY.
YEAH, I KNOW. KELTON'S GIVING ME HIS DISCOUNT AFTER SCHOOL.
Vicious whisper
LYNN KAY
KEYBOARDS, PROGRAMMING
RANDALL KAY
THE GUITARS
V
VOX, WITCHCRAFT
BRACE
PERCUSSION
AFTER SCHOOL?
AFTER SCHOOL.
BOLLOCKS.
BOLLOCKS?
BOLLOCKS.
"BOLLOCKS" IS NOT AN ARGUMENT.
OKAY, HOW ABOUT THIS FOR AN ARGUMENT: I'LL HATE YOU FOREVER IF YOU DON'T GET YOUR PERKY LITTLE ASS IN MY CAR...
TOOT SWEET!
SHE MEANS IT!
...
WOW.
HISSSS..

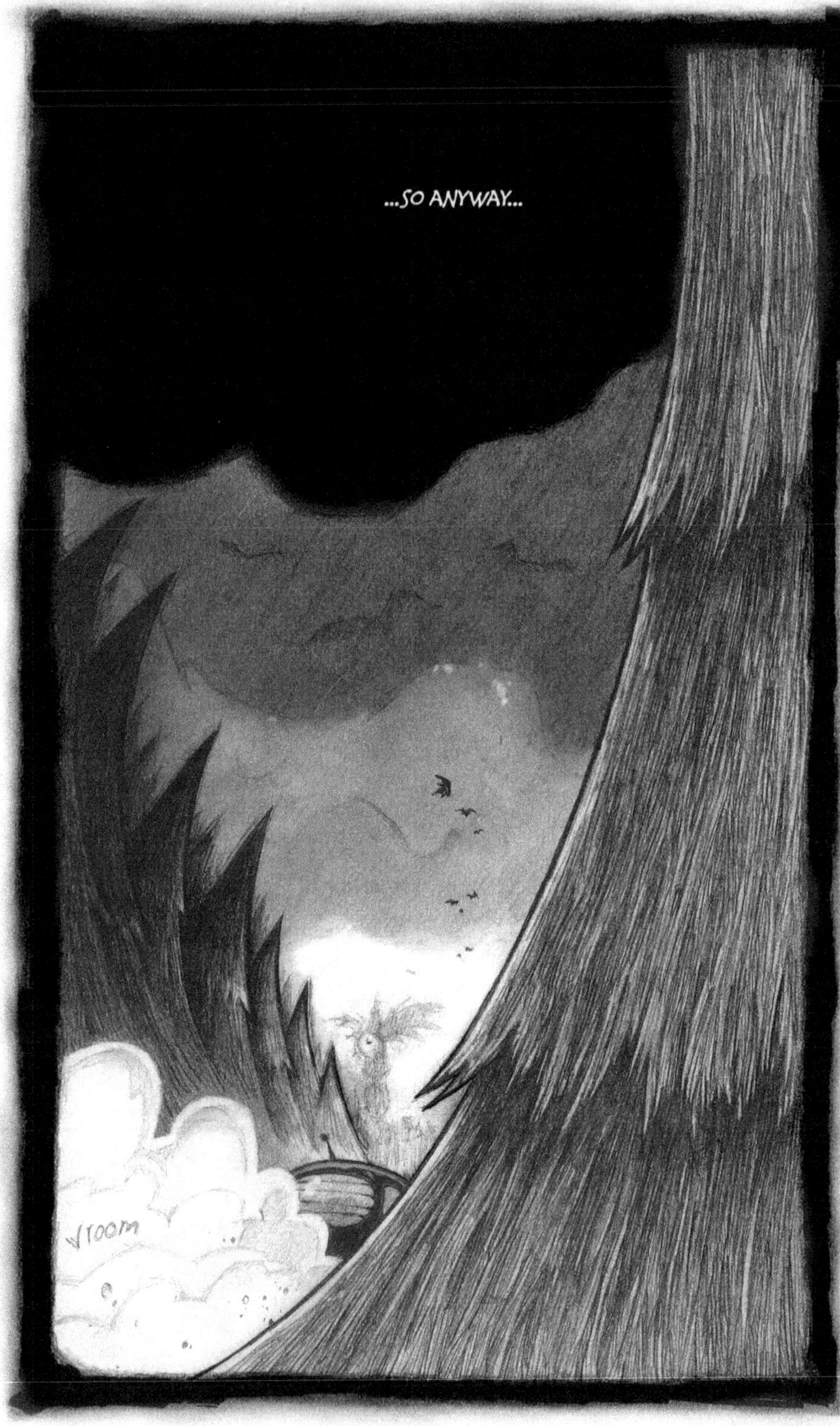
...SO ANYWAY...
vroom

THIS IS SOME CRAP I MADE FOR KELTON'S 'ZINE:
"FEARFUL THING: THE JOURNAL OF THE UNDERGROUND."

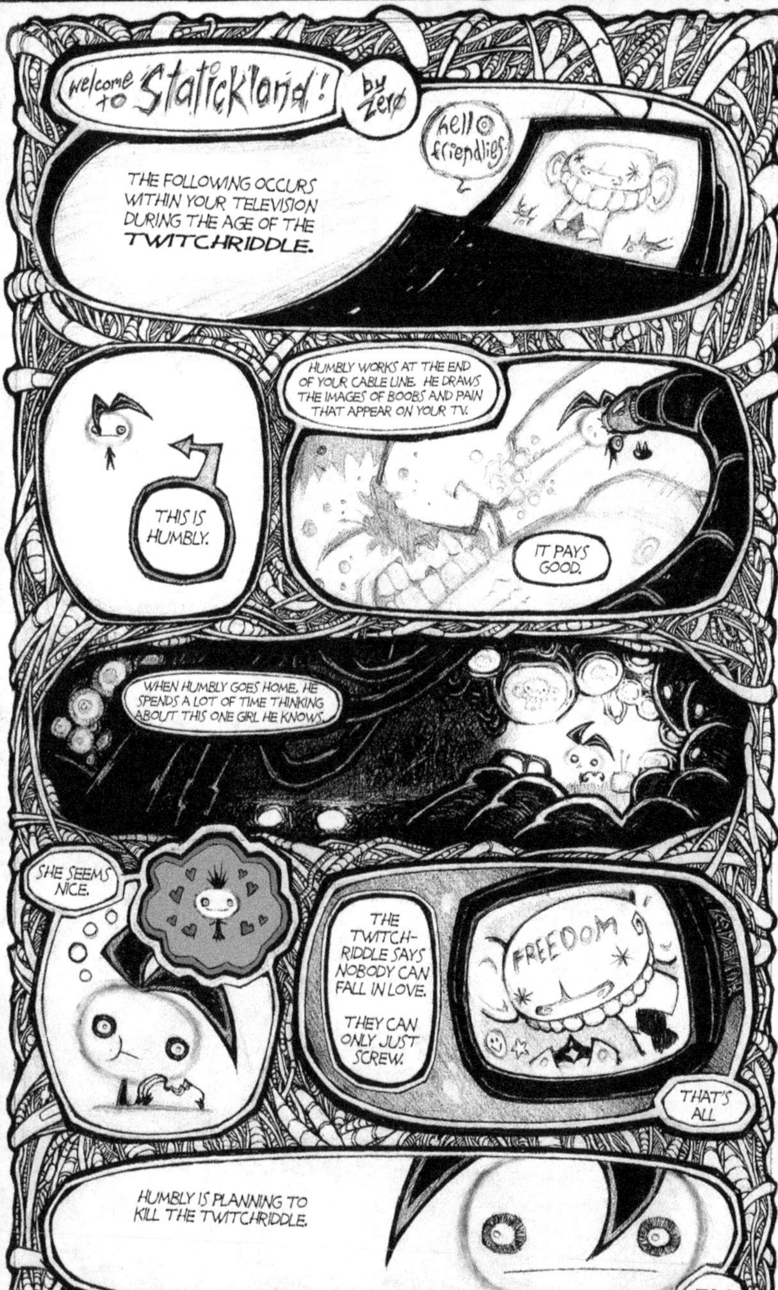
welcome to Statickland! by zerø
hello friendlies
THE FOLLOWING OCCURS WITHIN YOUR TELEVISION DURING THE AGE OF THE TWITCHRIDDLE.
THIS IS HUMBLY.
HUMBLY WORKS AT THE END OF YOUR CABLE LINE. HE DRAWS THE IMAGES OF BOOBS AND PAIN THAT APPEAR ON YOUR TV.
IT PAYS GOOD.
WHEN HUMBLY GOES HOME, HE SPENDS A LOT OF TIME THINKING ABOUT THIS ONE GIRL HE KNOWS.
SHE SEEMS NICE.
THE TWITCH-RIDDLE SAYS NOBODY CAN FALL IN LOVE.
THEY CAN ONLY JUST SCREW.
FREEDOM
THAT'S ALL
HUMBLY IS PLANNING TO KILL THE TWITCHRIDDLE.
T.B.C.

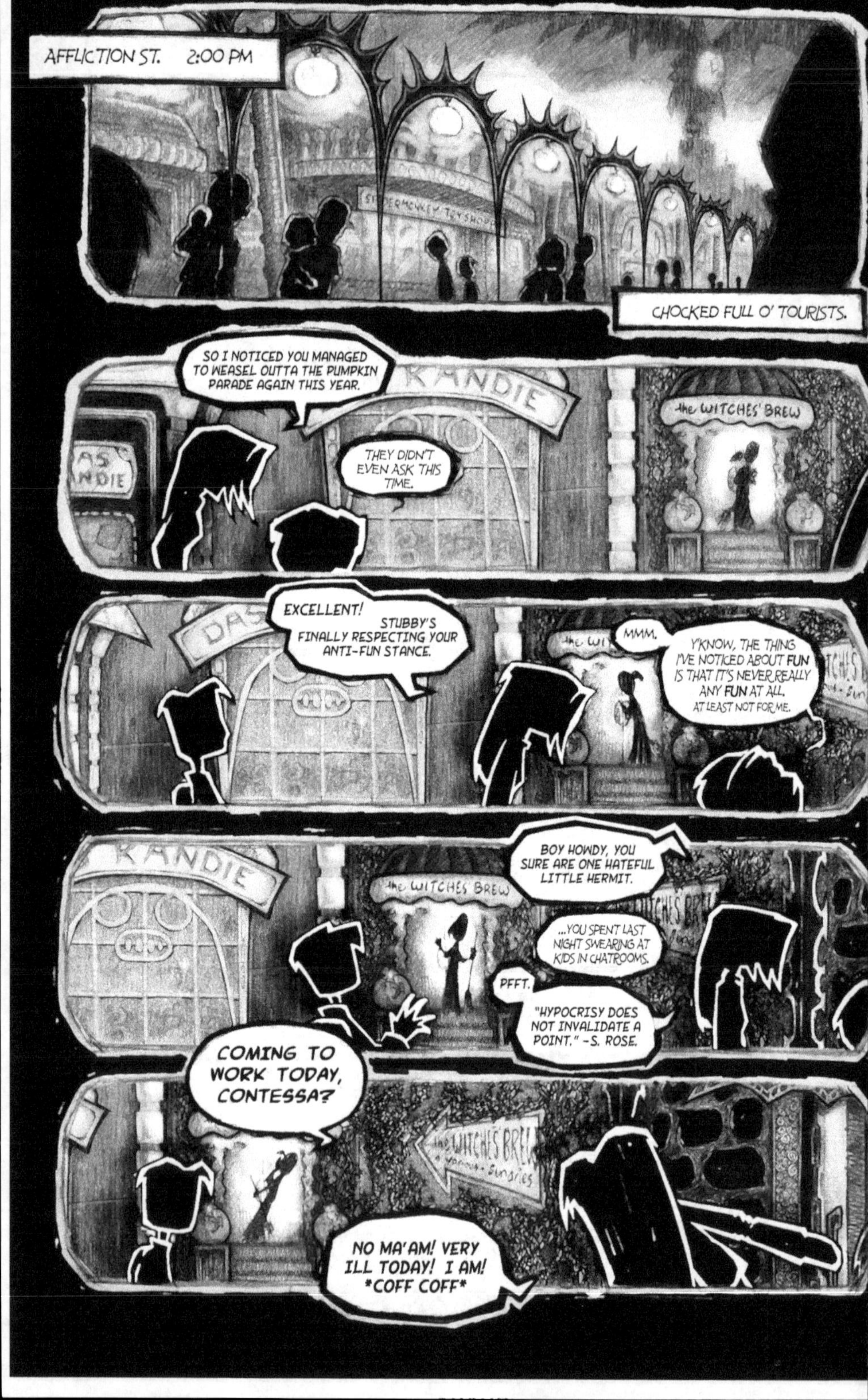
AFFLICTION ST. 2:00 PM
SPIDERMONKEY TOYSHOP
CHOCKED FULL O' TOURISTS.
SO I NOTICED YOU MANAGED TO WEASEL OUTTA THE PUMPKIN PARADE AGAIN THIS YEAR.
KANDIE
THEY DIDN'T EVEN ASK THIS TIME.
the WITCHES' BREW
EXCELLENT! STUBBY'S FINALLY RESPECTING YOUR ANTI-FUN STANCE.
MMM.
Y'KNOW, THE THING I'VE NOTICED ABOUT FUN IS THAT IT'S NEVER REALLY ANY FUN AT ALL. AT LEAST NOT FOR ME.
BOY HOWDY, YOU SURE ARE ONE HATEFUL LITTLE HERMIT.
...YOU SPENT LAST NIGHT SWEARING AT KIDS IN CHATROOMS.
PFFT.
"HYPOCRISY DOES NOT INVALIDATE A POINT." -S. ROSE.
COMING TO WORK TODAY, CONTESSA?
NO MA'AM! VERY ILL TODAY! I AM! *COFF COFF*

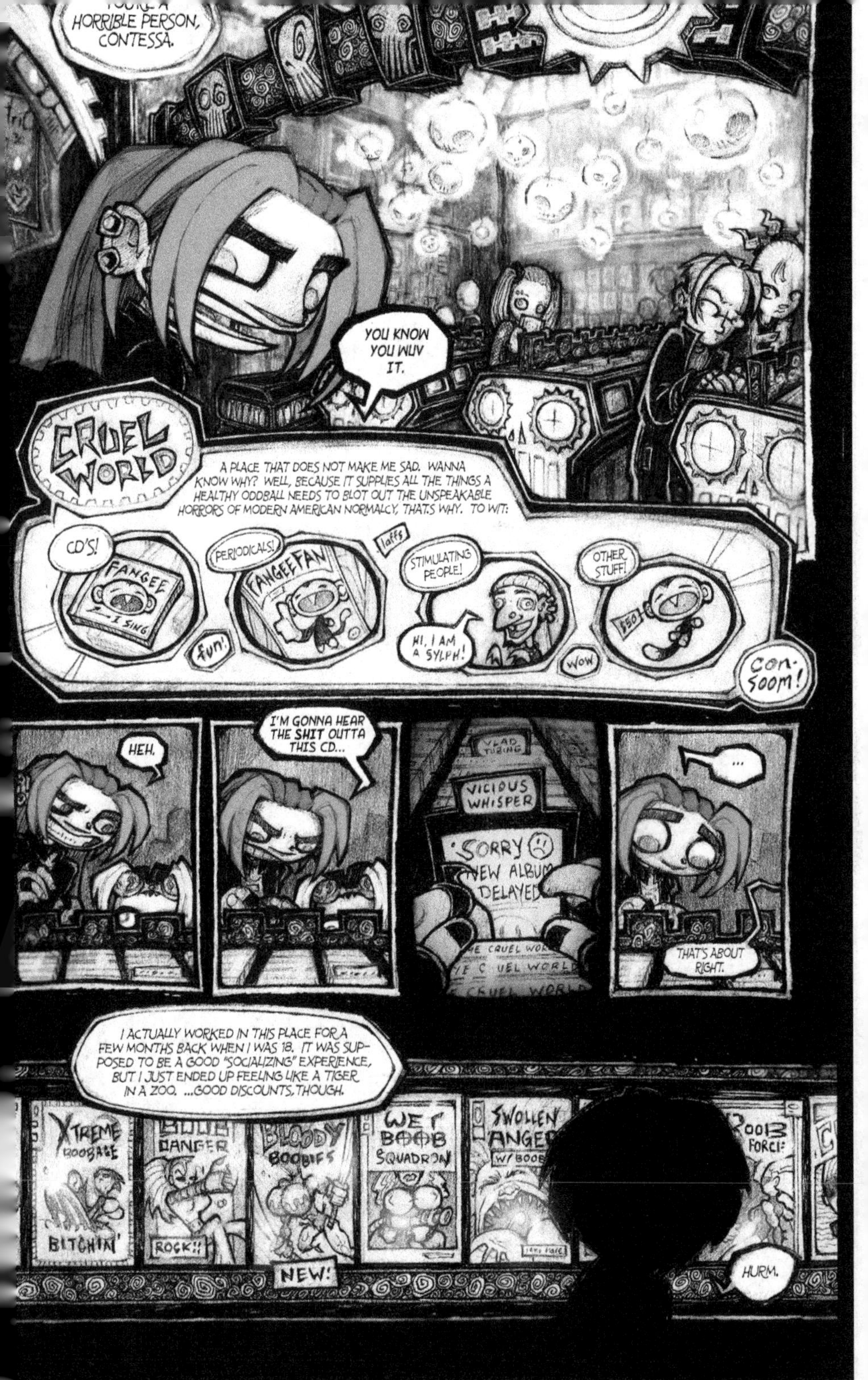
YOU'RE A HORRIBLE PERSON, CONTESSA.
YOU KNOW YOU WUV IT.
CRUEL WORLD
A PLACE THAT DOES NOT MAKE ME SAD. WANNA KNOW WHY? WELL, BECAUSE IT SUPPLIES ALL THE THINGS A HEALTHY ODDBALL NEEDS TO BLOT OUT THE UNSPEAKABLE HORRORS OF MODERN AMERICAN NORMALCY, THAT'S WHY. TO WIT:
CD'S!
FANGEE
I SING
fun!
PERIODICALS!
FANGEE FAN
laffs
STIMULATING PEOPLE!
HI, I AM A SYLPH!
wow
OTHER STUFF!
$50
con-soom!
HEH.
I'M GONNA HEAR THE SHIT OUTTA THIS CD...
VLAD TUBING
VICIOUS WHISPER
SORRY NEW ALBUM DELAYED
...
THAT'S ABOUT RIGHT.
I ACTUALLY WORKED IN THIS PLACE FOR A FEW MONTHS BACK WHEN I WAS 18. IT WAS SUPPOSED TO BE A GOOD "SOCIALIZING" EXPERIENCE, BUT I JUST ENDED UP FEELING LIKE A TIGER IN A ZOO. ...GOOD DISCOUNTS, THOUGH.
XTREME BOOBAGE
BITCHIN'
BOOB DANGER
ROCK!!
BLOODY BOOBIES
NEW!
WET BOOB SQUADRON
SWOLLEN ANGER W/ BOOB
HURM.

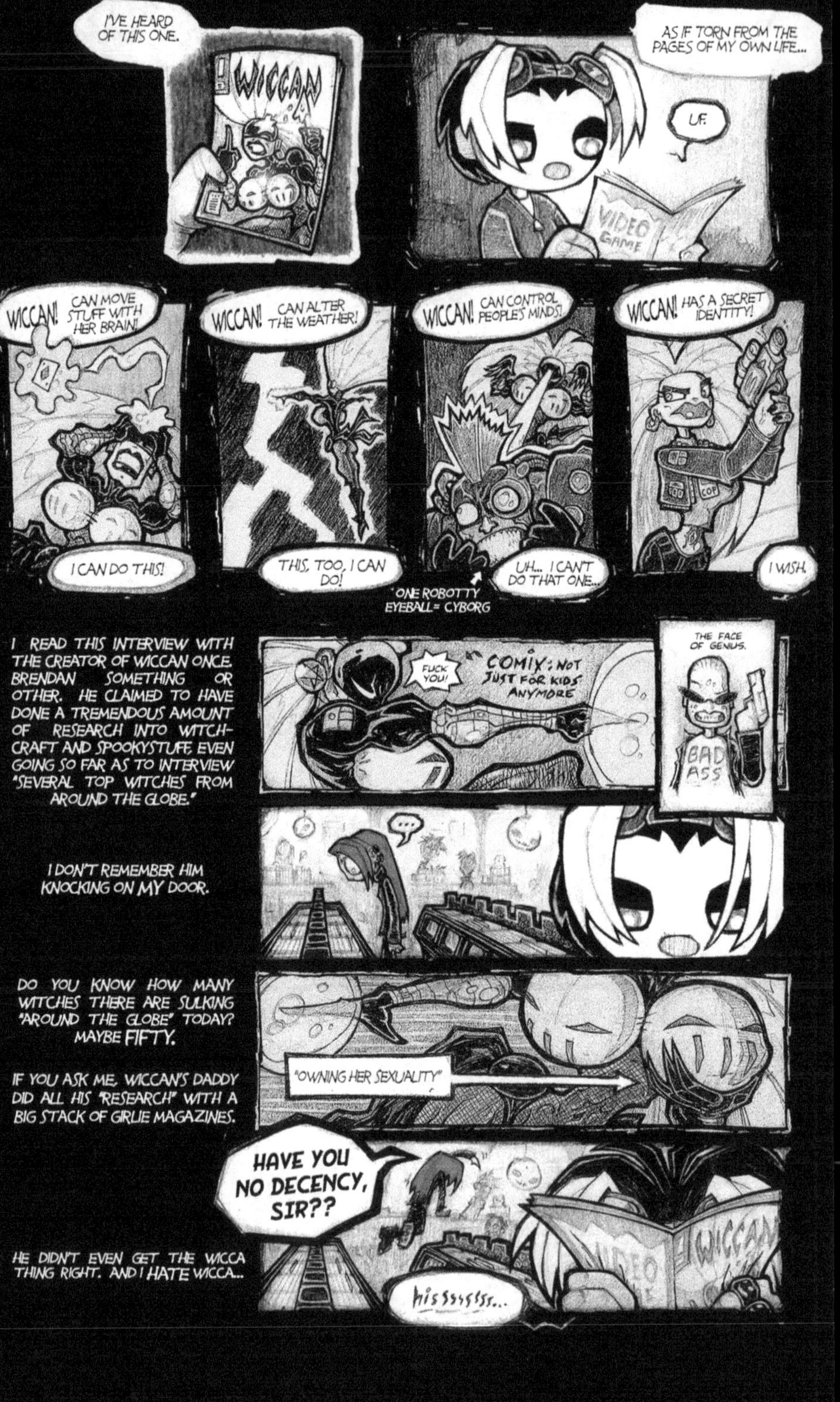
I'VE HEARD OF THIS ONE.
WICCAN
AS IF TORN FROM THE PAGES OF MY OWN LIFE...
UF.
VIDEO GAME
WICCAN! CAN MOVE STUFF WITH HER BRAIN!
I CAN DO THIS!
WICCAN! CAN ALTER THE WEATHER!
THIS, TOO, I CAN DO!
WICCAN! CAN CONTROL PEOPLE'S MINDS!
UH... I CAN'T DO THAT ONE...
*ONE ROBOTTY EYEBALL= CYBORG
WICCAN! HAS A SECRET IDENTITY!
COP
I WISH.
I READ THIS INTERVIEW WITH THE CREATOR OF WICCAN ONCE. BRENDAN SOMETHING OR OTHER. HE CLAIMED TO HAVE DONE A TREMENDOUS AMOUNT OF RESEARCH INTO WITCHCRAFT AND SPOOKYSTUFF, EVEN GOING SO FAR AS TO INTERVIEW "SEVERAL TOP WITCHES FROM AROUND THE GLOBE."
FUCK YOU!
COMIX: NOT JUST FOR KIDS ANYMORE
THE FACE OF GENIUS.
BAD ASS
I DON'T REMEMBER HIM KNOCKING ON MY DOOR.
DO YOU KNOW HOW MANY WITCHES THERE ARE SULKING "AROUND THE GLOBE" TODAY? MAYBE FIFTY.
IF YOU ASK ME, WICCAN'S DADDY DID ALL HIS "RESEARCH" WITH A BIG STACK OF GIRLIE MAGAZINES.
"OWNING HER SEXUALITY"
HAVE YOU NO DECENCY, SIR??
HE DIDN'T EVEN GET THE WICCA THING RIGHT. AND I HATE WICCA...
hissssssss...

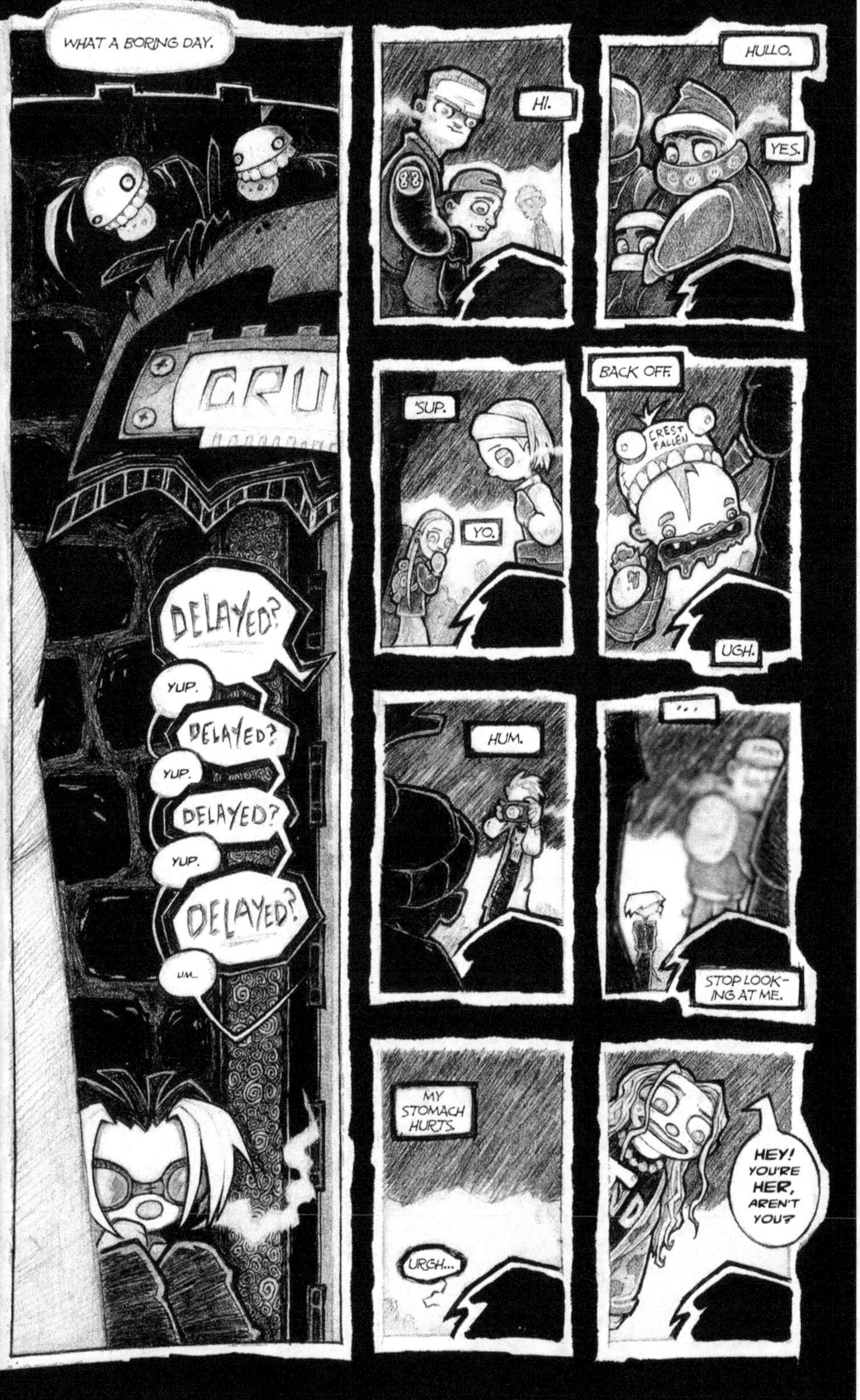
WHAT A BORING DAY.
GRU
DELAYED?
YUP.
DELAYED?
YUP.
DELAYED?
YUP.
DELAYED?
UM...
HI.
HULLO.
YES.
'SUP.
YO.
BACK OFF.
CREST FALLEN
UGH.
HUM.
...
STOP LOOKING AT ME.
MY STOMACH HURTS.
URGH...
HEY! YOU'RE HER, AREN'T YOU?

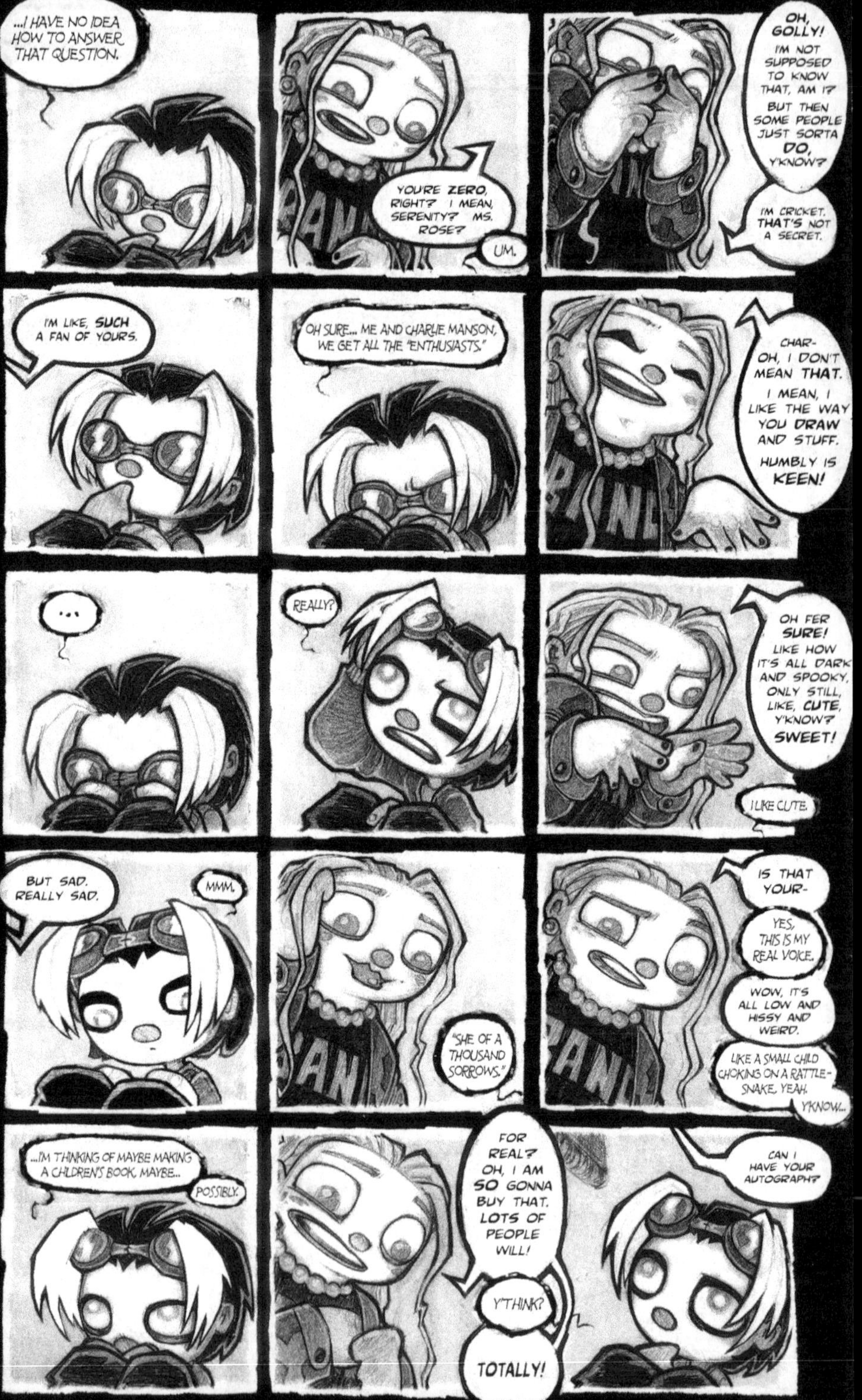
...I HAVE NO IDEA HOW TO ANSWER THAT QUESTION.
YOU'RE ZERO, RIGHT? I MEAN, SERENITY? MS. ROSE?
UM.
OH, GOLLY! I'M NOT SUPPOSED TO KNOW THAT, AM I? BUT THEN SOME PEOPLE JUST SORTA DO, Y'KNOW?
I'M CRICKET. THAT'S NOT A SECRET.
I'M LIKE, SUCH A FAN OF YOURS.
OH SURE... ME AND CHARLIE MANSON, WE GET ALL THE "ENTHUSIASTS."
CHAR- OH, I DON'T MEAN THAT. I MEAN, I LIKE THE WAY YOU DRAW AND STUFF. HUMBLY IS KEEN!
...
REALLY?
OH FER SURE! LIKE HOW IT'S ALL DARK AND SPOOKY, ONLY STILL, LIKE, CUTE, Y'KNOW? SWEET!
I LIKE CUTE.
BUT SAD. REALLY SAD.
MMM.
"SHE OF A THOUSAND SORROWS."
IS THAT YOUR-
YES, THIS IS MY REAL VOICE.
WOW, IT'S ALL LOW AND HISSY AND WEIRD.
LIKE A SMALL CHILD CHOKING ON A RATTLE-SNAKE, YEAH.
Y'KNOW...
...I'M THINKING OF MAYBE MAKING A CHILDREN'S BOOK, MAYBE...
POSSIBLY.
FOR REAL? OH, I AM SO GONNA BUY THAT. LOTS OF PEOPLE WILL!
Y'THINK?
TOTALLY!
CAN I HAVE YOUR AUTOGRAPH?

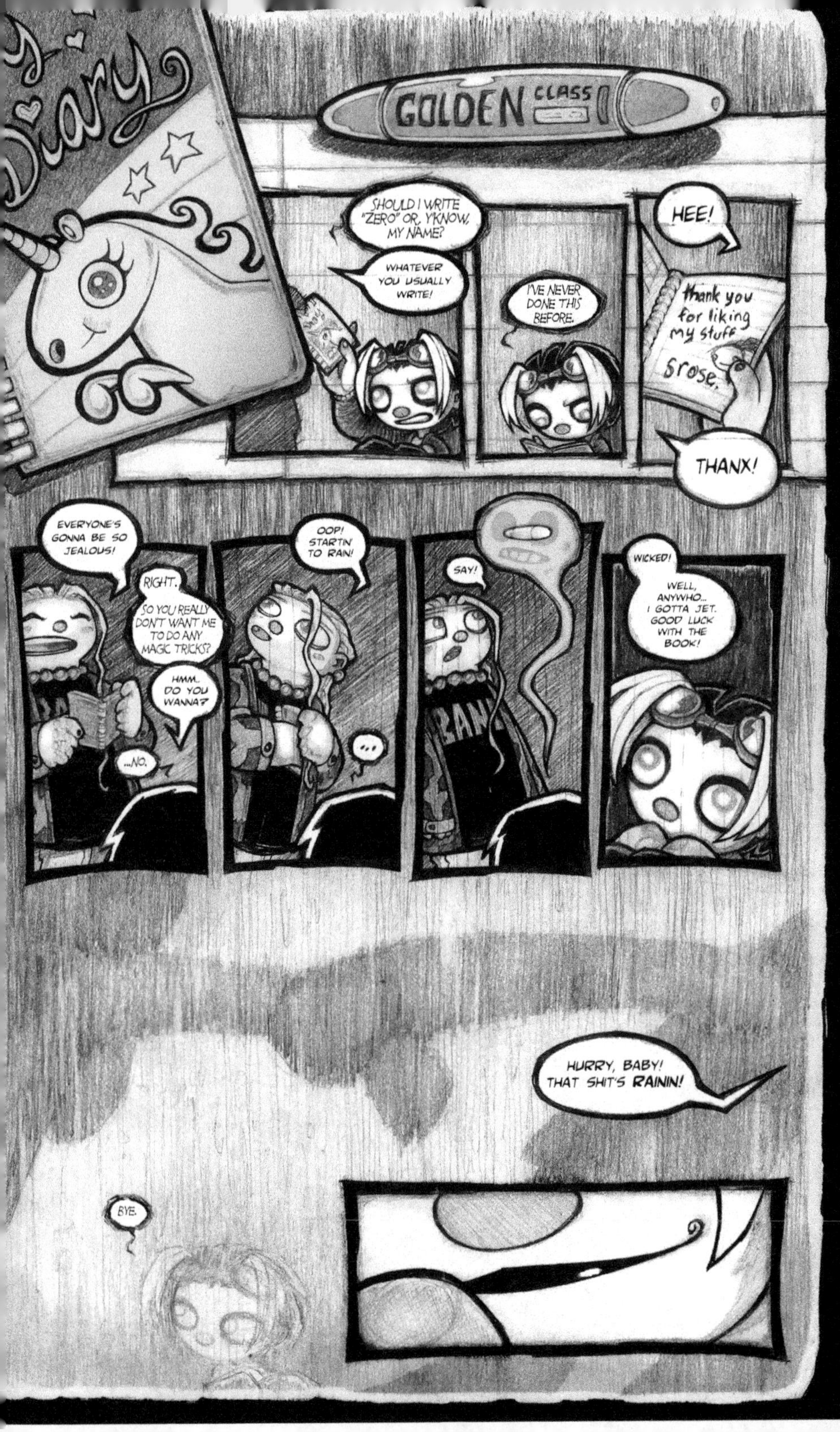
Diary
GOLDEN CLASS
SHOULD I WRITE "ZERO" OR, Y'KNOW, MY NAME?
WHATEVER YOU USUALLY WRITE!
I'VE NEVER DONE THIS BEFORE.
HEE!
thank you for liking my stuff
Srose.
THANX!
EVERYONE'S GONNA BE SO JEALOUS!
RIGHT.
SO YOU REALLY DON'T WANT ME TO DO ANY MAGIC TRICKS?
HMM.. DO YOU WANNA?
...NO.
OOP! STARTIN TO RAIN!
...
SAY!
WICKED!
WELL, ANYWHO... I GOTTA JET. GOOD LUCK WITH THE BOOK!
HURRY, BABY! THAT SHIT'S RAININ!
BYE.

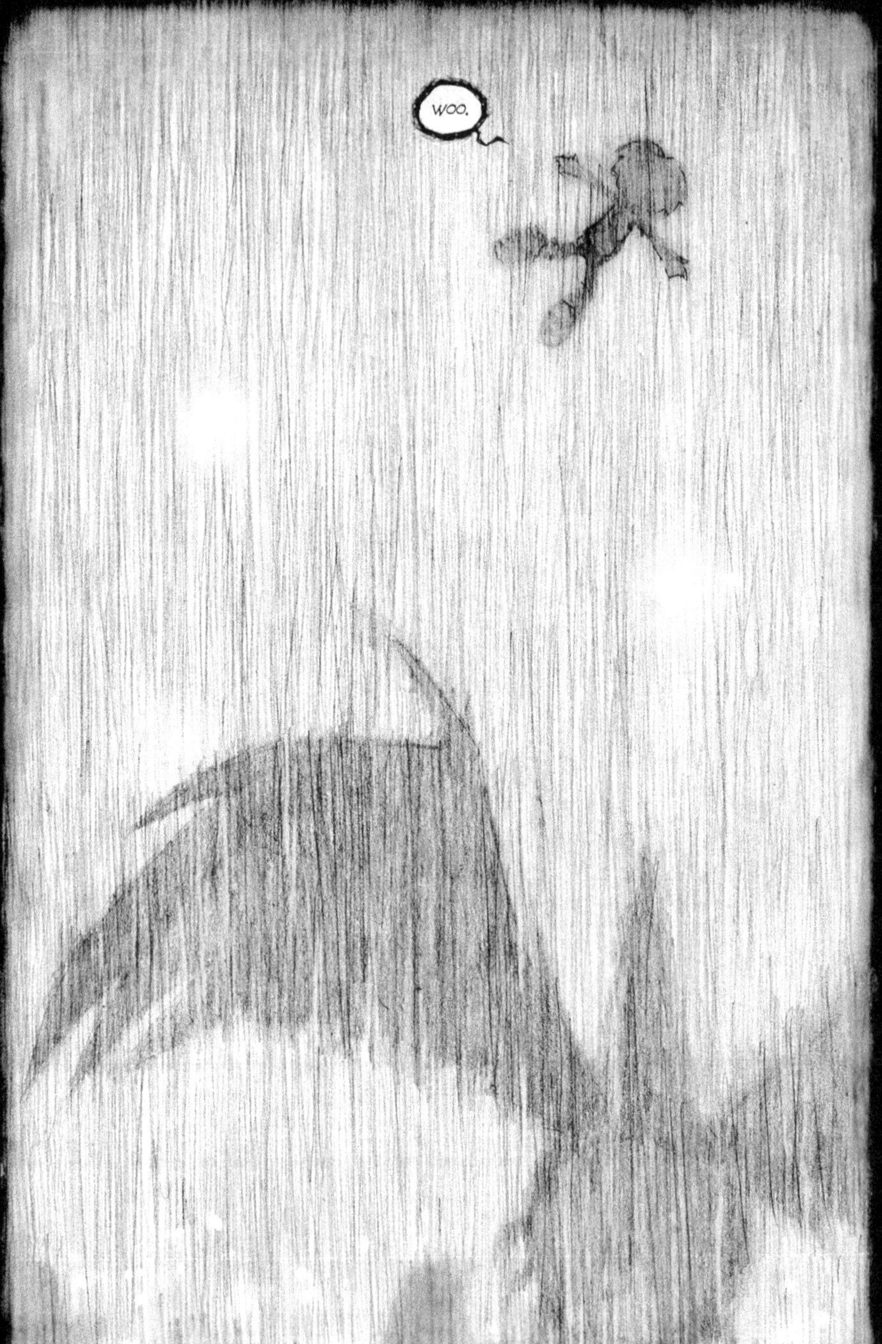
WOO.

...ISSUE TWO

Serenity Rose

the personal journals
of a local witch

..as told to aaron a.

issue number two:

"one thousand sorrows"

"starring"

SERA: SERA IS THE YOUNGEST, SHORTEST, AND SNARLIEST OF THE 5 AMERICAN WITCHES. I THINK. RECENTLY SHE'S BEGUN WEARING GOGGLES ALL HOURS OF THE DAY AND REFERRING TO HERSELF IN THE 3RD PERSON. (NOTE: SERENITY IS NOT A TEENAGER.)

TESS: CONTESSA NATALYA RUBIKOV HAS BEEN SERA'S CLOSEST FRIEND SINCE THE AGE OF EIGHT. HER HOBBIES INCLUDE HAMMERING, WELDING, CARVING, DRILLING, PUNCHING, HACKING AND LAUGHING DERISIVELY AT THE MISFORTUNE OF OTHERS. SHE'S A REAL SWEETHEART, THAT TESS.

KELTON: MR. DEWEY DWAYNE KELTON IS A PROFESSIONAL WORRYWART. IN HIS SPARE TIME HE PUBLISHES A 'ZINE, WRITES LEFTIST POLITICAL ESSAYS, AND PLAYS BASS IN A LOCAL POP PUNK OUTFIT CALLED "THE SPASTIC RASCALS". OH, AND HE WEEPS. ALWAYS THE WEEPING.

MARY ANN: MARY ANN IS SERA'S SPUNKY LITTLE SISTER. SHE IS COMPLETELY IRRELEVANT FOR OUR PURPOSES THIS EVENING.

serenity rose comics:
where cute is always victorious.

SATURDAY, NOV. 2

DEAR DIARIES ARE STUPID...

from *An Incomplete History of Crestfallen: A Peek at the Innards*
by Dr. Martha M. Luftig Passionless University Press, 1998.

"When, in 1661, the Crestfallen Coven pulled up half their wee island town and floated it across the pond to the New Old World, they brought their pets with them. First in number were tiny goblins, kept to act as messengers, assistants, and, quite often, as low-rent jesters. Next were towering trolls, imported to patrol the vast Inconsolable Wood in search of uninvited eyes. Third, dull-witted ogres, put to work exclusively as construction equipment. Fourth, the gnomes. And of cause there were others, a seemingly endless menagerie of spell-cast fauna (and flora), their nature and functions limited only by the imaginations of the seven witching famiies...

And so we see that with goblins to keep the houses, ogres to lift the stones, and trolls to mind the borders, the citizenry of Crestfallen was left free to pursoue the life of the mind, to actively engage themselves with the political, the social, the scientific and the magical, the artistic, the religious, and all of the other important issues of the day..."

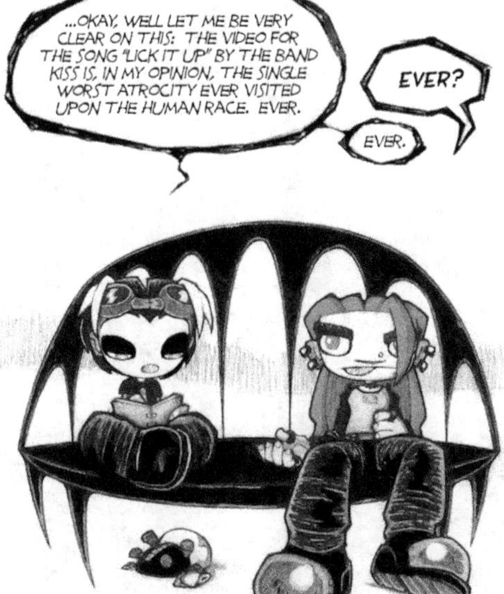

...OKAY, WELL LET ME BE VERY CLEAR ON THIS: THE VIDEO FOR THE SONG "LICK IT UP" BY THE BAND KISS IS, IN MY OPINION, THE SINGLE WORST ATROCITY EVER VISITED UPON THE HUMAN RACE. EVER.
EVER?
EVER.

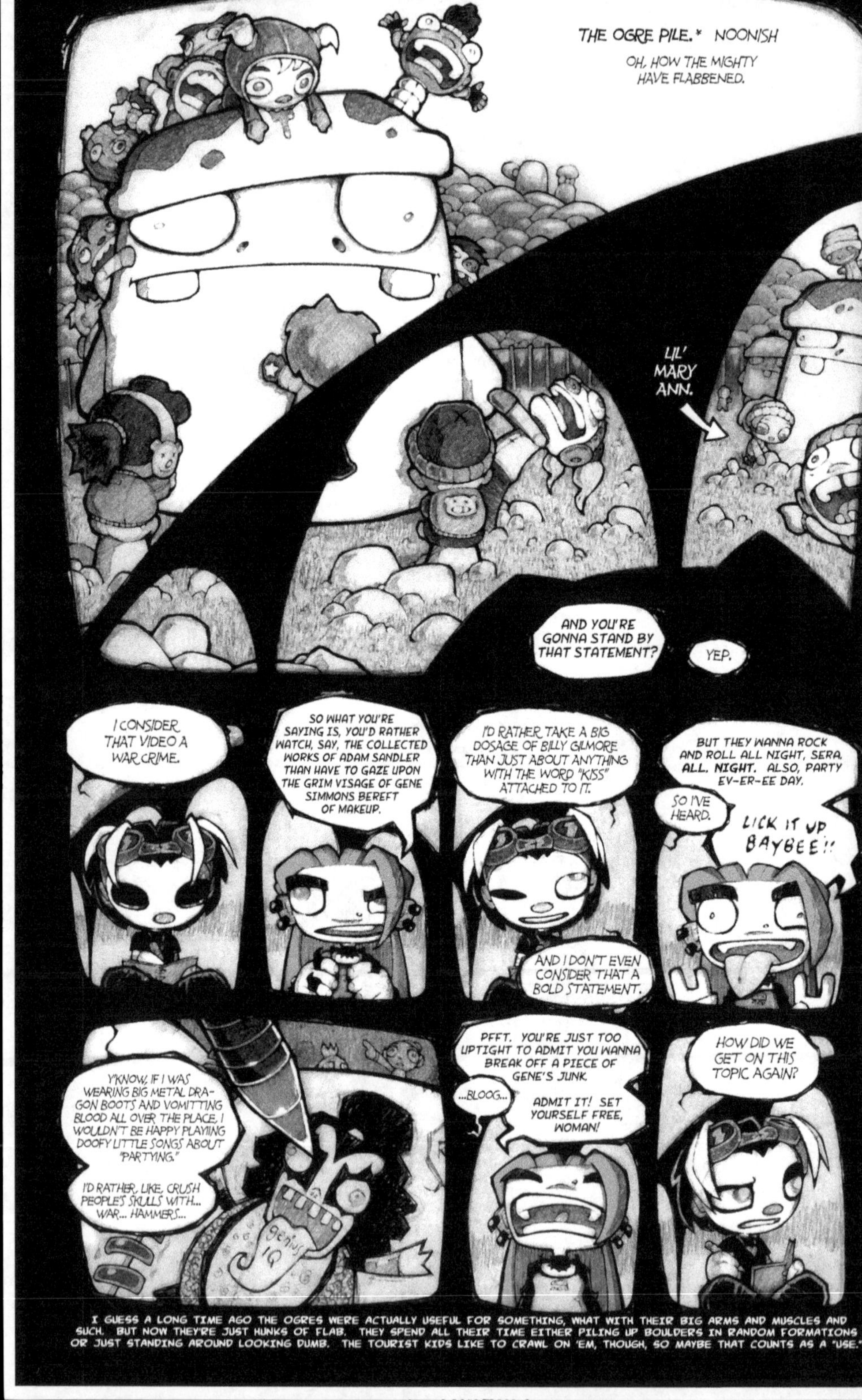
THE OGRE PILE.* NOONISH
OH, HOW THE MIGHTY HAVE FLABBENED.
LIL' MARY ANN.
AND YOU'RE GONNA STAND BY THAT STATEMENT?
YEP.
I CONSIDER THAT VIDEO A WAR CRIME.
SO WHAT YOU'RE SAYING IS, YOU'D RATHER WATCH, SAY, THE COLLECTED WORKS OF ADAM SANDLER THAN HAVE TO GAZE UPON THE GRIM VISAGE OF GENE SIMMONS BEREFT OF MAKEUP.
I'D RATHER TAKE A BIG DOSAGE OF BILLY GILMORE THAN JUST ABOUT ANYTHING WITH THE WORD "KISS" ATTACHED TO IT.
AND I DON'T EVEN CONSIDER THAT A BOLD STATEMENT.
BUT THEY WANNA ROCK AND ROLL ALL NIGHT, SERA. ALL. NIGHT. ALSO, PARTY EV-ER-EE DAY.
SO I'VE HEARD.
LICK IT UP BAYBEE!!
Y'KNOW, IF I WAS WEARING BIG METAL DRAGON BOOTS AND VOMITTING BLOOD ALL OVER THE PLACE, I WOULDN'T BE HAPPY PLAYING DOOFY LITTLE SONGS ABOUT "PARTYING."
I'D RATHER, LIKE, CRUSH PEOPLE'S SKULLS WITH... WAR... HAMMERS...
genius IQ
PFFT. YOU'RE JUST TOO UPTIGHT TO ADMIT YOU WANNA BREAK OFF A PIECE OF GENE'S JUNK.
...BLOOG...
ADMIT IT! SET YOURSELF FREE, WOMAN!
HOW DID WE GET ON THIS TOPIC AGAIN?

I GUESS A LONG TIME AGO THE OGRES WERE ACTUALLY USEFUL FOR SOMETHING, WHAT WITH THEIR BIG ARMS AND MUSCLES AND SUCH. BUT NOW THEY'RE JUST HUNKS OF FLAB. THEY SPEND ALL THEIR TIME EITHER PILING UP BOULDERS IN RANDOM FORMATIONS OR JUST STANDING AROUND LOOKING DUMB. THE TOURIST KIDS LIKE TO CRAWL ON 'EM, THOUGH, SO MAYBE THAT COUNTS AS A "USE."

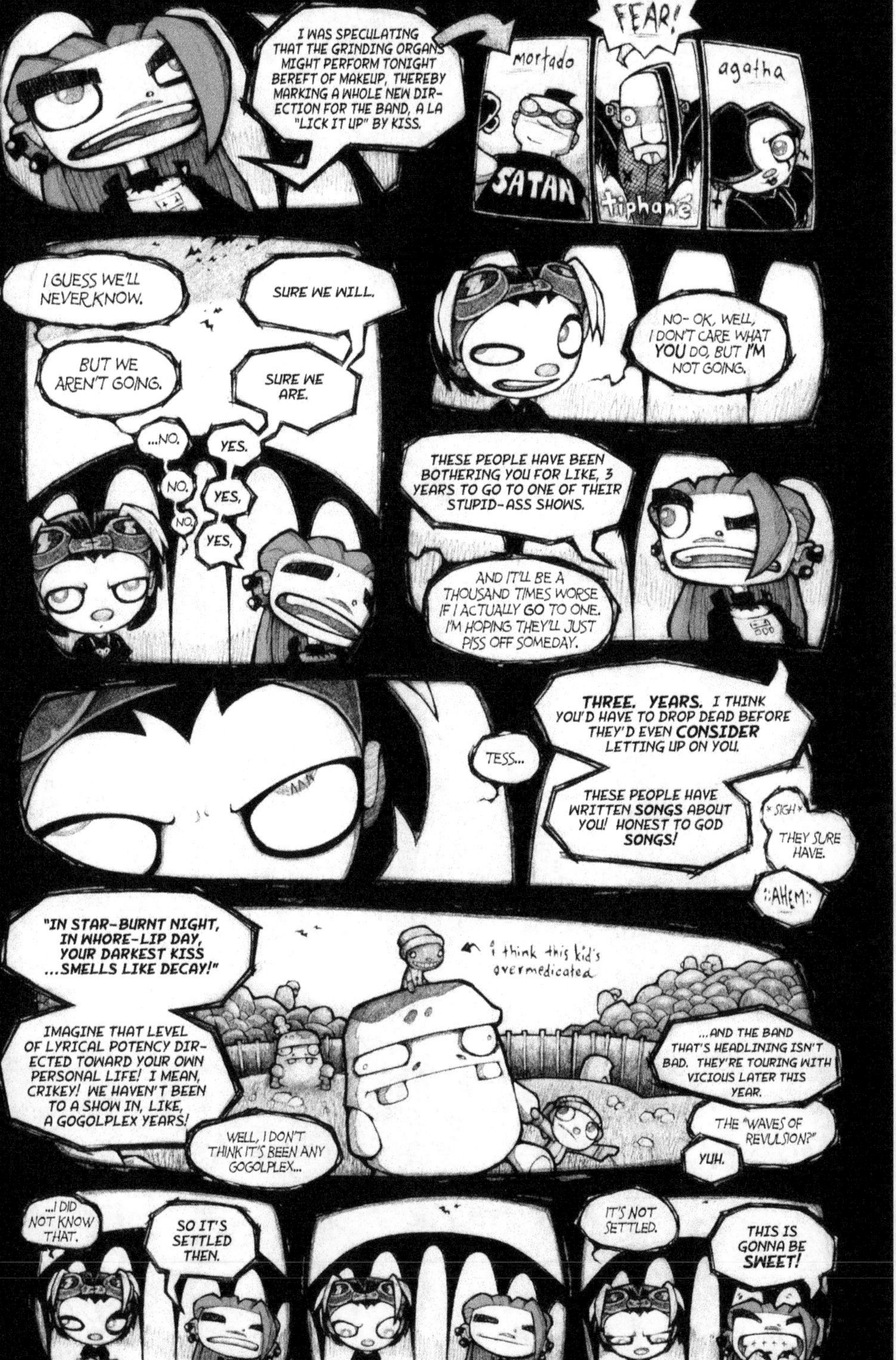
I WAS SPECULATING THAT THE GRINDING ORGANS MIGHT PERFORM TONIGHT BEREFT OF MAKEUP, THEREBY MARKING A WHOLE NEW DIRECTION FOR THE BAND, A LA "LICK IT UP" BY KISS.
FEAR!
mortado
SATAN
tiphane
agatha
I GUESS WE'LL NEVER KNOW.
SURE WE WILL.
BUT WE AREN'T GOING.
SURE WE ARE.
...NO.
YES.
NO.
YES,
NO.
YES,
NO- OK, WELL, I DON'T CARE WHAT YOU DO, BUT I'M NOT GOING.
THESE PEOPLE HAVE BEEN BOTHERING YOU FOR LIKE, 3 YEARS TO GO TO ONE OF THEIR STUPID-ASS SHOWS.
AND IT'LL BE A THOUSAND TIMES WORSE IF I ACTUALLY GO TO ONE. I'M HOPING THEY'LL JUST PISS OFF SOMEDAY.
TESS...
THREE. YEARS. I THINK YOU'D HAVE TO DROP DEAD BEFORE THEY'D EVEN CONSIDER LETTING UP ON YOU.
THESE PEOPLE HAVE WRITTEN SONGS ABOUT YOU! HONEST TO GOD SONGS!
SIGH THEY SURE HAVE.
::AHEM::
"IN STAR-BURNT NIGHT, IN WHORE-LIP DAY, YOUR DARKEST KISS ...SMELLS LIKE DECAY!"
i think this kid's overmedicated
IMAGINE THAT LEVEL OF LYRICAL POTENCY DIRECTED TOWARD YOUR OWN PERSONAL LIFE! I MEAN, CRIKEY! WE HAVEN'T BEEN TO A SHOW IN, LIKE, A GOGOLPLEX YEARS!
WELL, I DON'T THINK IT'S BEEN ANY GOGOLPLEX...
...AND THE BAND THAT'S HEADLINING ISN'T BAD. THEY'RE TOURING WITH VICIOUS LATER THIS YEAR.
THE "WAVES OF REVULSION?"
YUH.
...I DID NOT KNOW THAT.
SO IT'S SETTLED THEN.
IT'S NOT SETTLED.
THIS IS GONNA BE SWEET!

NOTE: ALL VIEWS EXPRESSED HEREIN HAVE BEEN EXCEEDINGLY WELL-CONSIDERED, ESPECIALLY THAT PART ABOUT GENE SIMMONS AND SUCKING.

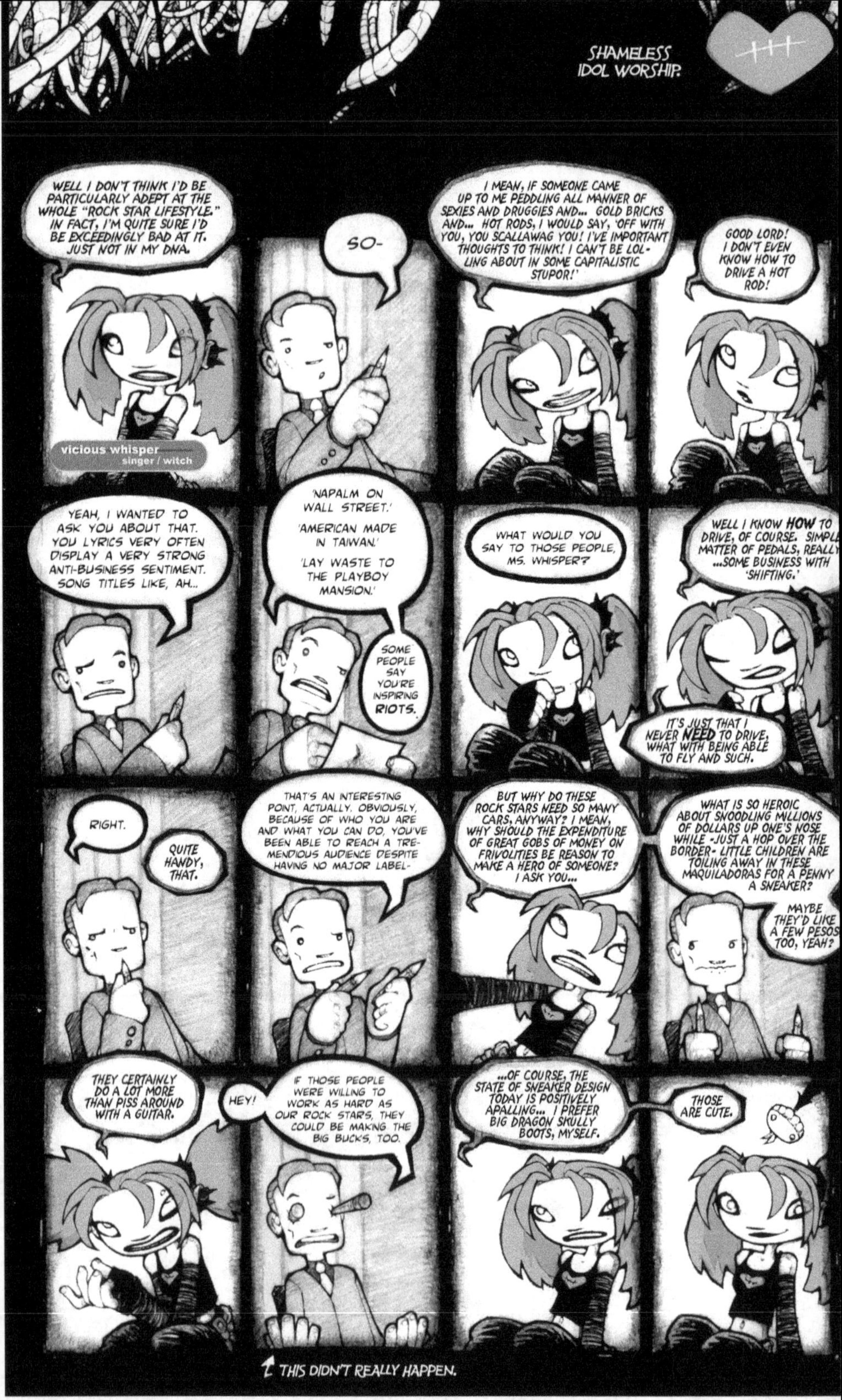
SHAMELESS IDOL WORSHIP.
WELL I DON'T THINK I'D BE PARTICULARLY ADEPT AT THE WHOLE "ROCK STAR LIFESTYLE." IN FACT, I'M QUITE SURE I'D BE EXCEEDINGLY BAD AT IT. JUST NOT IN MY DNA.
vicious whisper
singer / witch
SO-
I MEAN, IF SOMEONE CAME UP TO ME PEDDLING ALL MANNER OF SEXIES AND DRUGGIES AND... GOLD BRICKS AND... HOT RODS, I WOULD SAY, 'OFF WITH YOU, YOU SCALLAWAG YOU! I'VE IMPORTANT THOUGHTS TO THINK! I CAN'T BE LOL-LING ABOUT IN SOME CAPITALISTIC STUPOR!'
GOOD LORD! I DON'T EVEN KNOW HOW TO DRIVE A HOT ROD!
YEAH, I WANTED TO ASK YOU ABOUT THAT. YOU LYRICS VERY OFTEN DISPLAY A VERY STRONG ANTI-BUSINESS SENTIMENT. SONG TITLES LIKE, AH...
'NAPALM ON WALL STREET.' 'AMERICAN MADE IN TAIWAN.' 'LAY WASTE TO THE PLAYBOY MANSION.'
SOME PEOPLE SAY YOU'RE INSPIRING RIOTS.
WHAT WOULD YOU SAY TO THOSE PEOPLE, MS. WHISPER?
WELL I KNOW HOW TO DRIVE, OF COURSE. SIMPL MATTER OF PEDALS, REALL ...SOME BUSINESS WITH 'SHIFTING.'
IT'S JUST THAT I NEVER NEED TO DRIVE, WHAT WITH BEING ABLE TO FLY AND SUCH.
RIGHT.
QUITE HANDY, THAT.
THAT'S AN INTERESTING POINT, ACTUALLY. OBVIOUSLY, BECAUSE OF WHO YOU ARE AND WHAT YOU CAN DO, YOU'VE BEEN ABLE TO REACH A TRE-MENDIOUS AUDIENCE DESPITE HAVING NO MAJOR LABEL-
BUT WHY DO THESE ROCK STARS NEED SO MANY CARS, ANYWAY? I MEAN, WHY SHOULD THE EXPENDITURE OF GREAT GOBS OF MONEY ON FRIVOLITIES BE REASON TO MAKE A HERO OF SOMEONE? I ASK YOU...
WHAT IS SO HEROIC ABOUT SNOODLING MILLIONS OF DOLLARS UP ONE'S NOSE WHILE -JUST A HOP OVER THE BORDER- LITTLE CHILDREN ARE TOILING AWAY IN THESE MAQUILADORAS FOR A PENNY A SNEAKER?
MAYBE THEY'D LIKE A FEW PESOS TOO, YEAH?
THEY CERTAINLY DO A LOT MORE THAN PISS AROUND WITH A GUITAR.
HEY!
IF THOSE PEOPLE WERE WILLING TO WORK AS HARD AS OUR ROCK STARS, THEY COULD BE MAKING THE BIG BUCKS, TOO.
...OF COURSE, THE STATE OF SNEAKER DESIGN TODAY IS POSITIVELY APALLING... I PREFER BIG DRAGON SKULLY BOOTS, MYSELF.
THOSE ARE CUTE.
THIS DIDN'T REALLY HAPPEN.

excerpts: "an incomplete history of crestfallen."

The Crestfallens were not, however, responsible for bringing one supernatural species to the New Old World; the legendary "Shame of the Balkans", the vampire, was almost certainly imported with the more "traditional" colonists.

The origins of the vampiric affliction remain clouded, but the best evidence points to the late 13th Century and a breakaway sect of the Knight Templar, the so-called "Order of Silver". According to legend, the Order conspired with an unidentified Slavic warlock to unleash a terrible "plague of possession" across Europe, a plague only they, with their secret holy armaments, would be pious enough to contain. The Order's near total obscurity today speaks to the success of their bid for fame... And yet their terrible fanged legacy lives on.

valentine?

But although the origins of the affliction may be unclear, what is crystal clear is this: the vampire is in the venom. Every cell of the creature's body is infused with this venom, a terrible poison that is transferred from body to body through the elongated canines of the afflicted, a venom that seizes control of the victim's body upon physical death. The venom gives the vampire tremendous physical strength, extraordinary agility, and the ability to rapidly heal any wound inflicted by anything save silver or flame. Sunlight will burn the beast, as will any blessed objects (the oft-cited holy water, for example). The secrets of the Order of Silver thus revealed. During the day, the sleepless creature must keep to the shadows, often accumulating in "nests" o up to fifty, trembling from a need known only to the most pathological of drug addicts. But note: the vampire does not live on blood. It does not, in fact, live at all. But it needs. And this unholy need for blood drives every other concern from the vampire's mind, devolving the hapless creature into a primitive, animal state that could not be further removed from the elegant aristocrat of Stoker's novel.

lie

U.S. line mag.

The SSI (Supernatural Shield Initiative) estimates there may be as many as 10,000 vampires prowling the streets of America today.

"the count in colombia: the curse takes a bite out of the americas" U.S. line may 2000

→ excerpts:

The SSI (Supernatural Shield Initiative) has compiled "strong evidence" that at least seven countries in Central and South America are home to no fewer than 60 "blood cells", each capable of producing up to 4000 hits of The Curse every day. Indeed, reports have come in from Panama of a single cell housing perhaps 1000 vampires, all sedated with a combination of pig's blood and animal tranquilizers, each completely exsanguinated at a rate of once a week. And just one pint of pure blood can fetch nearly 10,000 dollars on the black market, with an investment by the seller of virtually nil.

SSI head Dr. Corliss Huske paints a grim portrait of The Curse's effect on the region: "We've seen cases where entire villages have been rounded up, marched to the cells, pumped full of vampire toxin and hung to death right in front of their families. 2-300 dead in a day. The local authorities are doing what they can, but the whole thing's just gotten too big." And it's getting worse. On the streets of Bogota, abductions by armed gangs of "sanguinistas" have become almost commonplace. Similiar situations are developing in Ecuador, Peru, and northern Brazil.

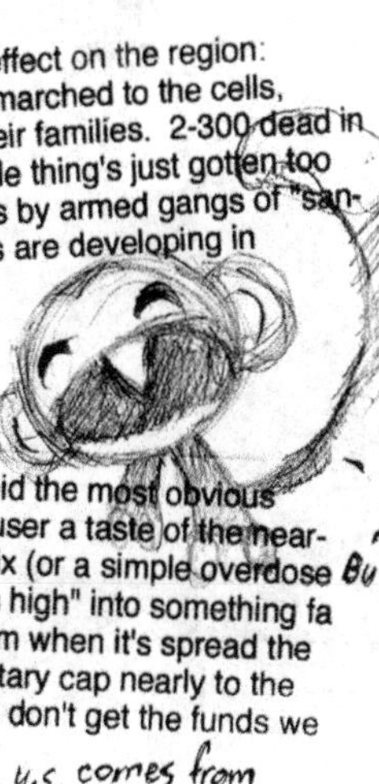

HIYA!! AH'M FAN-GEE™ TH' DRACUKEY!!®
AH'M CUTE AS A BUTTON!

Once harvested, the vampire's blood must be carefully diluted to avoid the most obvious danger. In small quantities mixed with human blood, it can give the user a taste of the near-orgasmic rush of a vampire feeding on its victim. But an improper mix (or a simple overdose as is becoming more and more common) can easily turn a "harmless high" into something far more sinister. Huske: "We have enough trouble containing vampirism when it's spread the old fashioned way. The Curse is pushing our already strained budgetary cap nearly to the breaking point." Another source within the SSI is more blunt: "If we don't get the funds we need, five years from now Dracula could be President." ?

fact: at least 70% of the curse consumed in the U.S. comes from vampires chained up in the spacious suburban basements of SSI bigshots.

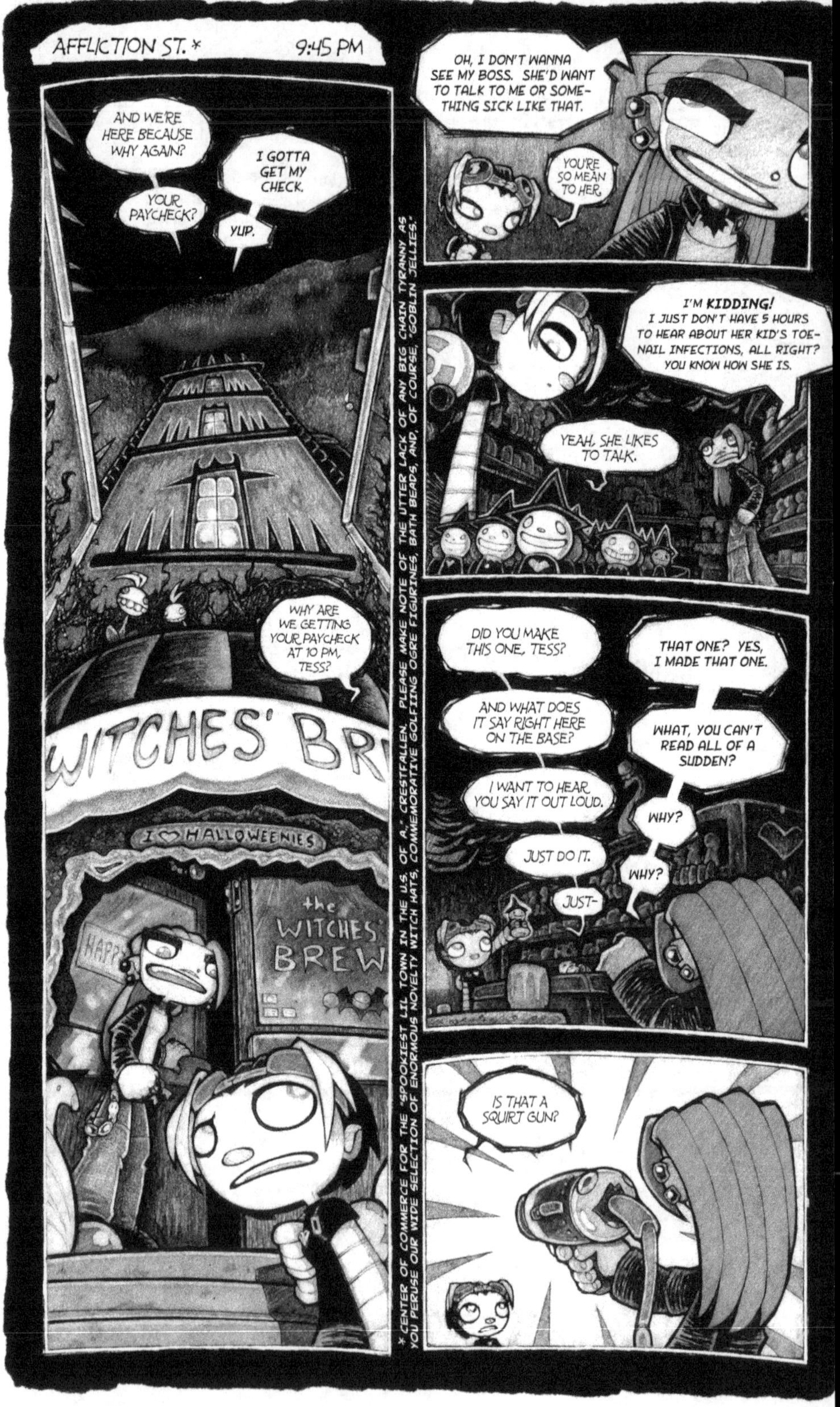
AFFLICTION ST.* 9:45 PM
AND WE'RE HERE BECAUSE WHY AGAIN?
I GOTTA GET MY CHECK.
YOUR PAYCHECK?
YUP.
WHY ARE WE GETTING YOUR PAYCHECK AT 10 PM, TESS?
WITCHES' BR
I ♡ HALLOWEENIES
the WITCHES' BREW
OH, I DON'T WANNA SEE MY BOSS. SHE'D WANT TO TALK TO ME OR SOMETHING SICK LIKE THAT.
YOU'RE SO MEAN TO HER.
I'M KIDDING! I JUST DON'T HAVE 5 HOURS TO HEAR ABOUT HER KID'S TOENAIL INFECTIONS, ALL RIGHT? YOU KNOW HOW SHE IS.
YEAH, SHE LIKES TO TALK.
DID YOU MAKE THIS ONE, TESS?
THAT ONE? YES, I MADE THAT ONE.
AND WHAT DOES IT SAY RIGHT HERE ON THE BASE?
WHAT, YOU CAN'T READ ALL OF A SUDDEN?
I WANT TO HEAR YOU SAY IT OUT LOUD.
WHY?
JUST DO IT.
WHY?
JUST-
IS THAT A SQUIRT GUN?
* CENTER OF COMMERCE FOR THE "SPOOKIEST LIL TOWN IN THE U.S. OF A," CRESTFALLEN. PLEASE MAKE NOTE OF THE UTTER LACK OF ANY BIG CHAIN TYRANNY AS YOU PERUSE OUR WIDE SELECTION OF ENORMOUS NOVELTY WITCH HATS, COMMEMORATIVE GOLFIING OGRE FIGURINES, BATH BEADS, AND, OF COURSE, "GOBLIN JELLIES."

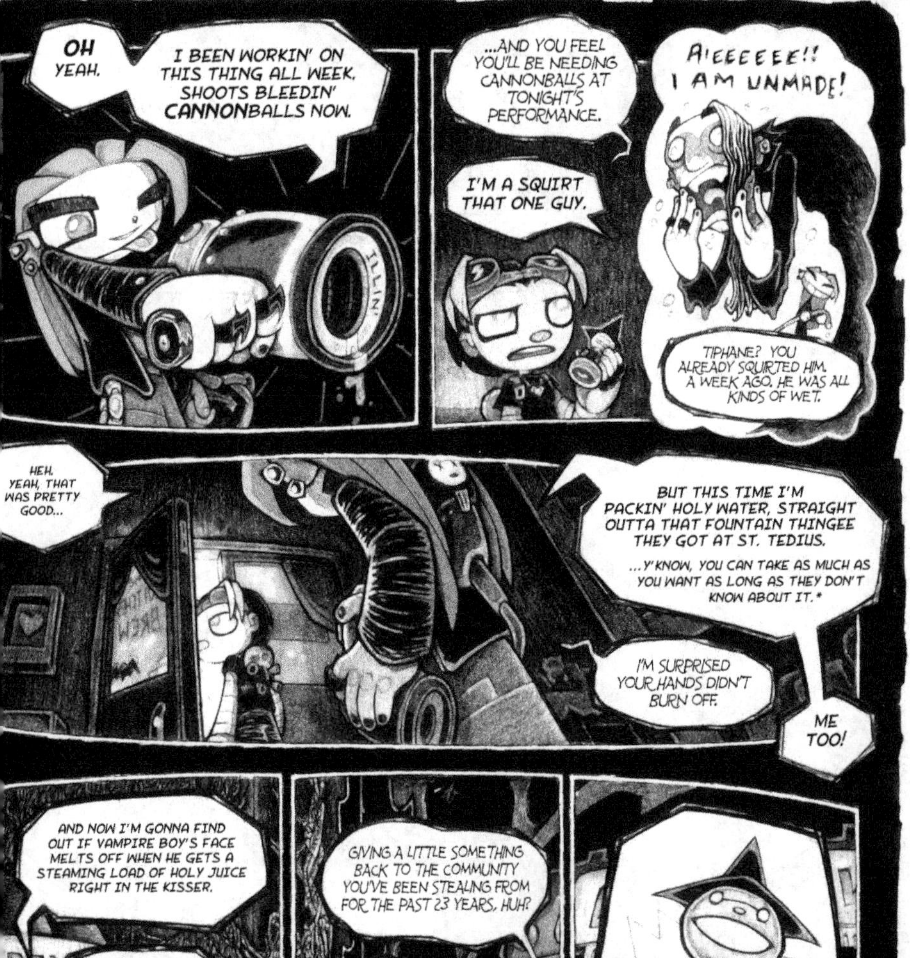
OH YEAH.
I BEEN WORKIN' ON THIS THING ALL WEEK. SHOOTS BLEEDIN' CANNONBALLS NOW.
...AND YOU FEEL YOU'LL BE NEEDING CANNONBALLS AT TONIGHT'S PERFORMANCE.
I'M A SQUIRT THAT ONE GUY.
AIEEEEEE!! I AM UNMADE!
TIPHANE? YOU ALREADY SQUIRTED HIM. A WEEK AGO. HE WAS ALL KINDS OF WET.
HEH. YEAH, THAT WAS PRETTY GOOD...
BUT THIS TIME I'M PACKIN' HOLY WATER, STRAIGHT OUTTA THAT FOUNTAIN THINGEE THEY GOT AT ST. TEDIUS.
...Y'KNOW, YOU CAN TAKE AS MUCH AS YOU WANT AS LONG AS THEY DON'T KNOW ABOUT IT.*
I'M SURPRISED YOUR HANDS DIDN'T BURN OFF.
ME TOO!
AND NOW I'M GONNA FIND OUT IF VAMPIRE BOY'S FACE MELTS OFF WHEN HE GETS A STEAMING LOAD OF HOLY JUICE RIGHT IN THE KISSER.
Y'KNOW, I'M NOT SURE HE REALLY THINKS HE'S A VAMPIRE. IT'S JUST SOMETHING TO SAY.
JUST MAKIN' SURE. PUBLIC SERVICE, REALLY.
GIVING A LITTLE SOMETHING BACK TO THE COMMUNITY YOU'VE BEEN STEALING FROM FOR THE PAST 23 YEARS, HUH?
OH, I THINK I'VE EARNED WHAT I'VE GOT.
Y'THINK?
GRAMMAS PUT A SPELL ON YOUR ♡
...

* I LATER DISCOVERED THE MOISTURE IN QUESTION WAS PROCURED DURING SUNDAY SERVICES WITH HER GRAMPA, WHO ENTREATED HER TO TEST IT OUT ON "THAT GODDAMN FATHER MULCAHY AND HIS GODDAMN FACIAL HAIRS."

SEZ GRAMPA RUBIKOV: "THAT'S A GOOD GAG!"

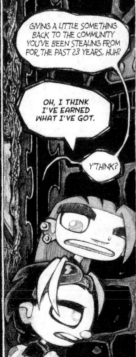

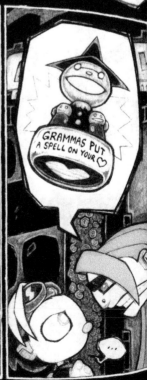

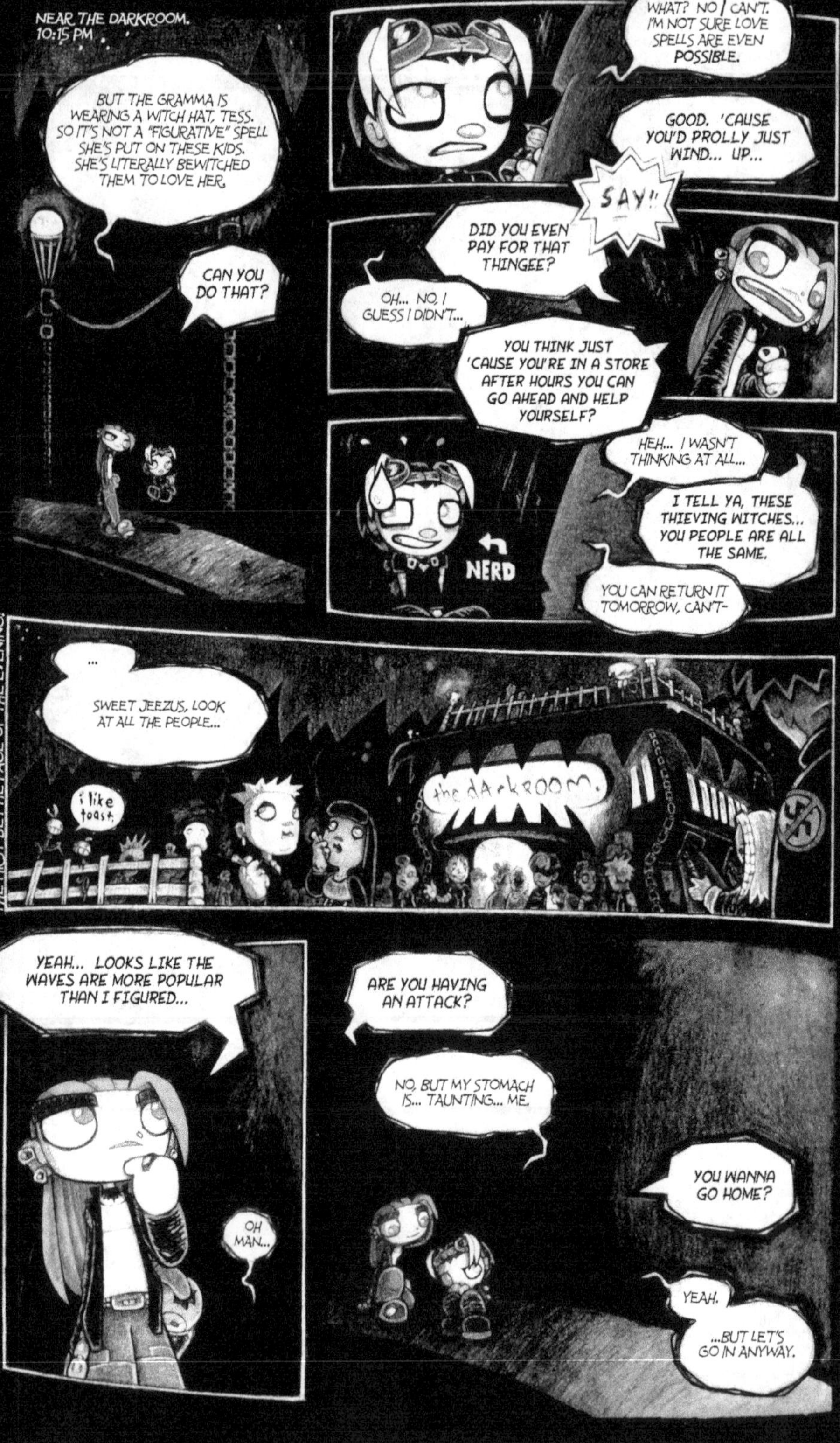
NEAR THE DARKROOM. 10:15 PM
BUT THE GRAMMA IS WEARING A WITCH HAT, TESS. SO IT'S NOT A "FIGURATIVE" SPELL SHE'S PUT ON THESE KIDS. SHE'S LITERALLY BEWITCHED THEM TO LOVE HER.
CAN YOU DO THAT?
WHAT? NO I CAN'T. I'M NOT SURE LOVE SPELLS ARE EVEN POSSIBLE.
GOOD. 'CAUSE YOU'D PROLLY JUST WIND... UP...
SAY!!
DID YOU EVEN PAY FOR THAT THINGEE?
OH... NO, I GUESS I DIDN'T...
YOU THINK JUST 'CAUSE YOU'RE IN A STORE AFTER HOURS YOU CAN GO AHEAD AND HELP YOURSELF?
NERD
HEH... I WASN'T THINKING AT ALL...
I TELL YA, THESE THIEVING WITCHES... YOU PEOPLE ARE ALL THE SAME.
YOU CAN RETURN IT TOMORROW, CAN'T-
THE FIRST BETTIE PAGE OF THE EVENING!
...
SWEET JEEZUS, LOOK AT ALL THE PEOPLE...
i like toast.
the dArkROOm.
YEAH... LOOKS LIKE THE WAVES ARE MORE POPULAR THAN I FIGURED...
OH MAN...
ARE YOU HAVING AN ATTACK?
NO, BUT MY STOMACH IS... TAUNTING... ME.
YOU WANNA GO HOME?
YEAH.
...BUT LET'S GO IN ANYWAY.

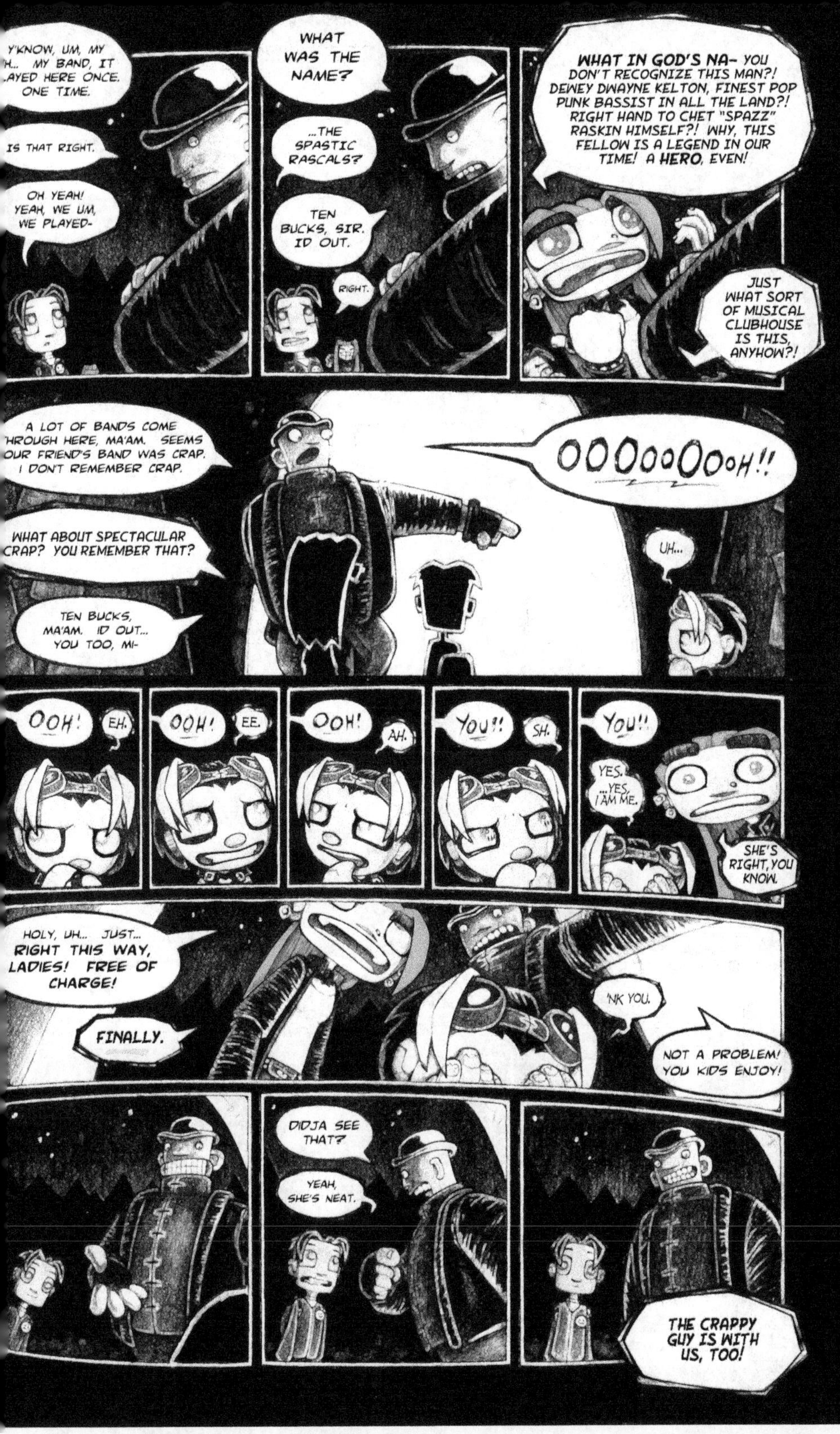

Y'KNOW, UM, MY UH... MY BAND, IT PLAYED HERE ONCE. ONE TIME.
IS THAT RIGHT.
OH YEAH! YEAH, WE UM, WE PLAYED-
WHAT WAS THE NAME?
...THE SPASTIC RASCALS?
TEN BUCKS, SIR. ID OUT.
RIGHT.
WHAT IN GOD'S NA- YOU DON'T RECOGNIZE THIS MAN?! DEWEY DWAYNE KELTON, FINEST POP PUNK BASSIST IN ALL THE LAND?! RIGHT HAND TO CHET "SPAZZ" RASKIN HIMSELF?! WHY, THIS FELLOW IS A LEGEND IN OUR TIME! A HERO, EVEN!
JUST WHAT SORT OF MUSICAL CLUBHOUSE IS THIS, ANYHOW?!
A LOT OF BANDS COME THROUGH HERE, MA'AM. SEEMS OUR FRIEND'S BAND WAS CRAP. I DON'T REMEMBER CRAP.
WHAT ABOUT SPECTACULAR CRAP? YOU REMEMBER THAT?
TEN BUCKS, MA'AM. ID OUT... YOU TOO, MI-
OOOOOOOOOH!!
UH...
OOH!
EH.
OOH!
EE.
OOH!
AH.
YOU!!
SH.
YOU!!
YES. ...YES, I AM ME.
SHE'S RIGHT, YOU KNOW.
HOLY, UH... JUST... RIGHT THIS WAY, LADIES! FREE OF CHARGE!
FINALLY.
'NK YOU.
NOT A PROBLEM! YOU KIDS ENJOY!
DIDJA SEE THAT?
YEAH, SHE'S NEAT.
THE CRAPPY GUY IS WITH US, TOO!

and so...

1. WOUNDED IN (SHAVING) ACTION 2. INDUSTRIAL DUDE HAIRCUT, STANDARD ISSUE 3. WORKS AT KINKO'S (HA HA HA! I HAVE DEFLATED THE SELF-IMPORTANT EGOTISM OF THE GOTH SCENE IN ONE BOLDLY ORIGINAL WITTICISM! CUTS LIKE A KNIFE, CHARLIE!) 4. WRITES EROTIC FANFIC FEATURING CENOBITES AND MONCHICHI 5. ABSOLUTELY CONVINCED HIS LIFE WOULD BE GREATLY IMPROVED BY CYBERNETIC IMPLANTS 6. CONSIDERED 'BLADE' TO BE THE PINNACLE OF AMERICAN CINEMA... UNTIL HE SAW 'BLADE 2' 7. JUST CAME TO MAKE FUN. 8. PRACTICING FOR BAND PHOTOS 9. "MAGICK" WITH A "K" 10. ONCE CHOKED ON GLENN DANZIG'S VOMIT. 11. WRITING A SCREENPLAY THAT EXPOSES THE DARK UNDERBELLY OF SUBURBIA 12. HAS PAINSTAKINGLY RECREATED THE COVER OF SKINNY PUPPY'S "TOO DARK PARK" IN BLACKLIGHT PAINT ACROSS ALL FOUR WALLS OF HIS BEDROOM 13. FALSE COWBOY 14. "IN MY DREAM, I AM THE WIZARD MASTER!" AND SHAME ON YOU IF YOU GOT THAT REFERENCE

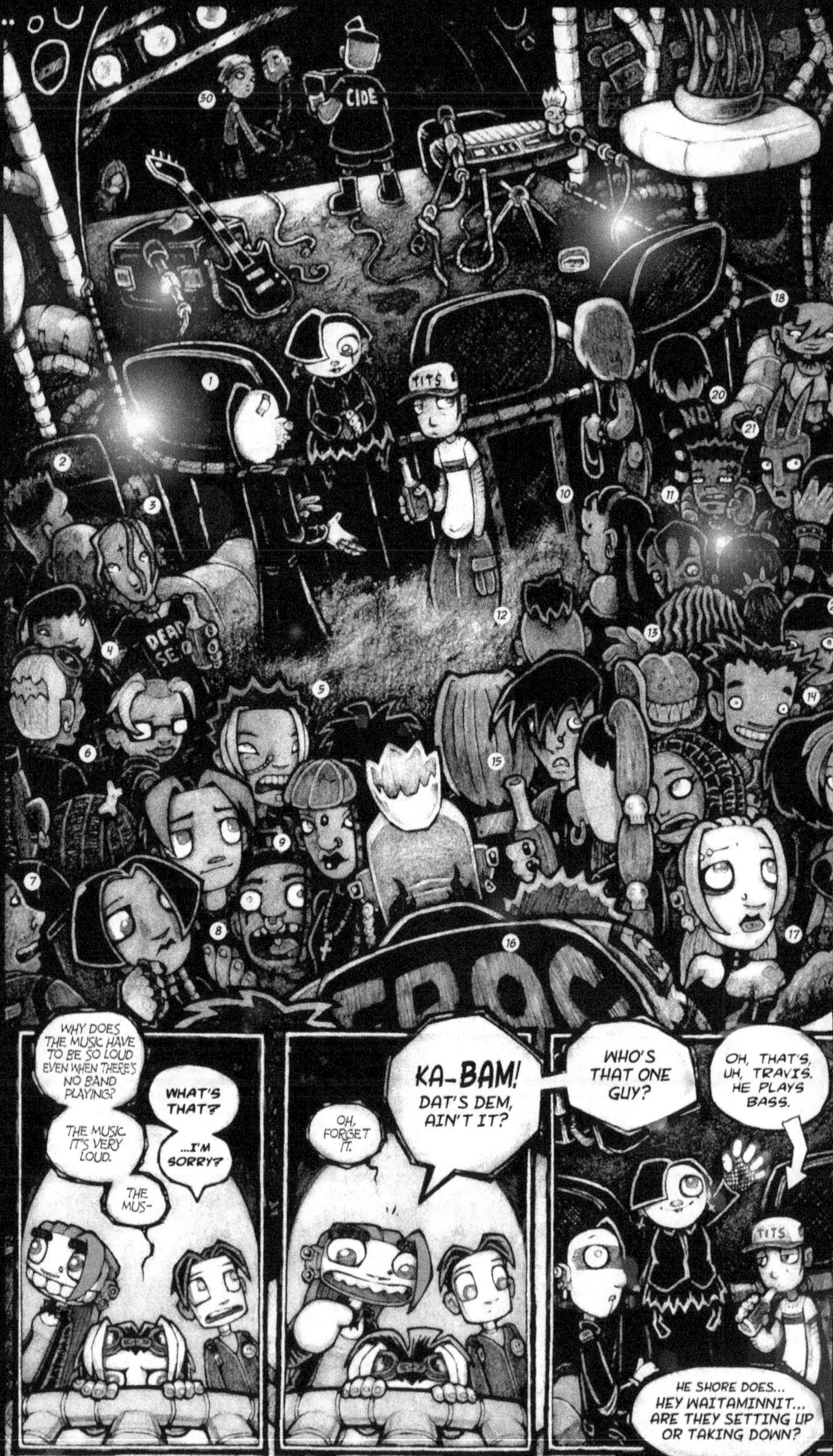

WHY DOES THE MUSIC HAVE TO BE SO LOUD EVEN WHEN THERE'S NO BAND PLAYING?
WHAT'S THAT?
THE MUSIC. IT'S VERY LOUD.
...I'M SORRY?
THE MUS-
OH, FORGET IT.
KA-BAM! DAT'S DEM, AIN'T IT?
WHO'S THAT ONE GUY?
OH, THAT'S, UH, TRAVIS. HE PLAYS BASS.
HE SHORE DOES... HEY WAITAMINNIT... ARE THEY SETTING UP OR TAKING DOWN?

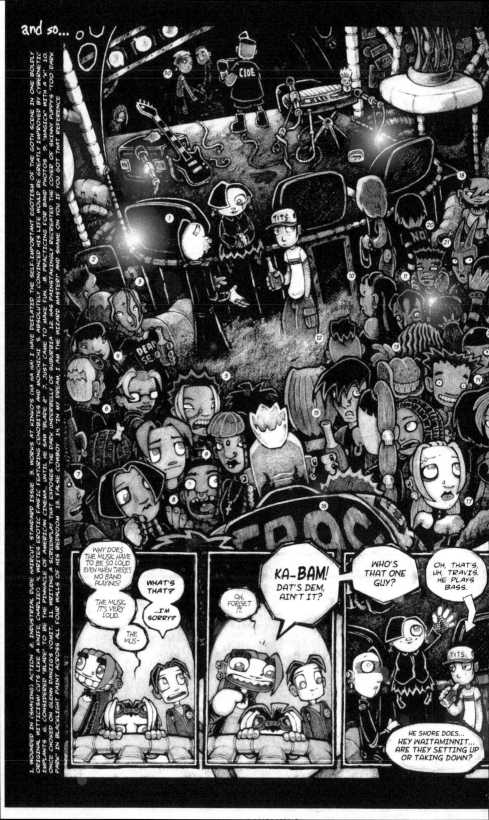

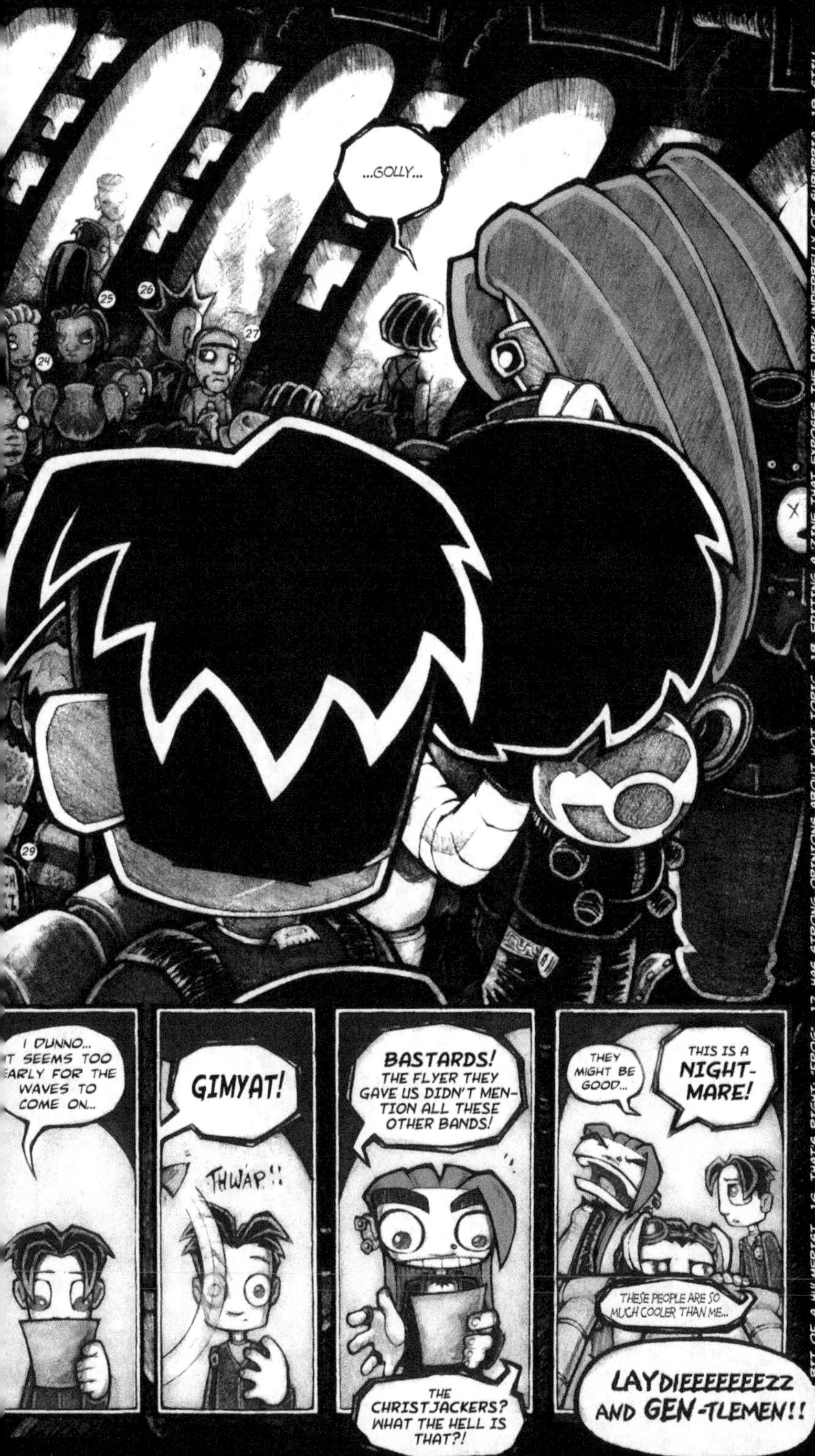
...GOLLY...
I DUNNO... T SEEMS TOO ARLY FOR THE WAVES TO COME ON...
GIMYAT!
THWAP!!
BASTARDS! THE FLYER THEY GAVE US DIDN'T MENTION ALL THESE OTHER BANDS!
THE CHRISTJACKERS? WHAT THE HELL IS THAT?!
THEY MIGHT BE GOOD...
THIS IS A NIGHTMARE!
THESE PEOPLE ARE SO MUCH COOLER THAN ME...
LAYDIEEEEEEEZZ AND GEN-TLEMEN!!

BIT OF A HULMERIST 16. THAT'S RIGHT: "FROG" 17. HAS STRONG OPINIONS ABOUT HOT TOPIC 18. EDITING A ZINE THAT EXPOSES THE DARK UNDERBELLY OF SUBURBIA 19. STILL CAN'T BELIEVE THE BOUNCER DIDN'T FIND HIS BUTTERFLY KNIFE 20. HAS SOME PHOTOGRAPHS OF MASSIVE GENITAL INJURIES HE'S PRETTY SURE JHONEN WILL FIND AMUSING WHEN THEY MEET SOMEDAY 21. JESUS FREAK 22. WWW.NAKEDPICTURESOFMEANDMYGIRLFRIENDGETTINGBIZZAY.COM 23. ACTUAL QUOTE: "MY GREATEST DREAM IN LIFE IS TO SOMEDAY GIVE BIRTH TO STILLBORN TRIPLETS." 24. CAN'T SEEM TO RECONCILE HER OVERALL DISAGREEMENT WITH MARILYN MANSON'S MUSIC OUTPUT WITH HER OVERALL AGREEMENT WITH MARILYN MANSON'S INTERVIEW OUTPUT 25. ACTUALLY ANGRY THEY'RE PLAYING SHIT FROM, LIKE, 10 YEARS AGO 26. THE SPIRIT OF '76 27. THERE'S THAT GUY AGAIN. AGAIN. 6 SHOWS IN A ROW, TESS! 28. RECORDING A CONCEPT ALBUM THAT EXPOSES THE DARK UNDERBELLY OF SUBURBIA 29. SORTA LIKES THE SUBURBS, ACTUALLY 30. HAS SEEN WORSE. BUT NOT MUCH WORSE.

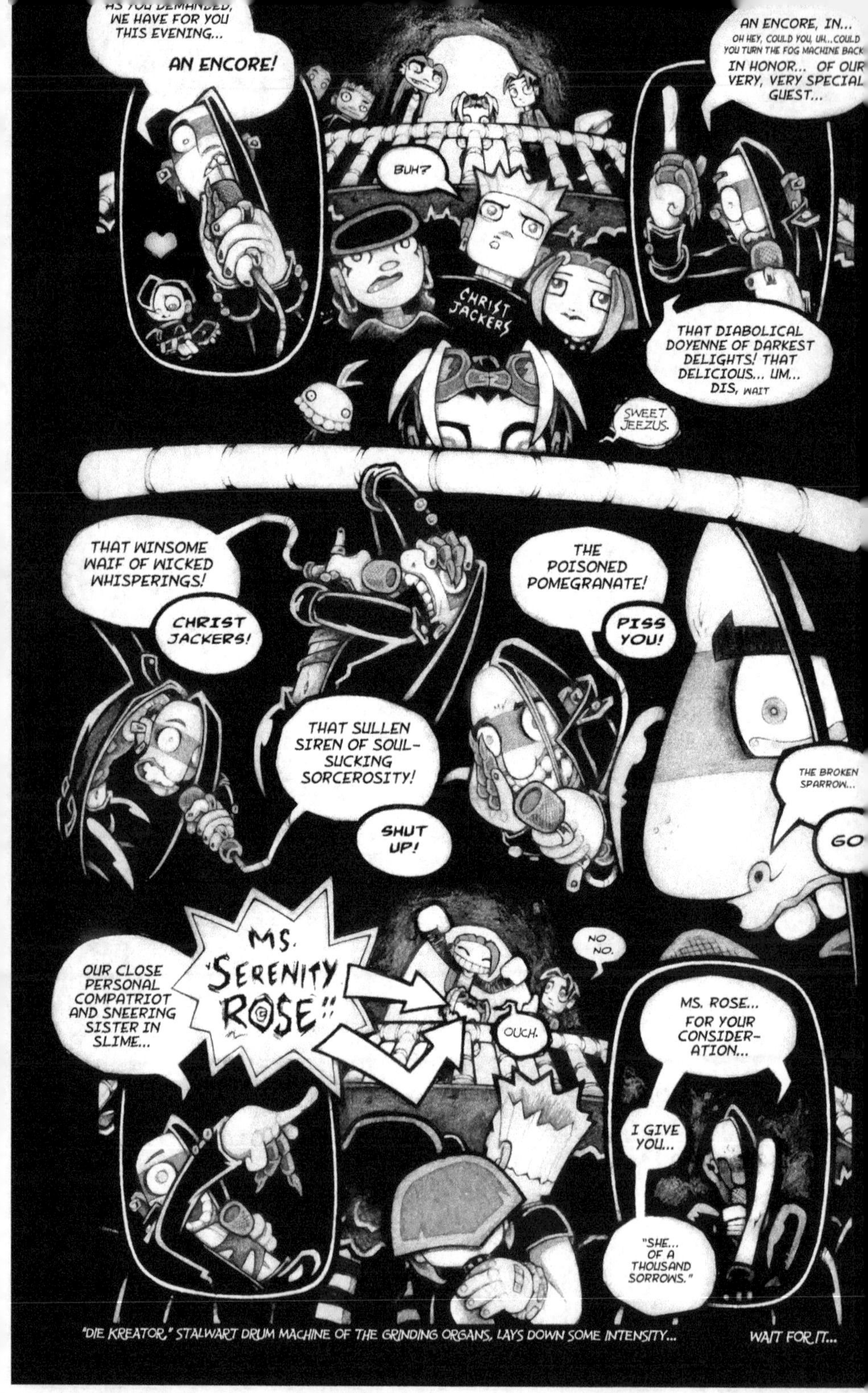
AS YOU DEMANDED, WE HAVE FOR YOU THIS EVENING...
AN ENCORE!
AN ENCORE, IN...
OH HEY, COULD YOU, UH...COULD YOU TURN THE FOG MACHINE BACK
IN HONOR... OF OUR VERY, VERY SPECIAL GUEST...
BUH?
CHRIST JACKERS
THAT DIABOLICAL DOYENNE OF DARKEST DELIGHTS! THAT DELICIOUS... UM... DIS, WAIT
SWEET JEEZUS.
THAT WINSOME WAIF OF WICKED WHISPERINGS!
CHRIST JACKERS!
THE POISONED POMEGRANATE!
PISS YOU!
THAT SULLEN SIREN OF SOUL-SUCKING SORCEROSITY!
SHUT UP!
THE BROKEN SPARROW...
GO
OUR CLOSE PERSONAL COMPATRIOT AND SNEERING SISTER IN SLIME...
MS. 'SERENITY ROSE'!!
NO NO.
OUCH.
MS. ROSE... FOR YOUR CONSIDER-ATION...
I GIVE YOU...
"SHE... OF A THOUSAND SORROWS."
"DIE KREATOR," STALWART DRUM MACHINE OF THE GRINDING ORGANS, LAYS DOWN SOME INTENSITY...
WAIT FOR IT...

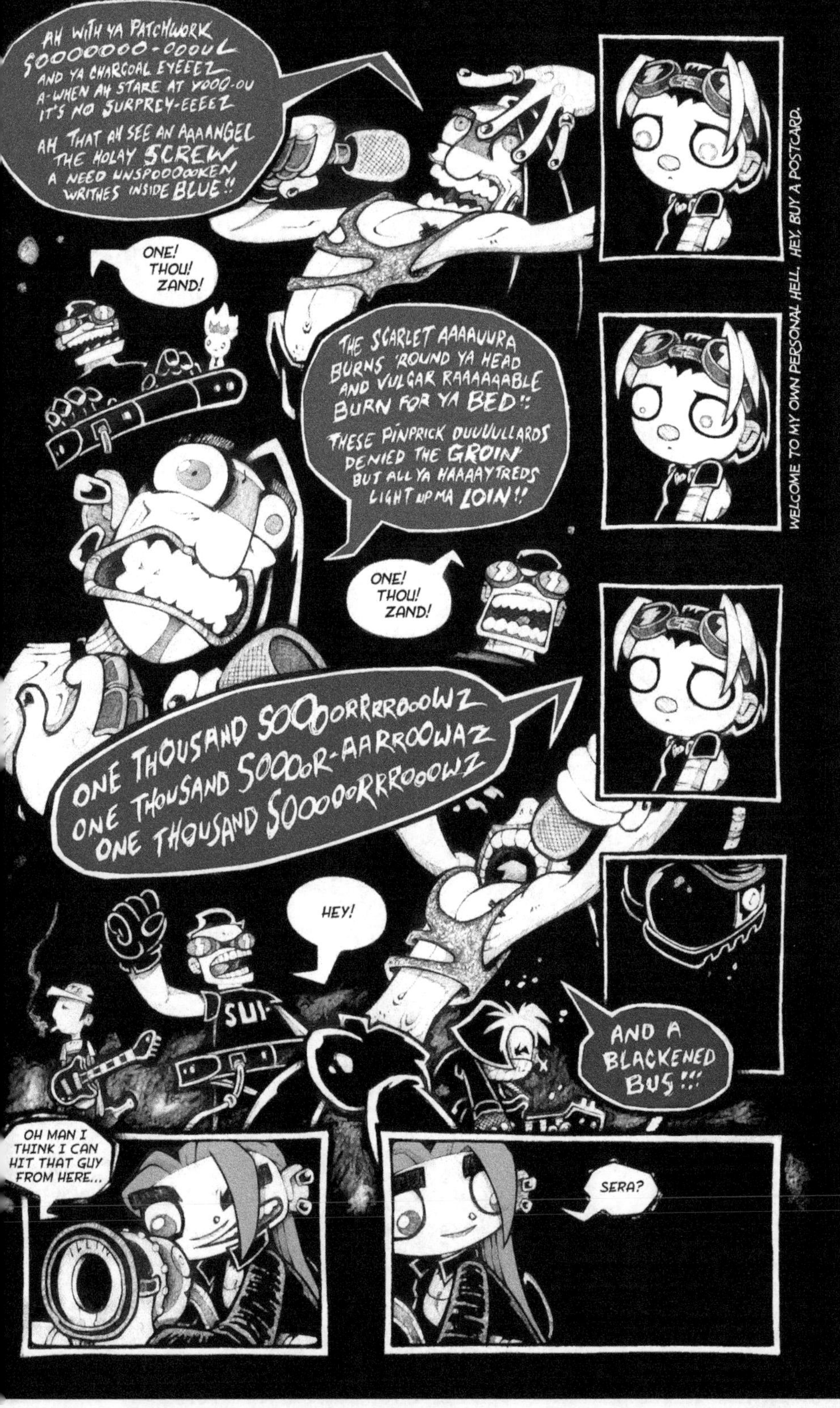
AH WITH YA PATCHWORK SOOOOOOO-OOOUL AND YA CHARCOAL EYEEEZ A-WHEN AH STARE AT YOOO-OU IT'S NO SURPREY-EEEEZ AH THAT AH SEE AN AAAANGEL THE HOLAY SCREW A NEED UNSPOOOOOKEN WRITHES INSIDE BLUE!!
ONE! THOU! ZAND!
THE SCARLET AAAAUURA BURNS 'ROUND YA HEAD AND VULGAR RAAAAAABLE BURN FOR YA BED!! THESE PINPRICK DUUUULLARDS DENIED THE GROIN BUT ALL YA HAAAAYTREDS LIGHT UP MA LOIN!!
ONE! THOU! ZAND!
ONE THOUSAND SOOOORRRROOOWZ ONE THOUSAND SOOOOR-AARROOWAZ ONE THOUSAND SOOOOORRROOOWZ
HEY!
SUI
AND A BLACKENED BUS!!!
OH MAN I THINK I CAN HIT THAT GUY FROM HERE...
SERA?
WELCOME TO MY OWN PERSONAL HELL. HEY, BUY A POSTCARD.

FROM FEARFUL THING: THE JOURNAL OF THE UNDERSIDE #2 (D.D. KELTON, ED.) DRAWED BY ME.

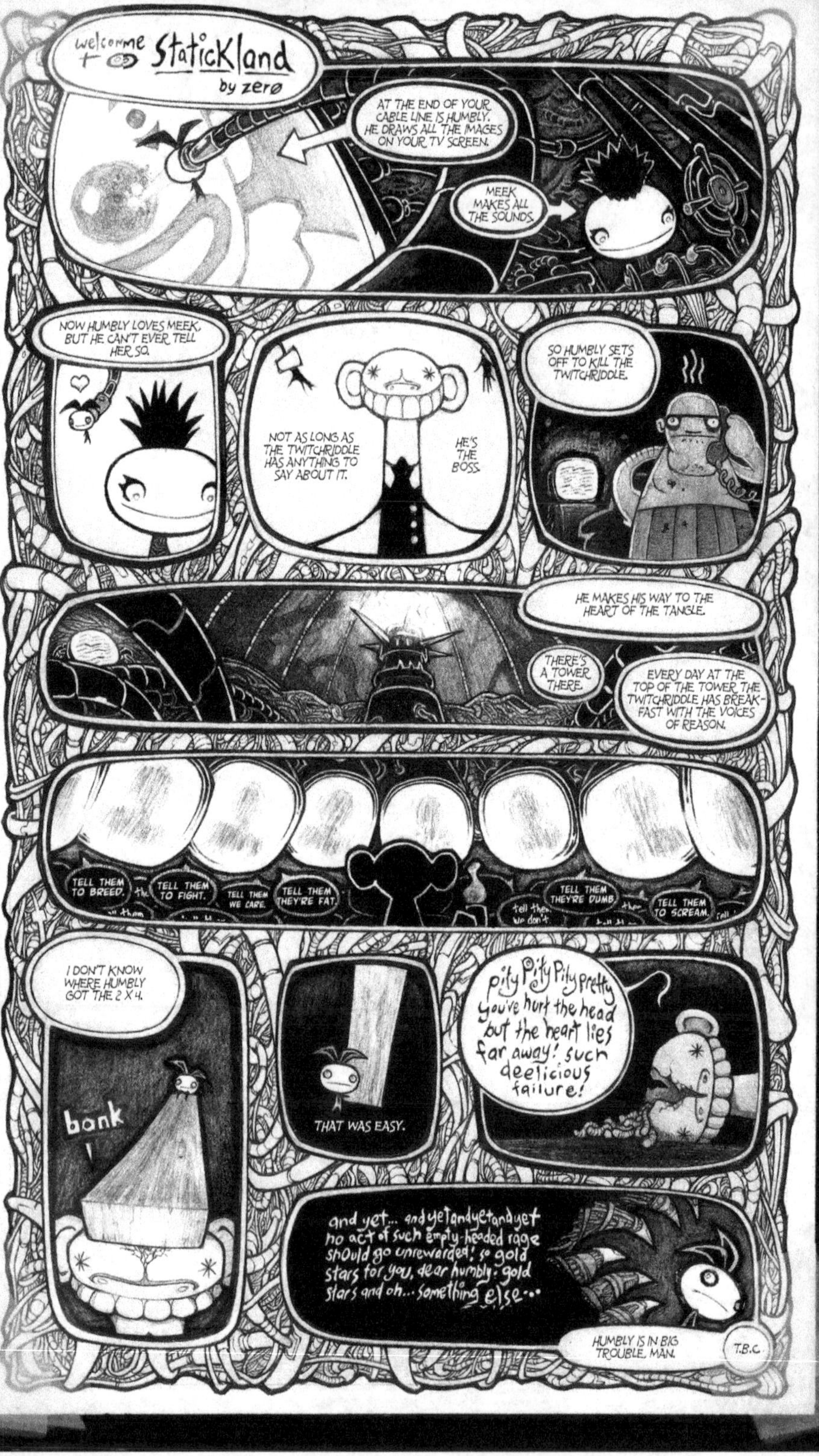
welcome to Statickland
by zerø
AT THE END OF YOUR CABLE LINE IS HUMBLY. HE DRAWS ALL THE IMAGES ON YOUR TV SCREEN.
MEEK MAKES ALL THE SOUNDS.
NOW HUMBLY LOVES MEEK, BUT HE CAN'T EVER TELL HER SO.
NOT AS LONG AS THE TWITCHRIDDLE HAS ANYTHING TO SAY ABOUT IT.
HE'S THE BOSS.
SO HUMBLY SETS OFF TO KILL THE TWITCHRIDDLE.
HE MAKES HIS WAY TO THE HEART OF THE TANGLE.
THERE'S A TOWER THERE.
EVERY DAY AT THE TOP OF THE TOWER THE TWITCHRIDDLE HAS BREAK-FAST WITH THE VOICES OF REASON.
TELL THEM TO BREED.
TELL THEM TO FIGHT.
TELL THEM WE CARE.
TELL THEM THEY'RE FAT.
TELL THEM THEY'RE DUMB.
TELL THEM TO SCREAM.
I DON'T KNOW WHERE HUMBLY GOT THE 2 X 4.
bank
THAT WAS EASY.
pity pity pity pretty you've hurt the head but the heart lies far away! such deelicious failure!
and yet... and yetandyetandyet no act of such empty-headed rage should go unrewarded! so gold stars for you, dear humbly. gold stars and oh... something else...
HUMBLY IS IN BIG TROUBLE, MAN.
T.B.C.

I SPEND THE NEXT COUPLE HOURS ON THE ROOF.

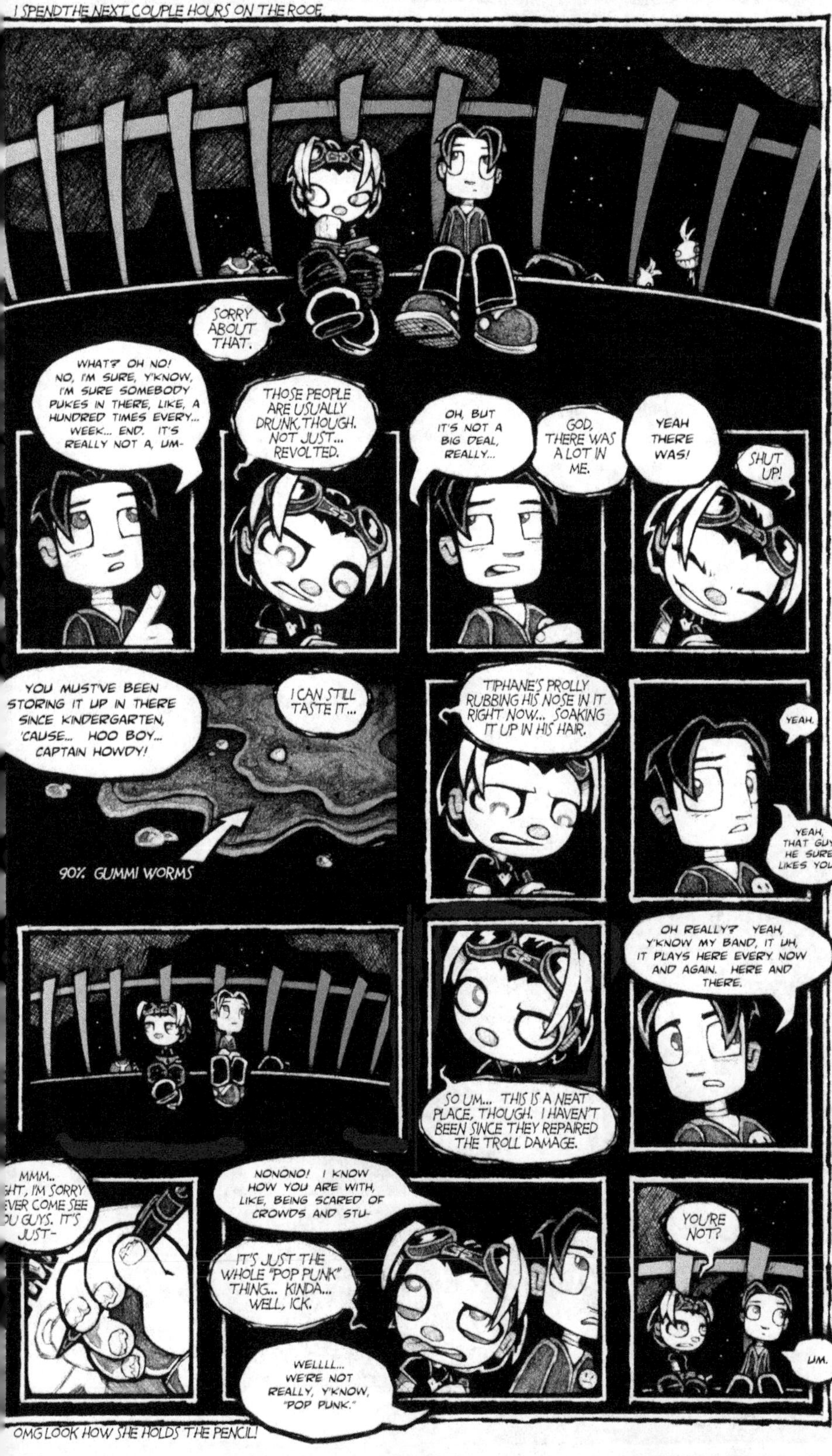
SORRY ABOUT THAT.
WHAT? OH NO! NO, I'M SURE, Y'KNOW, I'M SURE SOMEBODY PUKES IN THERE, LIKE, A HUNDRED TIMES EVERY... WEEK... END. IT'S REALLY NOT A, UM-
THOSE PEOPLE ARE USUALLY DRUNK, THOUGH. NOT JUST... REVOLTED.
OH, BUT IT'S NOT A BIG DEAL, REALLY...
GOD, THERE WAS A LOT IN ME.
YEAH THERE WAS!
SHUT UP!
YOU MUST'VE BEEN STORING IT UP IN THERE SINCE KINDERGARTEN, 'CAUSE... HOO BOY... CAPTAIN HOWDY!
I CAN STILL TASTE IT...
90% GUMMI WORMS
TIPHANE'S PROLLY RUBBING HIS NOSE IN IT RIGHT NOW... SOAKING IT UP IN HIS HAIR.
YEAH.
YEAH, THAT GUY, HE SURE LIKES YOU...
SO UM... THIS IS A NEAT PLACE, THOUGH. I HAVEN'T BEEN SINCE THEY REPAIRED THE TROLL DAMAGE.
OH REALLY? YEAH, Y'KNOW MY BAND, IT UH, IT PLAYS HERE EVERY NOW AND AGAIN. HERE AND THERE.
MMM.. GHT, I'M SORRY EVER COME SEE OU GUYS. IT'S JUST-
NONONO! I KNOW HOW YOU ARE WITH, LIKE, BEING SCARED OF CROWDS AND STU-
IT'S JUST THE WHOLE "POP PUNK" THING... KINDA... WELL, ICK.
WELLLL... WE'RE NOT REALLY, Y'KNOW, "POP PUNK."
YOU'RE NOT?
UM.

OMG LOOK HOW SHE HOLDS THE PENCIL!

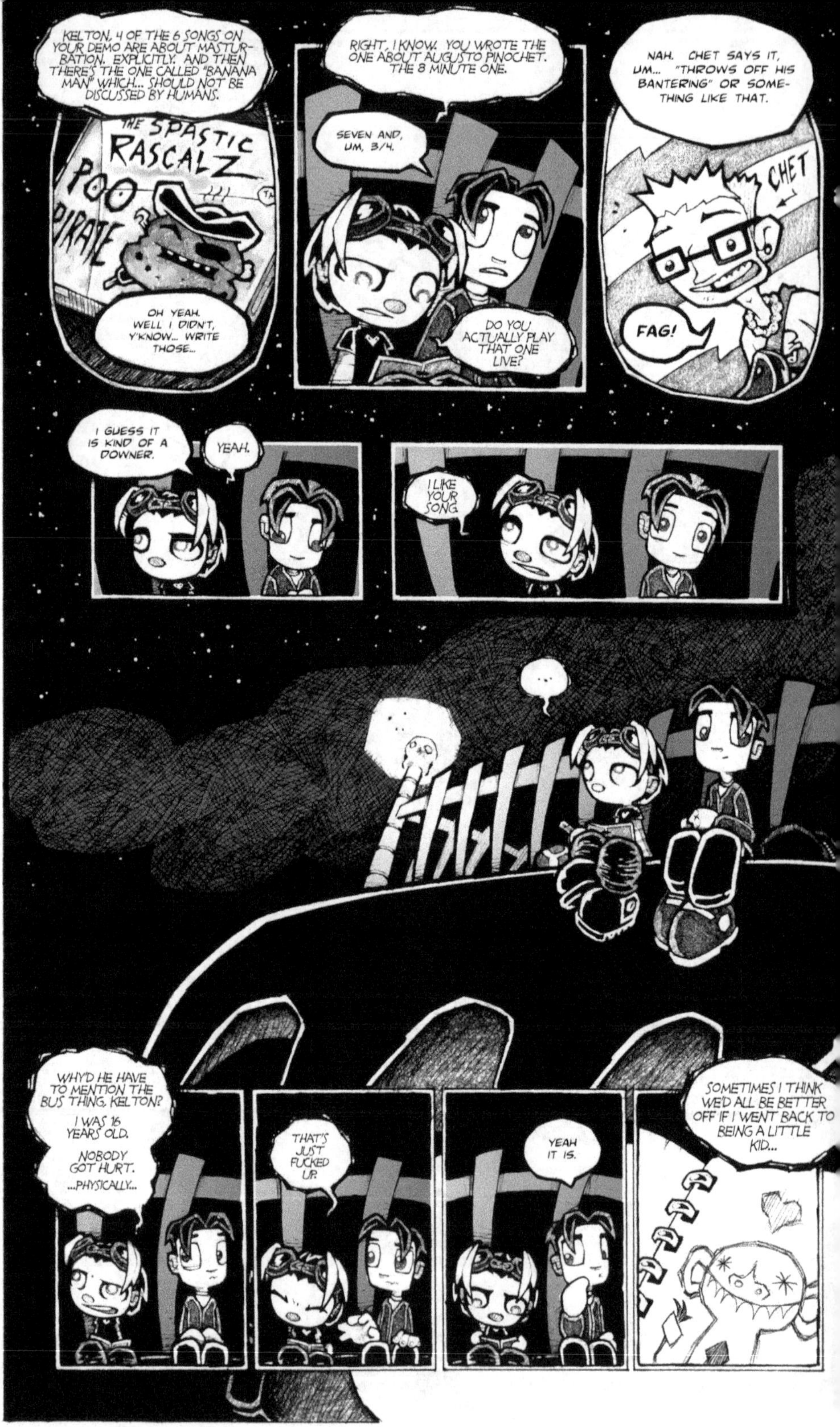
KELTON, 4 OF THE 6 SONGS ON YOUR DEMO ARE ABOUT MASTURBATION. EXPLICITLY. AND THEN THERE'S THE ONE CALLED "BANANA MAN" WHICH... SHOULD NOT BE DISCUSSED BY HUMANS.
THE SPASTIC RASCALZ
POO PIRATE
OH YEAH. WELL I DIDN'T, Y'KNOW... WRITE THOSE...
RIGHT, I KNOW. YOU WROTE THE ONE ABOUT AUGUSTO PINOCHET. THE 8 MINUTE ONE.
SEVEN AND, UM, 3/4.
DO YOU ACTUALLY PLAY THAT ONE LIVE?
NAH. CHET SAYS IT, UM... "THROWS OFF HIS BANTERING" OR SOMETHING LIKE THAT.
CHET
FAG!
I GUESS IT IS KIND OF A DOWNER.
YEAH.
I LIKE YOUR SONG
WHY'D HE HAVE TO MENTION THE BUS THING, KELTON?
I WAS 16 YEARS OLD.
NOBODY GOT HURT.
...PHYSICALLY...
THAT'S JUST FUCKED UP.
YEAH IT IS.
SOMETIMES I THINK WE'D ALL BE BETTER OFF IF I WENT BACK TO BEING A LITTLE KID...

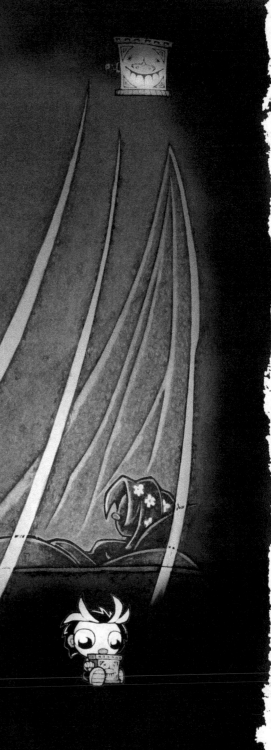

...I REMEMBER I USED TO HAVE THIS OLD JACK IN THE BOX WHEN I WAS LIKE FOUR YEARS OLD OR WHATEVER. IT HAD THIS SICKENING SMILEY MONKEY FACE ON IT THAT WAS JUST ABSOLUTELY TERRIFYIING TO ME, WITH THESE BIG CHOMPERS, AND LITTLE... ANUS... EYES... I DUNNO, IT WAS FREAKISH. BUT I LOVED THE SONG IT WOULD MAKE. YOU KNOW, THAT SIMPLE "POP GOES THE WEASEL" TUNE. I LOVED IT... EXCEPT I WAS AFRAID THAT IF I LET THE SONG PLAY ALL THE WAY TO THE END, THAT HORRIBLE MONKEYMAN WOULD COME BURSTING OUT AND... LIKE... I DUNNO, EAT MY TEETH OR WHATEVER. SOMETHING BAD.

SO ANYWAY, WHAT I WOULD DO WAS, I WOULD SIT ON THE FLOOR IN MY MOM'S ROOM —WHEN SHE WAS SICK, RIGHT— AND I WOULD TURN THE CRANK AND LISTEN TO THE SONG AND GET IT ALL THE WAY UP TO THE POINT OF DEATH... AND THEN I WOULD HAND IT UP TO MY MOM AND HIDE UNDER THE COVERS. SHE WOULD FIGHT THE MONKEYMAN FOR ME AND GIVE IT BACK AND WE'D START ALL OVER AGAIN.

HEH. THAT'S SWEET.

AND THIS WOULD GO ON FOR HOURS. BUT SHE NEVER COMPLAINED, EVEN THOUGH SHE WAS REALLY, REALLY, REALLY SICK... I MEAN, GOD, SHE MUST'VE HAD TO LISTEN TO THAT SONG MAYBE SIX THOUSAND TIMES... MAYBE MORE.

GOLLY!

YEAH. WEIRD. HUH?

CRAZY.

THAT'S STILL ONE OF MY FAVORITE MOM MEMORIES... AND YOU KNOW THE REALLY STRANGE PART? I'VE STILL NEVER ACTUALLY SEEN THE MONKEYMAN IN HIS POPPED OUT FORM. I'M NOT EVEN SURE WHERE THAT THING WENT OFF TO.

YOU SHOULD—

HEY SERA!

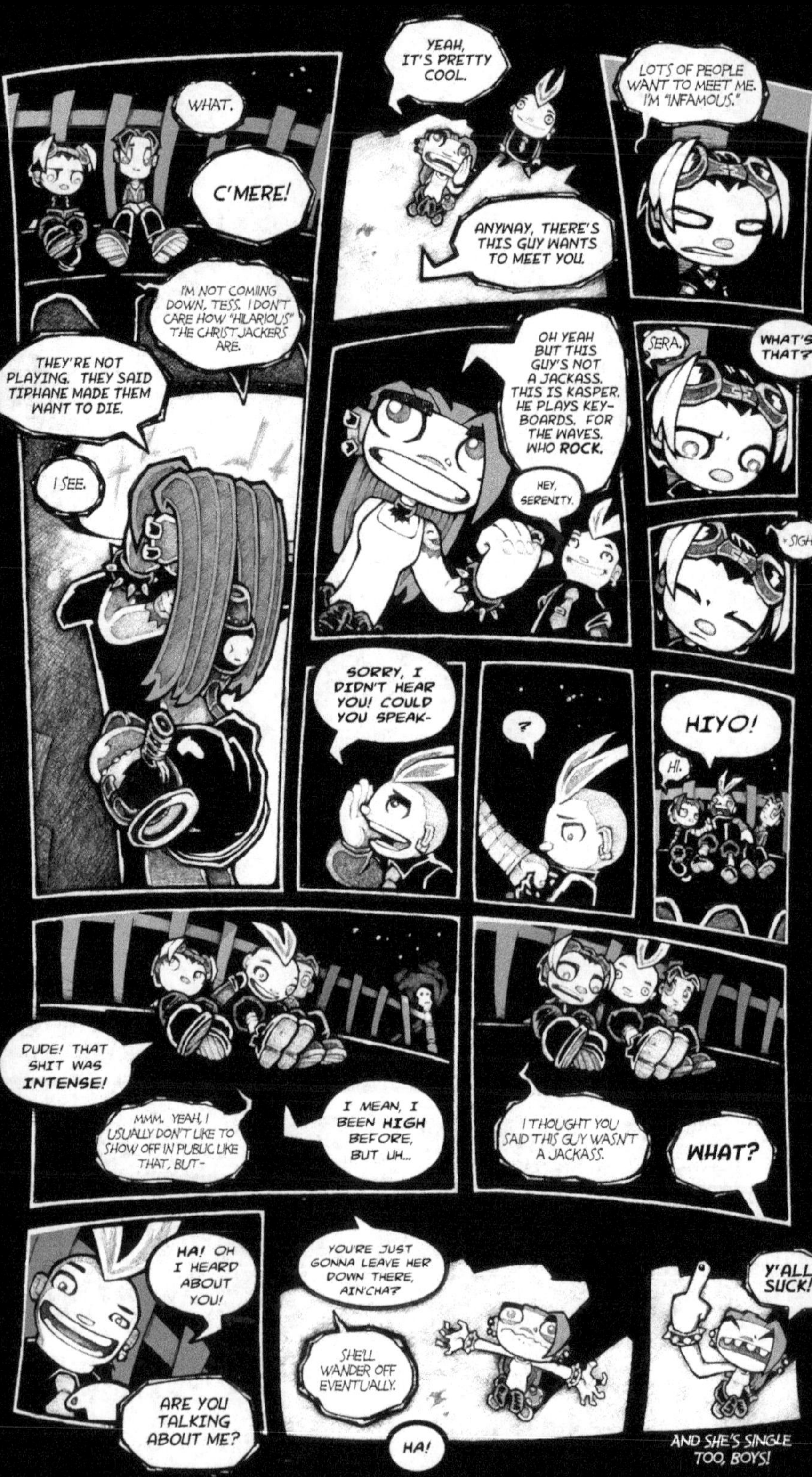
WHAT.
C'MERE!
YEAH, IT'S PRETTY COOL.
ANYWAY, THERE'S THIS GUY WANTS TO MEET YOU.
LOTS OF PEOPLE WANT TO MEET ME. I'M "INFAMOUS."
I'M NOT COMING DOWN, TESS. I DON'T CARE HOW "HILARIOUS" THE CHRISTJACKERS ARE.
THEY'RE NOT PLAYING. THEY SAID TIPHANE MADE THEM WANT TO DIE.
I SEE.
OH YEAH BUT THIS GUY'S NOT A JACKASS. THIS IS KASPER. HE PLAYS KEY-BOARDS. FOR THE WAVES. WHO ROCK.
HEY, SERENITY.
SERA.
WHAT'S THAT?
SIGH
SORRY, I DIDN'T HEAR YOU! COULD YOU SPEAK-
?
HIYO!
HI.
DUDE! THAT SHIT WAS INTENSE!
MMM. YEAH, I USUALLY DON'T LIKE TO SHOW OFF IN PUBLIC LIKE THAT, BUT-
I MEAN, I BEEN HIGH BEFORE, BUT UH...
I THOUGHT YOU SAID THIS GUY WASN'T A JACKASS.
WHAT?
HA! OH I HEARD ABOUT YOU!
ARE YOU TALKING ABOUT ME?
YOU'RE JUST GONNA LEAVE HER DOWN THERE, AIN'CHA?
SHE'LL WANDER OFF EVENTUALLY.
HA!
Y'ALL SUCK!
AND SHE'S SINGLE TOO, BOYS!

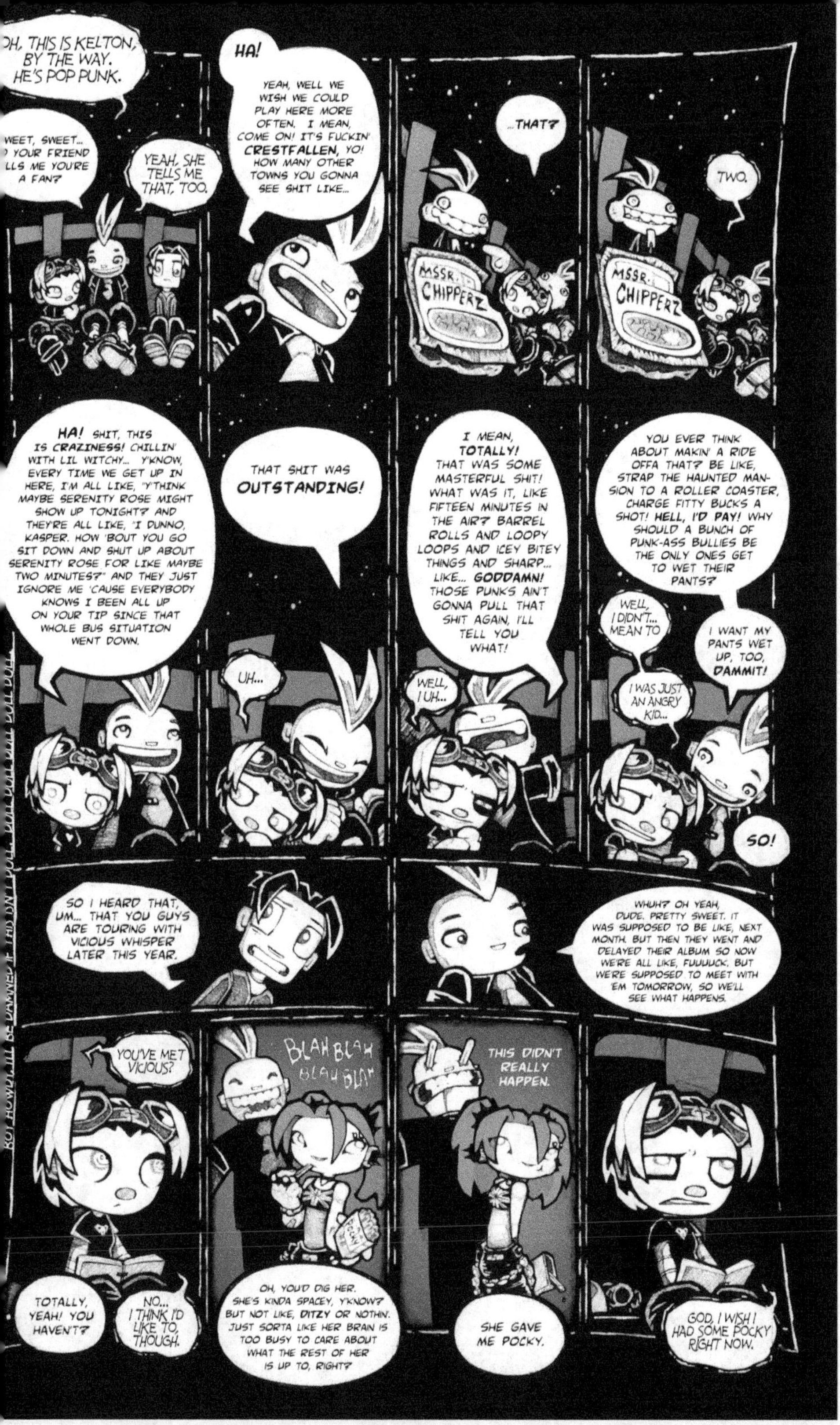

OH, THIS IS KELTON, BY THE WAY. HE'S POP PUNK.
WEET, SWEET... O YOUR FRIEND LLS ME YOU'RE A FAN?
YEAH, SHE TELLS ME THAT, TOO.
HA!
YEAH, WELL WE WISH WE COULD PLAY HERE MORE OFTEN. I MEAN, COME ON! IT'S FUCKIN' CRESTFALLEN, YO! HOW MANY OTHER TOWNS YOU GONNA SEE SHIT LIKE...
...THAT?
MSSR. CHIPPERZ
TWO.
MSSR. CHIPPERZ
HA! SHIT, THIS IS CRAZINESS! CHILLIN' WITH LIL WITCHY... Y'KNOW, EVERY TIME WE GET UP IN HERE, I'M ALL LIKE, "Y'THINK MAYBE SERENITY ROSE MIGHT SHOW UP TONIGHT? AND THEY'RE ALL LIKE, "I DUNNO, KASPER. HOW 'BOUT YOU GO SIT DOWN AND SHUT UP ABOUT SERENITY ROSE FOR LIKE MAYBE TWO MINUTES?" AND THEY JUST IGNORE ME 'CAUSE EVERYBODY KNOWS I BEEN ALL UP ON YOUR TIP SINCE THAT WHOLE BUS SITUATION WENT DOWN.
THAT SHIT WAS OUTSTANDING!
UH...
I MEAN, TOTALLY! THAT WAS SOME MASTERFUL SHIT! WHAT WAS IT, LIKE FIFTEEN MINUTES IN THE AIR? BARREL ROLLS AND LOOPY LOOPS AND ICEY BITEY THINGS AND SHARP... LIKE... GODDAMN! THOSE PUNKS AIN'T GONNA PULL THAT SHIT AGAIN, I'LL TELL YOU WHAT!
WELL, I UH...
YOU EVER THINK ABOUT MAKIN' A RIDE OFFA THAT? BE LIKE, STRAP THE HAUNTED MANSION TO A ROLLER COASTER, CHARGE FITTY BUCKS A SHOT! HELL, I'D PAY! WHY SHOULD A BUNCH OF PUNK-ASS BULLIES BE THE ONLY ONES GET TO WET THEIR PANTS?
WELL, I DIDN'T... MEAN TO
I WAS JUST AN ANGRY KID...
I WANT MY PANTS WET UP, TOO, DAMMIT!
SO!
SO I HEARD THAT, UM... THAT YOU GUYS ARE TOURING WITH VICIOUS WHISPER LATER THIS YEAR.
WHUH? OH YEAH, DUDE. PRETTY SWEET. IT WAS SUPPOSED TO BE LIKE, NEXT MONTH. BUT THEN THEY WENT AND DELAYED THEIR ALBUM SO NOW WE'RE ALL LIKE, FUUUUCK. BUT WE'RE SUPPOSED TO MEET WITH 'EM TOMORROW, SO WE'LL SEE WHAT HAPPENS.
YOU'VE MET VICIOUS?
TOTALLY, YEAH! YOU HAVEN'T?
NO... I THINK I'D LIKE TO, THOUGH.
BLAH BLAH BLAH BLAH
OH, YOU'D DIG HER. SHE'S KINDA SPACEY, Y'KNOW? BUT NOT LIKE, DITZY OR NOTHIN'. JUST SORTA LIKE HER BRAIN IS TOO BUSY TO CARE ABOUT WHAT THE REST OF HER IS UP TO, RIGHT?
THIS DIDN'T REALLY HAPPEN.
SHE GAVE ME POCKY.
GOD, I WISH I HAD SOME POCKY RIGHT NOW.

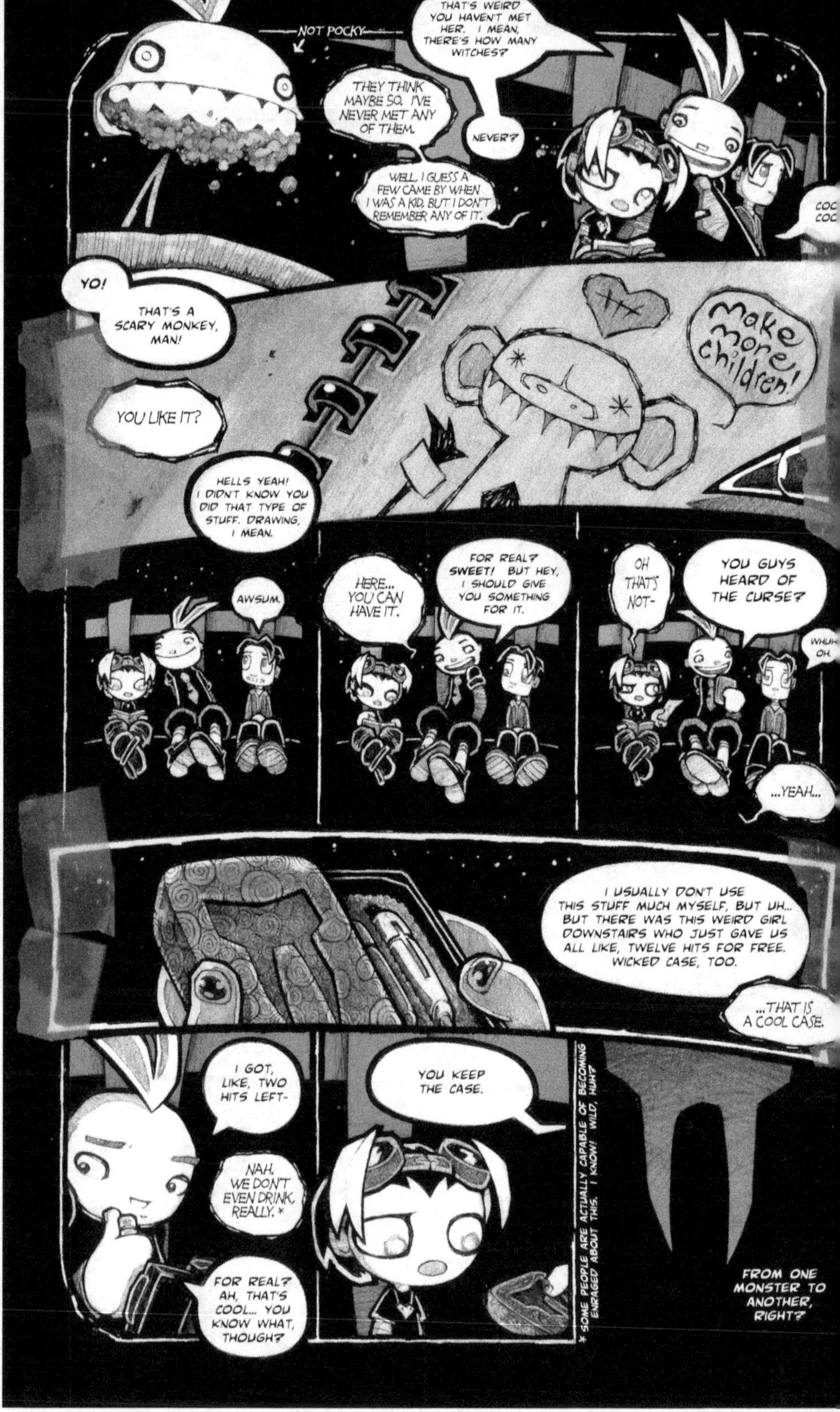
NOT POCKY
THEY THINK MAYBE SO. I'VE NEVER MET ANY OF THEM.
THAT'S WEIRD YOU HAVEN'T MET HER. I MEAN, THERE'S HOW MANY WITCHES?
NEVER?
WELL, I GUESS A FEW CAME BY WHEN I WAS A KID, BUT I DON'T REMEMBER ANY OF IT.
YO! THAT'S A SCARY MONKEY, MAN!
YOU LIKE IT?
Make more children!
HELLS YEAH! I DIDN'T KNOW YOU DID THAT TYPE OF STUFF. DRAWING, I MEAN.
AWSUM.
HERE... YOU CAN HAVE IT.
FOR REAL? SWEET! BUT HEY, I SHOULD GIVE YOU SOMETHING FOR IT.
OH THAT'S NOT-
YOU GUYS HEARD OF THE CURSE?
WHUH OH.
...YEAH...
I USUALLY DON'T USE THIS STUFF MUCH MYSELF, BUT UH... BUT THERE WAS THIS WEIRD GIRL DOWNSTAIRS WHO JUST GAVE US ALL LIKE, TWELVE HITS FOR FREE. WICKED CASE, TOO.
...THAT IS A COOL CASE.
I GOT, LIKE, TWO HITS LEFT-
NAH. WE DON'T EVEN DRINK, REALLY. *
FOR REAL? AH, THAT'S COOL... YOU KNOW WHAT, THOUGH?
YOU KEEP THE CASE.
* SOME PEOPLE ARE ACTUALLY CAPABLE OF BECOMING ENRAGED ABOUT THIS. I KNOW! WILD, HUH?
FROM ONE MONSTER TO ANOTHER, RIGHT?

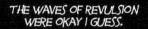

THE WAVES OF REVULSION
WERE OKAY I GUESS.

KINIDA NEW WAVEY.

THEY GOT ABOUT
8 MINUTES INTO THEIR
"BELA LUGOSI IS DEAD"
COVER BEFORE THE
SINGER REALLY STARTED
FEELING THAT
BAD CURSE.

...OH
COME ON,
NOW...

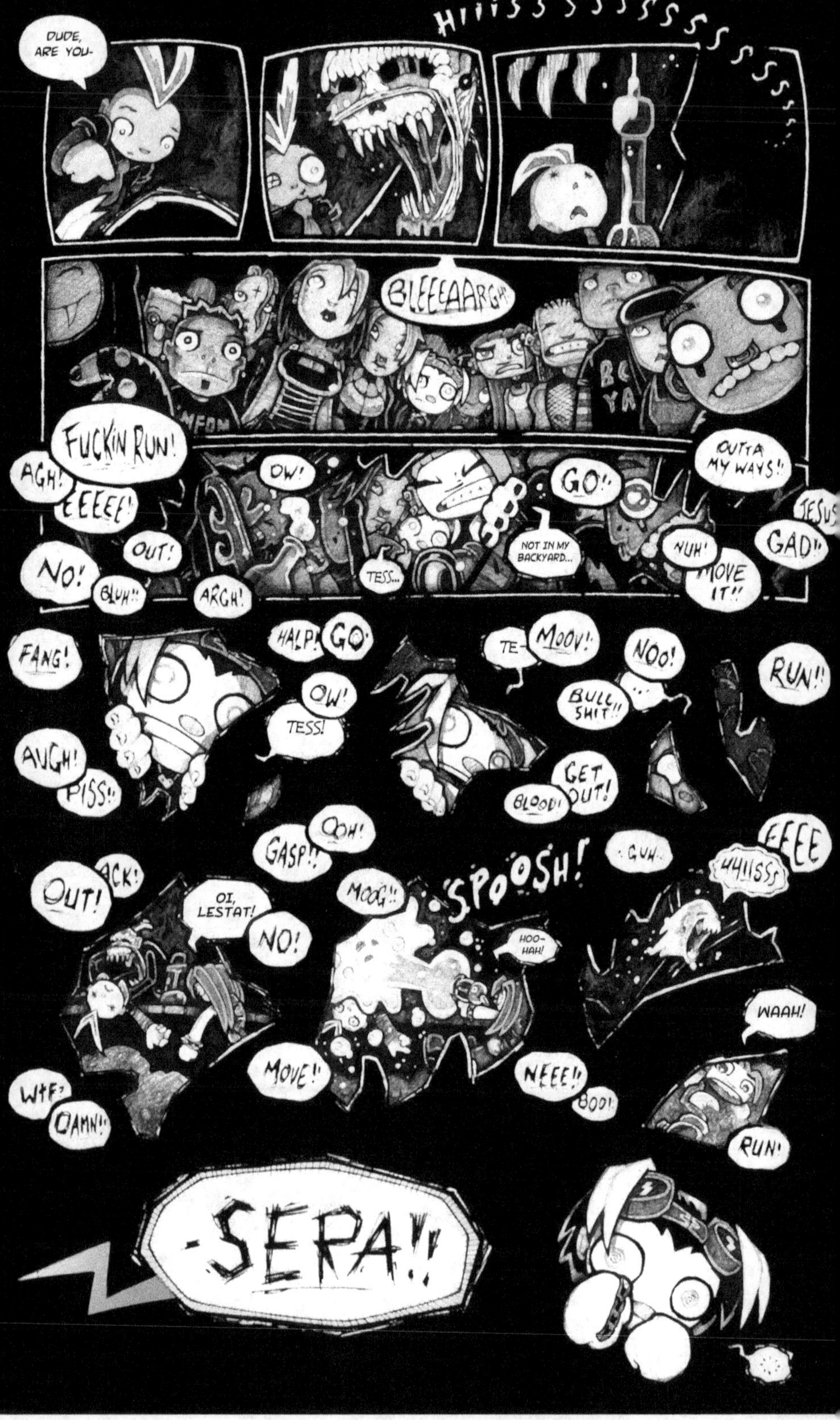

DUDE, ARE YOU-
HIIISSSSSSSSSSSSSSS
BLEEEAARGH!
FUCKIN RUN!
AGH!
EEEEE!
OW!
GO!!
OUTTA MY WAYS!!
OUT!
NO!
BLUH!!
ARGH!
TESS...
NOT IN MY BACKYARD...
NUH!
MOVE IT!!
GAD!!
FANG!
HALP!
GO
OW!
TESS!
TE-
MOOV!
NOO!
BULL SHIT!!
RUN!!
AUGH!
PISS!!
GET OUT!
BLOOD!
OOH!
GASP!!
GUH
EEEE
ACK!
OUT!
OI, LESTAT!
MOOG!!
SPOOSH!
NO!
HOO-HAH!
WAAH!
MOVE!!
NEEE!!
BOO!
WTF?
DAMN!!
RUN!
-SERA!!

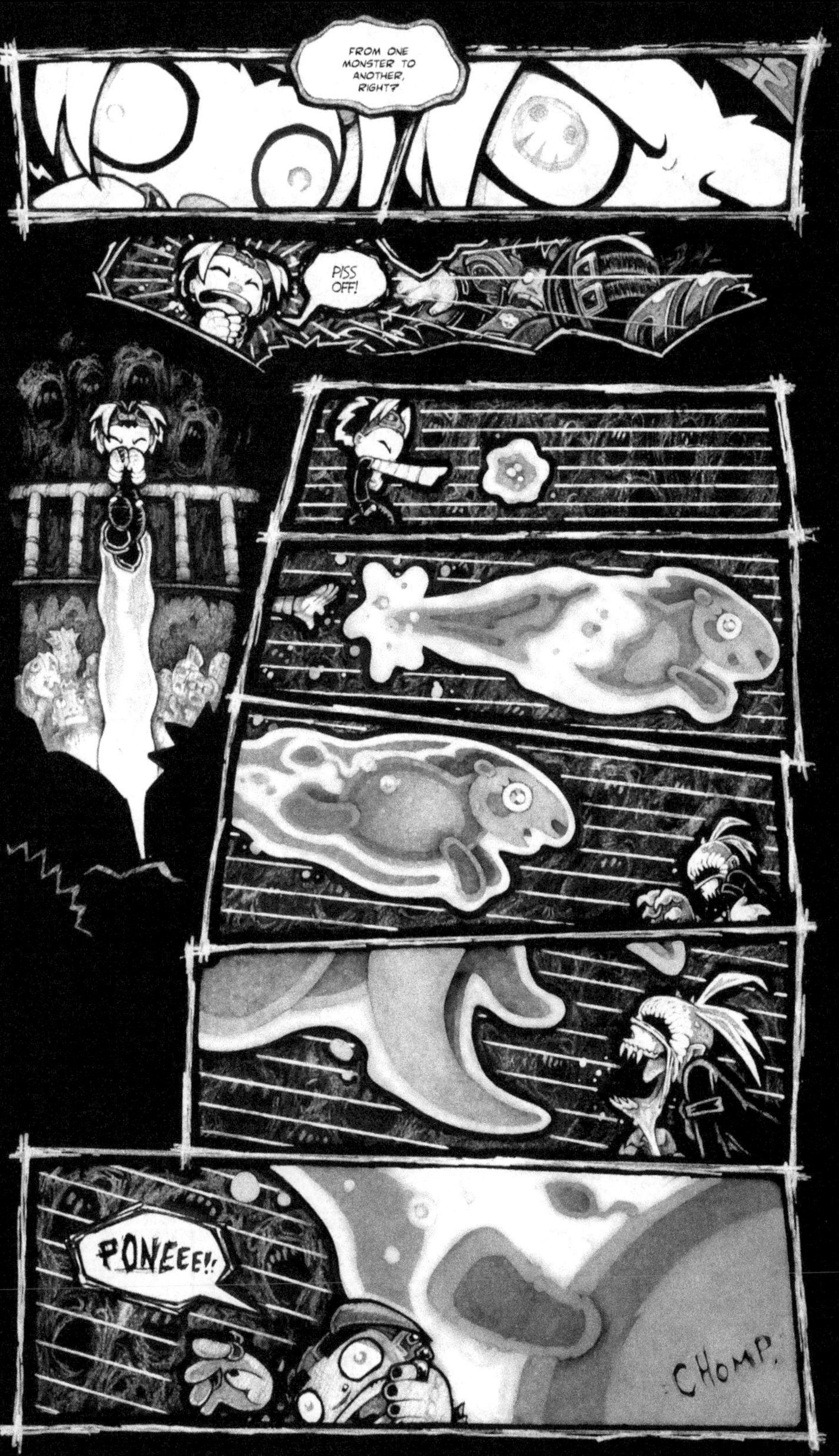
FROM ONE MONSTER TO ANOTHER, RIGHT?
PISS OFF!
PONEEE!!
CHOMP.

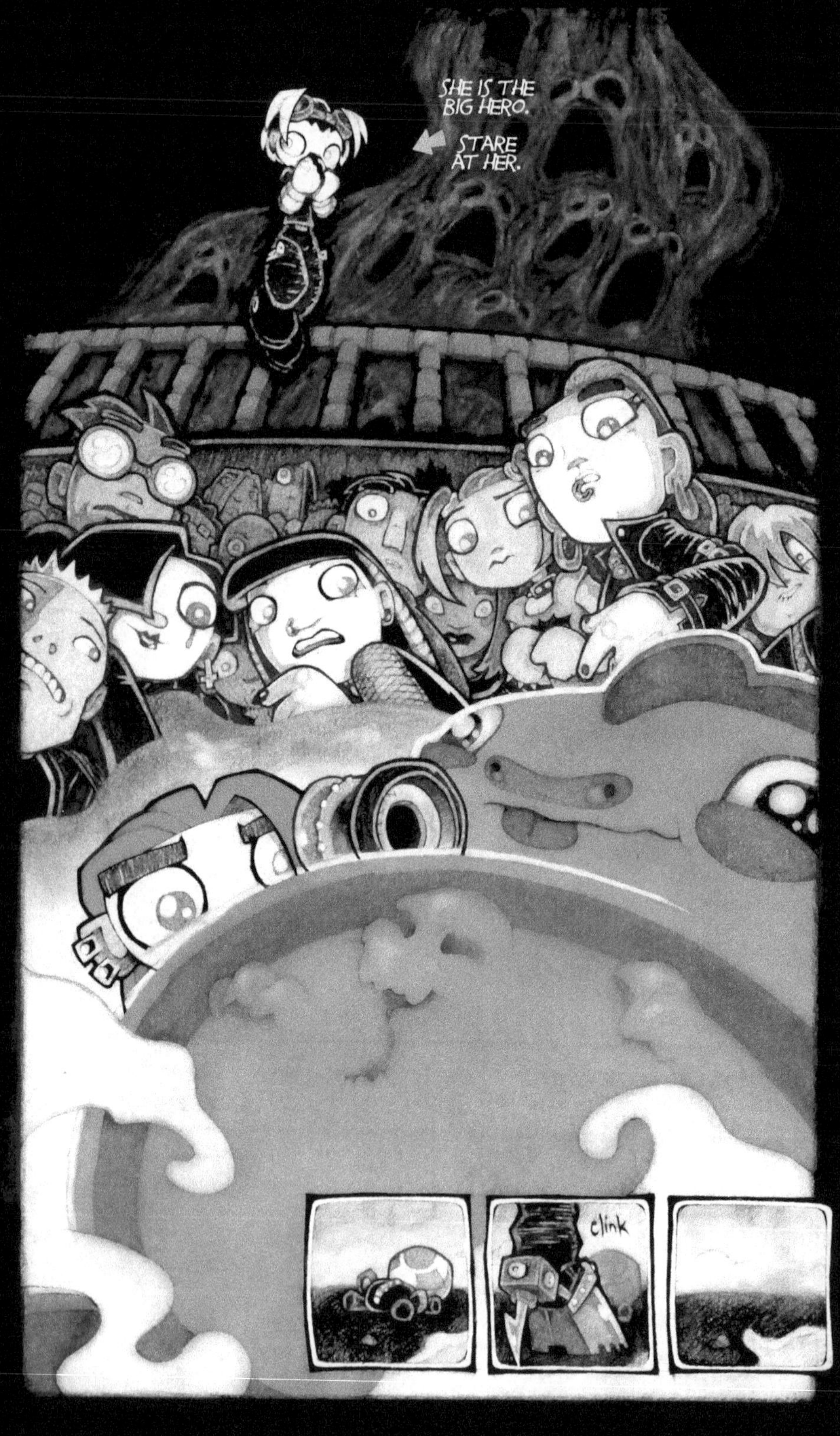
SHE IS THE BIG HERO.
STARE AT HER.
clink

...ISSUE THREE

Serenity Rose

the personal journals
of a local witch

...as told to **aaron a.**
with assists by gofflin

issue number three:

"forked tongues"

"Starring"

SERA (SHOWN HERE REACTING TO SOMETHING IN THE UPPER LEFT): SERENITY ELIZABETH "SERA" ROSE IS A WITCH, A PAINTER, A PART-TIME COLLEGE STUDENT AND 4'10" ALL AT THE SAME TIME. IN HER SPARE HOURS, SHE ENJOYS FLOATING, NAPPING, PLAYING STRATEGO AND DEFENDING HERSELF AGAINST ALLEGATIONS THAT SHE "TOTALLY HATES LIFE." ONE TIME SHE ATE A WHOLE WATERMELON ALL BY HERSELF.

TESS (SHOWN HERE CHEWING ON A SMALL BUNNY RABBIT): CONTESSA NATALYA "TESS" RUBIKOV IS SERA'S CLOSEST AND MOST TENACIOUS FRIEND/ENEMY. SHE HAS AN ENORMOUS SMILING SUN GUY TATTOOED ON HER LEFT SHOULDER, TWO HOLES IN EACH EAR, AND A THREE-INCH SCREWDRIVER SHANK PERMANENTLY WEDGED IN THE TOP OF HER SKULL. APPROACH WITH CAUTION.

KELTON (SHOWN HERE ON HIS NIGHTLY VISIT WITH MORPHEUS, GOD OF SLEEP): MR. DEWEY DWAYNE KELTON HAS BEEN STEADILY NOODLING HIS WAY INTO SERA'S LIFE FOR THE PAST TWO YEARS. WHEN HE'S NOT BUGGING MS. ROSE FOR MORE CARTOONS TO FILL HIS LEFTIST POLITICAL 'ZINE, "FEARFUL THING," MR. KELTON CAN BE FOUND DILLIGENTLY PREPARING DOUBLE-DARK CHOCOLATE MINT TEA LATTES AT THE LOCAL CRESTFALLEN "SCAREBUCKS" COFFEE HOUSE.

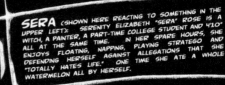

VICIOUS WHISPER (SHOWN HERE CRAWLING ON THE CEILING FOR SOME REASON): PERHAPS THE MOST FAMOUS WITCH IN THE WORLD, ANGLO/JAPANESE PERKIGOFF VICIOUS WHISPER (OR "V" TO HER PALS) IS A SINGER, PERFORMER, AND ALL AROUND RABBLE-ROUSER. SHE'S COOL, CONFIDENT, AND EVERYTHING OUR GIRL SERA WISHES SHE COULD BE. ALSO: SHE'S NOT IN THIS ISSUE VERY MUCH.

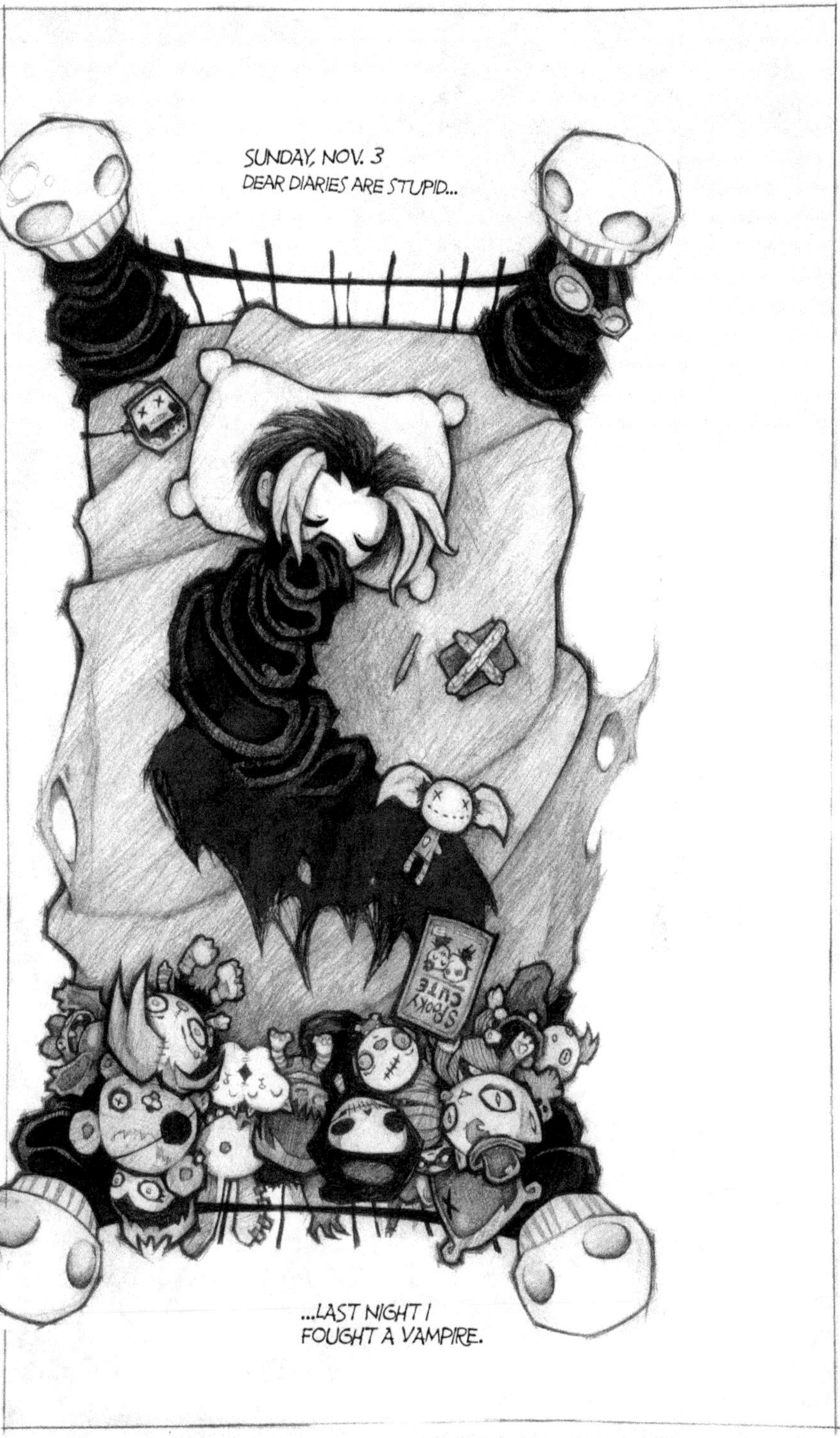
SUNDAY, NOV. 3
DEAR DIARIES ARE STUPID...
SPOOKY CUTE
...LAST NIGHT I
FOUGHT A VAMPIRE.

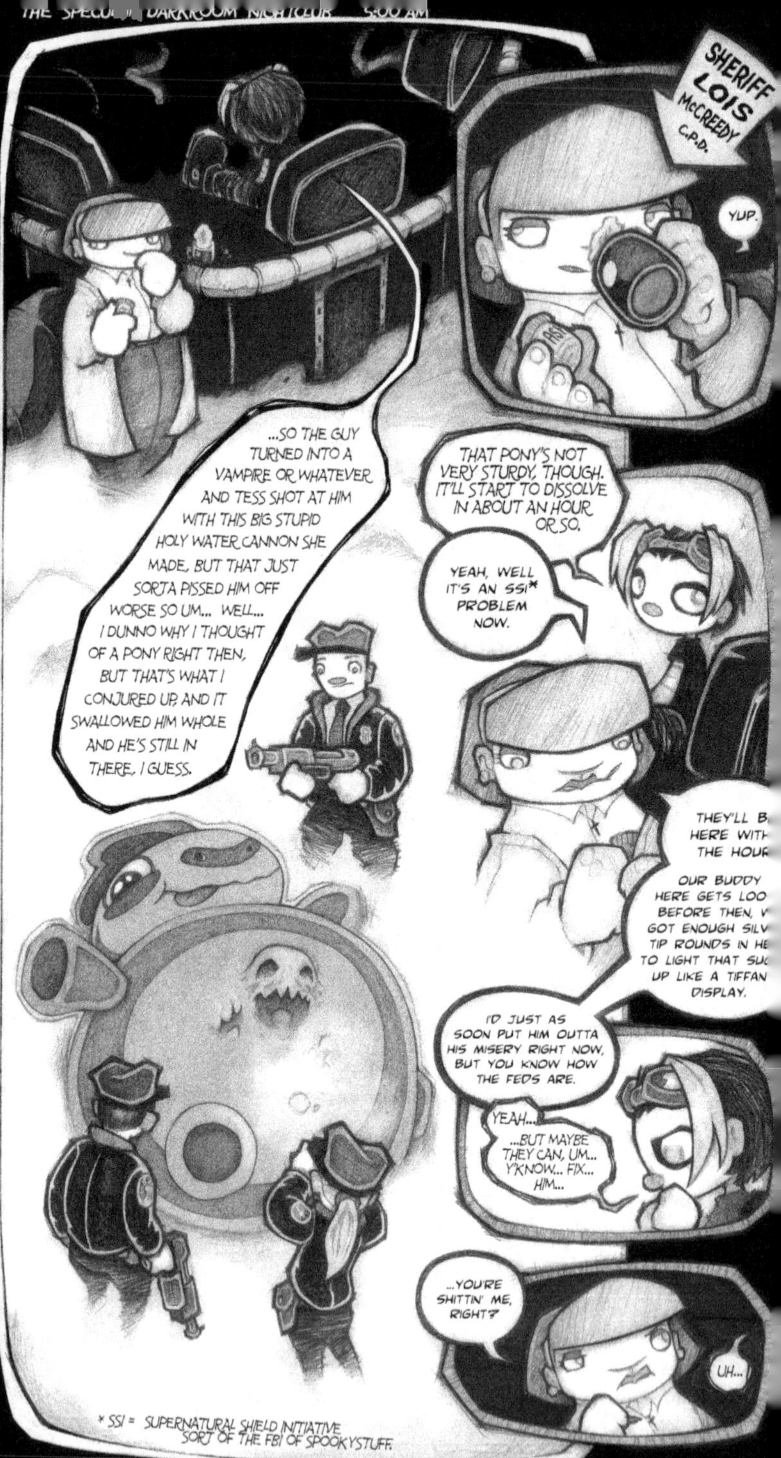
THE SPECU DARKROOM NIGHTCLUB 5:00 AM
SHERIFF LOIS McCREEDY C.P.D.
YUP.
...SO THE GUY TURNED INTO A VAMPIRE OR WHATEVER AND TESS SHOT AT HIM WITH THIS BIG STUPID HOLY WATER CANNON SHE MADE, BUT THAT JUST SORTA PISSED HIM OFF WORSE SO UM... WELL... I DUNNO WHY I THOUGHT OF A PONY RIGHT THEN, BUT THAT'S WHAT I CONJURED UP, AND IT SWALLOWED HIM WHOLE AND HE'S STILL IN THERE, I GUESS.
THAT PONY'S NOT VERY STURDY, THOUGH. IT'LL START TO DISSOLVE IN ABOUT AN HOUR OR SO.
YEAH, WELL IT'S AN SSI* PROBLEM NOW.
THEY'LL B HERE WITH THE HOUR
OUR BUDDY HERE GETS LOO BEFORE THEN, W GOT ENOUGH SILV TIP ROUNDS IN HE TO LIGHT THAT SUC UP LIKE A TIFFAN DISPLAY.
I'D JUST AS SOON PUT HIM OUTTA HIS MISERY RIGHT NOW, BUT YOU KNOW HOW THE FEDS ARE.
YEAH...
...BUT MAYBE THEY CAN, UM... Y'KNOW... FIX... HIM...
...YOU'RE SHITTIN' ME, RIGHT?
UH...
* SSI = SUPERNATURAL SHIELD INITIATIVE SORT OF THE FBI OF SPOOKYSTUFF.

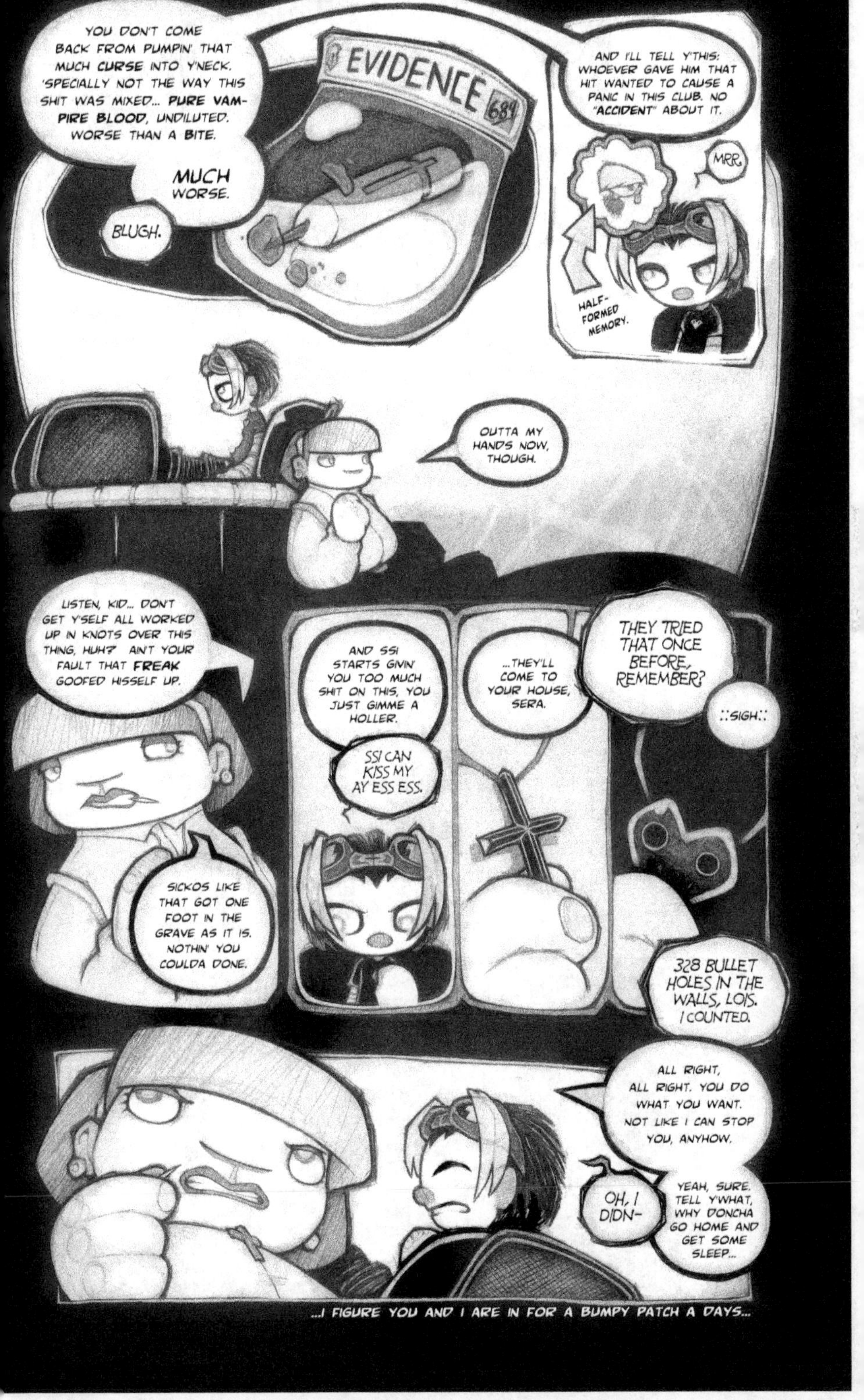
YOU DON'T COME BACK FROM PUMPIN' THAT MUCH CURSE INTO Y'NECK. 'SPECIALLY NOT THE WAY THIS SHIT WAS MIXED... PURE VAMPIRE BLOOD, UNDILUTED. WORSE THAN A BITE.
MUCH WORSE.
BLUGH.
EVIDENCE 684
AND I'LL TELL Y'THIS: WHOEVER GAVE HIM THAT HIT WANTED TO CAUSE A PANIC IN THIS CLUB. NO "ACCIDENT" ABOUT IT.
MRR.
HALF-FORMED MEMORY.
OUTTA MY HANDS NOW, THOUGH.
LISTEN, KID... DON'T GET Y'SELF ALL WORKED UP IN KNOTS OVER THIS THING, HUH? AIN'T YOUR FAULT THAT FREAK GOOFED HISSELF UP.
SICKOS LIKE THAT GOT ONE FOOT IN THE GRAVE AS IT IS. NOTHIN' YOU COULDA DONE.
AND SSI STARTS GIVIN' YOU TOO MUCH SHIT ON THIS, YOU JUST GIMME A HOLLER.
SSI CAN KISS MY AY ESS ESS.
...THEY'LL COME TO YOUR HOUSE, SERA.
THEY TRIED THAT ONCE BEFORE, REMEMBER?
::SIGH::
328 BULLET HOLES IN THE WALLS, LOIS. I COUNTED.
ALL RIGHT, ALL RIGHT. YOU DO WHAT YOU WANT. NOT LIKE I CAN STOP YOU, ANYHOW.
OH, I DIDN-
YEAH, SURE. TELL Y'WHAT, WHY DONCHA GO HOME AND GET SOME SLEEP...
...I FIGURE YOU AND I ARE IN FOR A BUMPY PATCH A DAYS...

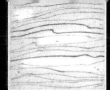

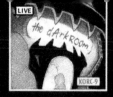

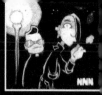

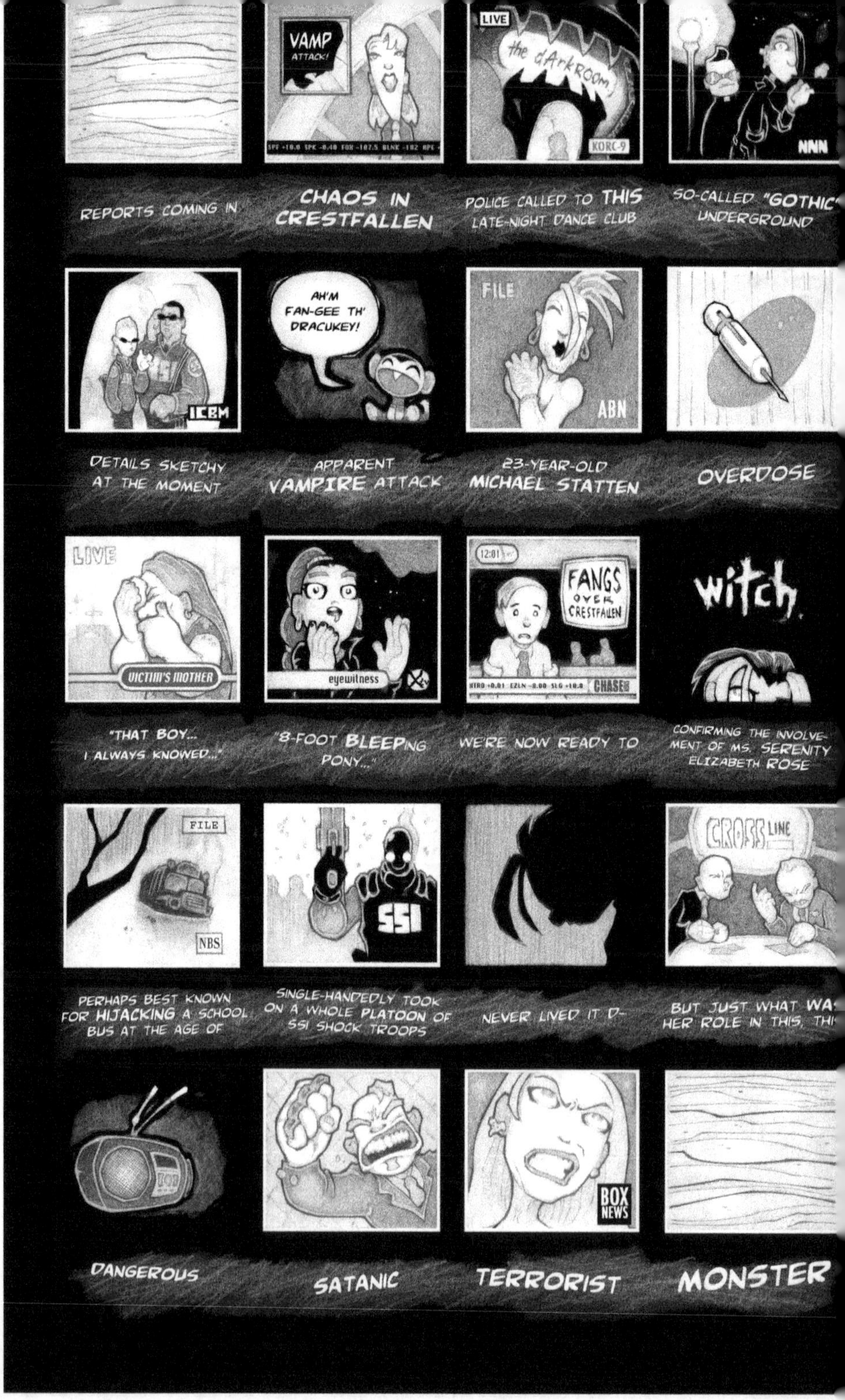

REPORTS COMING IN
VAMP ATTACK!
CHAOS IN CRESTFALLEN
LIVE
the dArkROOM
KORC-9
POLICE CALLED TO THIS LATE-NIGHT DANCE CLUB
NNN
SO-CALLED "GOTHIC" UNDERGROUND
ICBM
DETAILS SKETCHY AT THE MOMENT
AH'M FAN-GEE TH' DRACUKEY!
APPARENT VAMPIRE ATTACK
FILE
ABN
23-YEAR-OLD MICHAEL STATTEN
OVERDOSE
LIVE
VICTIM'S MOTHER
"THAT BOY... I ALWAYS KNOWED..."
eyewitness
"8-FOOT BLEEPING PONY..."
12:01
FANGS OVER CRESTFALLEN
CHASE
WE'RE NOW READY TO
witch.
CONFIRMING THE INVOLVEMENT OF MS. SERENITY ELIZABETH ROSE
FILE
NBS
PERHAPS BEST KNOWN FOR HIJACKING A SCHOOL BUS AT THE AGE OF
SSI
SINGLE-HANDEDLY TOOK ON A WHOLE PLATOON OF SSI SHOCK TROOPS
NEVER LIVED IT D-
CROSS LINE
BUT JUST WHAT WA HER ROLE IN THIS, TH
DANGEROUS
SATANIC
BOX NEWS
TERRORIST
MONSTER

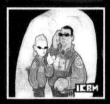

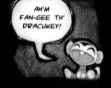

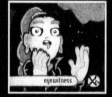

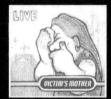

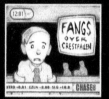

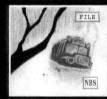

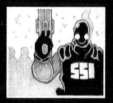

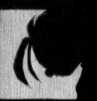

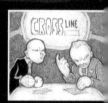

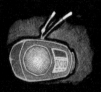

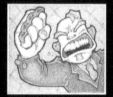

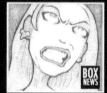

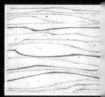

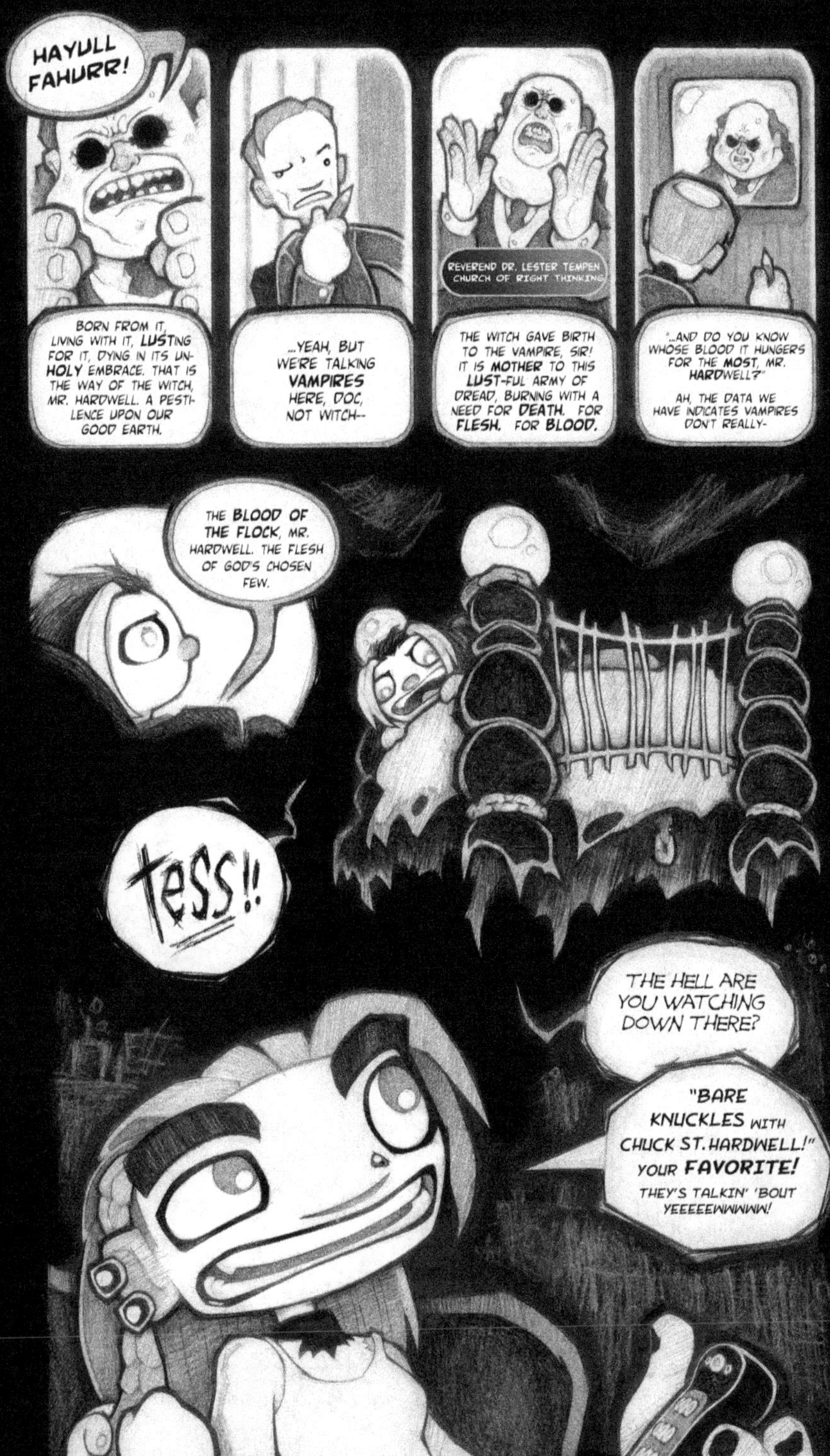
HAYULL FAHURR!
BORN FROM IT, LIVING WITH IT, LUSTING FOR IT, DYING IN ITS UN-HOLY EMBRACE. THAT IS THE WAY OF THE WITCH, MR. HARDWELL. A PESTI-LENCE UPON OUR GOOD EARTH.
...YEAH, BUT WE'RE TALKING VAMPIRES HERE, DOC, NOT WITCH--
REVEREND DR. LESTER TEMPEN CHURCH OF RIGHT THINKING
THE WITCH GAVE BIRTH TO THE VAMPIRE, SIR! IT IS MOTHER TO THIS LUST-FUL ARMY OF DREAD, BURNING WITH A NEED FOR DEATH. FOR FLESH. FOR BLOOD.
"...AND DO YOU KNOW WHOSE BLOOD IT HUNGERS FOR THE MOST, MR. HARDWELL?"
AH, THE DATA WE HAVE INDICATES VAMPIRES DON'T REALLY-
THE BLOOD OF THE FLOCK, MR. HARDWELL. THE FLESH OF GOD'S CHOSEN FEW.
tess!!
THE HELL ARE YOU WATCHING DOWN THERE?
"BARE KNUCKLES WITH CHUCK ST. HARDWELL!" YOUR FAVORITE!
THEY'S TALKIN' 'BOUT YEEEEEWWWWW!

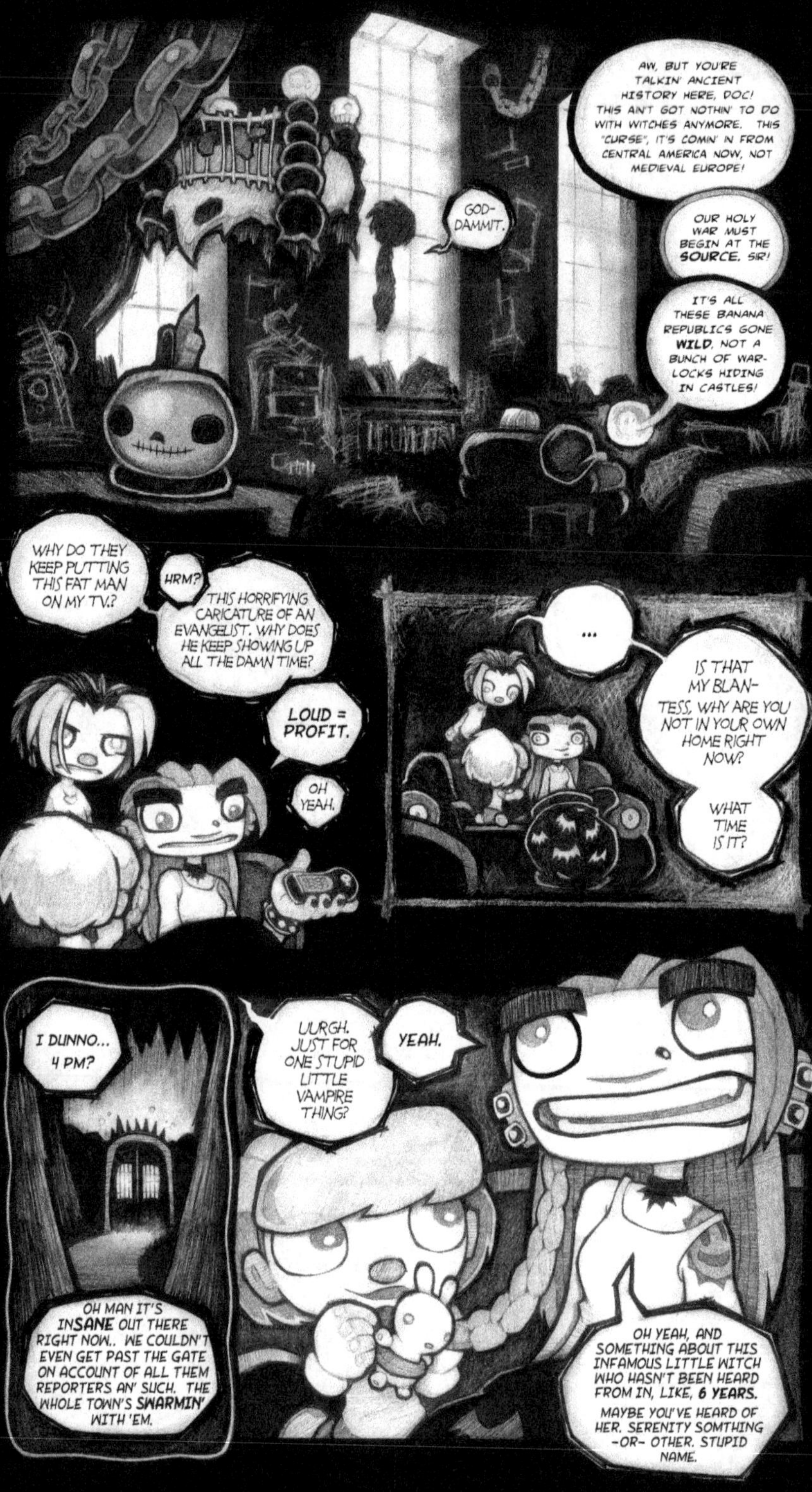

AW, BUT YOU'RE TALKIN' ANCIENT HISTORY HERE, DOC! THIS AIN'T GOT NOTHIN' TO DO WITH WITCHES ANYMORE. THIS "CURSE", IT'S COMIN' IN FROM CENTRAL AMERICA NOW, NOT MEDIEVAL EUROPE!
GOD-DAMMIT.
OUR HOLY WAR MUST BEGIN AT THE SOURCE, SIR!
IT'S ALL THESE BANANA REPUBLICS GONE WILD, NOT A BUNCH OF WAR-LOCKS HIDING IN CASTLES!
WHY DO THEY KEEP PUTTING THIS FAT MAN ON MY TV.?
HRM?
THIS HORRIFYING CARICATURE OF AN EVANGELIST. WHY DOES HE KEEP SHOWING UP ALL THE DAMN TIME?
LOUD = PROFIT.
OH YEAH.
...
IS THAT MY BLAN-TESS, WHY ARE YOU NOT IN YOUR OWN HOME RIGHT NOW?
WHAT TIME IS IT?
I DUNNO... 4 PM?
OH MAN IT'S INSANE OUT THERE RIGHT NOW.. WE COULDN'T EVEN GET PAST THE GATE ON ACCOUNT OF ALL THEM REPORTERS AN' SUCH. THE WHOLE TOWN'S SWARMIN' WITH 'EM.
UURGH. JUST FOR ONE STUPID LITTLE VAMPIRE THING?
YEAH.
OH YEAH, AND SOMETHING ABOUT THIS INFAMOUS LITTLE WITCH WHO HASN'T BEEN HEARD FROM IN, LIKE, 6 YEARS.
MAYBE YOU'VE HEARD OF HER. SERENITY SOMTHING -OR- OTHER. STUPID NAME.

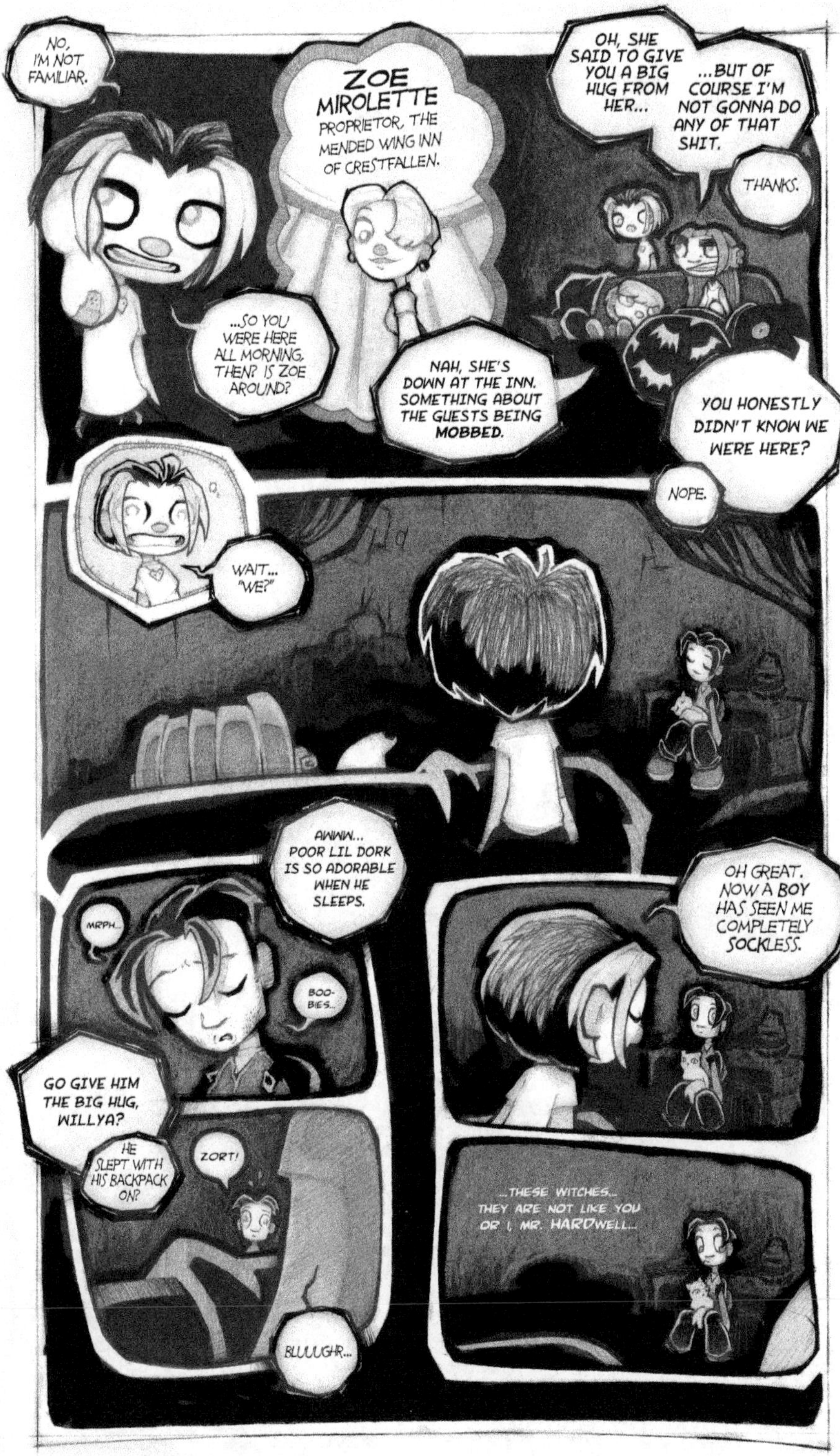
NO, I'M NOT FAMILIAR.
ZOE MIROLETTE
PROPRIETOR, THE MENDED WING INN OF CRESTFALLEN.
...SO YOU WERE HERE ALL MORNING, THEN? IS ZOE AROUND?
NAH, SHE'S DOWN AT THE INN. SOMETHING ABOUT THE GUESTS BEING MOBBED.
OH, SHE SAID TO GIVE YOU A BIG HUG FROM HER...
...BUT OF COURSE I'M NOT GONNA DO ANY OF THAT SHIT.
THANKS.
YOU HONESTLY DIDN'T KNOW WE WERE HERE?
NOPE.
WAIT... "WE?"
AWWW... POOR LIL DORK IS SO ADORABLE WHEN HE SLEEPS.
MRPH...
BOO-BIES...
GO GIVE HIM THE BIG HUG, WILLYA?
HE SLEPT WITH HIS BACKPACK ON?
ZORT!
BLUUUGHR...
OH GREAT. NOW A BOY HAS SEEN ME COMPLETELY SOCKLESS.
...THESE WITCHES... THEY ARE NOT LIKE YOU OR I, MR. HARDWELL...

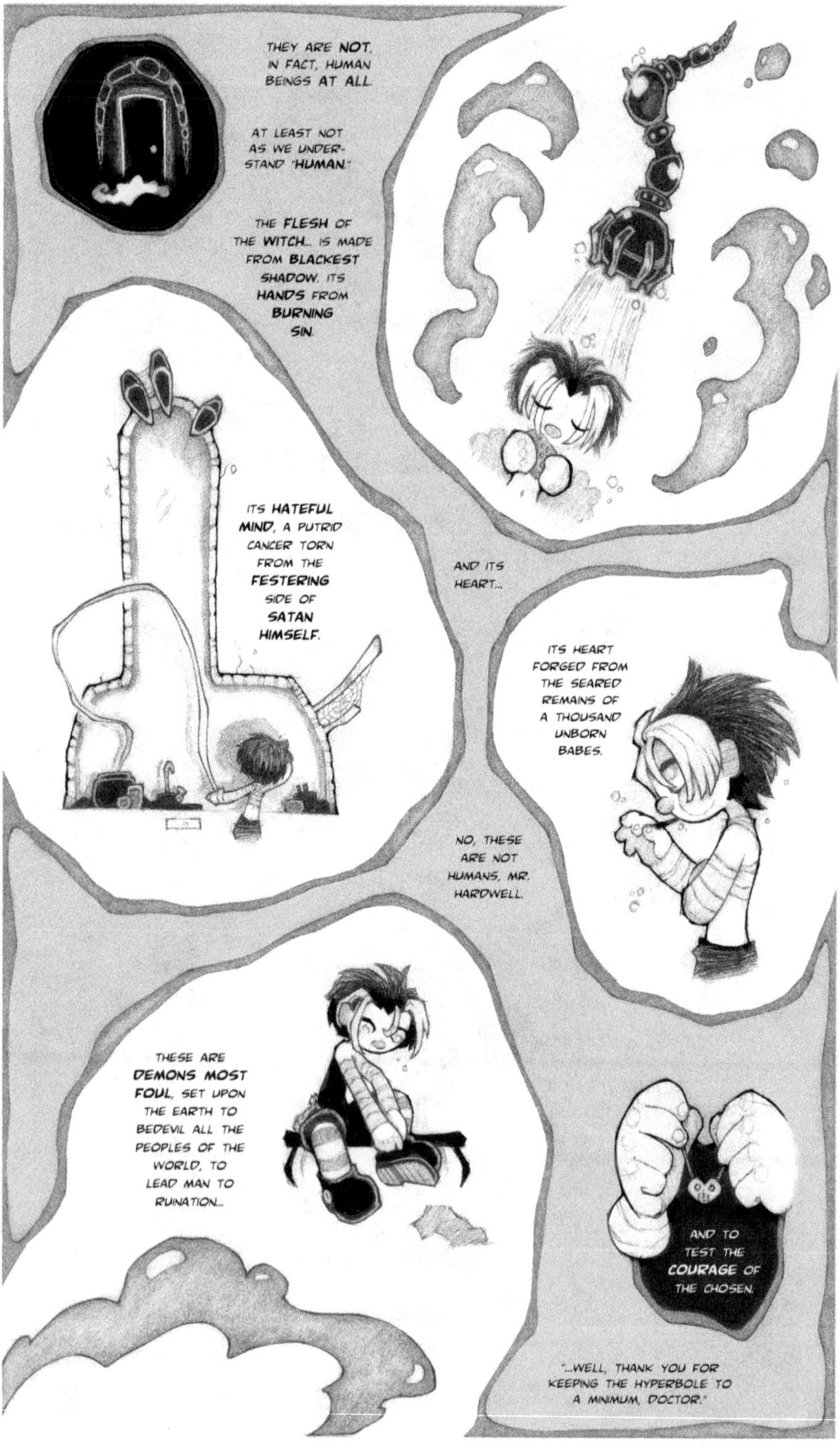
THEY ARE NOT, IN FACT, HUMAN BEINGS AT ALL.
AT LEAST NOT AS WE UNDER-STAND "HUMAN."
THE FLESH OF THE WITCH... IS MADE FROM BLACKEST SHADOW. ITS HANDS FROM BURNING SIN.
ITS HATEFUL MIND, A PUTRID CANCER TORN FROM THE FESTERING SIDE OF SATAN HIMSELF.
AND ITS HEART...
ITS HEART FORGED FROM THE SEARED REMAINS OF A THOUSAND UNBORN BABES.
NO, THESE ARE NOT HUMANS, MR. HARDWELL.
THESE ARE DEMONS MOST FOUL, SET UPON THE EARTH TO BEDEVIL ALL THE PEOPLES OF THE WORLD, TO LEAD MAN TO RUINATION...
AND TO TEST THE COURAGE OF THE CHOSEN.
"...WELL, THANK YOU FOR KEEPING THE HYPERBOLE TO A MINIMUM, DOCTOR."

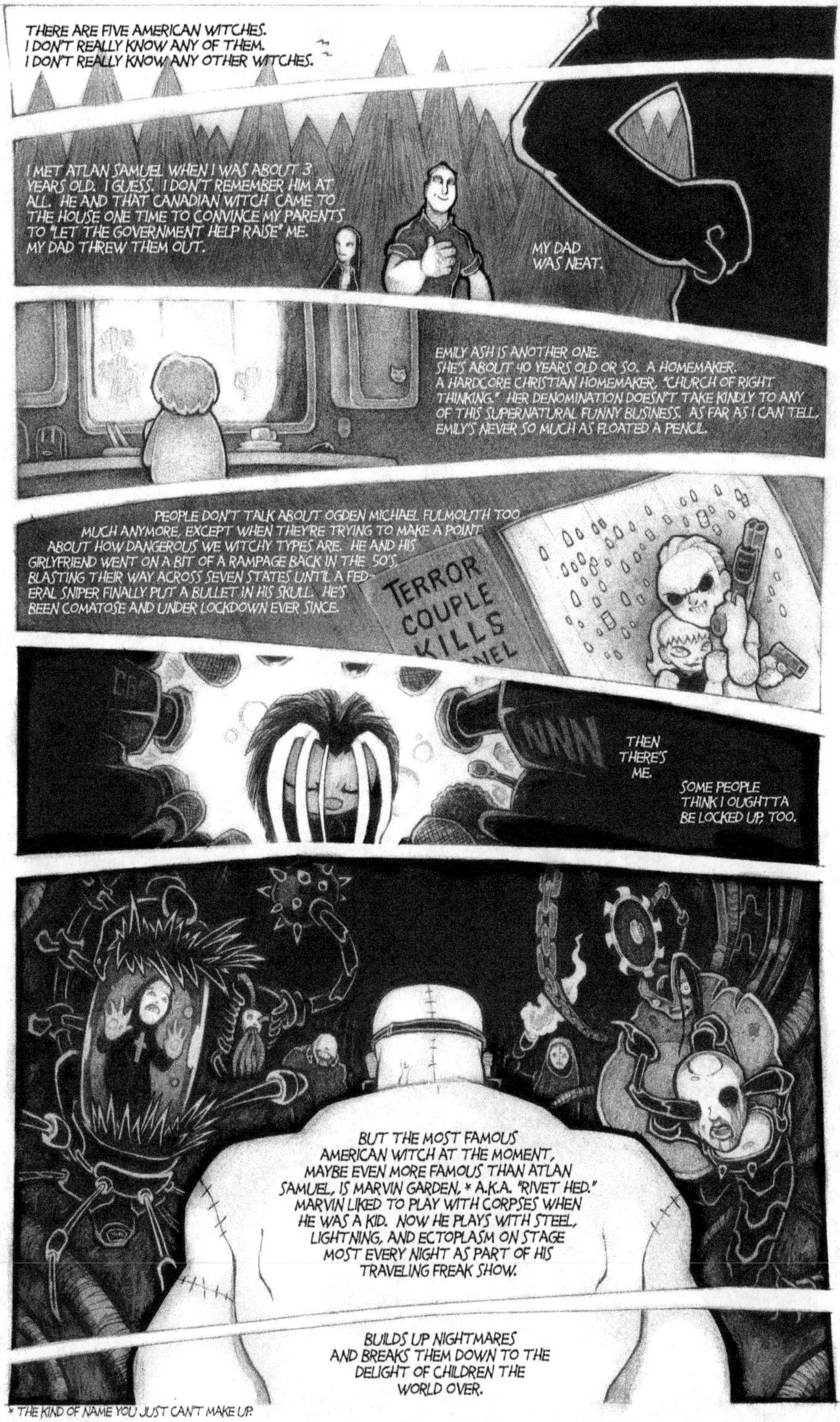

THERE ARE FIVE AMERICAN WITCHES.
I DON'T REALLY KNOW ANY OF THEM.
I DON'T REALLY KNOW ANY OTHER WITCHES.
I MET ATLAN SAMUEL WHEN I WAS ABOUT 3 YEARS OLD. I GUESS. I DON'T REMEMBER HIM AT ALL. HE AND THAT CANADIAN WITCH CAME TO THE HOUSE ONE TIME TO CONVINCE MY PARENTS TO "LET THE GOVERNMENT HELP RAISE" ME. MY DAD THREW THEM OUT.
MY DAD WAS NEAT.
EMILY ASH IS ANOTHER ONE. SHE'S ABOUT 40 YEARS OLD OR SO. A HOMEMAKER. A HARDCORE CHRISTIAN HOMEMAKER. "CHURCH OF RIGHT THINKING." HER DENOMINATION DOESN'T TAKE KINDLY TO ANY OF THIS SUPERNATURAL FUNNY BUSINESS. AS FAR AS I CAN TELL, EMILY'S NEVER SO MUCH AS FLOATED A PENCIL.
PEOPLE DON'T TALK ABOUT OGDEN MICHAEL FULMOUTH TOO MUCH ANYMORE, EXCEPT WHEN THEY'RE TRYING TO MAKE A POINT ABOUT HOW DANGEROUS WE WITCHY TYPES ARE. HE AND HIS GIRLYFRIEND WENT ON A BIT OF A RAMPAGE BACK IN THE 50'S, BLASTING THEIR WAY ACROSS SEVEN STATES UNTIL A FEDERAL SNIPER FINALLY PUT A BULLET IN HIS SKULL. HE'S BEEN COMATOSE AND UNDER LOCKDOWN EVER SINCE.
TERROR COUPLE KILLS
THEN THERE'S ME.
SOME PEOPLE THINK I OUGHTTA BE LOCKED UP, TOO.
BUT THE MOST FAMOUS AMERICAN WITCH AT THE MOMENT, MAYBE EVEN MORE FAMOUS THAN ATLAN SAMUEL, IS MARVIN GARDEN, * A.K.A. "RIVET HED." MARVIN LIKED TO PLAY WITH CORPSES WHEN HE WAS A KID. NOW HE PLAYS WITH STEEL, LIGHTNING, AND ECTOPLASM ON STAGE MOST EVERY NIGHT AS PART OF HIS TRAVELING FREAK SHOW.
BUILDS UP NIGHTMARES AND BREAKS THEM DOWN TO THE DELIGHT OF CHILDREN THE WORLD OVER.

* THE KIND OF NAME YOU JUST CAN'T MAKE UP.

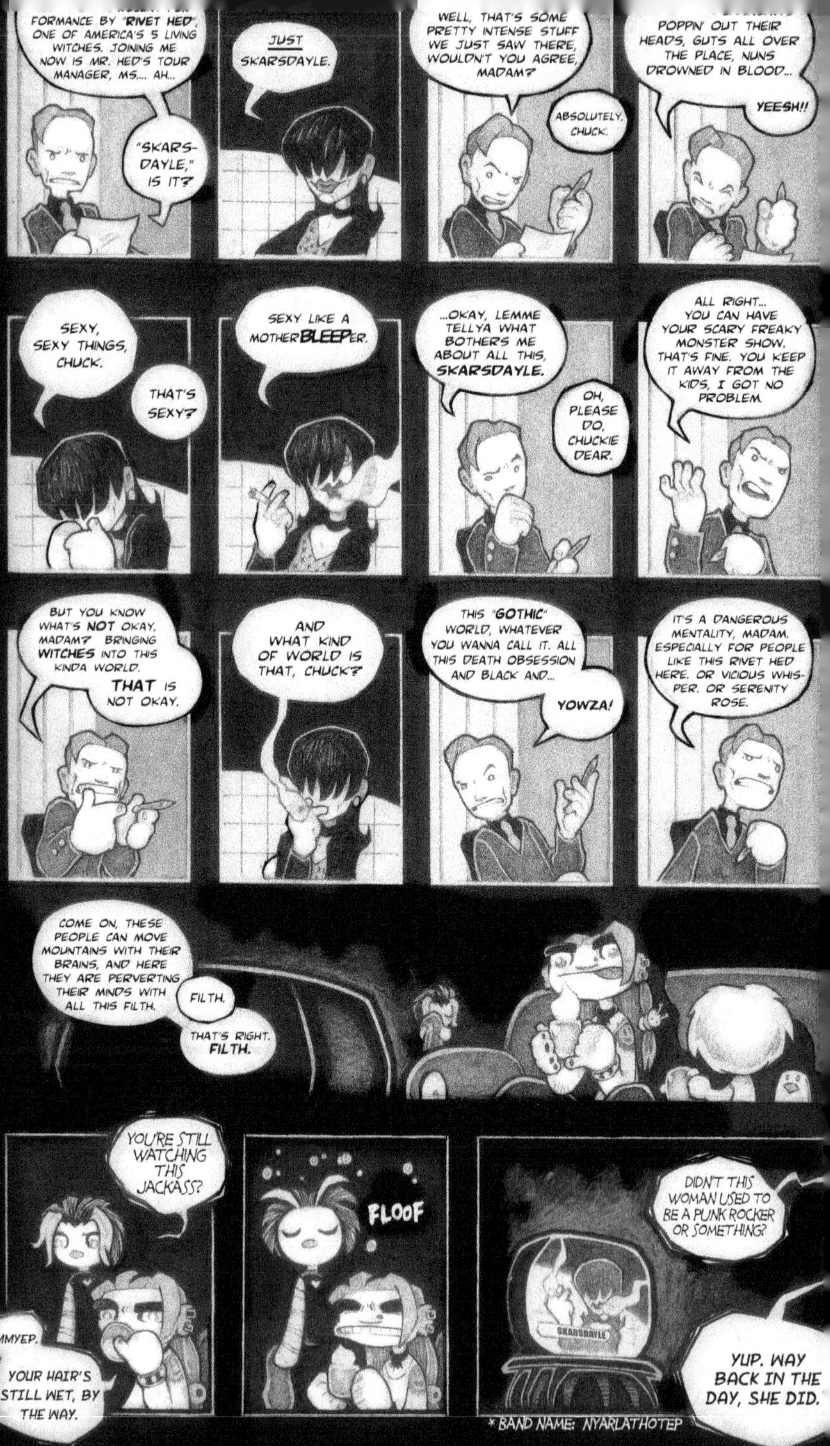
FORMANCE BY "RIVET HED", ONE OF AMERICA'S 5 LIVING WITCHES. JOINING ME NOW IS MR. HED'S TOUR MANAGER, MS.... AH...
"SKARS-DAYLE," IS IT?
JUST SKARSDAYLE.
WELL, THAT'S SOME PRETTY INTENSE STUFF WE JUST SAW THERE, WOULDN'T YOU AGREE, MADAM?
ABSOLUTELY, CHUCK.
POPPIN' OUT THEIR HEADS, GUTS ALL OVER THE PLACE, NUNS DROWNED IN BLOOD...
YEESH!!
SEXY, SEXY THINGS, CHUCK.
THAT'S SEXY?
SEXY LIKE A MOTHERBLEEPER.
...OKAY, LEMME TELLYA WHAT BOTHERS ME ABOUT ALL THIS, SKARSDAYLE.
OH, PLEASE DO, CHUCKIE DEAR.
ALL RIGHT... YOU CAN HAVE YOUR SCARY FREAKY MONSTER SHOW. THAT'S FINE. YOU KEEP IT AWAY FROM THE KIDS, I GOT NO PROBLEM.
BUT YOU KNOW WHAT'S NOT OKAY, MADAM? BRINGING WITCHES INTO THIS KINDA WORLD.
THAT IS NOT OKAY.
AND WHAT KIND OF WORLD IS THAT, CHUCK?
THIS "GOTHIC" WORLD, WHATEVER YOU WANNA CALL IT. ALL THIS DEATH OBSESSION AND BLACK AND...
YOWZA!
IT'S A DANGEROUS MENTALITY, MADAM. ESPECIALLY FOR PEOPLE LIKE THIS RIVET HED HERE. OR VICIOUS WHIS-PER. OR SERENITY ROSE.
COME ON, THESE PEOPLE CAN MOVE MOUNTAINS WITH THEIR BRAINS, AND HERE THEY ARE PERVERTING THEIR MINDS WITH ALL THIS FILTH.
FILTH.
THAT'S RIGHT. FILTH.
YOU'RE STILL WATCHING THIS JACKASS?
MMYEP.
YOUR HAIR'S STILL WET, BY THE WAY.
FLOOF
DIDN'T THIS WOMAN USED TO BE A PUNK ROCKER OR SOMETHING?
SKARSDAYLE
YUP. WAY BACK IN THE DAY, SHE DID.*
* BAND NAME: NYARLATHOTEP

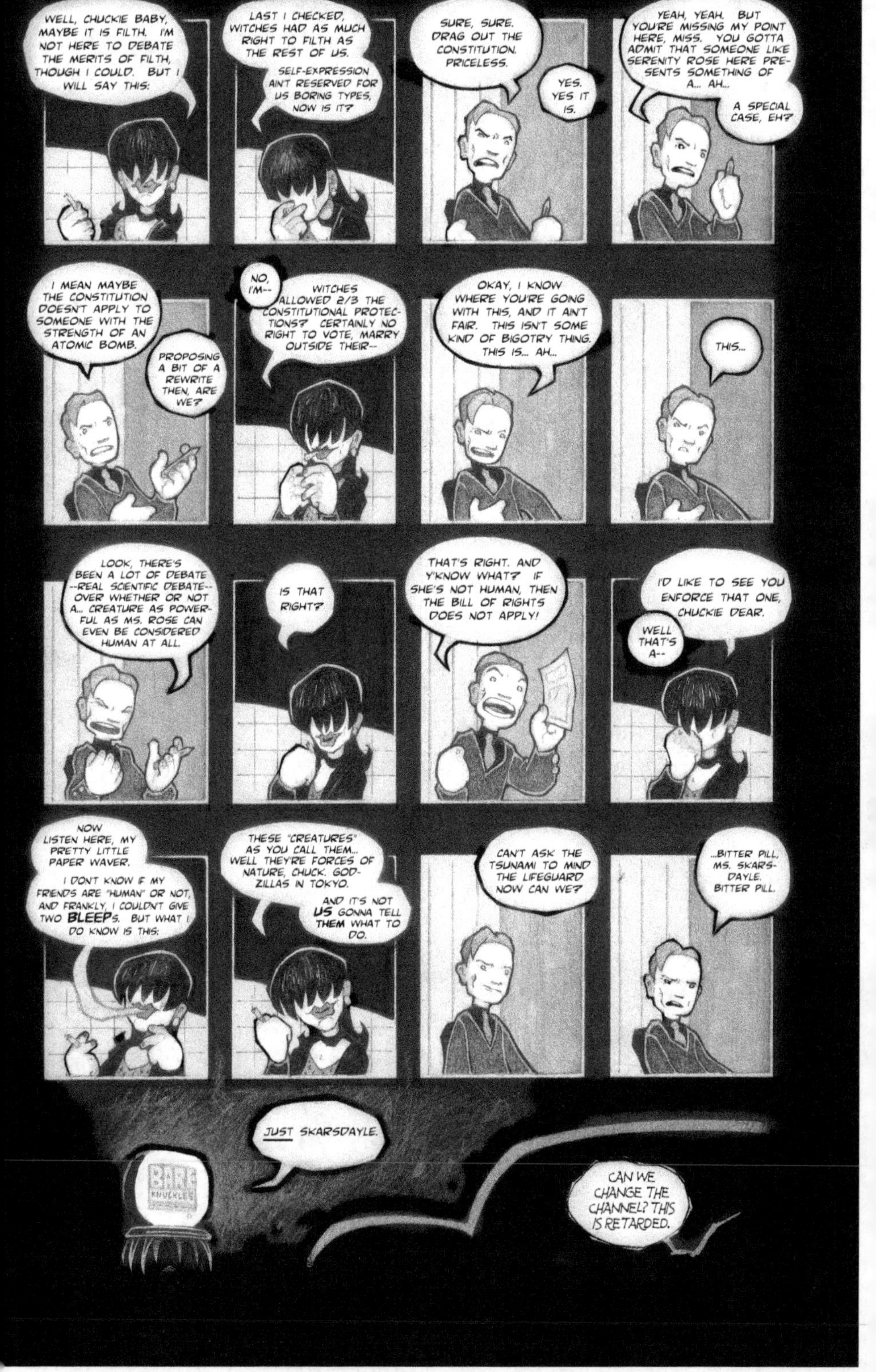
WELL, CHUCKIE BABY, MAYBE IT IS FILTH. I'M NOT HERE TO DEBATE THE MERITS OF FILTH, THOUGH I COULD. BUT I WILL SAY THIS:
LAST I CHECKED, WITCHES HAD AS MUCH RIGHT TO FILTH AS THE REST OF US.
SELF-EXPRESSION AIN'T RESERVED FOR US BORING TYPES, NOW IS IT?
SURE, SURE. DRAG OUT THE CONSTITUTION. PRICELESS.
YES. YES IT IS.
YEAH, YEAH. BUT YOU'RE MISSING MY POINT HERE, MISS. YOU GOTTA ADMIT THAT SOMEONE LIKE SERENITY ROSE HERE PRESENTS SOMETHING OF A... AH...
A SPECIAL CASE, EH?
I MEAN MAYBE THE CONSTITUTION DOESN'T APPLY TO SOMEONE WITH THE STRENGTH OF AN ATOMIC BOMB.
PROPOSING A BIT OF A REWRITE THEN, ARE WE?
NO, I'M--
WITCHES ALLOWED 2/3 THE CONSTITUTIONAL PROTECTIONS? CERTAINLY NO RIGHT TO VOTE, MARRY OUTSIDE THEIR--
OKAY, I KNOW WHERE YOU'RE GOING WITH THIS, AND IT AIN'T FAIR. THIS ISN'T SOME KIND OF BIGOTRY THING. THIS IS... AH...
THIS...
LOOK, THERE'S BEEN A LOT OF DEBATE --REAL SCIENTIFIC DEBATE-- OVER WHETHER OR NOT A... CREATURE AS POWERFUL AS MS. ROSE CAN EVEN BE CONSIDERED HUMAN AT ALL.
IS THAT RIGHT?
THAT'S RIGHT. AND Y'KNOW WHAT? IF SHE'S NOT HUMAN, THEN THE BILL OF RIGHTS DOES NOT APPLY!
I'D LIKE TO SEE YOU ENFORCE THAT ONE, CHUCKIE DEAR.
WELL THAT'S A--
NOW LISTEN HERE, MY PRETTY LITTLE PAPER WAVER.
I DON'T KNOW IF MY FRIENDS ARE "HUMAN" OR NOT, AND FRANKLY, I COULDN'T GIVE TWO BLEEPS. BUT WHAT I DO KNOW IS THIS:
THESE "CREATURES" AS YOU CALL THEM... WELL THEY'RE FORCES OF NATURE, CHUCK. GODZILLAS IN TOKYO.
AND IT'S NOT US GONNA TELL THEM WHAT TO DO.
CAN'T ASK THE TSUNAMI TO MIND THE LIFEGUARD NOW CAN WE?
...BITTER PILL, MS. SKARSDAYLE. BITTER PILL.
JUST SKARSDAYLE.
CAN WE CHANGE THE CHANNEL? THIS IS RETARDED.

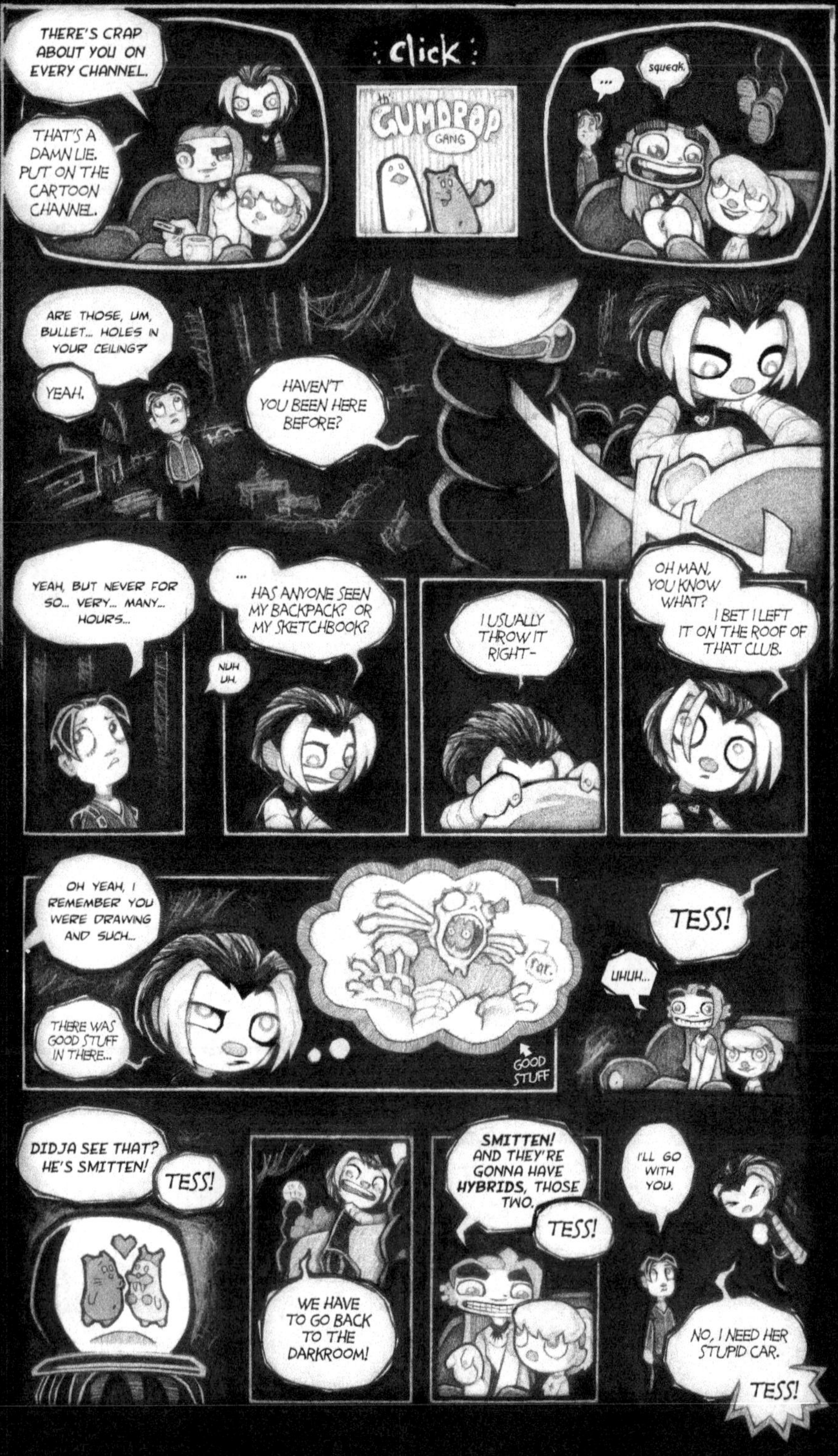
THERE'S CRAP ABOUT YOU ON EVERY CHANNEL.
THAT'S A DAMN LIE. PUT ON THE CARTOON CHANNEL.
click
th' GUMDROP GANG
...
squeak.
ARE THOSE, UM, BULLET... HOLES IN YOUR CEILING?
YEAH.
HAVEN'T YOU BEEN HERE BEFORE?
YEAH, BUT NEVER FOR SO... VERY... MANY... HOURS...
... HAS ANYONE SEEN MY BACKPACK? OR MY SKETCHBOOK?
NUH UH.
I USUALLY THROW IT RIGHT-
OH MAN, YOU KNOW WHAT?
I BET I LEFT IT ON THE ROOF OF THAT CLUB.
OH YEAH, I REMEMBER YOU WERE DRAWING AND SUCH...
THERE WAS GOOD STUFF IN THERE...
rar.
GOOD STUFF
TESS!
UHUH...
DIDJA SEE THAT? HE'S SMITTEN!
TESS!
WE HAVE TO GO BACK TO THE DARKROOM!
SMITTEN! AND THEY'RE GONNA HAVE HYBRIDS, THOSE TWO.
TESS!
I'LL GO WITH YOU.
NO, I NEED HER STUPID CAR.
TESS!

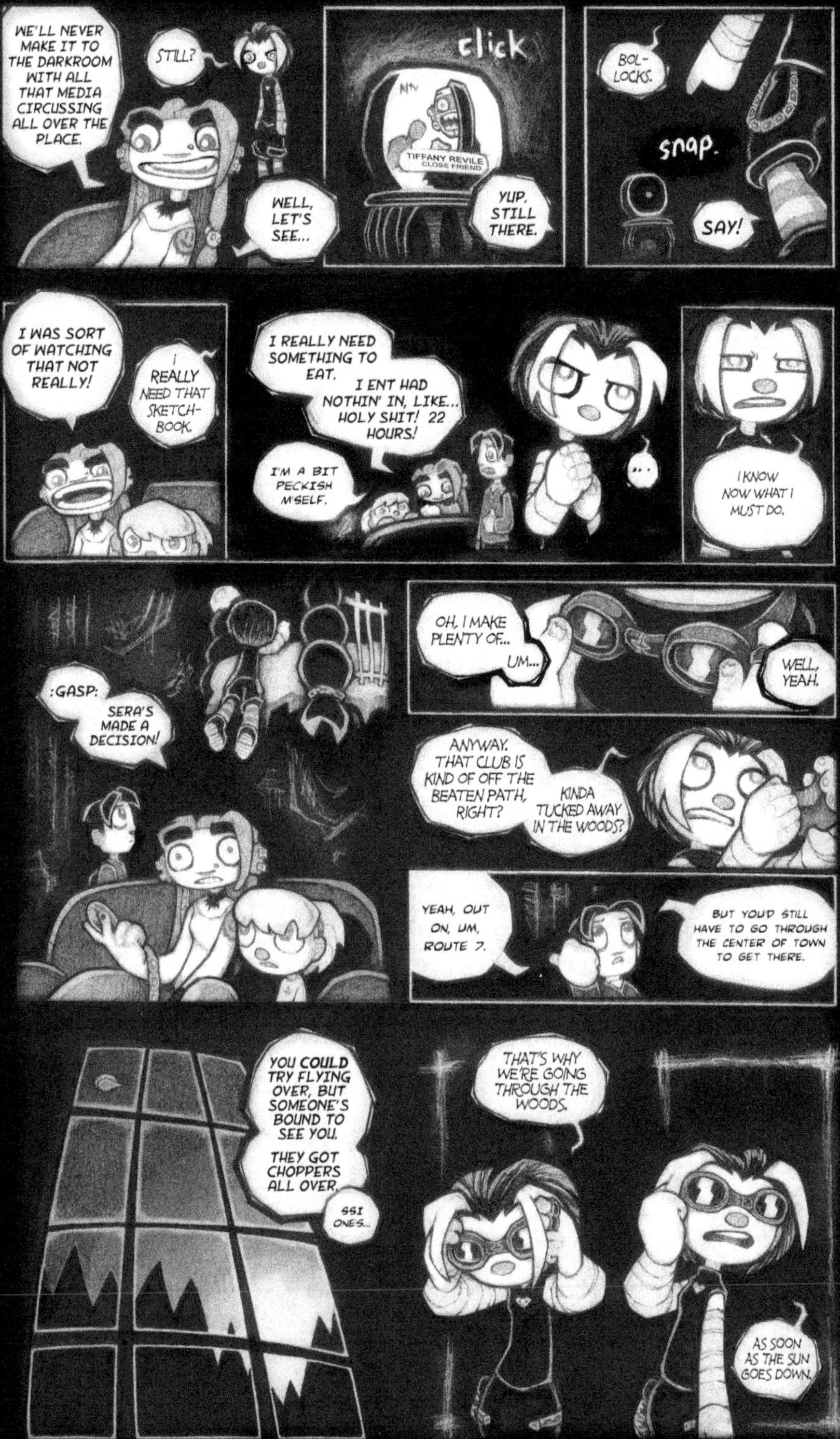
WE'LL NEVER MAKE IT TO THE DARKROOM WITH ALL THAT MEDIA CIRCUSSING ALL OVER THE PLACE.
STILL?
WELL, LET'S SEE...
click
TIFFANY REVILE
CLOSE FRIEND
YUP, STILL THERE.
BOL-LOCKS.
snap.
SAY!
I WAS SORT OF WATCHING THAT NOT REALLY!
I REALLY NEED THAT SKETCH-BOOK.
I REALLY NEED SOMETHING TO EAT.
I ENT HAD NOTHIN' IN, LIKE... HOLY SHIT! 22 HOURS!
I'M A BIT PECKISH M'SELF.
I KNOW NOW WHAT I MUST DO.
:GASP:
SERA'S MADE A DECISION!
OH, I MAKE PLENTY OF...
UM...
WELL, YEAH.
ANYWAY. THAT CLUB IS KIND OF OFF THE BEATEN PATH, RIGHT?
KINDA TUCKED AWAY IN THE WOODS?
YEAH, OUT ON, UM, ROUTE 7.
BUT YOU'D STILL HAVE TO GO THROUGH THE CENTER OF TOWN TO GET THERE.
YOU COULD TRY FLYING OVER, BUT SOMEONE'S BOUND TO SEE YOU.
THEY GOT CHOPPERS ALL OVER.
SSI ONES...
THAT'S WHY WE'RE GOING THROUGH THE WOODS.
AS SOON AS THE SUN GOES DOWN.

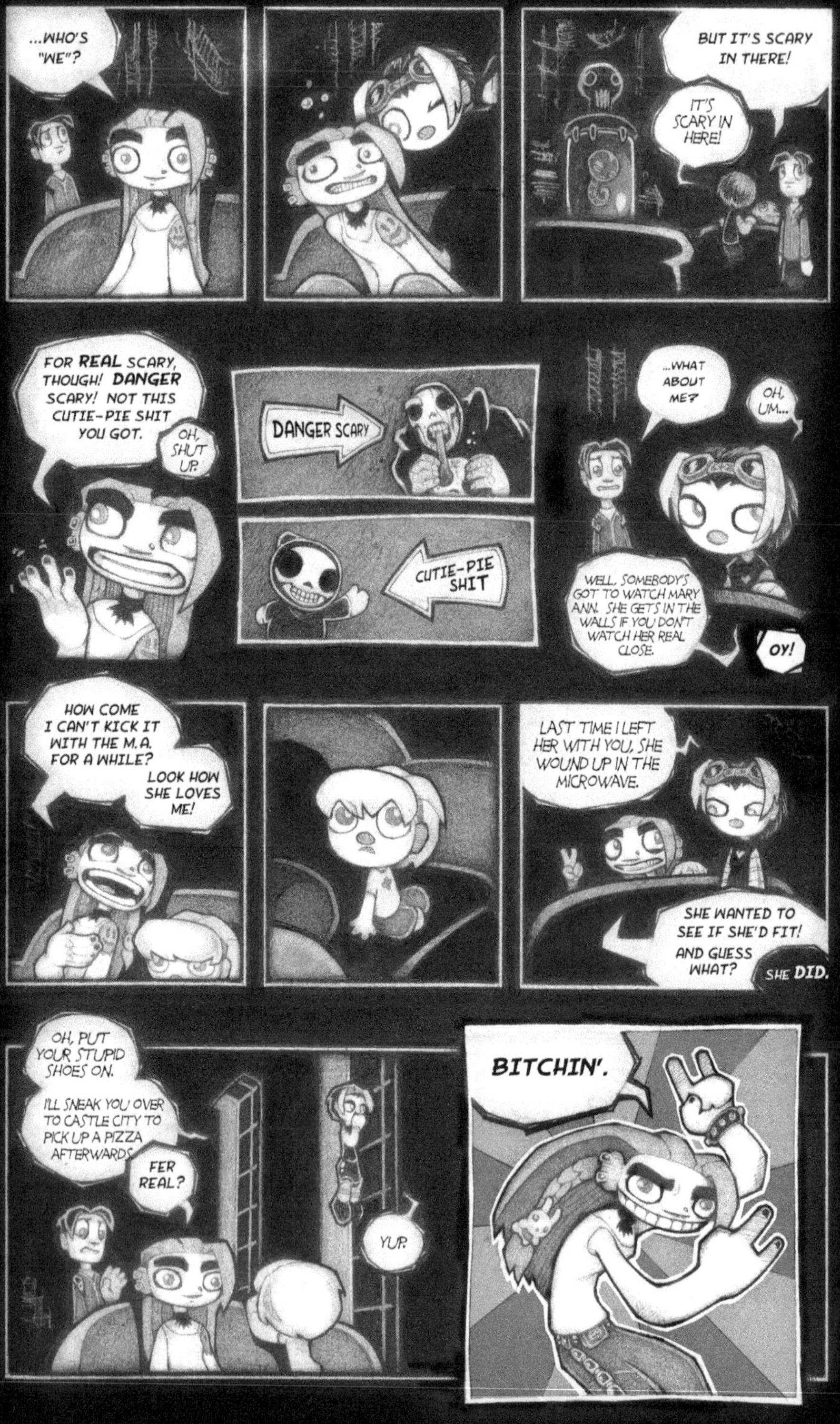

...WHO'S "WE"?
BUT IT'S SCARY IN THERE!
IT'S SCARY IN HERE!
FOR REAL SCARY, THOUGH! DANGER SCARY! NOT THIS CUTIE-PIE SHIT YOU GOT.
OH, SHUT UP.
DANGER SCARY
CUTIE-PIE SHIT
...WHAT ABOUT ME?
OH, UM...
WELL, SOMEBODY'S GOT TO WATCH MARY ANN. SHE GETS IN THE WALLS IF YOU DON'T WATCH HER REAL CLOSE.
OY!
HOW COME I CAN'T KICK IT WITH THE M.A. FOR A WHILE?
LOOK HOW SHE LOVES ME!
LAST TIME I LEFT HER WITH YOU, SHE WOUND UP IN THE MICROWAVE.
SHE WANTED TO SEE IF SHE'D FIT!
AND GUESS WHAT?
SHE DID.
OH, PUT YOUR STUPID SHOES ON.
I'LL SNEAK YOU OVER TO CASTLE CITY TO PICK UP A PIZZA AFTERWARDS.
FER REAL?
YUP.
BITCHIN'.

FEARFUL THING. THE JOURNAL OF THE UNDERSIDE #3 (D.D. KELTON, ED.) DRAWN BY

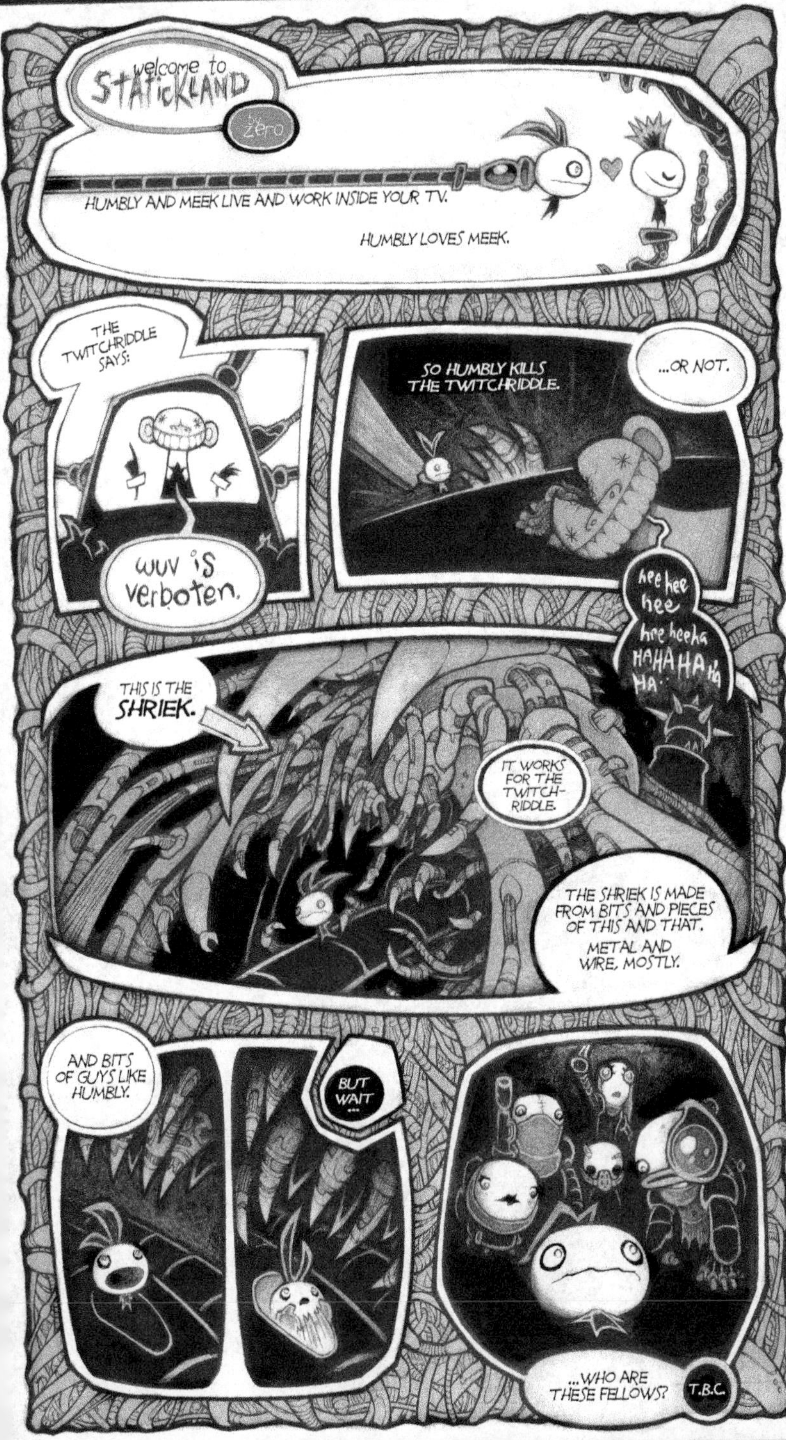

welcome to STATICKLAND
by zero
HUMBLY AND MEEK LIVE AND WORK INSIDE YOUR TV.
HUMBLY LOVES MEEK.
THE TWITCHRIDDLE SAYS:
wuv is verboten.
SO HUMBLY KILLS THE TWITCHRIDDLE.
...OR NOT.
hee hee hee hee heeha HAHAHAHA HA HA
THIS IS THE SHRIEK.
IT WORKS FOR THE TWITCH-RIDDLE.
THE SHRIEK IS MADE FROM BITS AND PIECES OF THIS AND THAT.
METAL AND WIRE, MOSTLY.
AND BITS OF GUYS LIKE HUMBLY.
BUT WAIT...
...WHO ARE THESE FELLOWS?
T.B.C.

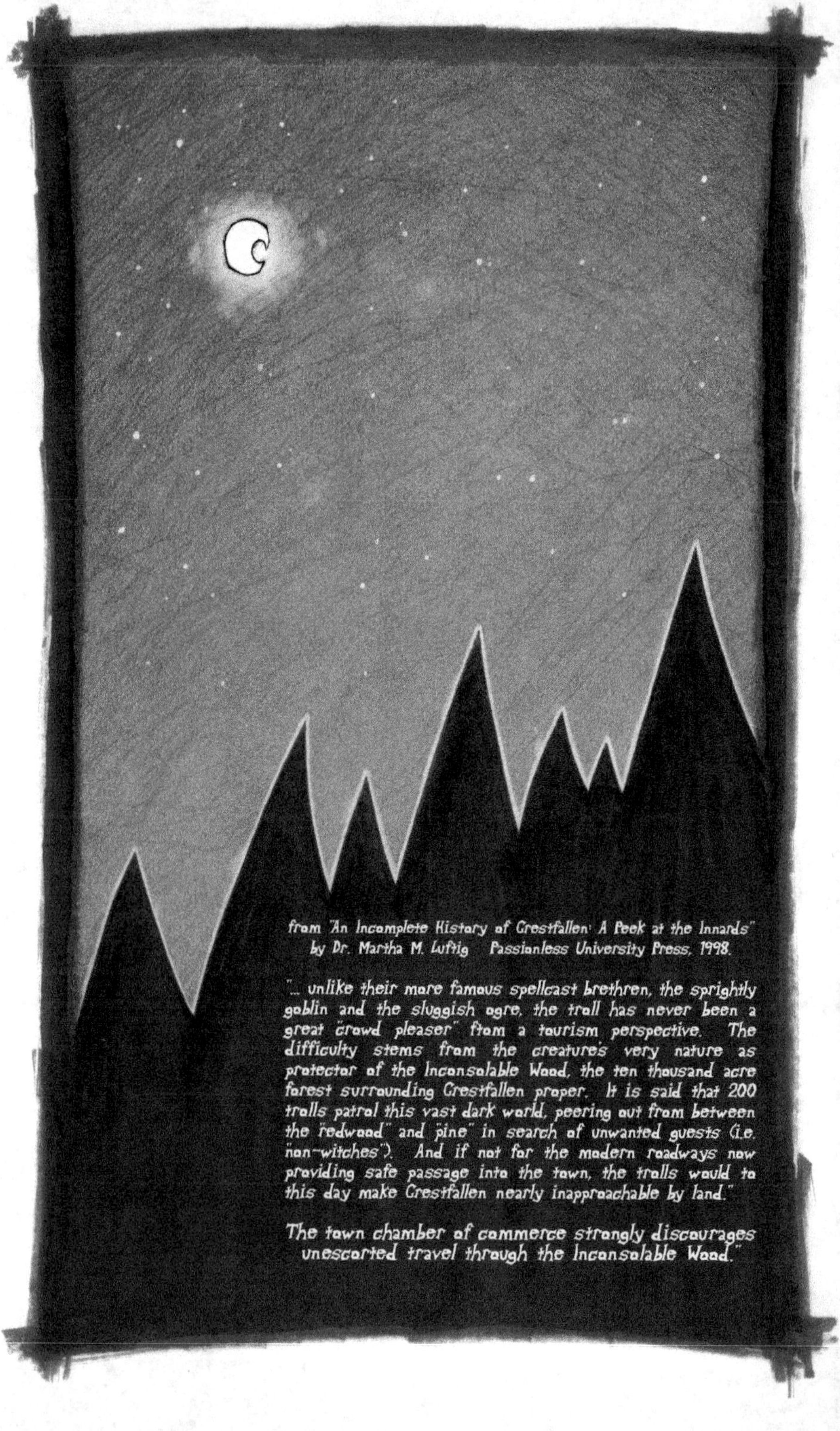
from "An Incomplete History of Crestfallen: A Peek at the Innards"
by Dr. Martha M. Luftig   Passionless University Press, 1998.
"... unlike their more famous spellcast brethren, the sprightly goblin and the sluggish ogre, the troll has never been a great "crowd pleaser" from a tourism perspective. The difficulty stems from the creature's very nature as protector of the Inconsolable Wood, the ten thousand acre forest surrounding Crestfallen proper. It is said that 200 trolls patrol this vast dark world, peering out from between the "redwood" and "pine" in search of unwanted guests (i.e. "non-witches"). And if not for the modern roadways now providing safe passage into the town, the trolls would to this day make Crestfallen nearly inapproachable by land."
The town chamber of commerce strongly discourages unescorted travel through the Inconsolable Wood."

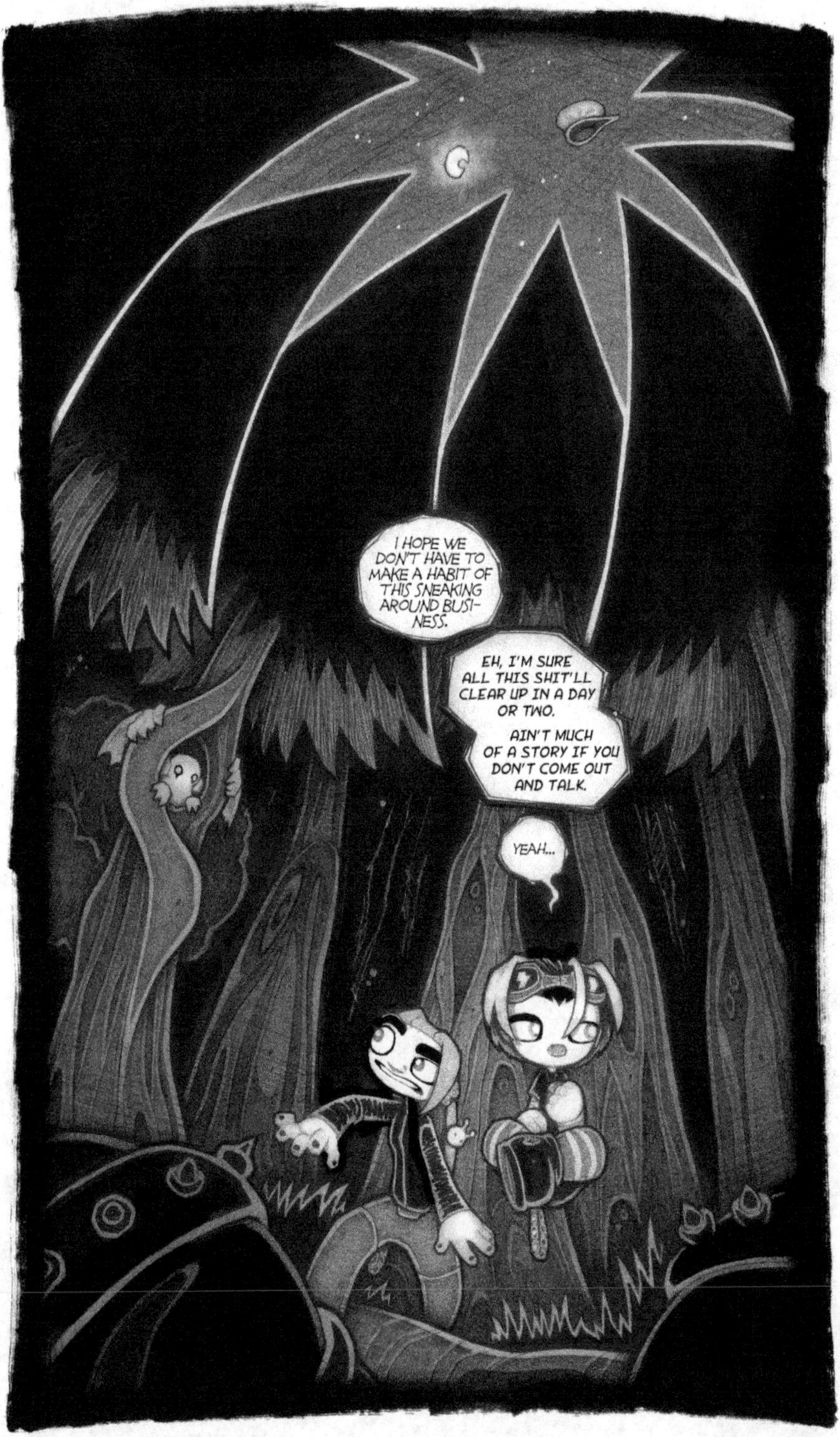
I HOPE WE DON'T HAVE TO MAKE A HABIT OF THIS SNEAKING AROUND BUSI-NESS.
EH, I'M SURE ALL THIS SHIT'LL CLEAR UP IN A DAY OR TWO.
AIN'T MUCH OF A STORY IF YOU DON'T COME OUT AND TALK.
YEAH...

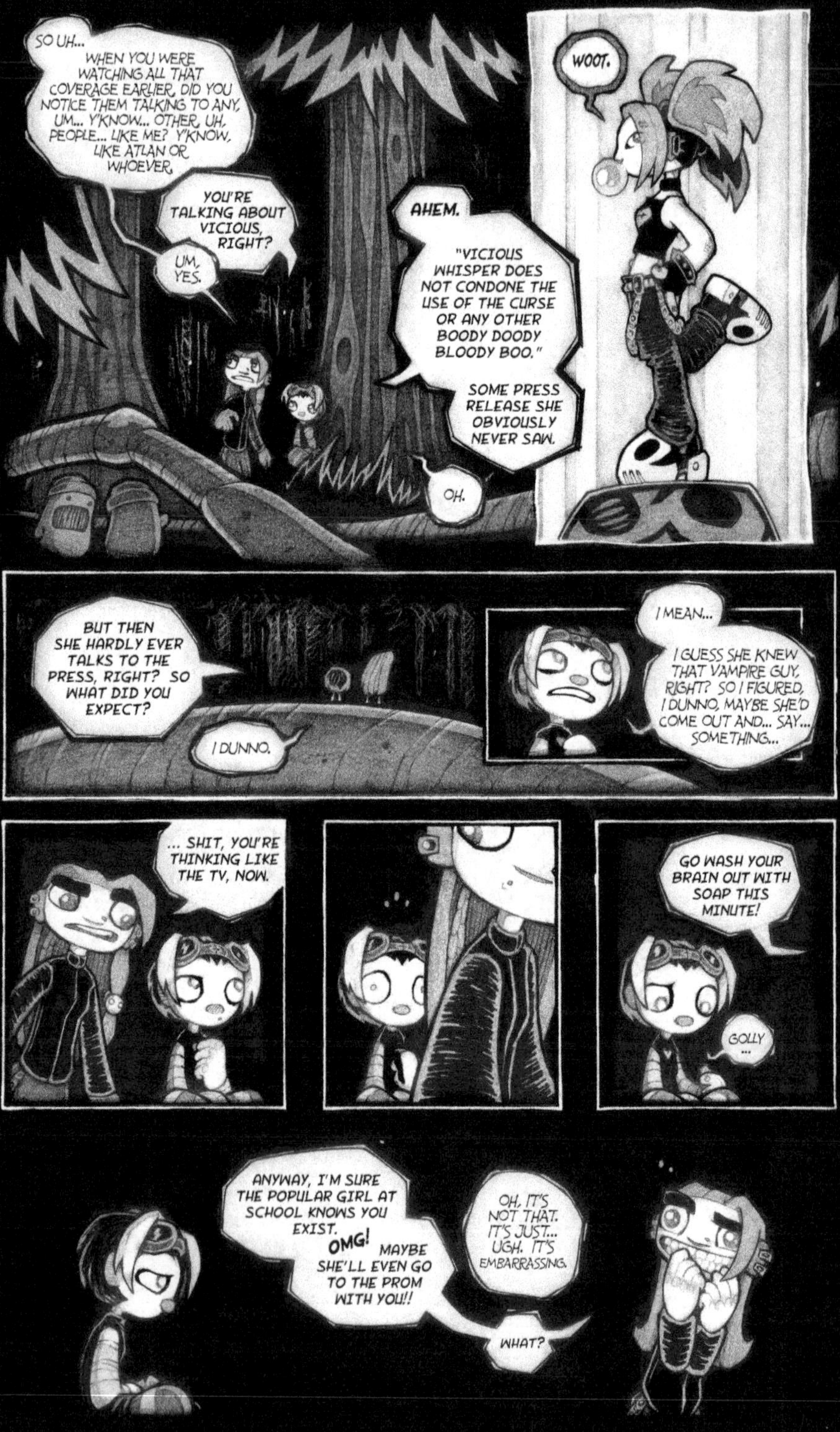
SO UH... WHEN YOU WERE WATCHING ALL THAT COVERAGE EARLIER, DID YOU NOTICE THEM TALKING TO ANY, UM... Y'KNOW... OTHER, UH, PEOPLE... LIKE ME? Y'KNOW, LIKE ATLAN OR WHOEVER.
YOU'RE TALKING ABOUT VICIOUS, RIGHT?
UM, YES.
AHEM.
"VICIOUS WHISPER DOES NOT CONDONE THE USE OF THE CURSE OR ANY OTHER BOODY DOODY BLOODY BOO."
SOME PRESS RELEASE SHE OBVIOUSLY NEVER SAW.
WOOT.
OH.
BUT THEN SHE HARDLY EVER TALKS TO THE PRESS, RIGHT? SO WHAT DID YOU EXPECT?
I DUNNO.
I MEAN...
I GUESS SHE KNEW THAT VAMPIRE GUY, RIGHT? SO I FIGURED, I DUNNO, MAYBE SHE'D COME OUT AND... SAY... SOMETHING...
... SHIT, YOU'RE THINKING LIKE THE TV, NOW.
GO WASH YOUR BRAIN OUT WITH SOAP THIS MINUTE!
GOLLY ...
ANYWAY, I'M SURE THE POPULAR GIRL AT SCHOOL KNOWS YOU EXIST.
OMG! MAYBE SHE'LL EVEN GO TO THE PROM WITH YOU!!
WHAT?
OH, IT'S NOT THAT. IT'S JUST... UGH. IT'S EMBARRASSING.

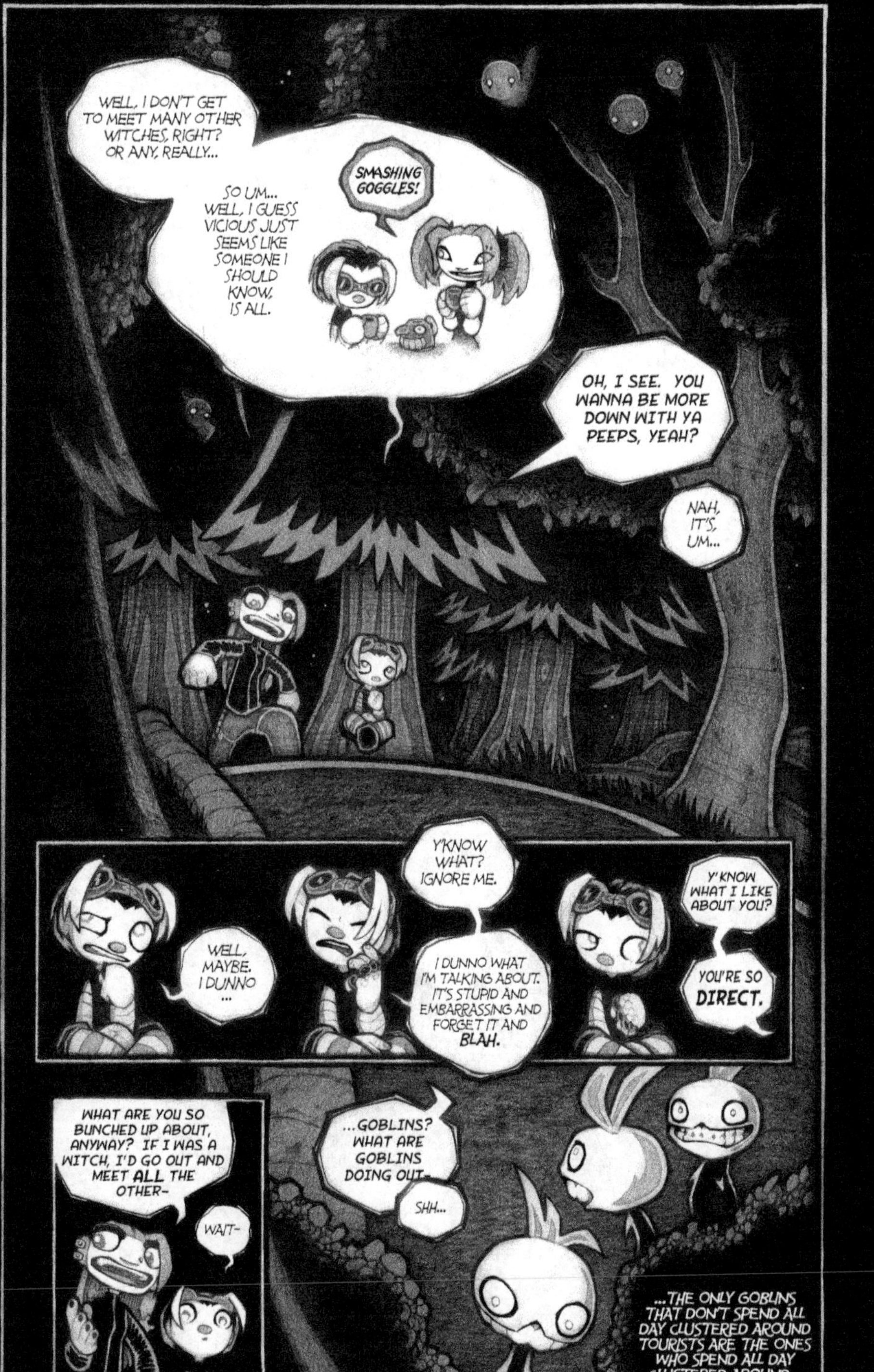

WELL, I DON'T GET TO MEET MANY OTHER WITCHES, RIGHT? OR ANY, REALLY...
SO UM... WELL, I GUESS VICIOUS JUST SEEMS LIKE SOMEONE I SHOULD KNOW, IS ALL.
SMASHING GOGGLES!
OH, I SEE. YOU WANNA BE MORE DOWN WITH YA PEEPS, YEAH?
NAH, IT'S, UM...
WELL, MAYBE. I DUNNO ...
Y'KNOW WHAT? IGNORE ME.
I DUNNO WHAT I'M TALKING ABOUT. IT'S STUPID AND EMBARRASSING AND FORGET IT AND BLAH.
Y' KNOW WHAT I LIKE ABOUT YOU?
YOU'RE SO DIRECT.
WHAT ARE YOU SO BUNCHED UP ABOUT, ANYWAY? IF I WAS A WITCH, I'D GO OUT AND MEET ALL THE OTHER-
WAIT-
...GOBLINS? WHAT ARE GOBLINS DOING OUT-
SHH...
...THE ONLY GOBLINS THAT DON'T SPEND ALL DAY CLUSTERED AROUND TOURISTS ARE THE ONES WHO SPEND ALL DAY CLUSTERED AROUND...

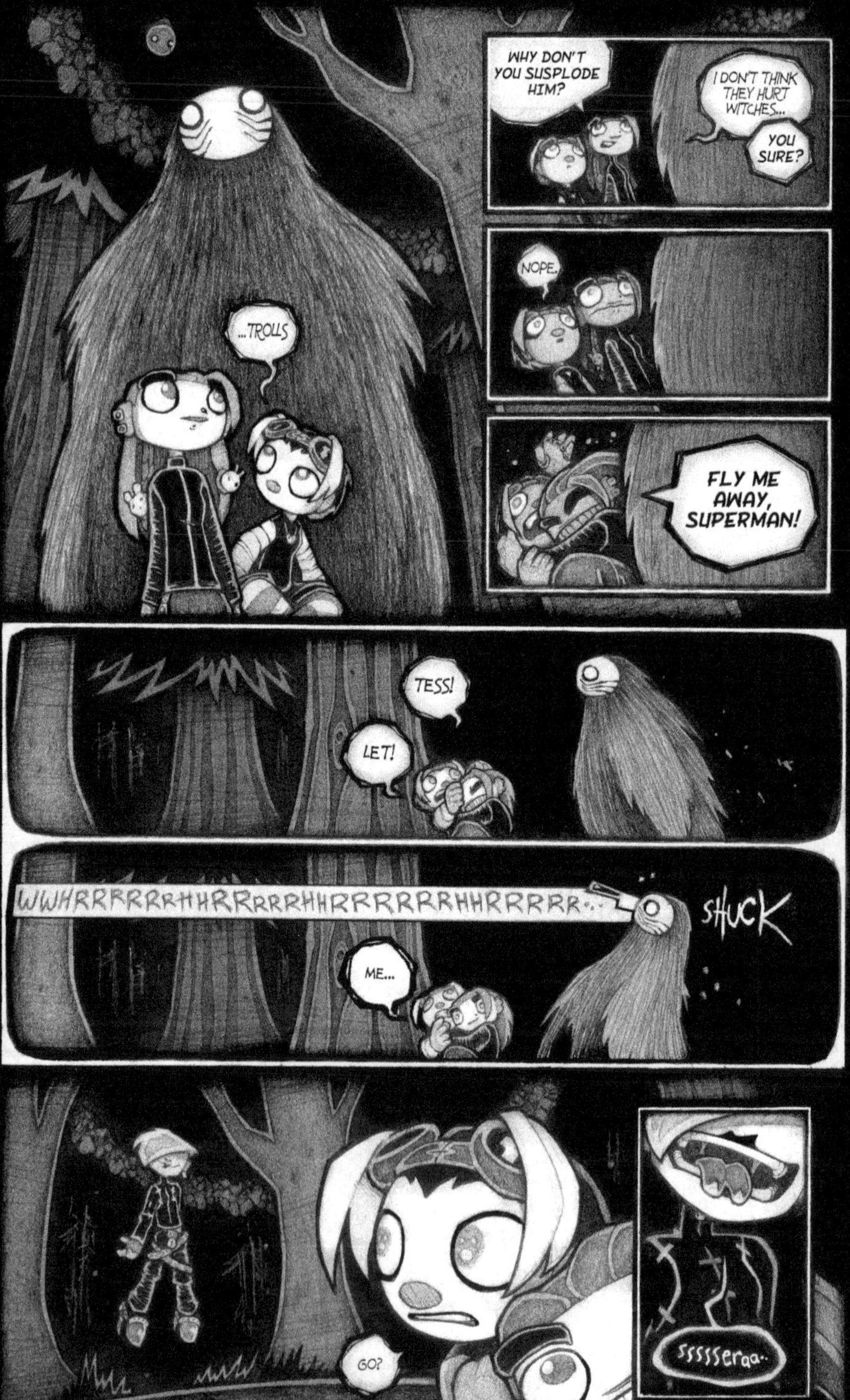
WHY DON'T YOU SUSPLODE HIM?
I DON'T THINK THEY HURT WITCHES...
YOU SURE?
...TROLLS
NOPE.
FLY ME AWAY, SUPERMAN!
TESS!
LET!
WWHRRRRRRHHRRRRRHHRRRRRRRHHRRRRRR..
SHUCK
ME...
GO?
SSSSSeraa..

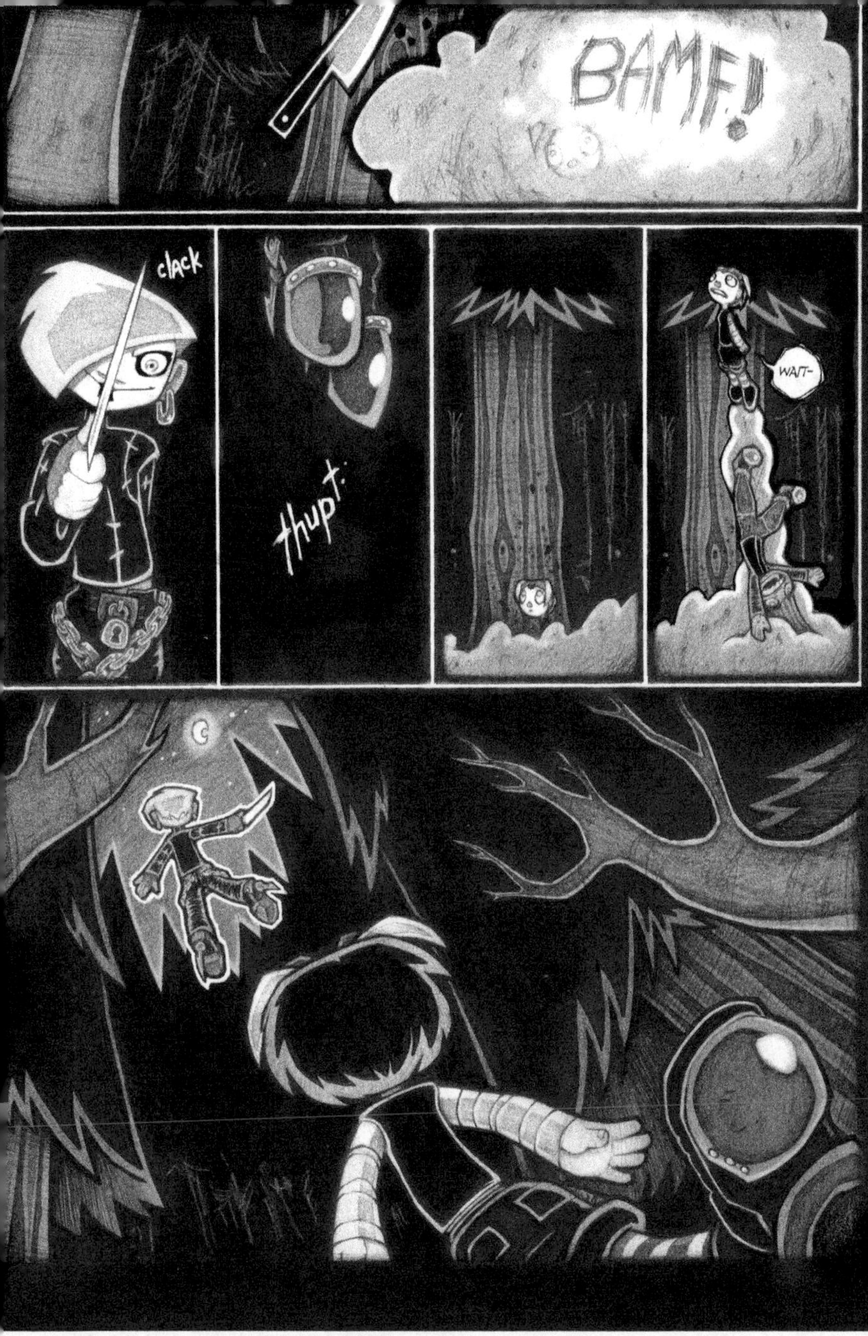
BAMF!
clack
thupt
WAIT-

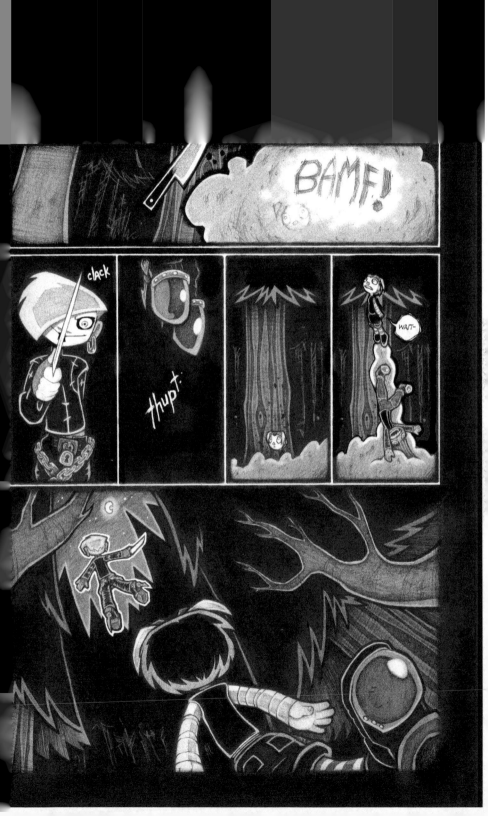

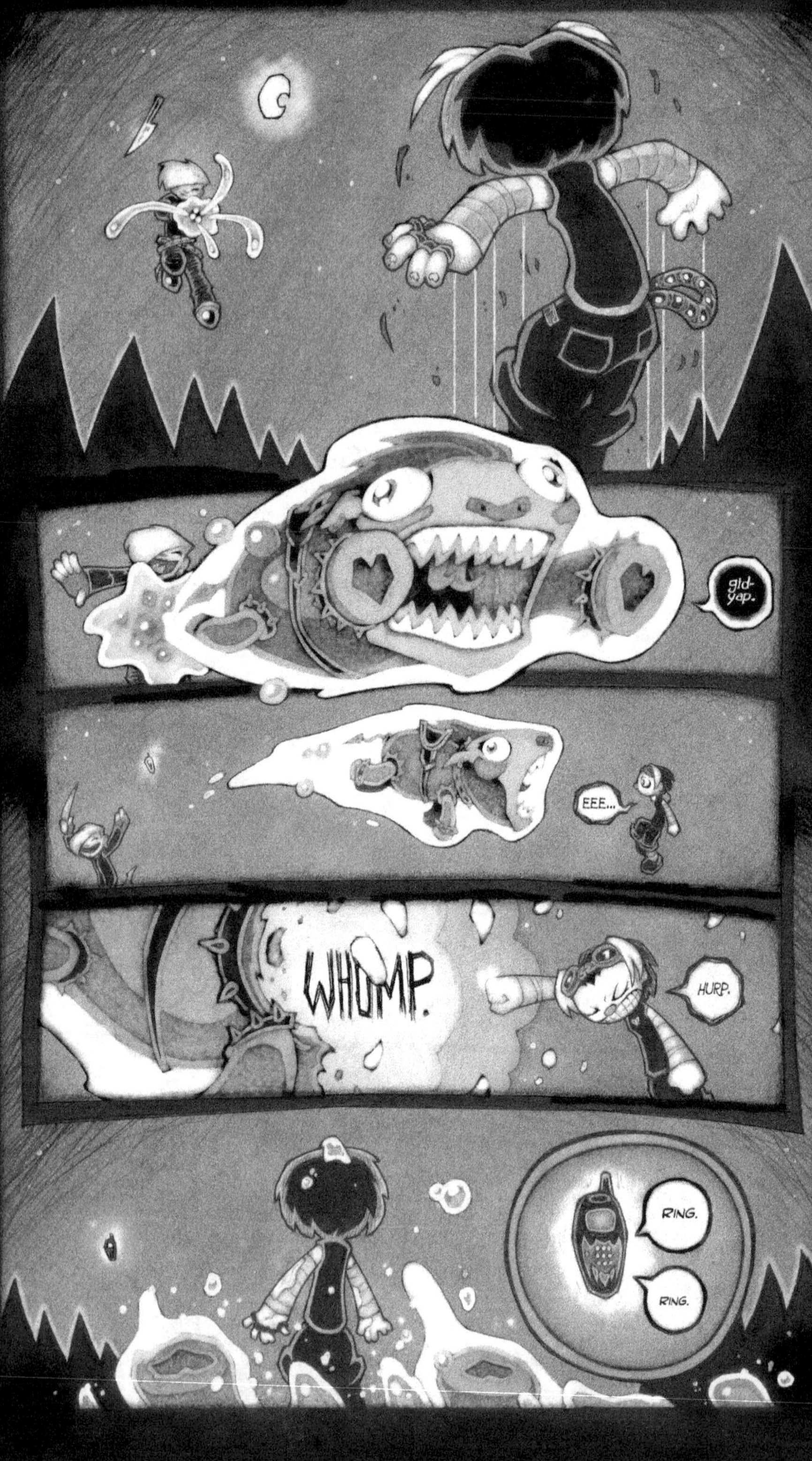
gid-yap.
EEE...
WHOMP.
HURP.
RING.
RING.

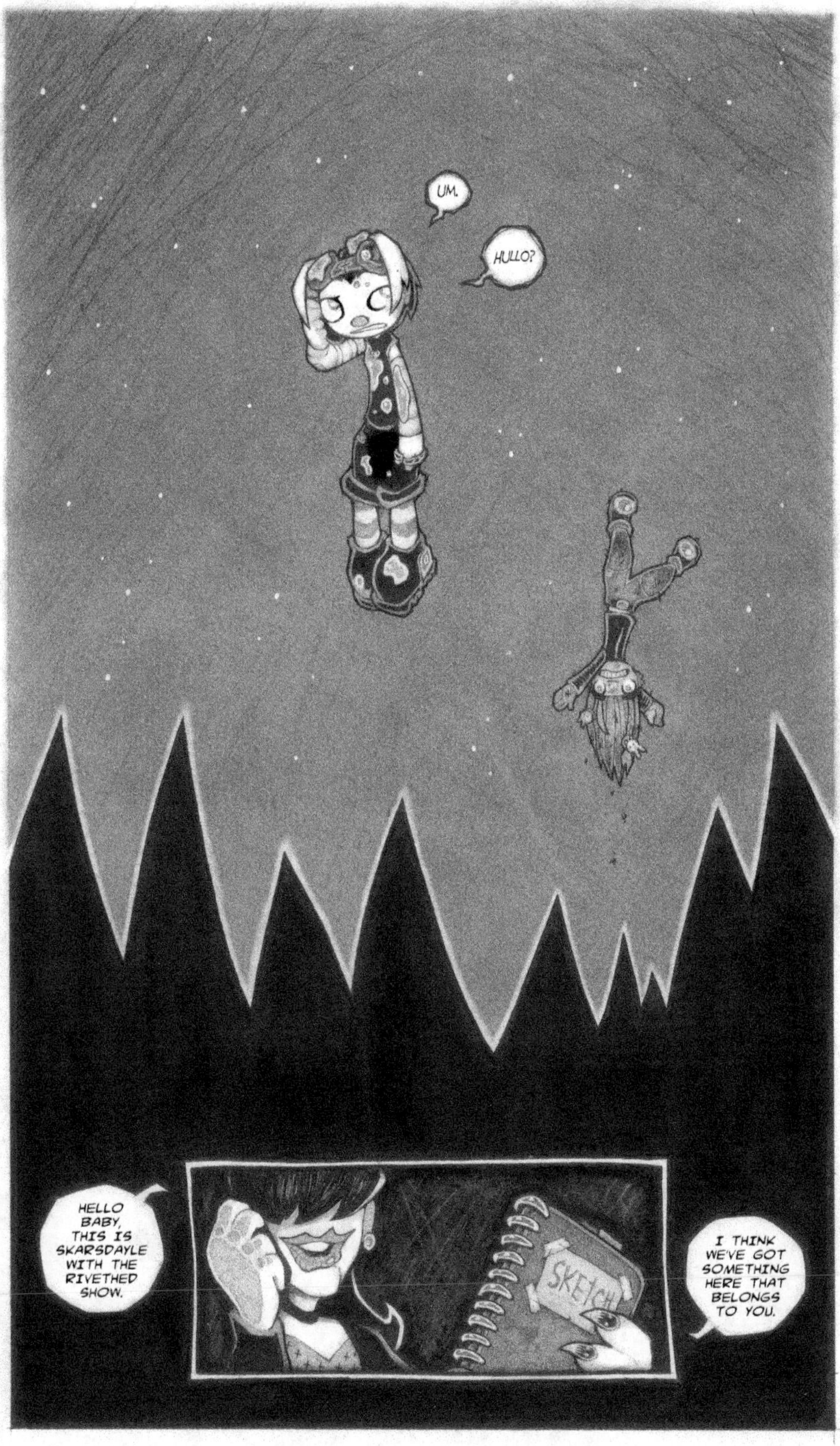
UM.
HULLO?
HELLO BABY, THIS IS SKARSDAYLE WITH THE RIVETHED SHOW.
SKETCH
I THINK WE'VE GOT SOMETHING HERE THAT BELONGS TO YOU.

WHILE WE WERE OUT:

I THINK
WHAT'S
REALLY
INTERESTING,
THOUGH...

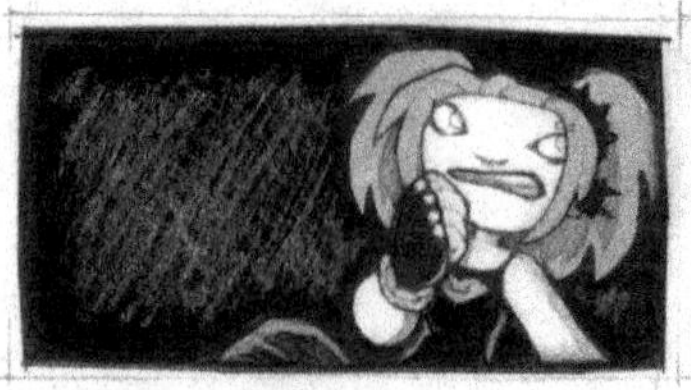

IS THAT
IN THE
MIDST OF
ALL THIS
HULLABALLOO,

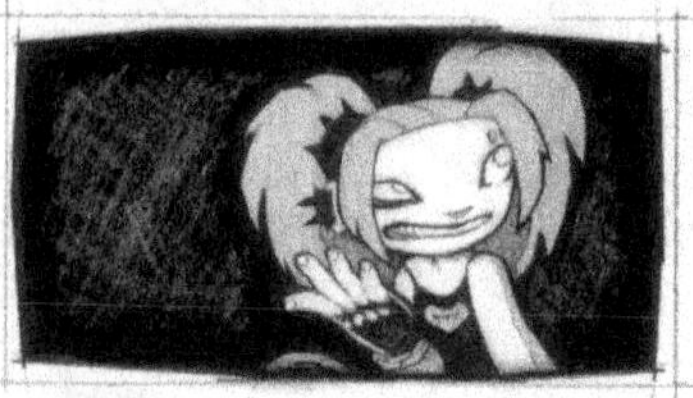

THIS FOOFARAW
ABOUT VAMPS
AND PONIES
AND HEAVEN
AND HELL,

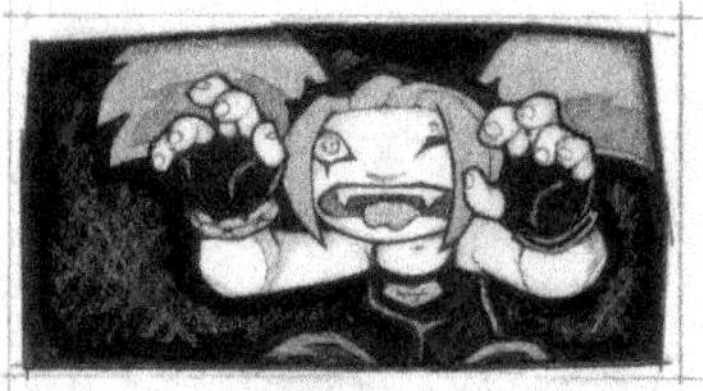

THAT
NOT ONE
PERSON HAS
MENTIONED
-NOT ONE-

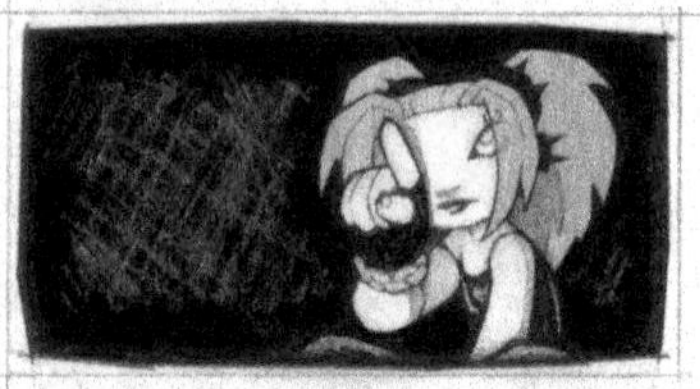

...THAT
THAT GIRL
WAS A
HERO.

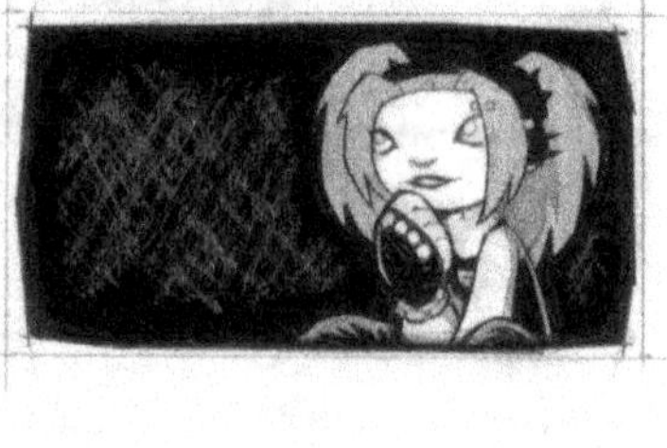

...ISSUE FOUR

Serenity Rose

the personal journals of a local witch

...as told to aaron a.
with assists by gofflin + casey

issue number four:

"scary monsters, super freaks"

"starring"

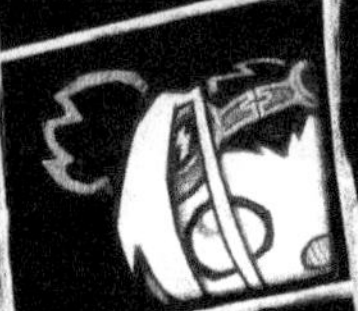

SERA "PUPPYNOSE" ROSE: SERENITY ELIZABETH "SERA" ROSE IS THE 10TH YOUNGEST, 8TH SHORTEST, 6TH "GOTHIEST," 22ND MOST POWERFUL, 38TH MOST RESPECTED AND 5TH MOST RECLUSIVE OF THE WORLD'S 50 KNOWN WITCHES. BUT WHEN IT COMES TO SMELLING LIKE FLOWERS, SHE'LL ALWAYS BE NUMBER ONE WITH ME.

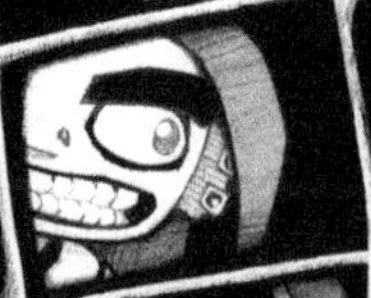

CONTESSA "SUNNYSIDE" RUBIKOV: CONTESSA NATALYA "TESS" RUBIKOV IS THE MOST UNPLEASANT PERSON IN CRESTFALLEN. SELF-PROCLAIMED, OF COURSE. MOST PEOPLE JUST KNOW HER AS "THAT ENORMOUS RED-HAIRED SASQUATCH THAT HANGS OUT WITH SERENITY ROSE." HER GOAL: 100% HATRED BY THE YEAR 2010.

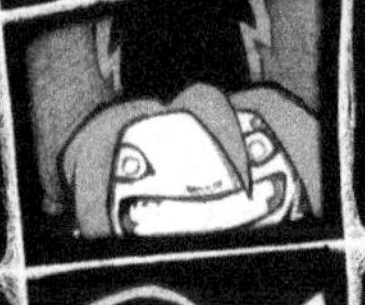

VICIOUS "NOT VISCOUS" WHISPER: SEE PAGE 87.

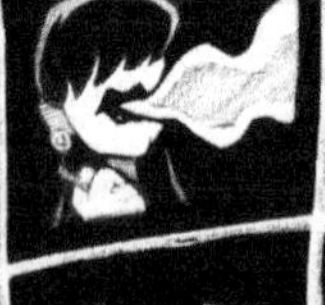

SKARSDAYLE: SEE PAGE 86.

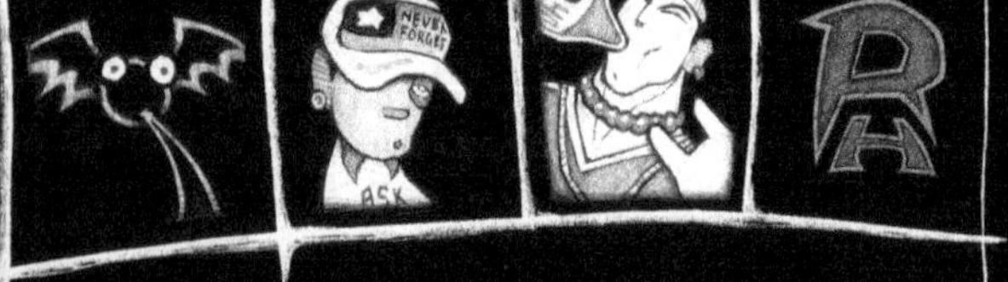

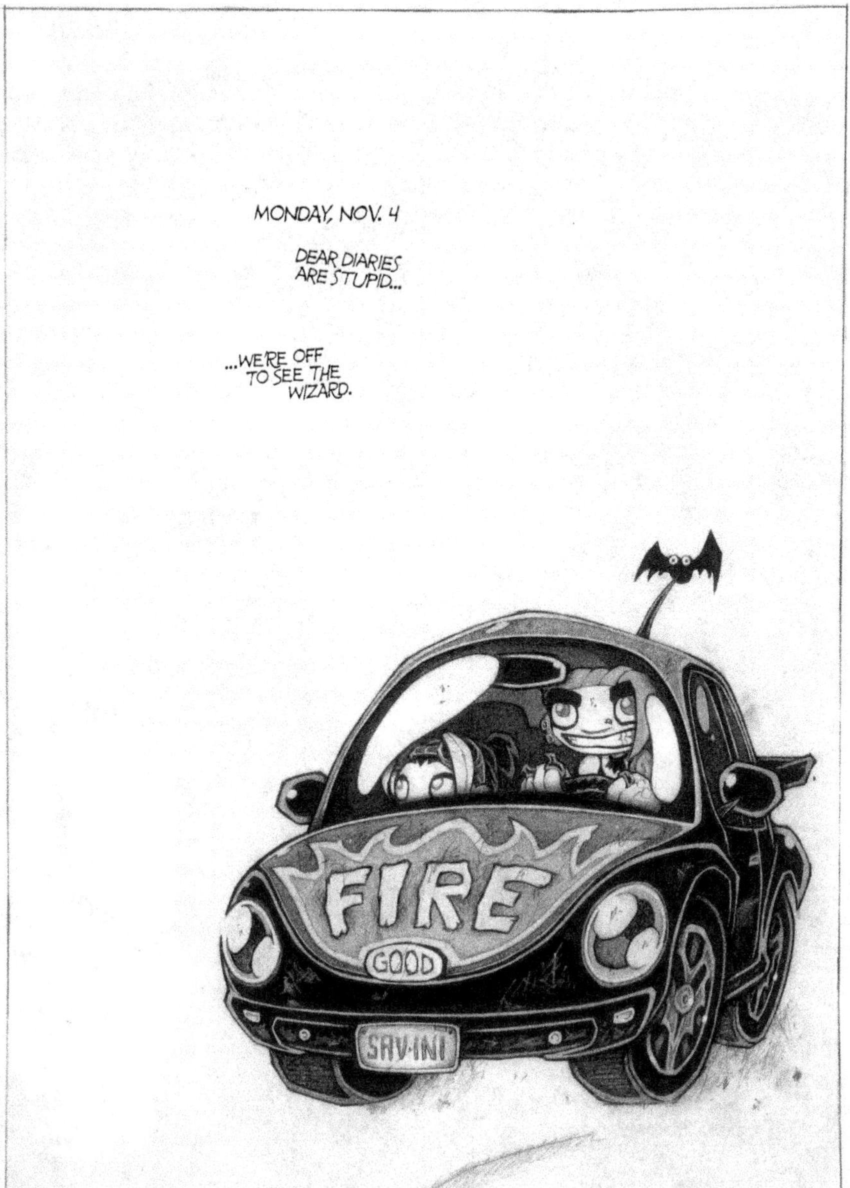
MONDAY, NOV. 4
DEAR DIARIES ARE STUPID...
...WE'RE OFF TO SEE THE WIZARD.
FIRE
GOOD
SAV-INI

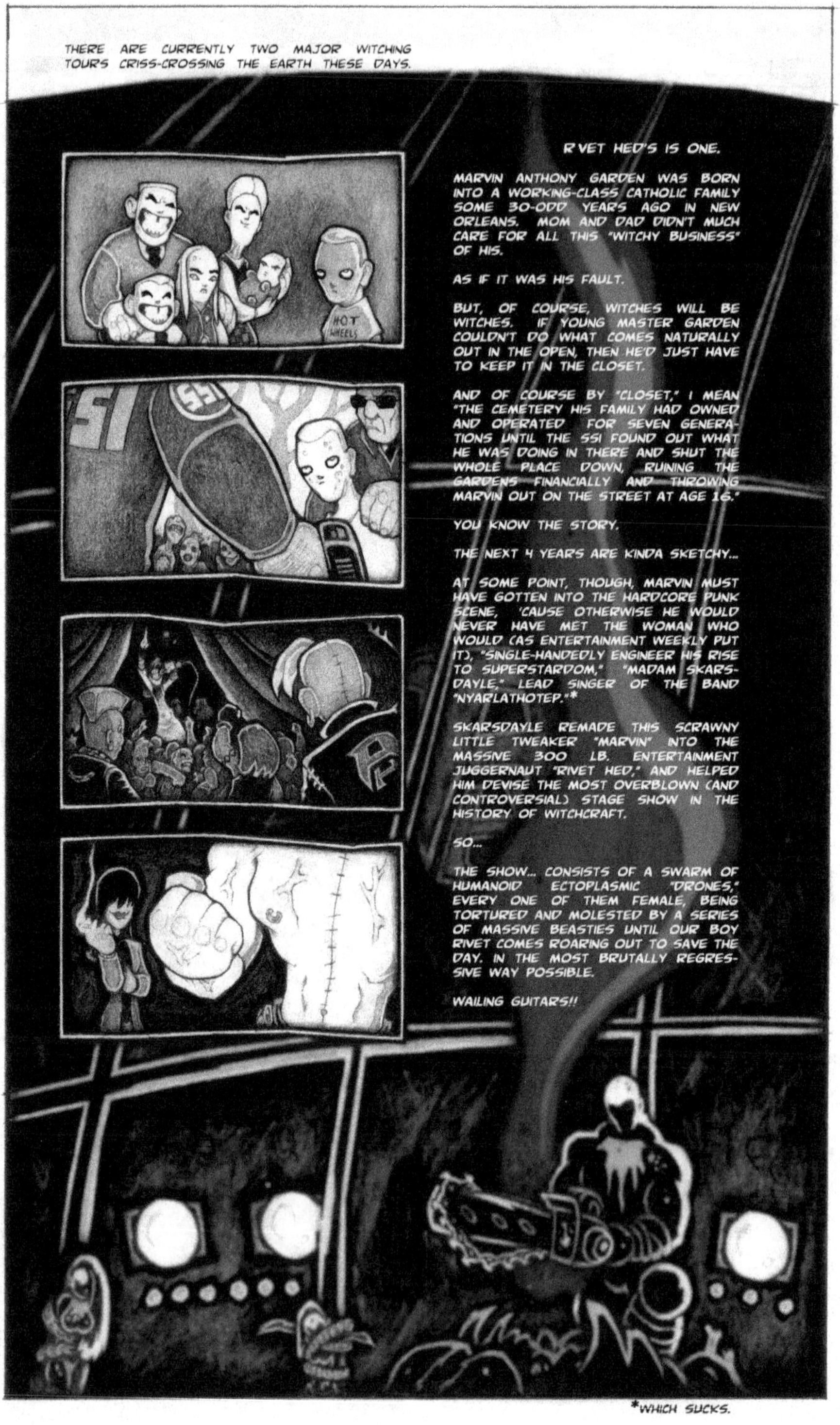
THERE ARE CURRENTLY TWO MAJOR WITCHING TOURS CRISS-CROSSING THE EARTH THESE DAYS.
RVET HED'S IS ONE.
MARVIN ANTHONY GARDEN WAS BORN INTO A WORKING-CLASS CATHOLIC FAMILY SOME 30-ODD YEARS AGO IN NEW ORLEANS. MOM AND DAD DIDN'T MUCH CARE FOR ALL THIS "WITCHY BUSINESS" OF HIS.
AS IF IT WAS HIS FAULT.
BUT, OF COURSE, WITCHES WILL BE WITCHES. IF YOUNG MASTER GARDEN COULDN'T DO WHAT COMES NATURALLY OUT IN THE OPEN, THEN HE'D JUST HAVE TO KEEP IT IN THE CLOSET.
AND OF COURSE BY "CLOSET," I MEAN "THE CEMETERY HIS FAMILY HAD OWNED AND OPERATED FOR SEVEN GENERATIONS UNTIL THE SSI FOUND OUT WHAT HE WAS DOING IN THERE AND SHUT THE WHOLE PLACE DOWN, RUINING THE GARDENS FINANCIALLY AND THROWING MARVIN OUT ON THE STREET AT AGE 16."
YOU KNOW THE STORY.
THE NEXT 4 YEARS ARE KINDA SKETCHY...
AT SOME POINT, THOUGH, MARVIN MUST HAVE GOTTEN INTO THE HARDCORE PUNK SCENE, 'CAUSE OTHERWISE HE WOULD NEVER HAVE MET THE WOMAN WHO WOULD (AS ENTERTAINMENT WEEKLY PUT IT), "SINGLE-HANDEDLY ENGINEER HIS RISE TO SUPERSTARDOM," "MADAM SKARSDAYLE," LEAD SINGER OF THE BAND "NYARLATHOTEP."*
SKARSDAYLE REMADE THIS SCRAWNY LITTLE TWEAKER "MARVIN" INTO THE MASSIVE 300 LB. ENTERTAINMENT JUGGERNAUT "RIVET HED," AND HELPED HIM DEVISE THE MOST OVERBLOWN (AND CONTROVERSIAL) STAGE SHOW IN THE HISTORY OF WITCHCRAFT.
SO...
THE SHOW... CONSISTS OF A SWARM OF HUMANOID ECTOPLASMIC "DRONES," EVERY ONE OF THEM FEMALE, BEING TORTURED AND MOLESTED BY A SERIES OF MASSIVE BEASTIES UNTIL OUR BOY RIVET COMES ROARING OUT TO SAVE THE DAY. IN THE MOST BRUTALLY REGRESSIVE WAY POSSIBLE.
WAILING GUITARS!!
HOT WHEELS
SSI
*WHICH SUCKS.

VICIOUS WHISPER'S SHOW IS T'OTHER.

VICTORIA "VICIOUS" WHISPER WAS BORN 33 YEARS AGO NEAR OXFORD, ENGLAND, TO THE FAMOUS BRITISH PHYSICIST RONALD WU AND THE EVEN FAMOUSER JAPANESE POP IDOL KIMI WHISPER.

BY ALL ACCOUNTS, RON AND KIMI WERE IDEALLY SUITED TO RAISE A YOUNG WITCH; THE TWO OF THEM ARE OPTIMISTIC, GENEROUS, OPEN-MINDED, AND INTIMATELY ACCQUAINTED WITH THE SUBTLE ART OF "FAME-MANAGEMENT" (NOT TO MENTION CHOCKED FULL O' ££). THEIR KID... WOULD BE THE ENVY OF WITCHES THE WORLD OVER.

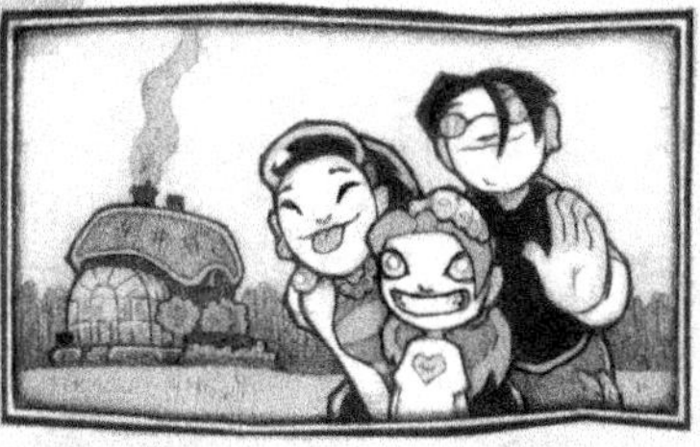

BUT YOUNG VICKIE WASN'T JUST SOME SPOILED RICH KID... RON AND KIMI WERE DETERMINED THEIR LIL TERROR LEARN ALL SHE COULD ABOUT THE DEVELOPMENT AND APPLICATION OF HER PARTICULAR ABILITIES, AND TO THAT END, THEY BROUGHT IN THE UK'S MOST FAMOUS WITCH, DAME GLAURIE THROPP, TO BE VICKIE'S TUTOR. YOU REMEMBER MS. THROPP. SHE WROTE ALL THOSE "MAD LORD FLUTTERBY" BOOKS YOU SPENT SO MUCH TIME STARING AT AS A WEE ONE. SUFFICE TO SAY, GLAURIE AND HER LITTLE "VICIOUS" SPENT A LOT OF TIME CONJURING BUTTERFLIES...

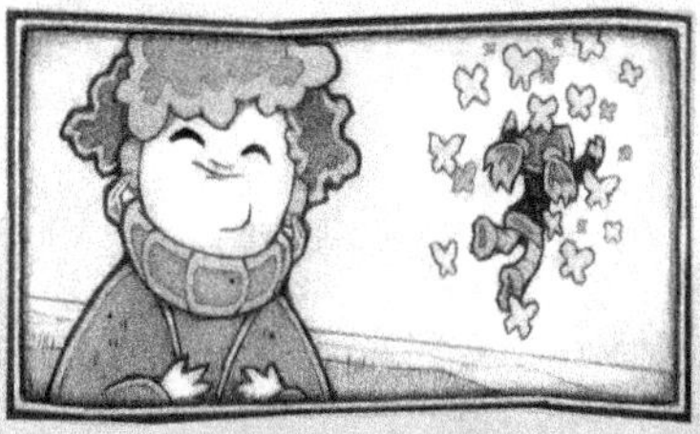

ANYWAY, VICKIE KEPT MOSTLY TO HERSELF DURING HER FORMATIVE YEARS, LOSING HERSELF IN A THOUSAND DIFFERENT INTELLECTUAL PURSUITS: LITERATURE, PHILOSOPHY, PHYSICS, DESIGN, PAINTING, HISTORY, BOTANY(?), SOCIOLOGY, AND, INCREASINGLY, MUSIC. IN FACT, WITH THE HELP OF HER MENTOR, SHE RECORDED A CD OF PECULIAR "FLUTTERBY"-INSPIRED SYNTHPOP SONGS, AND DISTRIBUTED IT ACROSS THE UK (CURRENT PRICE ON EBAY: £300)

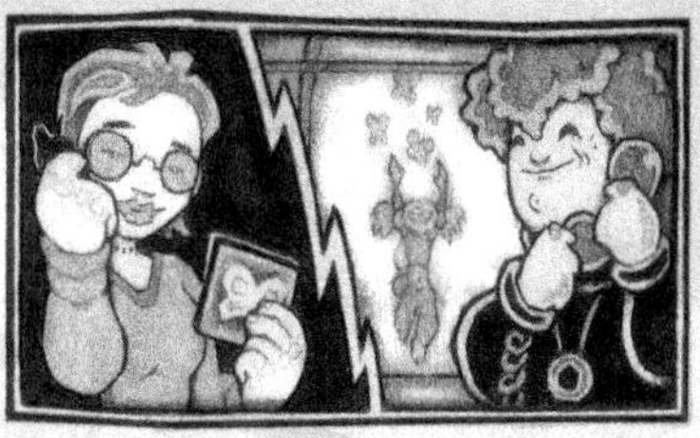

ONE PARTICULAR COPY OF "THE MAD LORD SESSIONS" WOUND UP IN THE HANDS OF ONE MS. LYNN KAY, FORMERLY OF THE INFAMOUS AGGRO-INDUSTRIAL BAND "DEAD AMERICA (REMEMBER HOW THEY ENDED UP?)." MS. KAY WAS, UNDERSTANDABLY, LOOKING TO TAKE HER ART IN A WHOLE NEW DIRECTION -A MORE PROGRESSIVE ONE- AND THOUGHT VICKIE MIGHT BE THE PERFECT PARTNER...

VICIOUS' SHOW... IS NOT UNLIKE WATCHING TWENTY OF THE MOST INCREDIBLE MUSIC VIDEOS YOU'VE EVER SEEN COME ALIVE ALL AROUND YOU. AND THAT'S ONLY ONE TENTH OF THE REASON I LOVE 'ER.*

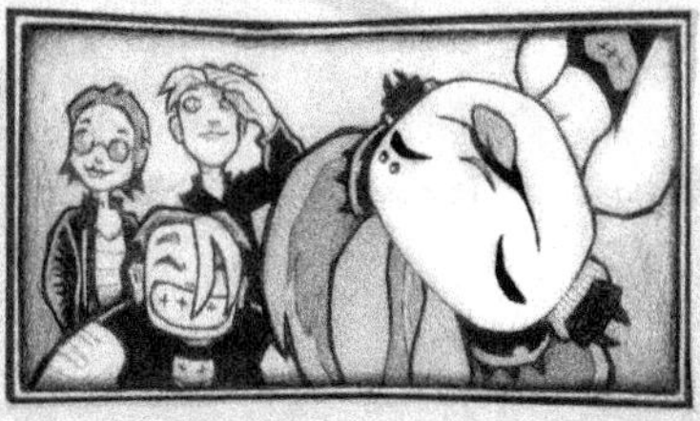

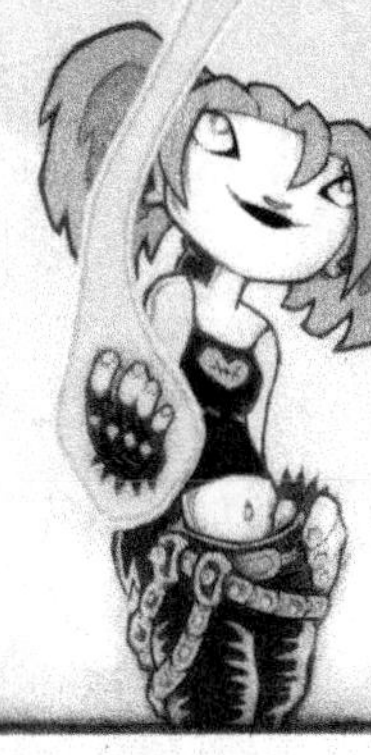

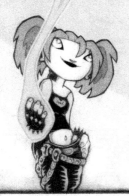

SO.

TWO WITCHES, TWO TOURS, TWO POINTS OF VIEW AS DIFFERENT AS NIGHT AND DAY, BUT BOTH APPEALING TO THE SAME DISAFFECTED OUTSIDER AUDIENCE. SOUNDS LIKE A RECIPE FOR GOOD STORYTELLING, EH?

SHAME I'M NOT IN THE BUSINESS OF TELLING STORIES...

*RIVET HED, OF COURSE, CALLS HER A "POINTLESS RIPOFF."

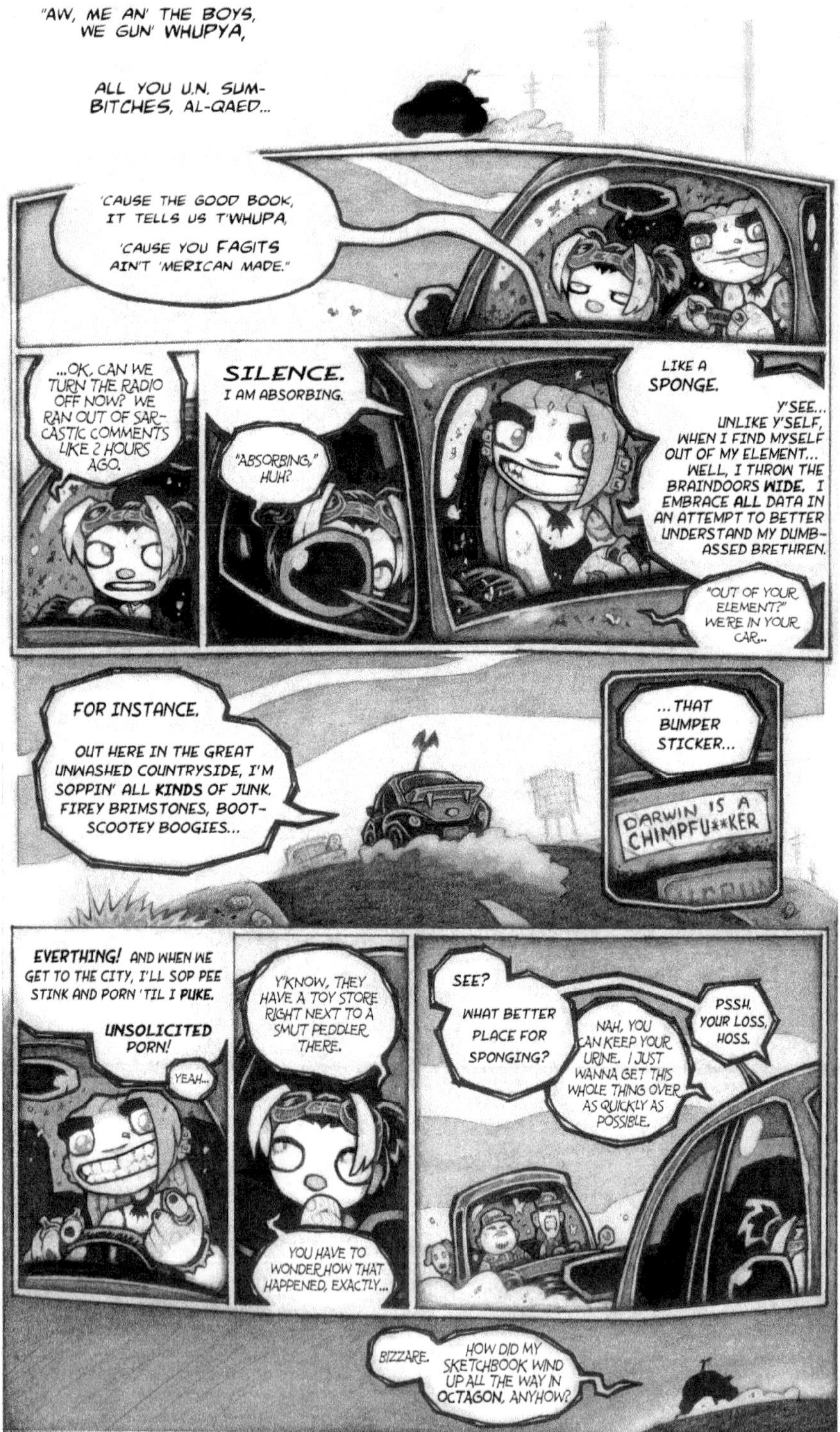

"AW, ME AN' THE BOYS, WE GUN' WHUPYA,
ALL YOU U.N. SUM-BITCHES, AL-QAED...
'CAUSE THE GOOD BOOK, IT TELLS US T'WHUPA,
'CAUSE YOU FAGITS AIN'T 'MERICAN MADE."
...OK, CAN WE TURN THE RADIO OFF NOW? WE RAN OUT OF SARCASTIC COMMENTS LIKE 2 HOURS AGO.
SILENCE. I AM ABSORBING.
"ABSORBING," HUH?
LIKE A SPONGE.
Y'SEE... UNLIKE Y'SELF, WHEN I FIND MYSELF OUT OF MY ELEMENT... WELL, I THROW THE BRAINDOORS WIDE. I EMBRACE ALL DATA IN AN ATTEMPT TO BETTER UNDERSTAND MY DUMB-ASSED BRETHREN.
"OUT OF YOUR ELEMENT?" WE'RE IN YOUR CAR...
FOR INSTANCE.
OUT HERE IN THE GREAT UNWASHED COUNTRYSIDE, I'M SOPPIN' ALL KINDS OF JUNK. FIREY BRIMSTONES, BOOT-SCOOTEY BOOGIES...
...THAT BUMPER STICKER...
DARWIN IS A CHIMPFU**KER
EVERTHING! AND WHEN WE GET TO THE CITY, I'LL SOP PEE STINK AND PORN 'TIL I PUKE.
UNSOLICITED PORN!
YEAH...
Y'KNOW, THEY HAVE A TOY STORE RIGHT NEXT TO A SMUT PEDDLER THERE.
YOU HAVE TO WONDER HOW THAT HAPPENED, EXACTLY...
SEE?
WHAT BETTER PLACE FOR SPONGING?
NAH, YOU CAN KEEP YOUR URINE. I JUST WANNA GET THIS WHOLE THING OVER AS QUICKLY AS POSSIBLE.
PSSH. YOUR LOSS, HOSS.
BIZZARE.
HOW DID MY SKETCHBOOK WIND UP ALL THE WAY IN OCTAGON, ANYHOW?

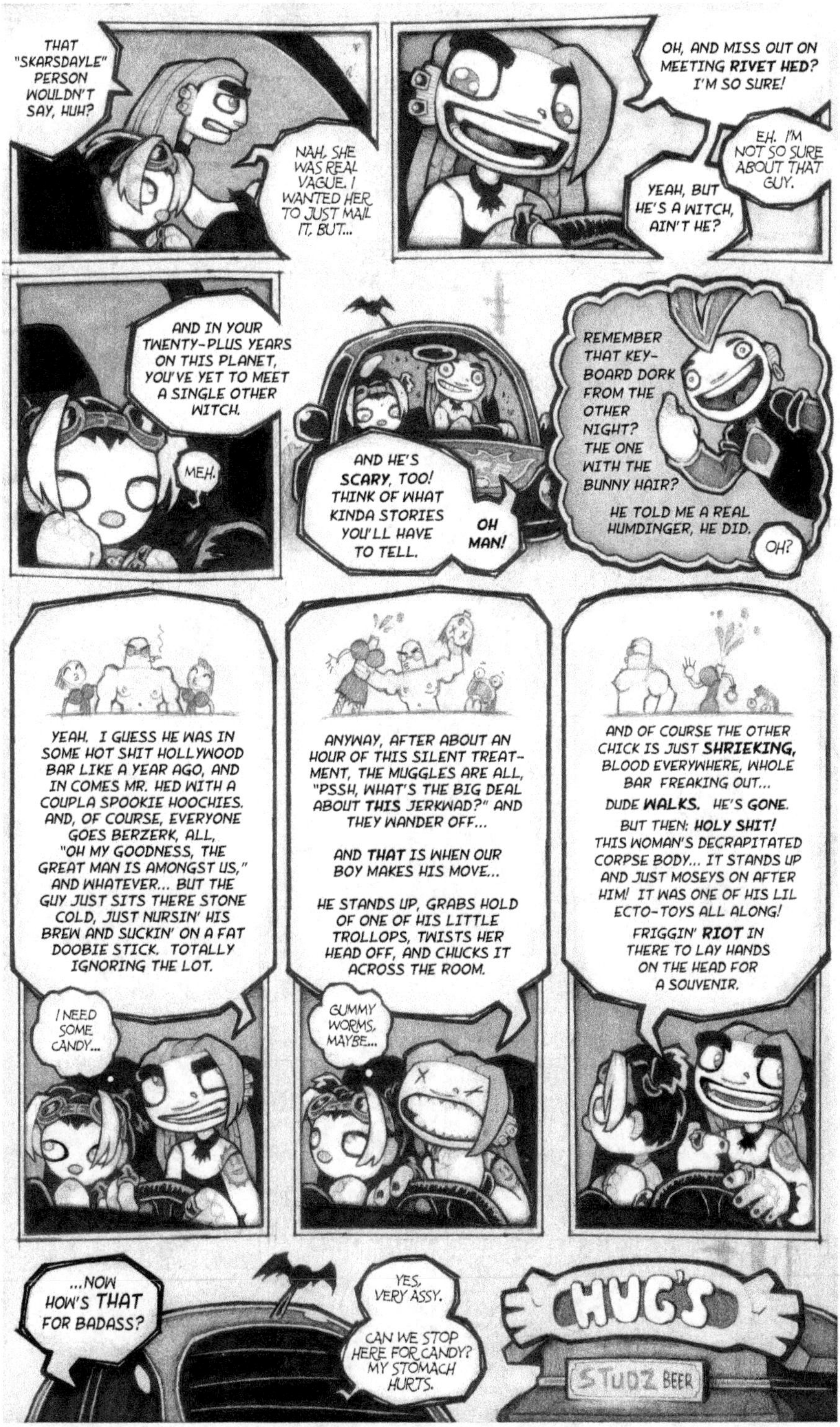

THAT "SKARSDAYLE" PERSON WOULDN'T SAY, HUH?
NAH, SHE WAS REAL VAGUE. I WANTED HER TO JUST MAIL IT, BUT...
OH, AND MISS OUT ON MEETING RIVET HED? I'M SO SURE!
EH. I'M NOT SO SURE ABOUT THAT GUY.
YEAH, BUT HE'S A WITCH, AIN'T HE?
AND IN YOUR TWENTY-PLUS YEARS ON THIS PLANET, YOU'VE YET TO MEET A SINGLE OTHER WITCH.
MEH.
AND HE'S SCARY, TOO! THINK OF WHAT KINDA STORIES YOU'LL HAVE TO TELL.
OH MAN!
REMEMBER THAT KEY-BOARD DORK FROM THE OTHER NIGHT? THE ONE WITH THE BUNNY HAIR?
HE TOLD ME A REAL HUMDINGER, HE DID.
OH?
YEAH. I GUESS HE WAS IN SOME HOT SHIT HOLLYWOOD BAR LIKE A YEAR AGO, AND IN COMES MR. HED WITH A COUPLA SPOOKIE HOOCHIES. AND, OF COURSE, EVERYONE GOES BERZERK, ALL, "OH MY GOODNESS, THE GREAT MAN IS AMONGST US," AND WHATEVER... BUT THE GUY JUST SITS THERE STONE COLD, JUST NURSIN' HIS BREW AND SUCKIN' ON A FAT DOOBIE STICK. TOTALLY IGNORING THE LOT.
I NEED SOME CANDY...
ANYWAY, AFTER ABOUT AN HOUR OF THIS SILENT TREATMENT, THE MUGGLES ARE ALL, "PSSH, WHAT'S THE BIG DEAL ABOUT THIS JERKWAD?" AND THEY WANDER OFF...
AND THAT IS WHEN OUR BOY MAKES HIS MOVE...
HE STANDS UP, GRABS HOLD OF ONE OF HIS LITTLE TROLLOPS, TWISTS HER HEAD OFF, AND CHUCKS IT ACROSS THE ROOM.
GUMMY WORMS, MAYBE...
AND OF COURSE THE OTHER CHICK IS JUST SHRIEKING, BLOOD EVERYWHERE, WHOLE BAR FREAKING OUT...
DUDE WALKS. HE'S GONE.
BUT THEN: HOLY SHIT! THIS WOMAN'S DECRAPITATED CORPSE BODY... IT STANDS UP AND JUST MOSEYS ON AFTER HIM! IT WAS ONE OF HIS LIL ECTO-TOYS ALL ALONG!
FRIGGIN' RIOT IN THERE TO LAY HANDS ON THE HEAD FOR A SOUVENIR.
...NOW HOW'S THAT FOR BADASS?
YES, VERY ASSY.
CAN WE STOP HERE FOR CANDY? MY STOMACH HURTS.
HUG'S
STUDZ BEER

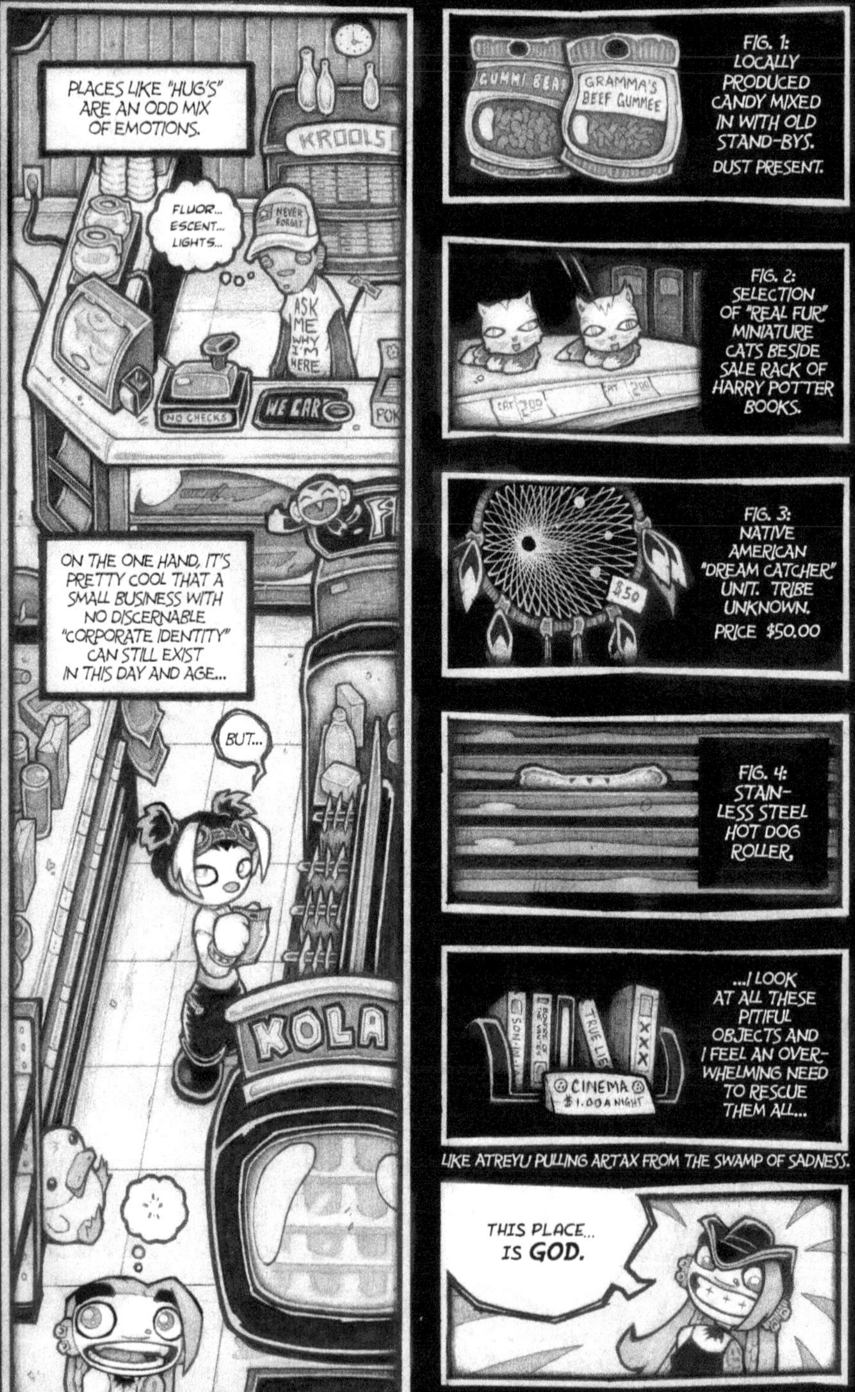
PLACES LIKE "HUG'S" ARE AN ODD MIX OF EMOTIONS.
KROOLS
FLUOR... ESCENT... LIGHTS...
NEVER FORGET
ASK ME WHY I'M HERE
NO CHECKS
ON THE ONE HAND, IT'S PRETTY COOL THAT A SMALL BUSINESS WITH NO DISCERNABLE "CORPORATE IDENTITY" CAN STILL EXIST IN THIS DAY AND AGE...
BUT...
KOLA
GRAMMA'S BEEF GUMMEE
FIG. 1: LOCALLY PRODUCED CANDY MIXED IN WITH OLD STAND-BYS.
DUST PRESENT.
FIG. 2: SELECTION OF "REAL FUR" MINIATURE CATS BESIDE SALE RACK OF HARRY POTTER BOOKS.
$50
FIG. 3: NATIVE AMERICAN "DREAM CATCHER" UNIT. TRIBE UNKNOWN.
PRICE $50.00
FIG. 4: STAIN-LESS STEEL HOT DOG ROLLER.
XXX
CINEMA $1.00 A NIGHT
...I LOOK AT ALL THESE PITIFUL OBJECTS AND I FEEL AN OVER-WHELMING NEED TO RESCUE THEM ALL...
LIKE ATREYU PULLING ARTAX FROM THE SWAMP OF SADNESS.
THIS PLACE... IS GOD.
...AND THEN THERE ARE THOSE WITH AN ENTIRELY DIFFERENT REACTION.

...YOU'RE GETTING A HAT?

DAMN SKIPPY. WHY SHOULDN'T I?

MMM! DUNNO. BECAUSE YOU'VE NEVER EXPRESSED THE SLIGHTEST INTEREST IN COWBOY CULTURE THUS FAR?

"COWBOY" NOTHIN'.

AH'M PSYCHOBILLY, BAYBEH!!

OH.

GONNA BETTIE PAGE M'BANGS AND EVERYTHING, I AM...

BUT FIRST,

I PEE.

GUMMI BRICKS

DING DING

SNICK SNICK

...AND SO OF COURSE WE HAVE **THE DUDES.** NO MATTER WHERE YOU GO, YOU ALWAYS END UP HAVING TO DEAL WITH SOME FORM OF DUDERY OR ANOTHER. **SPECIAL NOTE:** IN THIS SCENE I'VE REPLACED ALL THE SWEARS WITH LESS OBJECTIONABLE WORDS. NORMALLY I WOULDN'T, BUT... GEEZ, THESE GUYS WERE JUST EMBARRASSING...

DAY-UMN!

SNICK SNICK

FRANKIN FANGOT GOTTA TELL ME MAH BIZNISS FRANKIN... LIL' SOOT. FRANKIN GLASSES AN' SOOT...

SNICK SNICK

SOOT, BRAH, I FRANK **WHO** I WANT, **WHEN** I WANT. WHADDA FRANK HE CARES, I WANNA FRANK HIS GOD-SAM SISTAH?

SNICK SNICK SNICK

SOOOOOT... FRANKIN FANGOT PROLLY WANNA FRANK ME, BRAH. WANNA FRANK ME.

SNICK SNICK SNICK

FRANKIN'... SHOVE 'IS FRANKIN' FANGOT GLASSES UP HIS ACE, BRAH. AH MEAN, S—

OH SOOT, BRAH. CHECK IT OUT...

A: LOUSY EMINEM-STYLE BOWL CUT B: BLING C: COMICAL PORNO-JOKE JERSEY THING D: CROTCH GRAB DEFAULT E: THOSE "SANDALS" THAT LOOK TO HAVE MORE MATERIAL THAN A STANDARD PAIR OF SHOES F: TORTURED-BRIM HAT G: ONE OF THOSE SHIRTS THAT HAS SUPERHEROES (OR DRAGONBALLS) ALL THE FRANK OVER IT H: LARGE TROUSERS (STILL! SEE, TESS? SEE? IT HASN'T DIED YET!)

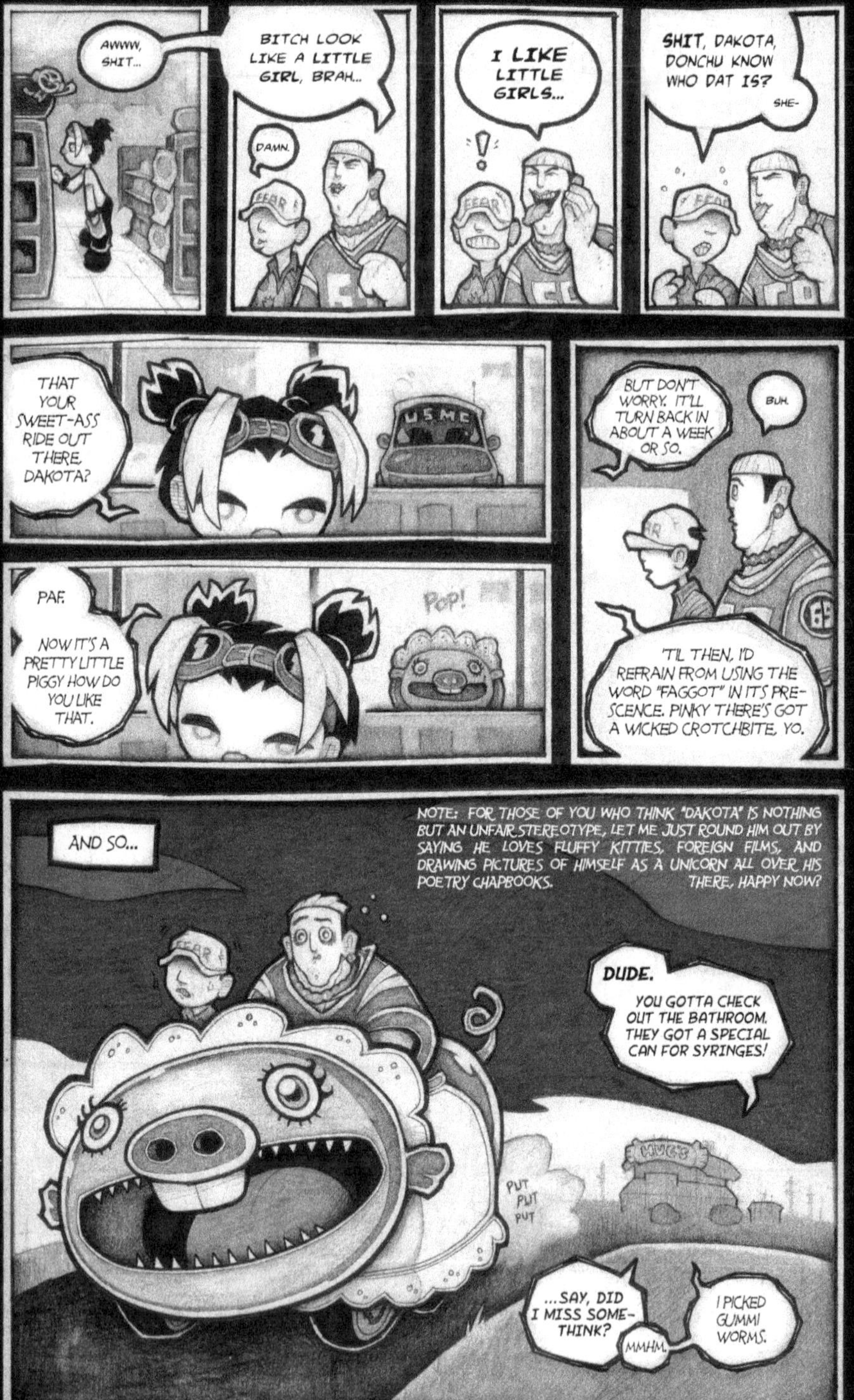
AWWW, SHIT...
BITCH LOOK LIKE A LITTLE GIRL, BRAH...
DAMN.
I LIKE LITTLE GIRLS...
!
SHIT, DAKOTA, DONCHU KNOW WHO DAT IS?
SHE-
THAT YOUR SWEET-ASS RIDE OUT THERE, DAKOTA?
USMC
BUT DON'T WORRY. IT'LL TURN BACK IN ABOUT A WEEK OR SO.
BUH.
PAF.
NOW IT'S A PRETTY LITTLE PIGGY HOW DO YOU LIKE THAT.
POP!
'TIL THEN, I'D REFRAIN FROM USING THE WORD "FAGGOT" IN ITS PRESCENCE. PINKY THERE'S GOT A WICKED CROTCHBITE, YO.
AND SO...
NOTE: FOR THOSE OF YOU WHO THINK "DAKOTA" IS NOTHING BUT AN UNFAIR STEREOTYPE, LET ME JUST ROUND HIM OUT BY SAYING HE LOVES FLUFFY KITTIES, FOREIGN FILMS, AND DRAWING PICTURES OF HIMSELF AS A UNICORN ALL OVER HIS POETRY CHAPBOOKS. THERE, HAPPY NOW?
DUDE.
YOU GOTTA CHECK OUT THE BATHROOM. THEY GOT A SPECIAL CAN FOR SYRINGES!
PUT PUT PUT
...SAY, DID I MISS SOMETHINK?
MMHM.
I PICKED GUMMI WORMS.

THE CITY OF OCTAGON 10:00 PM

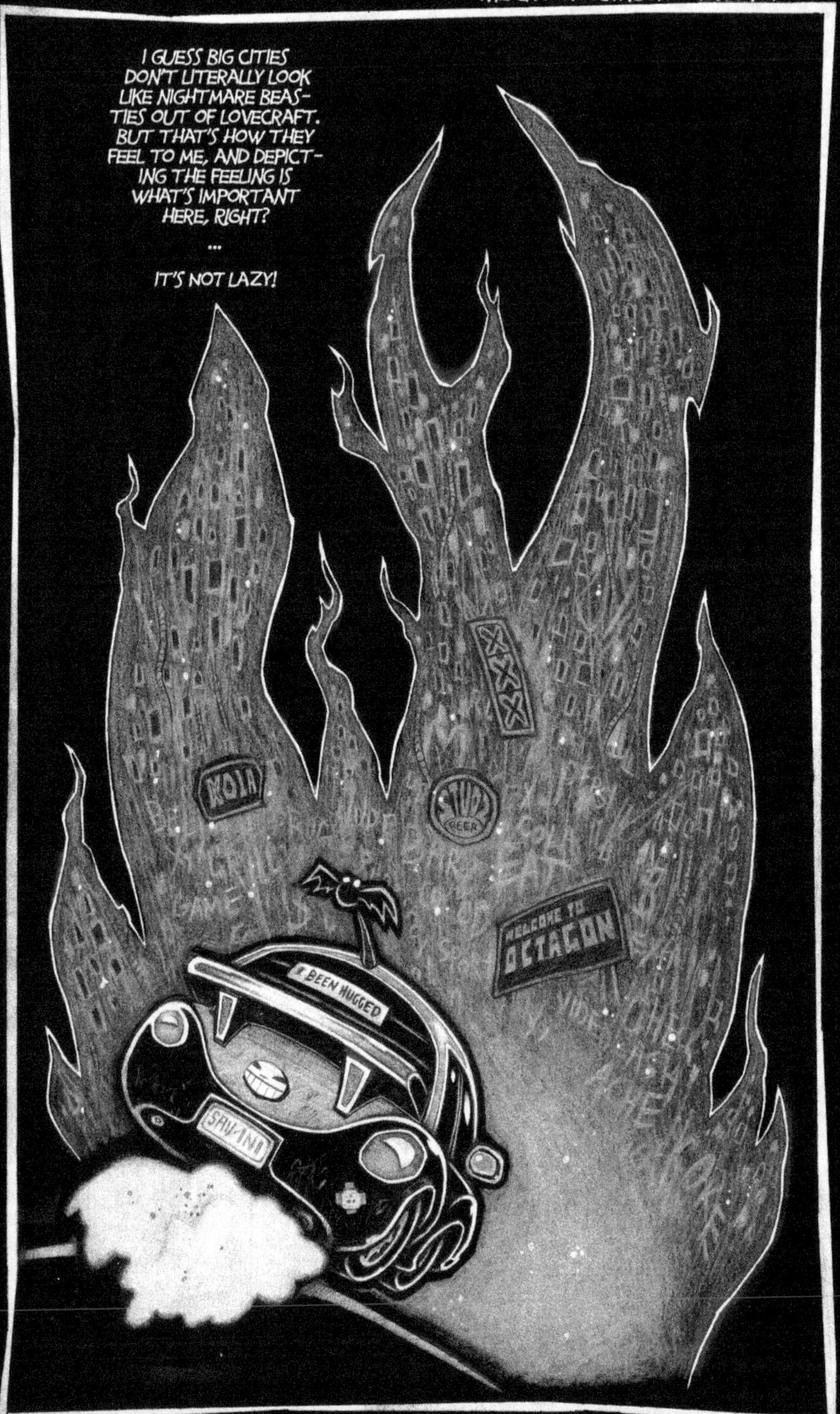
I GUESS BIG CITIES DON'T LITERALLY LOOK LIKE NIGHTMARE BEASTIES OUT OF LOVECRAFT. BUT THAT'S HOW THEY FEEL TO ME, AND DEPICTING THE FEELING IS WHAT'S IMPORTANT HERE, RIGHT?
...
IT'S NOT LAZY!
XXX
BEER
WELCOME TO OCTAGON
BEEN HUGGED
SAV-INI

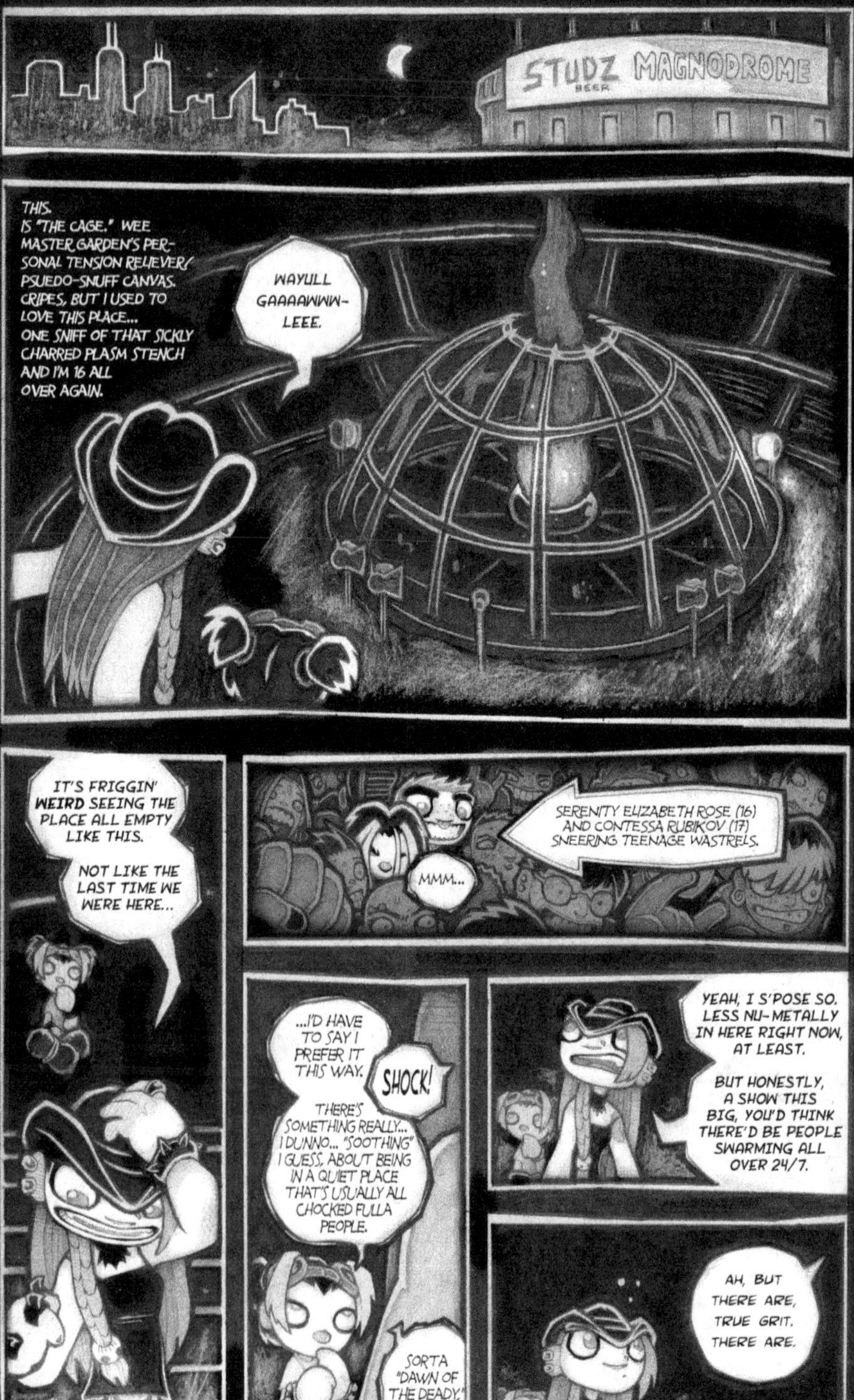

STUDZ BEER MAGNODROME
THIS. IS "THE CAGE." WEE MASTER GARDEN'S PERSONAL TENSION RELIEVER/ PSUEDO-SNUFF CANVAS. CRIPES, BUT I USED TO LOVE THIS PLACE... ONE SNIFF OF THAT SICKLY CHARRED PLASM STENCH AND I'M 16 ALL OVER AGAIN.
WAYULL GAAAAWWW-LEEE.
IT'S FRIGGIN' **WEIRD** SEEING THE PLACE ALL EMPTY LIKE THIS.
NOT LIKE THE LAST TIME WE WERE HERE...
SERENITY ELIZABETH ROSE (16) AND CONTESSA RUBIKOV (17) SNEERING TEENAGE WASTRELS.
MMM...
...I'D HAVE TO SAY I PREFER IT THIS WAY.
SHOCK!
THERE'S SOMETHING REALLY... I DUNNO... "SOOTHING" I GUESS, ABOUT BEING IN A QUIET PLACE THAT'S USUALLY ALL CHOCKED FULLA PEOPLE.
SORTA "DAWN OF THE DEADY," Y'KNOW?
YEAH, I S'POSE SO. LESS NU-METALLY IN HERE RIGHT NOW, AT LEAST.
BUT HONESTLY, A SHOW THIS BIG, YOU'D THINK THERE'D BE PEOPLE SWARMING ALL OVER 24/7.
AH, BUT THERE ARE, TRUE GRIT. THERE ARE.

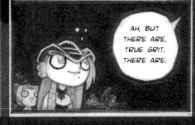

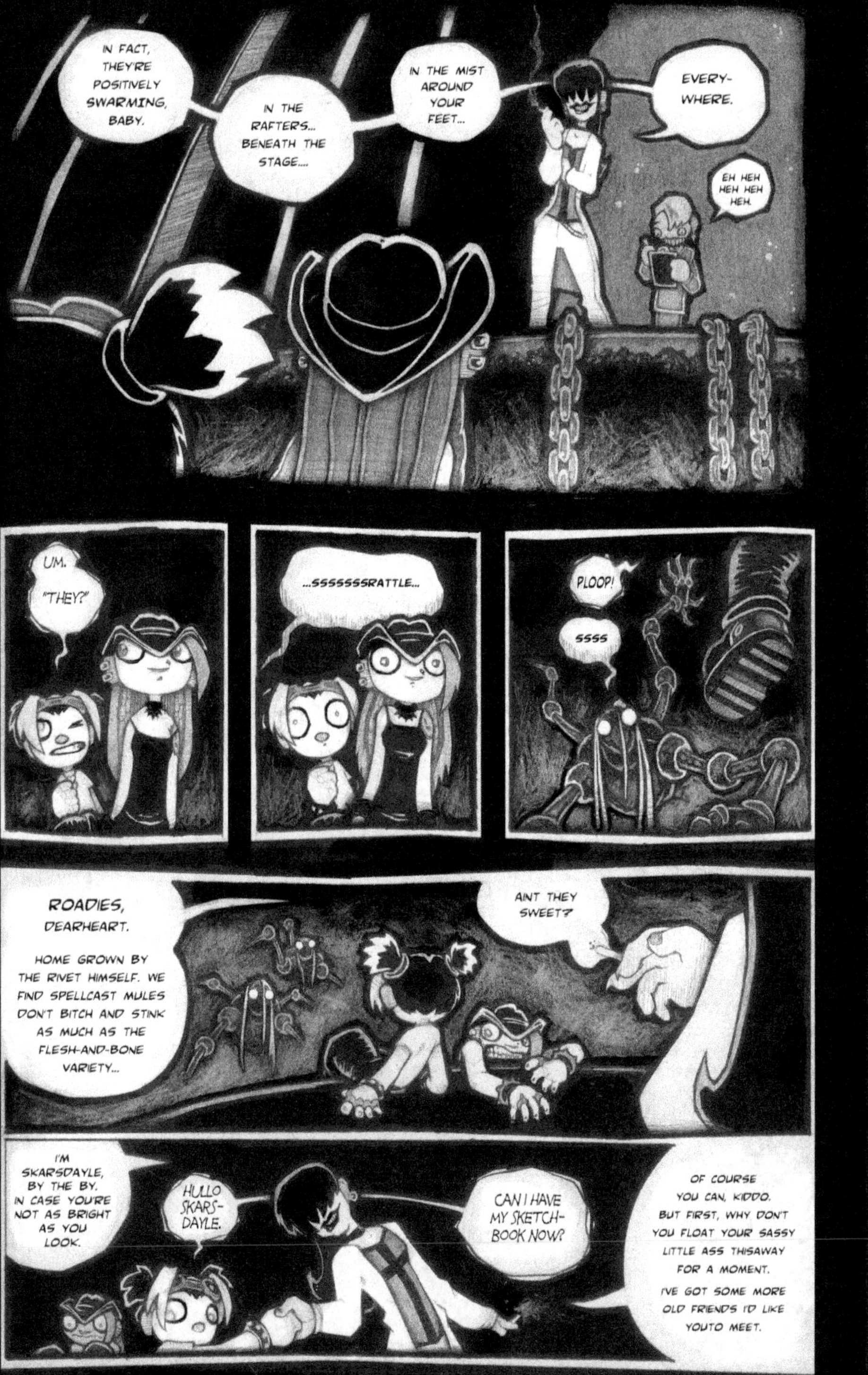

IN FACT, THEY'RE POSITIVELY SWARMING, BABY.
IN THE RAFTERS... BENEATH THE STAGE....
IN THE MIST AROUND YOUR FEET...
EVERY-WHERE.
EH HEH HEH HEH HEH.
UM.
"THEY?"
...SSSSSSSRATTLE...
PLOOP!
SSSS
ROADIES, DEARHEART.
HOME GROWN BY THE RIVET HIMSELF. WE FIND SPELLCAST MULES DON'T BITCH AND STINK AS MUCH AS THE FLESH-AND-BONE VARIETY...
AINT THEY SWEET?
I'M SKARSDAYLE, BY THE BY. IN CASE YOU'RE NOT AS BRIGHT AS YOU LOOK.
HULLO SKARS-DAYLE.
CAN I HAVE MY SKETCH-BOOK NOW?
OF COURSE YOU CAN, KIDDO. BUT FIRST, WHY DON'T YOU FLOAT YOUR SASSY LITTLE ASS THISAWAY FOR A MOMENT.
I'VE GOT SOME MORE OLD FRIENDS I'D LIKE YOUTO MEET.

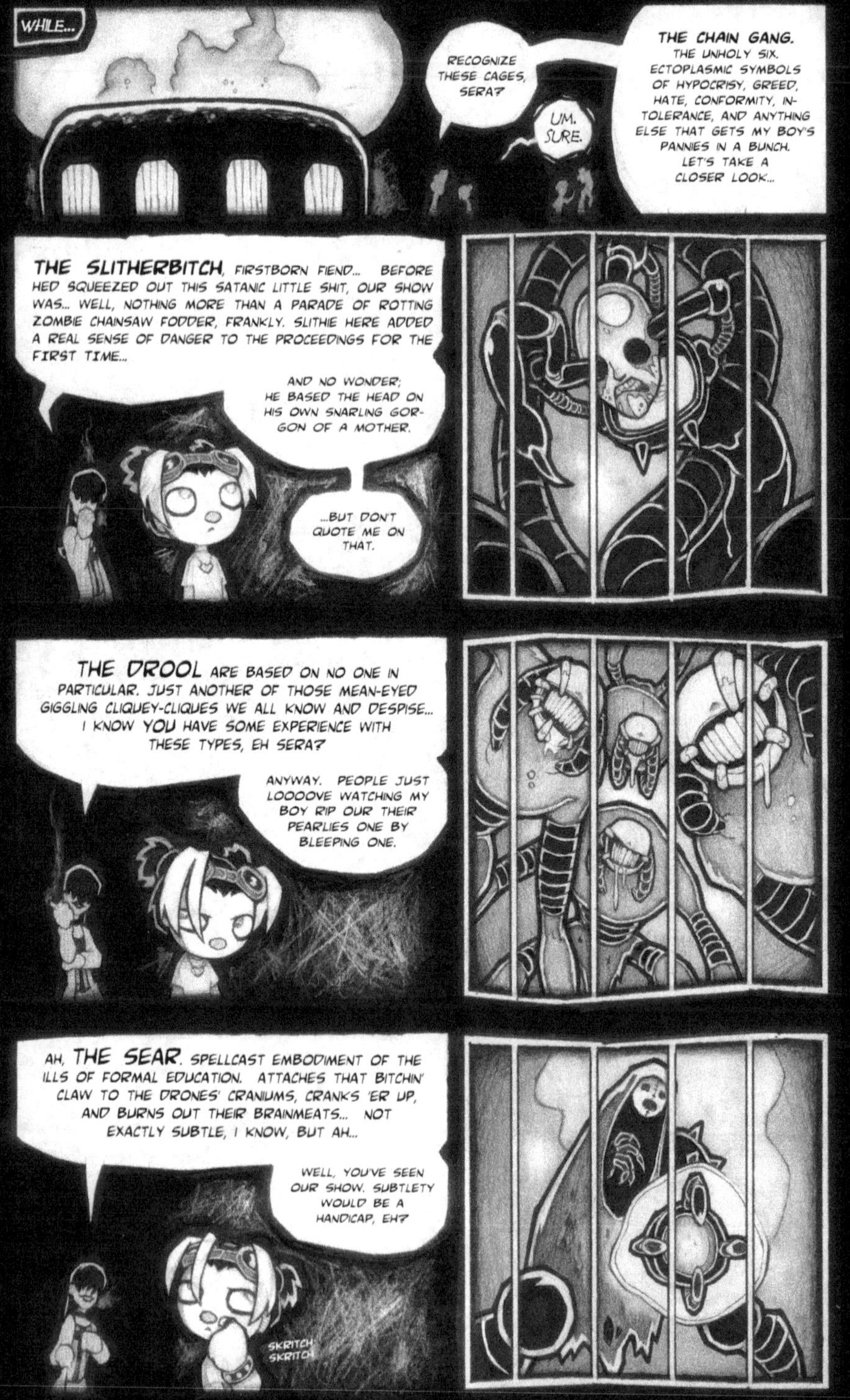
WHILE...
RECOGNIZE THESE CAGES, SERA?
UM. SURE.
THE CHAIN GANG. THE UNHOLY SIX. ECTOPLASMIC SYMBOLS OF HYPOCRISY, GREED, HATE, CONFORMITY, INTOLERANCE, AND ANYTHING ELSE THAT GETS MY BOY'S PANNIES IN A BUNCH. LET'S TAKE A CLOSER LOOK...
THE SLITHERBITCH, FIRSTBORN FIEND... BEFORE HED SQUEEZED OUT THIS SATANIC LITTLE SHIT, OUR SHOW WAS... WELL, NOTHING MORE THAN A PARADE OF ROTTING ZOMBIE CHAINSAW FODDER, FRANKLY. SLITHIE HERE ADDED A REAL SENSE OF DANGER TO THE PROCEEDINGS FOR THE FIRST TIME...
AND NO WONDER; HE BASED THE HEAD ON HIS OWN SNARLING GORGON OF A MOTHER.
...BUT DON'T QUOTE ME ON THAT.
THE DROOL ARE BASED ON NO ONE IN PARTICULAR. JUST ANOTHER OF THOSE MEAN-EYED GIGGLING CLIQUEY-CLIQUES WE ALL KNOW AND DESPISE... I KNOW YOU HAVE SOME EXPERIENCE WITH THESE TYPES, EH SERA?
ANYWAY. PEOPLE JUST LOOOOVE WATCHING MY BOY RIP OUR THEIR PEARLIES ONE BY BLEEPING ONE.
AH, THE SEAR. SPELLCAST EMBODIMENT OF THE ILLS OF FORMAL EDUCATION. ATTACHES THAT BITCHIN' CLAW TO THE DRONES' CRANIUMS, CRANKS 'ER UP, AND BURNS OUT THEIR BRAINMEATS... NOT EXACTLY SUBTLE, I KNOW, BUT AH...
WELL, YOU'VE SEEN OUR SHOW. SUBTLETY WOULD BE A HANDICAP, EH?
SKRITCH SKRITCH

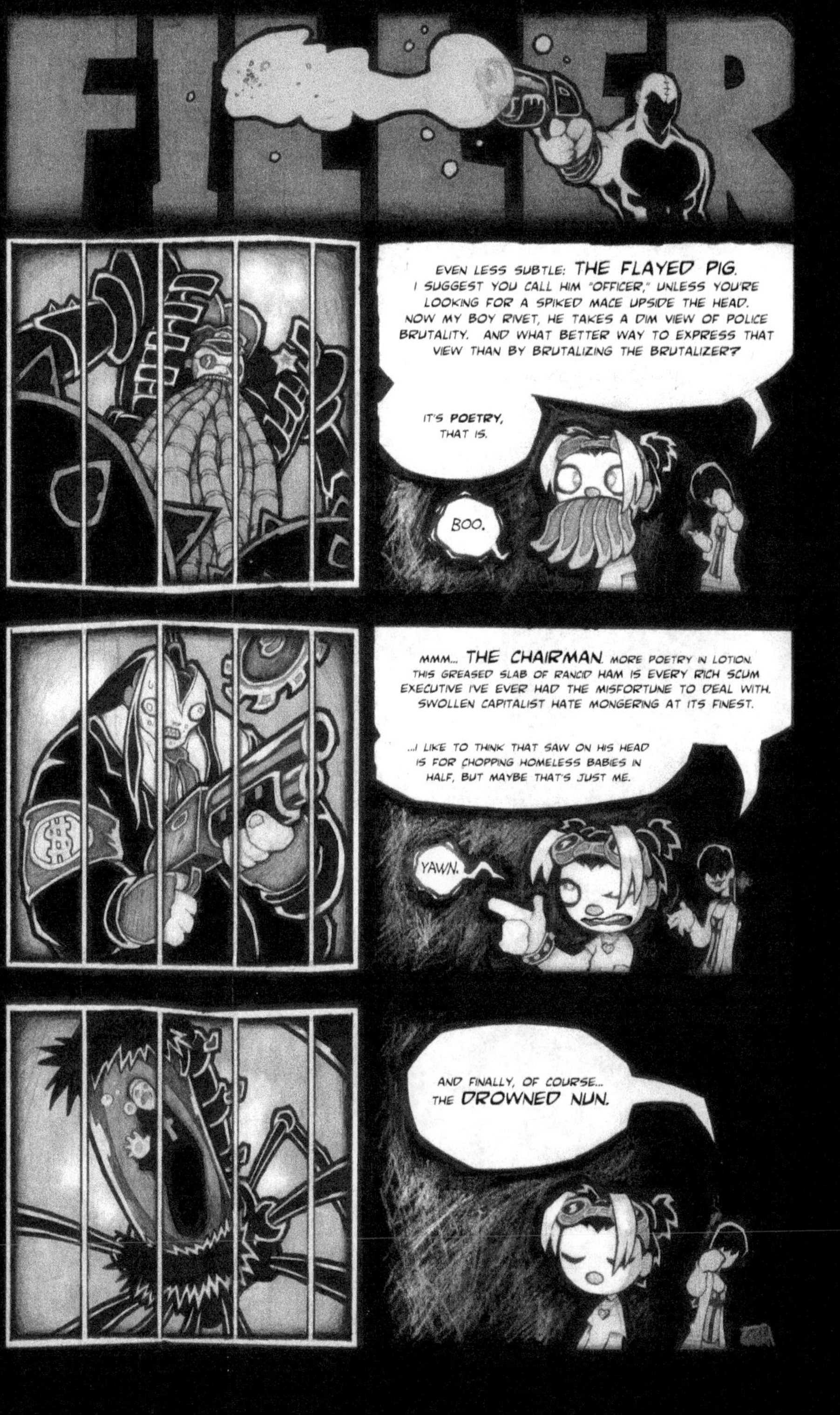
FILLER
EVEN LESS SUBTLE: THE FLAYED PIG. I SUGGEST YOU CALL HIM "OFFICER," UNLESS YOU'RE LOOKING FOR A SPIKED MACE UPSIDE THE HEAD. NOW MY BOY RIVET, HE TAKES A DIM VIEW OF POLICE BRUTALITY. AND WHAT BETTER WAY TO EXPRESS THAT VIEW THAN BY BRUTALIZING THE BRUTALIZER?
IT'S POETRY, THAT IS.
BOO.
MMM... THE CHAIRMAN. MORE POETRY IN LOTION. THIS GREASED SLAB OF RANCID HAM IS EVERY RICH SCUM EXECUTIVE I'VE EVER HAD THE MISFORTUNE TO DEAL WITH. SWOLLEN CAPITALIST HATE MONGERING AT ITS FINEST.
...I LIKE TO THINK THAT SAW ON HIS HEAD IS FOR CHOPPING HOMELESS BABIES IN HALF, BUT MAYBE THAT'S JUST ME.
YAWN.
AND FINALLY, OF COURSE... THE DROWNED NUN.

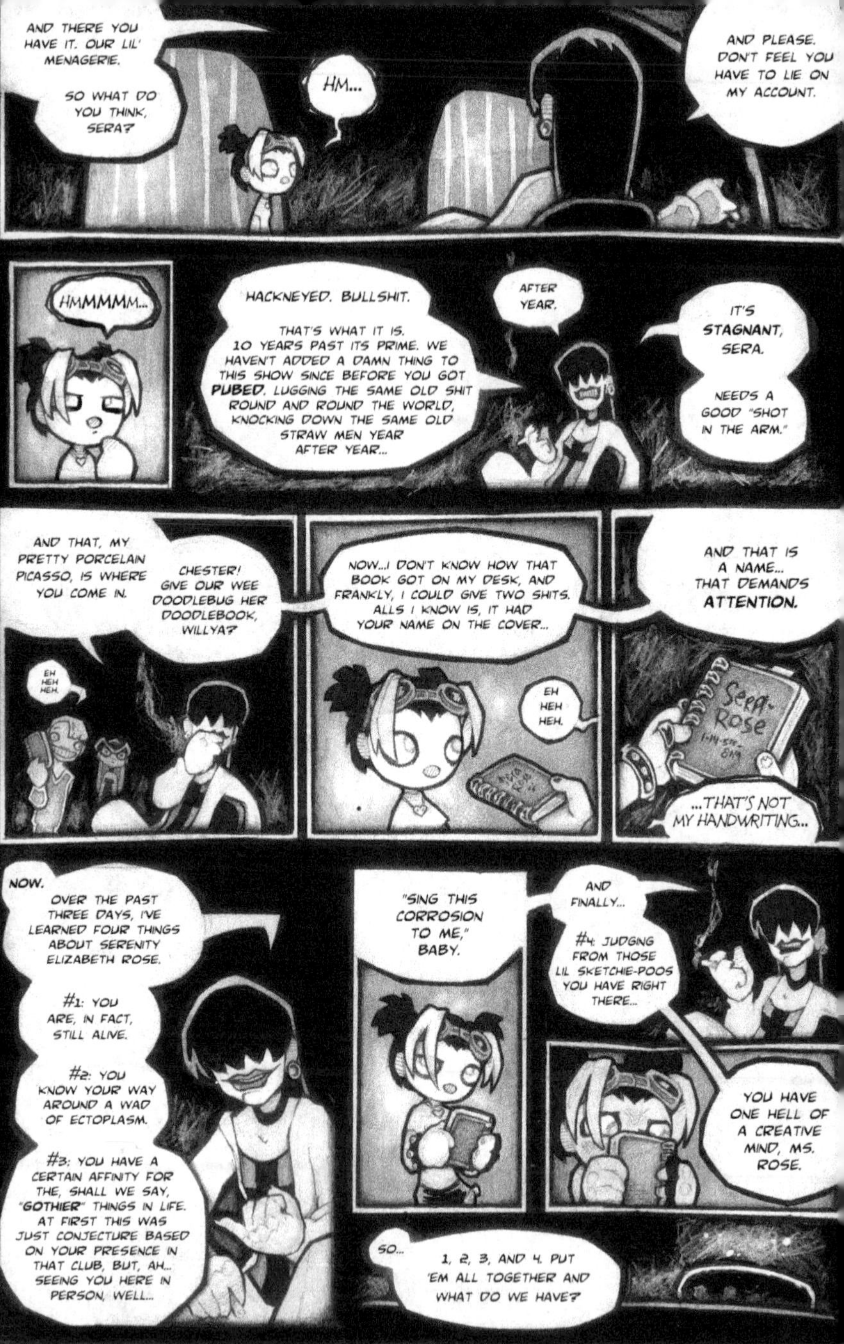

AND THERE YOU HAVE IT. OUR LIL' MENAGERIE.
SO WHAT DO YOU THINK, SERA?
HM...
AND PLEASE. DON'T FEEL YOU HAVE TO LIE ON MY ACCOUNT.
HMMMMM...
HACKNEYED. BULLSHIT.
THAT'S WHAT IT IS. 10 YEARS PAST ITS PRIME. WE HAVEN'T ADDED A DAMN THING TO THIS SHOW SINCE BEFORE YOU GOT PUBED. LUGGING THE SAME OLD SHIT ROUND AND ROUND THE WORLD, KNOCKING DOWN THE SAME OLD STRAW MEN YEAR AFTER YEAR...
AFTER YEAR.
IT'S STAGNANT, SERA.
NEEDS A GOOD "SHOT IN THE ARM."
AND THAT, MY PRETTY PORCELAIN PICASSO, IS WHERE YOU COME IN.
CHESTER! GIVE OUR WEE DOODLEBUG HER DOODLEBOOK, WILLYA?
EH HEH HEH.
NOW...I DON'T KNOW HOW THAT BOOK GOT ON MY DESK, AND FRANKLY, I COULD GIVE TWO SHITS. ALLS I KNOW IS, IT HAD YOUR NAME ON THE COVER...
EH HEH HEH.
AND THAT IS A NAME... THAT DEMANDS ATTENTION.
Sera-Rose
...THAT'S NOT MY HANDWRITING...
NOW.
OVER THE PAST THREE DAYS, I'VE LEARNED FOUR THINGS ABOUT SERENITY ELIZABETH ROSE.
#1: YOU ARE, IN FACT, STILL ALIVE.
#2: YOU KNOW YOUR WAY AROUND A WAD OF ECTOPLASM.
#3: YOU HAVE A CERTAIN AFFINITY FOR THE, SHALL WE SAY, "GOTHIER" THINGS IN LIFE. AT FIRST THIS WAS JUST CONJECTURE BASED ON YOUR PRESENCE IN THAT CLUB, BUT, AH... SEEING YOU HERE IN PERSON, WELL...
"SING THIS CORROSION TO ME," BABY.
AND FINALLY...
#4: JUDGING FROM THOSE LIL SKETCHIE-POOS YOU HAVE RIGHT THERE...
YOU HAVE ONE HELL OF A CREATIVE MIND, MS. ROSE.
SO...
1, 2, 3, AND 4. PUT 'EM ALL TOGETHER AND WHAT DO WE HAVE?
MMMM... SOMETHING I CAN USE.

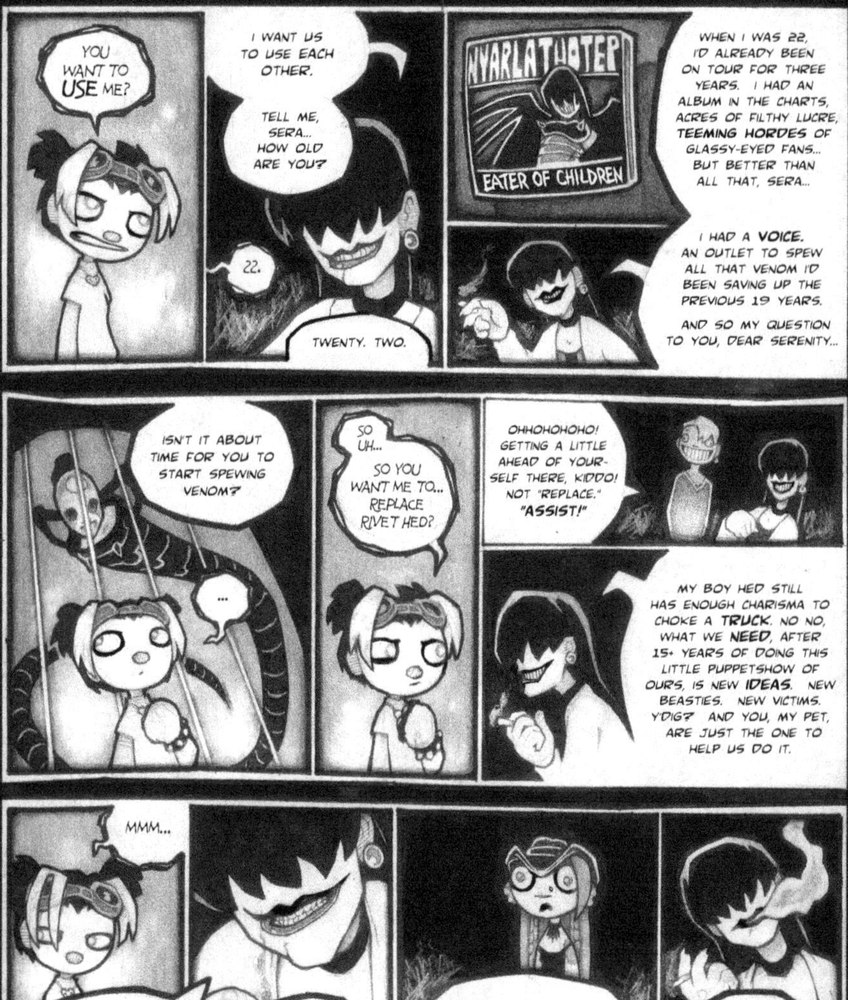
YOU WANT TO USE ME?
I WANT US TO USE EACH OTHER.
TELL ME, SERA... HOW OLD ARE YOU?
22.
TWENTY. TWO.
NYARLATHOTEP
EATER OF CHILDREN
WHEN I WAS 22, I'D ALREADY BEEN ON TOUR FOR THREE YEARS. I HAD AN ALBUM IN THE CHARTS, ACRES OF FILTHY LUCRE, TEEMING HORDES OF GLASSY-EYED FANS... BUT BETTER THAN ALL THAT, SERA...
I HAD A VOICE. AN OUTLET TO SPEW ALL THAT VENOM I'D BEEN SAVING UP THE PREVIOUS 19 YEARS.
AND SO MY QUESTION TO YOU, DEAR SERENITY...
ISN'T IT ABOUT TIME FOR YOU TO START SPEWING VENOM?
...
SO UH... SO YOU WANT ME TO... REPLACE RIVET HED?
OHHOHOHOHO! GETTING A LITTLE AHEAD OF YOURSELF THERE, KIDDO! NOT "REPLACE." "ASSIST!"
MY BOY HED STILL HAS ENOUGH CHARISMA TO CHOKE A TRUCK. NO NO, WHAT WE NEED, AFTER 15+ YEARS OF DOING THIS LITTLE PUPPETSHOW OF OURS, IS NEW IDEAS. NEW BEASTIES. NEW VICTIMS. Y'DIG? AND YOU, MY PET, ARE JUST THE ONE TO HELP US DO IT.
MMM...
LISTEN, SERA... DO YOU KNOW HOW MUCH MONEY THIS SHOW PULLED IN LAST YEAR?
EIGHTY. MILLION. DOLLARS.
AND THAT WAS AN OFF YEAR. WITH A BRAND NEW SET OF BEASTIES AND YOUR NAME ON THE MARQUEE, WE COULD DOUBLE THAT NUMBER WITH NARY A BEAD OF SWEAT.
AND LET ME ASSURE YOU: YOUR CUT WOULD NOT BE STINGY.
I DON'T NEED MONEY.
EXPERIENCE, THEN. THE OPPORTUNITY TO LEARN FROM ANOTHER WITCH.
HMM...
THAT REMINDS ME... IS RIVET HED EVEN HERE TODAY?
I MEAN... SHOULDN'T I BE TALKING TO HIM... AS WELL?
OF COURSE YOU SHOULD, BABY!

SERENITY ROSE COMICS: THE ULTIMATE EXPERIENCE IN GRUELING WORD BALLOONS!

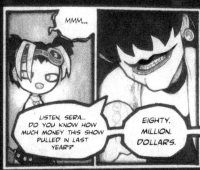

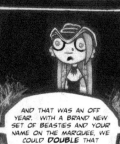

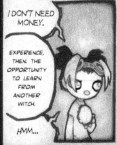

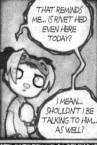

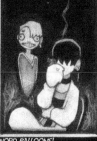

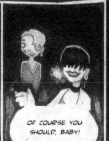

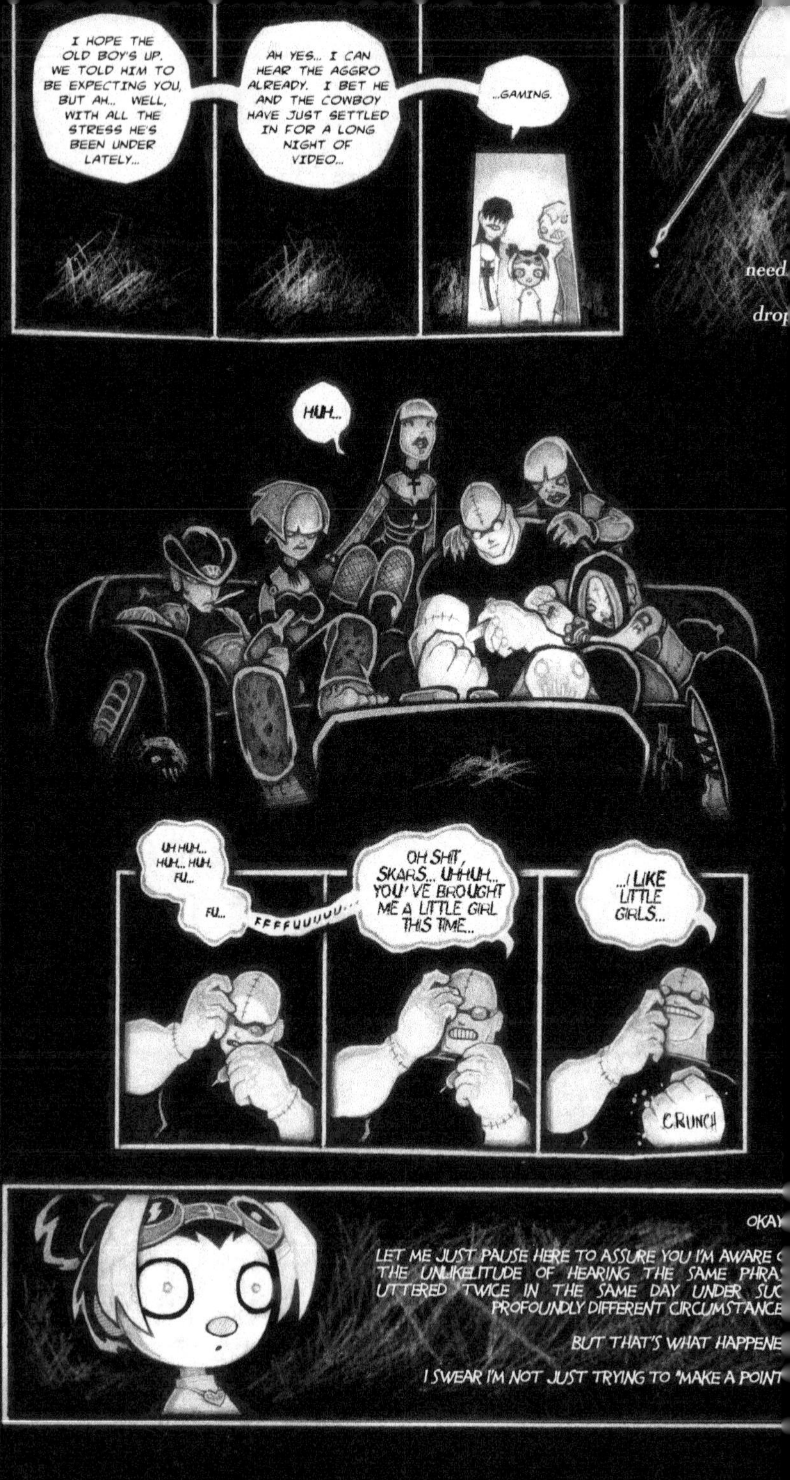
I HOPE THE OLD BOY'S UP. WE TOLD HIM TO BE EXPECTING YOU, BUT AH... WELL, WITH ALL THE STRESS HE'S BEEN UNDER LATELY...
AH YES... I CAN HEAR THE AGGRO ALREADY. I BET HE AND THE COWBOY HAVE JUST SETTLED IN FOR A LONG NIGHT OF VIDEO...
...GAMING.
HUH...
UH HUH... HUH... HUH, FU...
FU...
FFFFUUUUUU...
OH SHIT, SKARS... UHHUH... YOU'VE BROUGHT ME A LITTLE GIRL THIS TIME...
...I LIKE LITTLE GIRLS...
CRUNCH
OKAY
LET ME JUST PAUSE HERE TO ASSURE YOU I'M AWARE O
THE UNLIKELITUDE OF HEARING THE SAME PHRAS
UTTERED TWICE IN THE SAME DAY UNDER SUC
PROFOUNDLY DIFFERENT CIRCUMSTANCE
BUT THAT'S WHAT HAPPENE
I SWEAR I'M NOT JUST TRYING TO "MAKE A POINT

need

drop

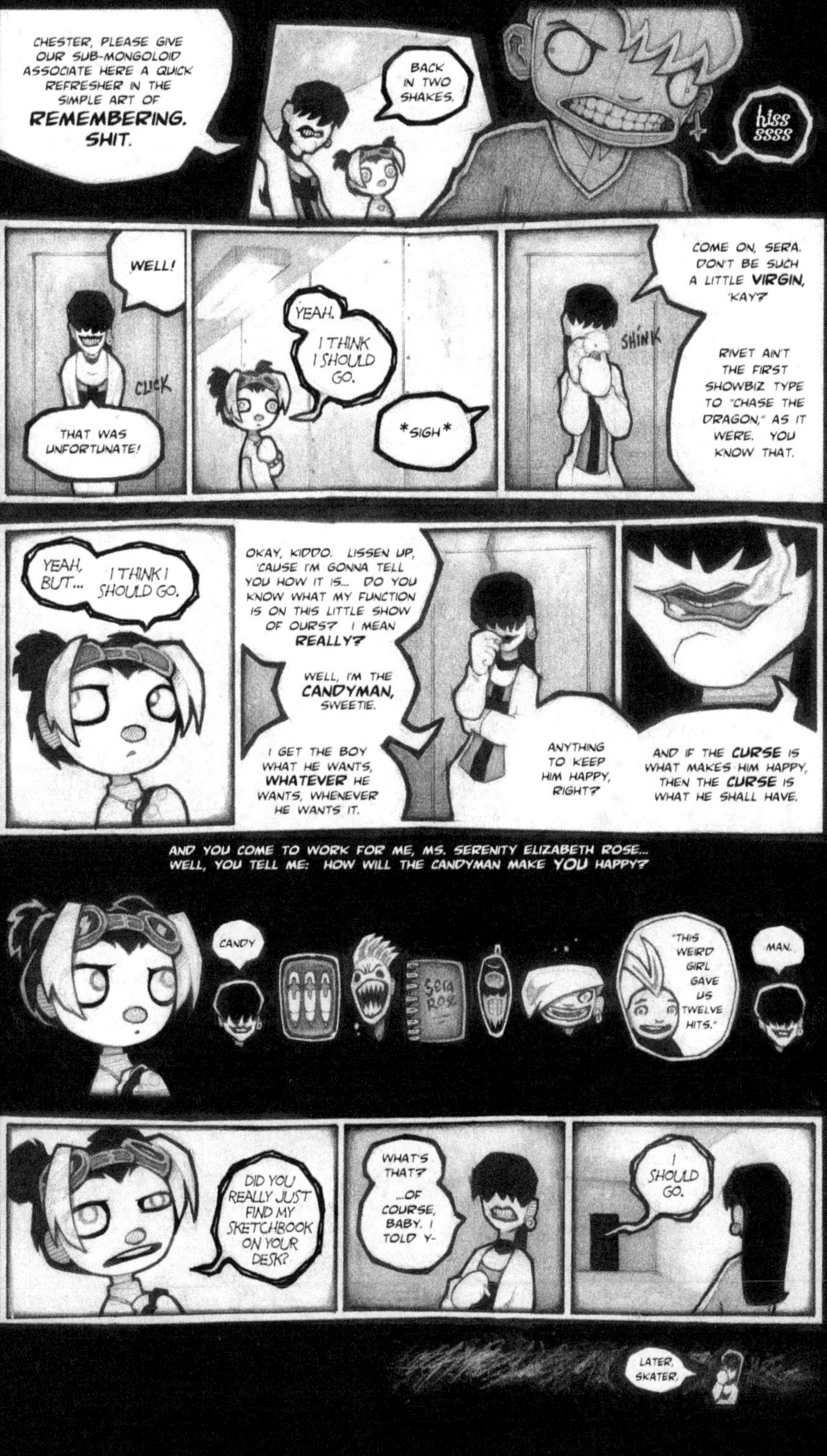

CHESTER, PLEASE GIVE OUR SUB-MONGOLOID ASSOCIATE HERE A QUICK REFRESHER IN THE SIMPLE ART OF REMEMBERING. SHIT.
BACK IN TWO SHAKES.
hiss ssss
WELL!
CLICK
THAT WAS UNFORTUNATE!
YEAH.
I THINK I SHOULD GO.
SIGH
SHINK
COME ON, SERA. DON'T BE SUCH A LITTLE VIRGIN, 'KAY?
RIVET AIN'T THE FIRST SHOWBIZ TYPE TO "CHASE THE DRAGON," AS IT WERE. YOU KNOW THAT.
YEAH, BUT...
I THINK I SHOULD GO.
OKAY, KIDDO. LISSEN UP, 'CAUSE I'M GONNA TELL YOU HOW IT IS... DO YOU KNOW WHAT MY FUNCTION IS ON THIS LITTLE SHOW OF OURS? I MEAN REALLY?
WELL, I'M THE CANDYMAN, SWEETIE.
I GET THE BOY WHAT HE WANTS, WHATEVER HE WANTS, WHENEVER HE WANTS IT.
ANYTHING TO KEEP HIM HAPPY, RIGHT?
AND IF THE CURSE IS WHAT MAKES HIM HAPPY, THEN THE CURSE IS WHAT HE SHALL HAVE.
AND YOU COME TO WORK FOR ME, MS. SERENITY ELIZABETH ROSE...
WELL, YOU TELL ME: HOW WILL THE CANDYMAN MAKE YOU HAPPY?
CANDY
Sera Rose
"THIS WEIRD GIRL GAVE US TWELVE HITS."
MAN.
DID YOU REALLY JUST FIND MY SKETCHBOOK ON YOUR DESK?
WHAT'S THAT?
...OF COURSE, BABY. I TOLD Y-
I SHOULD GO.
LATER, SKATER.

FROM FEARFUL THING: THE JOURNAL OF THE UNDERSIDE #4 (D.D. KELTON, ED.) DRAWED BY ME.

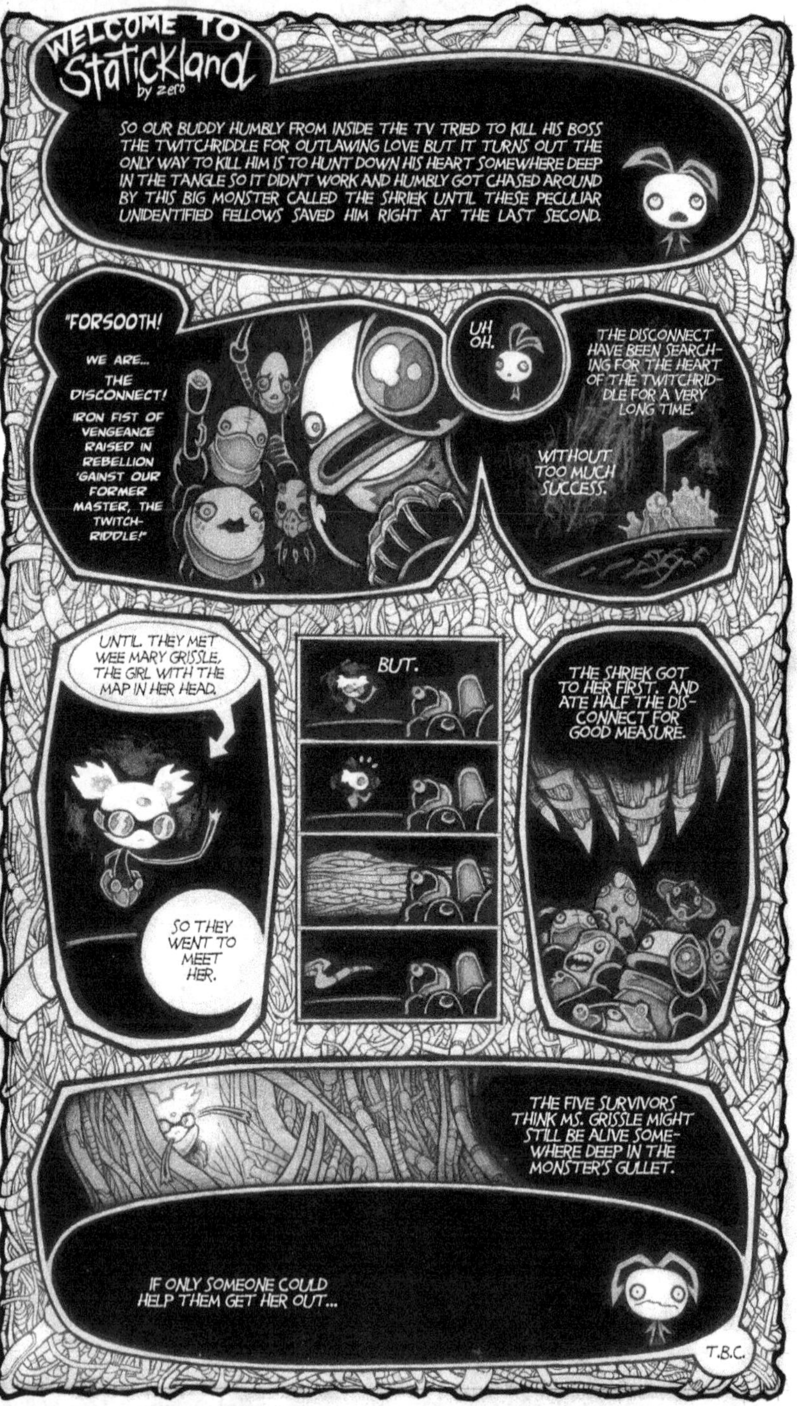
WELCOME TO Statickland by zero
SO OUR BUDDY HUMBLY FROM INSIDE THE TV TRIED TO KILL HIS BOSS THE TWITCHRIDDLE FOR OUTLAWING LOVE BUT IT TURNS OUT THE ONLY WAY TO KILL HIM IS TO HUNT DOWN HIS HEART SOMEWHERE DEEP IN THE TANGLE SO IT DIDN'T WORK AND HUMBLY GOT CHASED AROUND BY THIS BIG MONSTER CALLED THE SHRIEK UNTIL THESE PECULIAR UNIDENTIFIED FELLOWS SAVED HIM RIGHT AT THE LAST SECOND.
"FORSOOTH!
WE ARE... THE DISCONNECT!
IRON FIST OF VENGEANCE RAISED IN REBELLION 'GAINST OUR FORMER MASTER, THE TWITCH-RIDDLE!"
UH OH.
THE DISCONNECT HAVE BEEN SEARCHING FOR THE HEART OF THE TWITCHRIDDLE FOR A VERY LONG TIME.
WITHOUT TOO MUCH SUCCESS.
UNTIL THEY MET WEE MARY GRISSLE, THE GIRL WITH THE MAP IN HER HEAD.
SO THEY WENT TO MEET HER.
BUT.
THE SHRIEK GOT TO HER FIRST. AND ATE HALF THE DISCONNECT FOR GOOD MEASURE.
THE FIVE SURVIVORS THINK MS. GRISSLE MIGHT STILL BE ALIVE SOMEWHERE DEEP IN THE MONSTER'S GULLET.
IF ONLY SOMEONE COULD HELP THEM GET HER OUT...
T.B.C.

THIS PAGE HAS NO DISCERNABLE CENTER OF INTEREST. MY APOLOGIES.

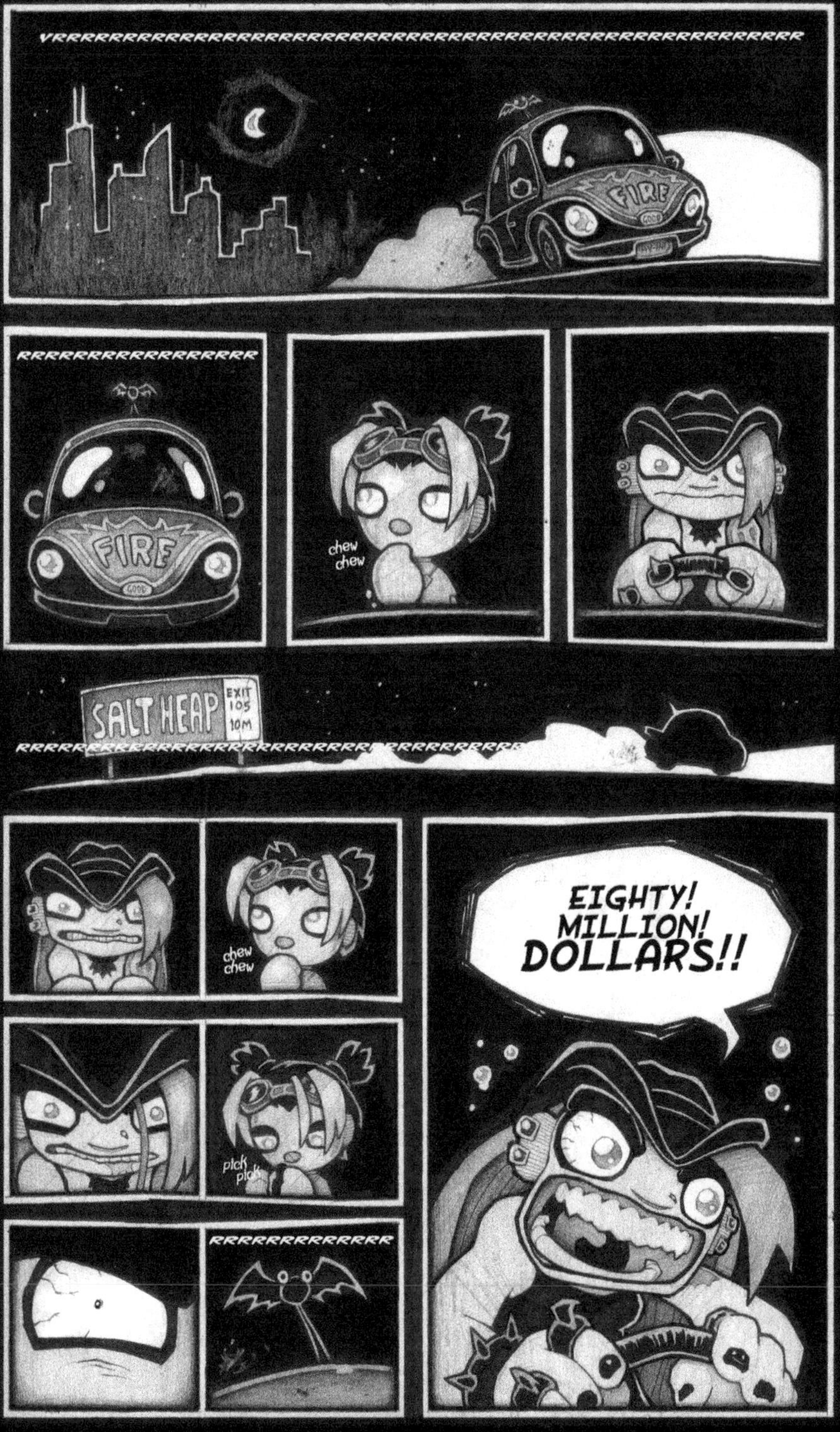

VRRRRRRRRRRRRRRRRRRRRRRRRRRRRRRRRRRRRRRRRRRRRRRRRRRRRRR
FIRE
RRRRRRRRRRRRRRRRRRR
FIRE
chew chew
SALT HEAP
EXIT 105 10M
chew chew
pick pick
RRRRRRRRRRRRR
EIGHTY! MILLION! DOLLARS!!

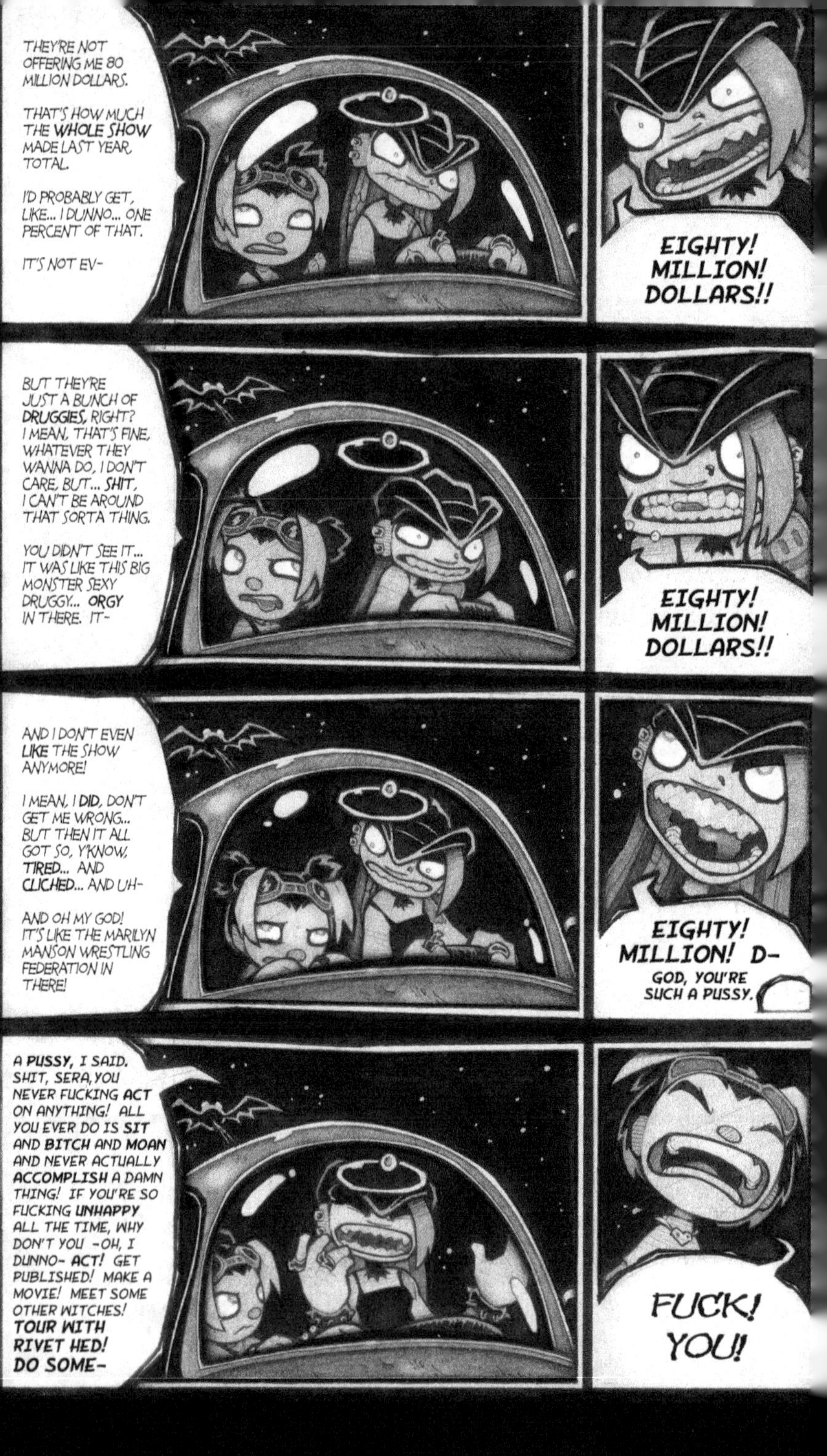
THEY'RE NOT OFFERING ME 80 MILLION DOLLARS.
THAT'S HOW MUCH THE WHOLE SHOW MADE LAST YEAR, TOTAL.
I'D PROBABLY GET, LIKE... I DUNNO... ONE PERCENT OF THAT.
IT'S NOT EV-
EIGHTY! MILLION! DOLLARS!!
BUT THEY'RE JUST A BUNCH OF DRUGGIES, RIGHT? I MEAN, THAT'S FINE, WHATEVER THEY WANNA DO, I DON'T CARE, BUT... SHIT, I CAN'T BE AROUND THAT SORTA THING.
YOU DIDN'T SEE IT... IT WAS LIKE THIS BIG MONSTER SEXY DRUGGY... ORGY IN THERE. IT-
EIGHTY! MILLION! DOLLARS!!
AND I DON'T EVEN LIKE THE SHOW ANYMORE!
I MEAN, I DID, DON'T GET ME WRONG... BUT THEN IT ALL GOT SO, Y'KNOW, TIRED... AND CLICHED... AND UH-
AND OH MY GOD! IT'S LIKE THE MARILYN MANSON WRESTLING FEDERATION IN THERE!
EIGHTY! MILLION! D-
GOD, YOU'RE SUCH A PUSSY.
A PUSSY, I SAID. SHIT, SERA, YOU NEVER FUCKING ACT ON ANYTHING! ALL YOU EVER DO IS SIT AND BITCH AND MOAN AND NEVER ACTUALLY ACCOMPLISH A DAMN THING! IF YOU'RE SO FUCKING UNHAPPY ALL THE TIME, WHY DON'T YOU -OH, I DUNNO- ACT! GET PUBLISHED! MAKE A MOVIE! MEET SOME OTHER WITCHES! TOUR WITH RIVET HED! DO SOME-
FUCK! YOU!

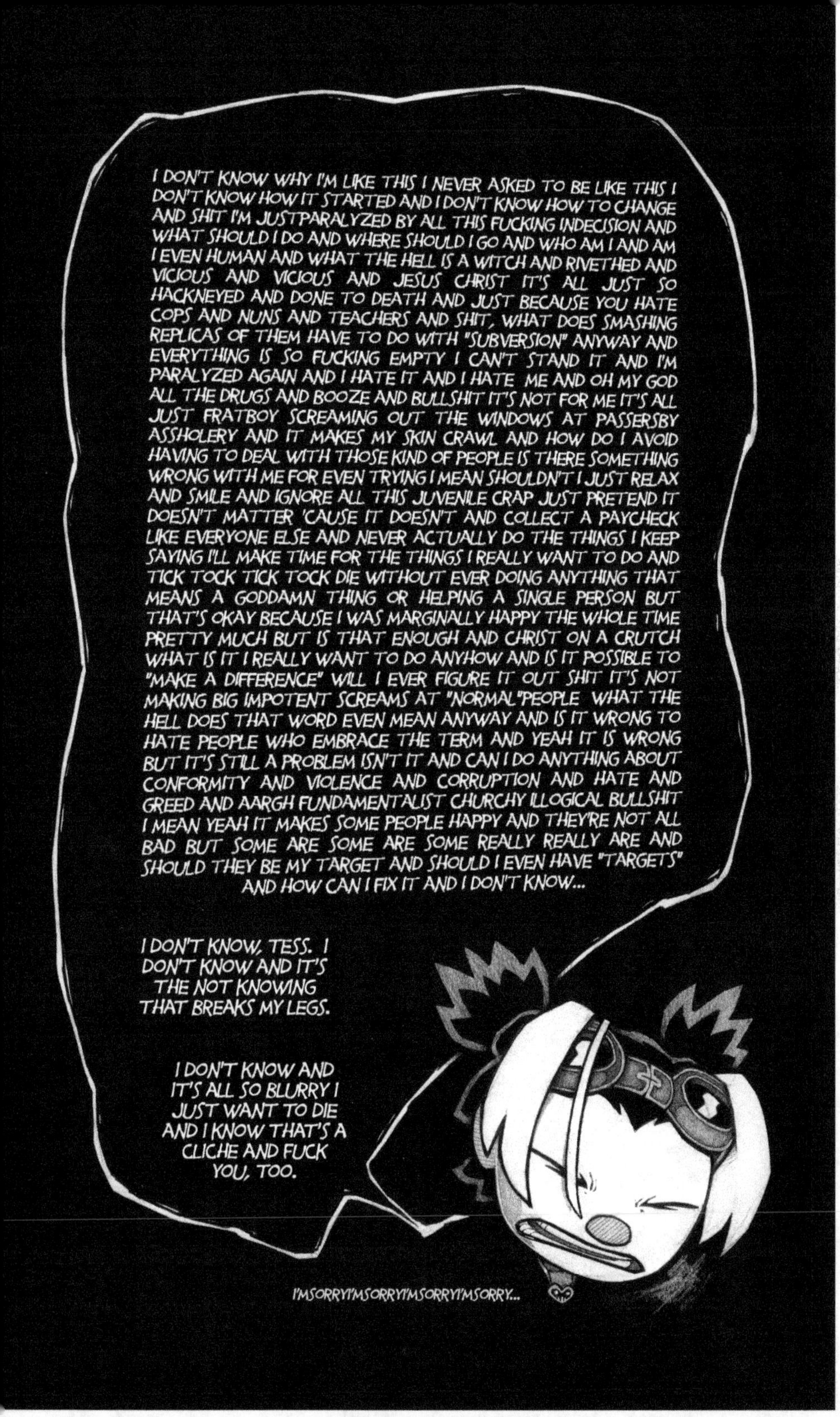
I DON'T KNOW WHY I'M LIKE THIS I NEVER ASKED TO BE LIKE THIS I DON'T KNOW HOW IT STARTED AND I DON'T KNOW HOW TO CHANGE AND SHIT I'M JUSTPARALYZED BY ALL THIS FUCKING INDECISION AND WHAT SHOULD I DO AND WHERE SHOULD I GO AND WHO AM I AND AM I EVEN HUMAN AND WHAT THE HELL IS A WITCH AND RIVETHED AND VICIOUS AND VICIOUS AND JESUS CHRIST IT'S ALL JUST SO HACKNEYED AND DONE TO DEATH AND JUST BECAUSE YOU HATE COPS AND NUNS AND TEACHERS AND SHIT, WHAT DOES SMASHING REPLICAS OF THEM HAVE TO DO WITH "SUBVERSION" ANYWAY AND EVERYTHING IS SO FUCKING EMPTY I CAN'T STAND IT AND I'M PARALYZED AGAIN AND I HATE IT AND I HATE ME AND OH MY GOD ALL THE DRUGS AND BOOZE AND BULLSHIT IT'S NOT FOR ME IT'S ALL JUST FRATBOY SCREAMING OUT THE WINDOWS AT PASSERSBY ASSHOLERY AND IT MAKES MY SKIN CRAWL AND HOW DO I AVOID HAVING TO DEAL WITH THOSE KIND OF PEOPLE IS THERE SOMETHING WRONG WITH ME FOR EVEN TRYING I MEAN SHOULDN'T I JUST RELAX AND SMILE AND IGNORE ALL THIS JUVENILE CRAP JUST PRETEND IT DOESN'T MATTER 'CAUSE IT DOESN'T AND COLLECT A PAYCHECK LIKE EVERYONE ELSE AND NEVER ACTUALLY DO THE THINGS I KEEP SAYING I'LL MAKE TIME FOR THE THINGS I REALLY WANT TO DO AND TICK TOCK TICK TOCK DIE WITHOUT EVER DOING ANYTHING THAT MEANS A GODDAMN THING OR HELPING A SINGLE PERSON BUT THAT'S OKAY BECAUSE I WAS MARGINALLY HAPPY THE WHOLE TIME PRETTY MUCH BUT IS THAT ENOUGH AND CHRIST ON A CRUTCH WHAT IS IT I REALLY WANT TO DO ANYHOW AND IS IT POSSIBLE TO "MAKE A DIFFERENCE" WILL I EVER FIGURE IT OUT SHIT IT'S NOT MAKING BIG IMPOTENT SCREAMS AT "NORMAL"PEOPLE WHAT THE HELL DOES THAT WORD EVEN MEAN ANYWAY AND IS IT WRONG TO HATE PEOPLE WHO EMBRACE THE TERM AND YEAH IT IS WRONG BUT IT'S STILL A PROBLEM ISN'T IT AND CAN I DO ANYTHING ABOUT CONFORMITY AND VIOLENCE AND CORRUPTION AND HATE AND GREED AND AARGH FUNDAMENTALIST CHURCHY ILLOGICAL BULLSHIT I MEAN YEAH IT MAKES SOME PEOPLE HAPPY AND THEY'RE NOT ALL BAD BUT SOME ARE SOME ARE SOME REALLY REALLY ARE AND SHOULD THEY BE MY TARGET AND SHOULD I EVEN HAVE "TARGETS" AND HOW CAN I FIX IT AND I DON'T KNOW...
I DON'T KNOW, TESS. I DON'T KNOW AND IT'S THE NOT KNOWING THAT BREAKS MY LEGS.
I DON'T KNOW AND IT'S ALL SO BLURRY I JUST WANT TO DIE AND I KNOW THAT'S A CLICHE AND FUCK YOU, TOO.
I'MSORRYI'MSORRYI'MSORRYI'MSORRY...

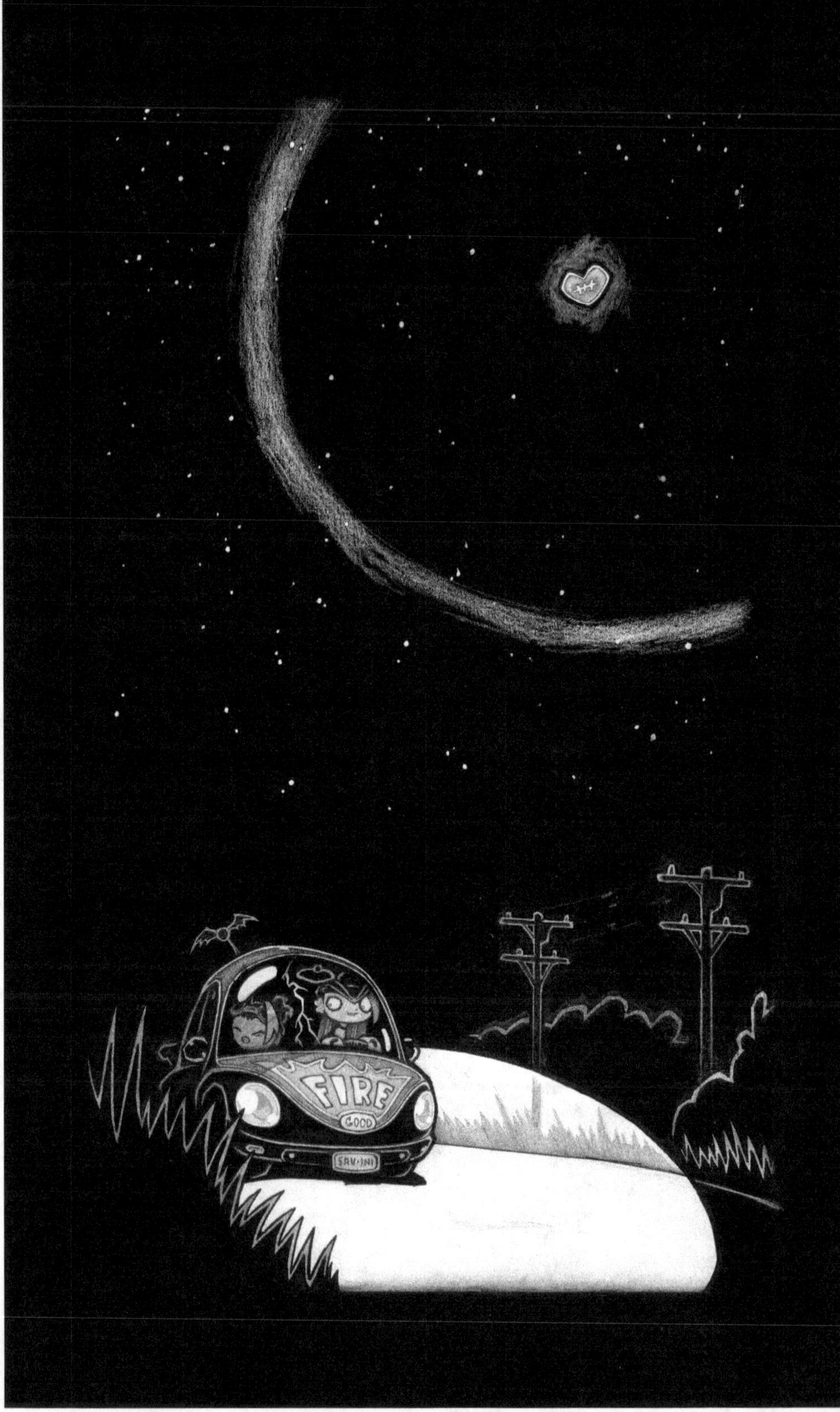
FIRE
GOOD

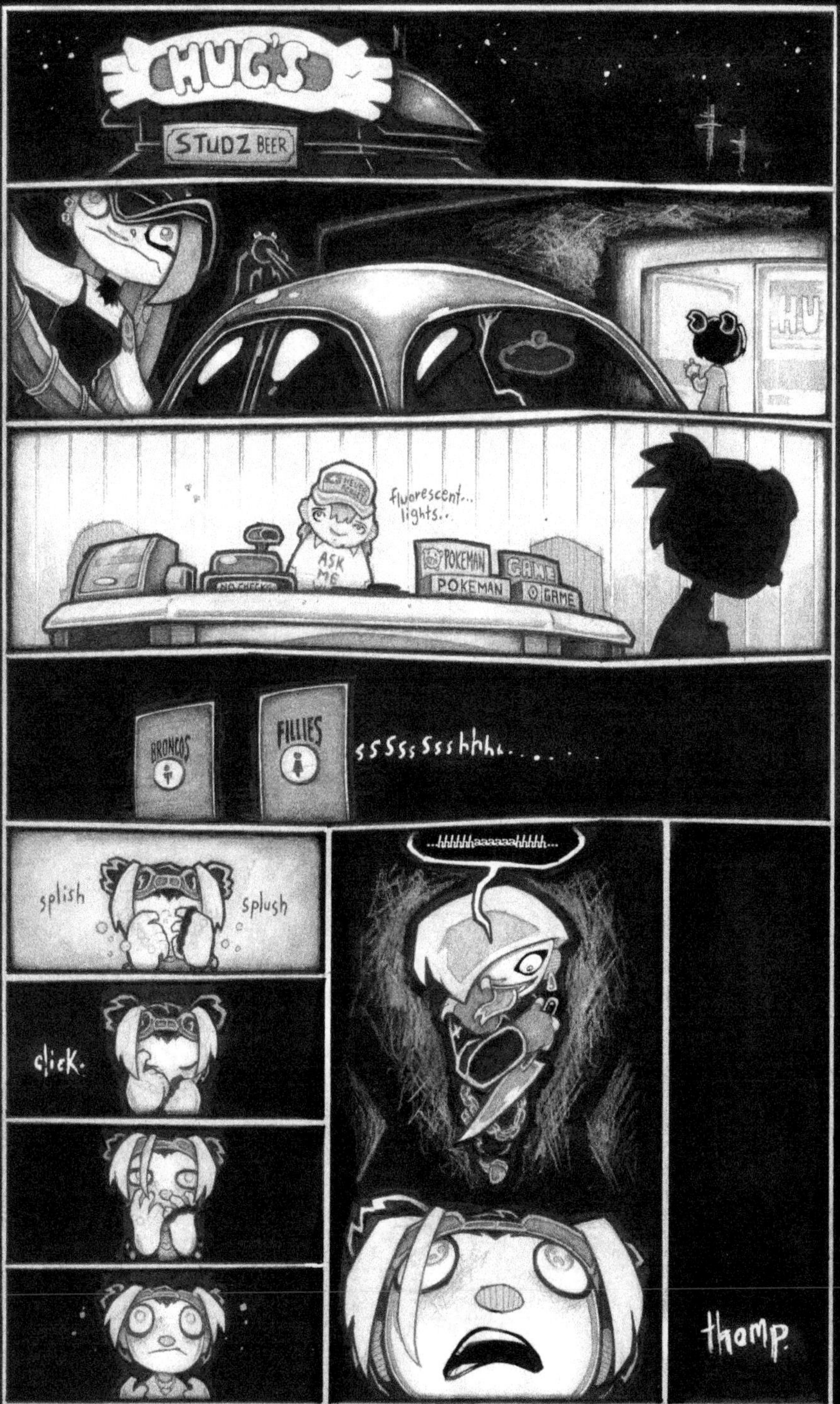
HUG'S
STUDZ BEER
fluorescent... lights..
ASK ME
POKEMAN
GAME
POKEMAN
GAME
BRONCOS
FILLIES
sSSsSsshhh.......
splish
splush
click.
...hhhhhaaaaaahhhhh...
thomp.

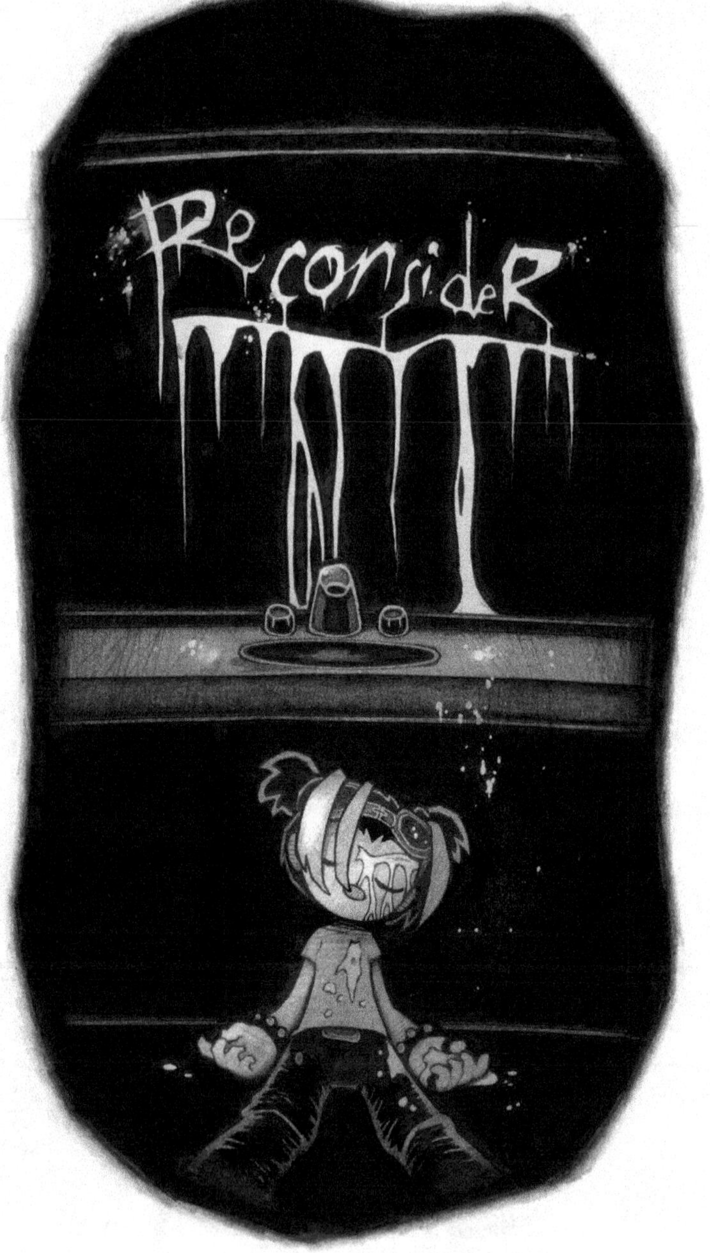
Reconsider

...ISSUE FIVE

Serenity Rose

the personal journals
of a local witch

...as told to aaron a.

issue number five:

"answers
and not."

"starring"

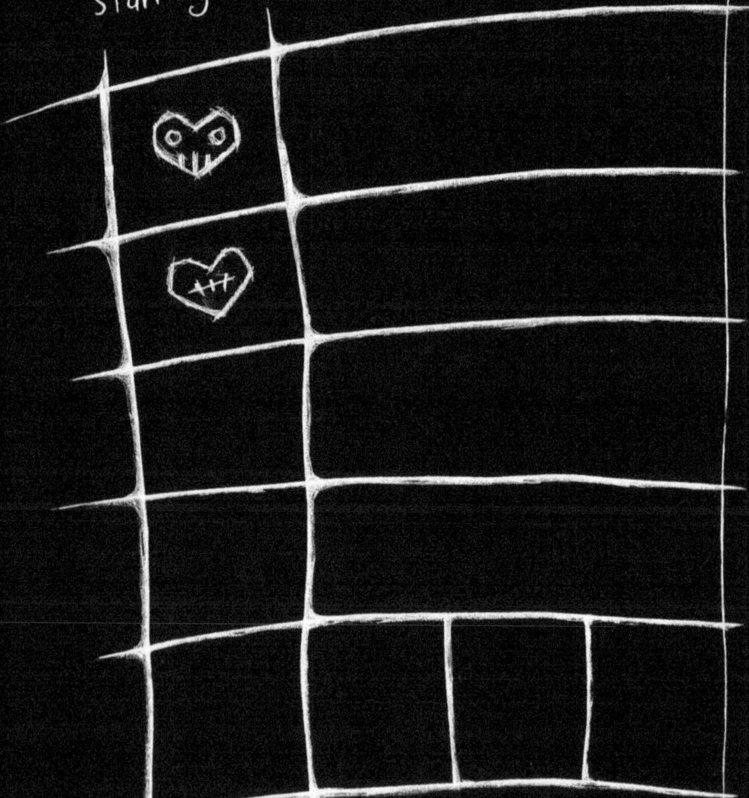

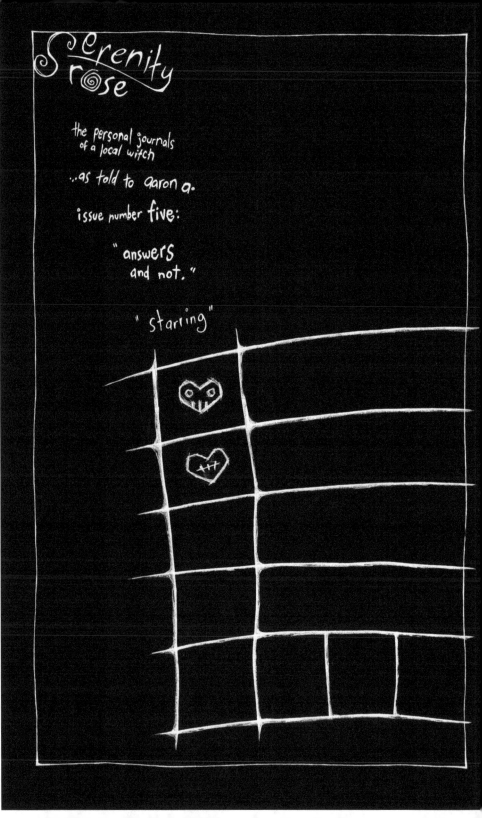

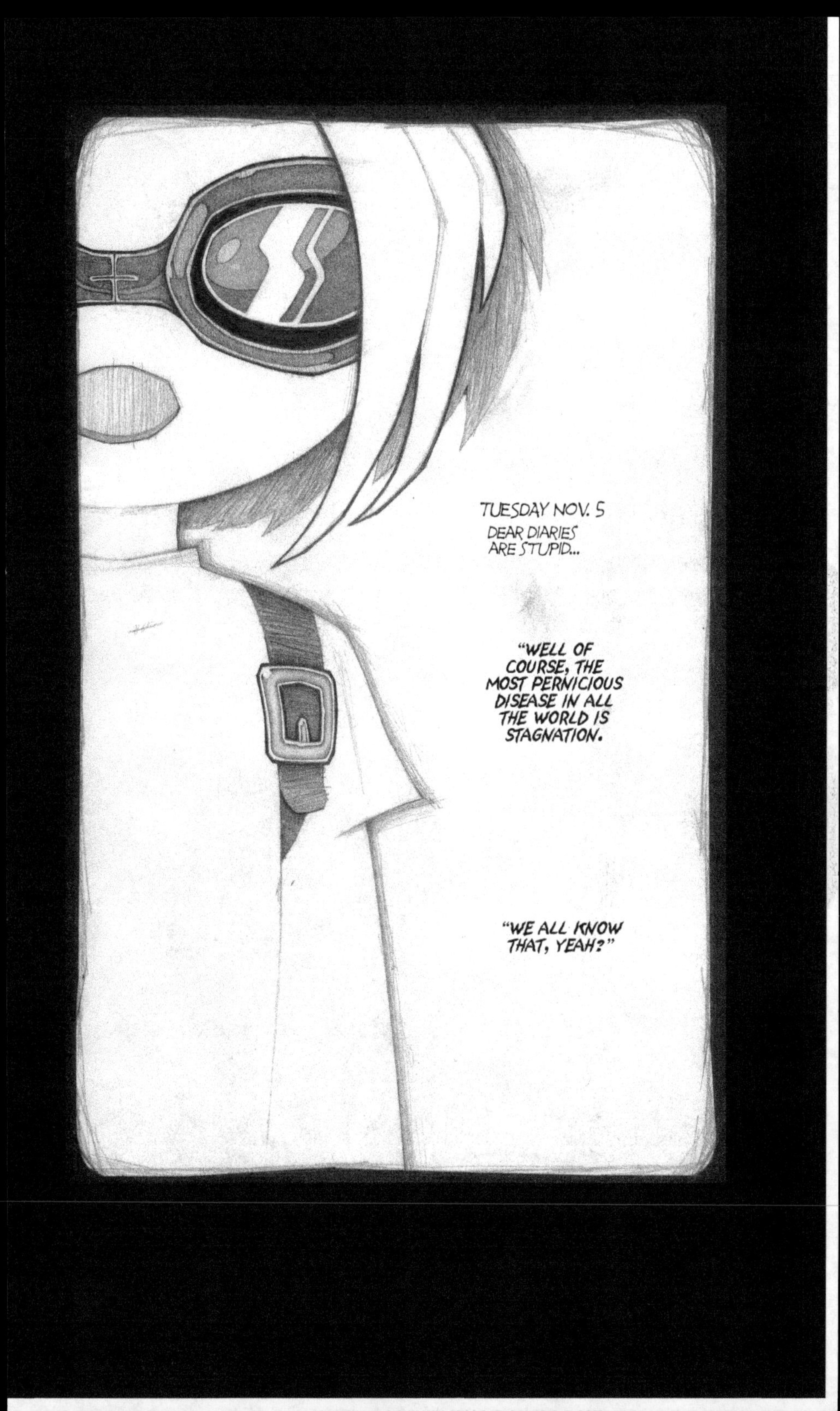
TUESDAY NOV. 5
DEAR DIARIES ARE STUPID...
"WELL OF COURSE, THE MOST PERNICIOUS DISEASE IN ALL THE WORLD IS STAGNATION.
"WE ALL KNOW THAT, YEAH?"

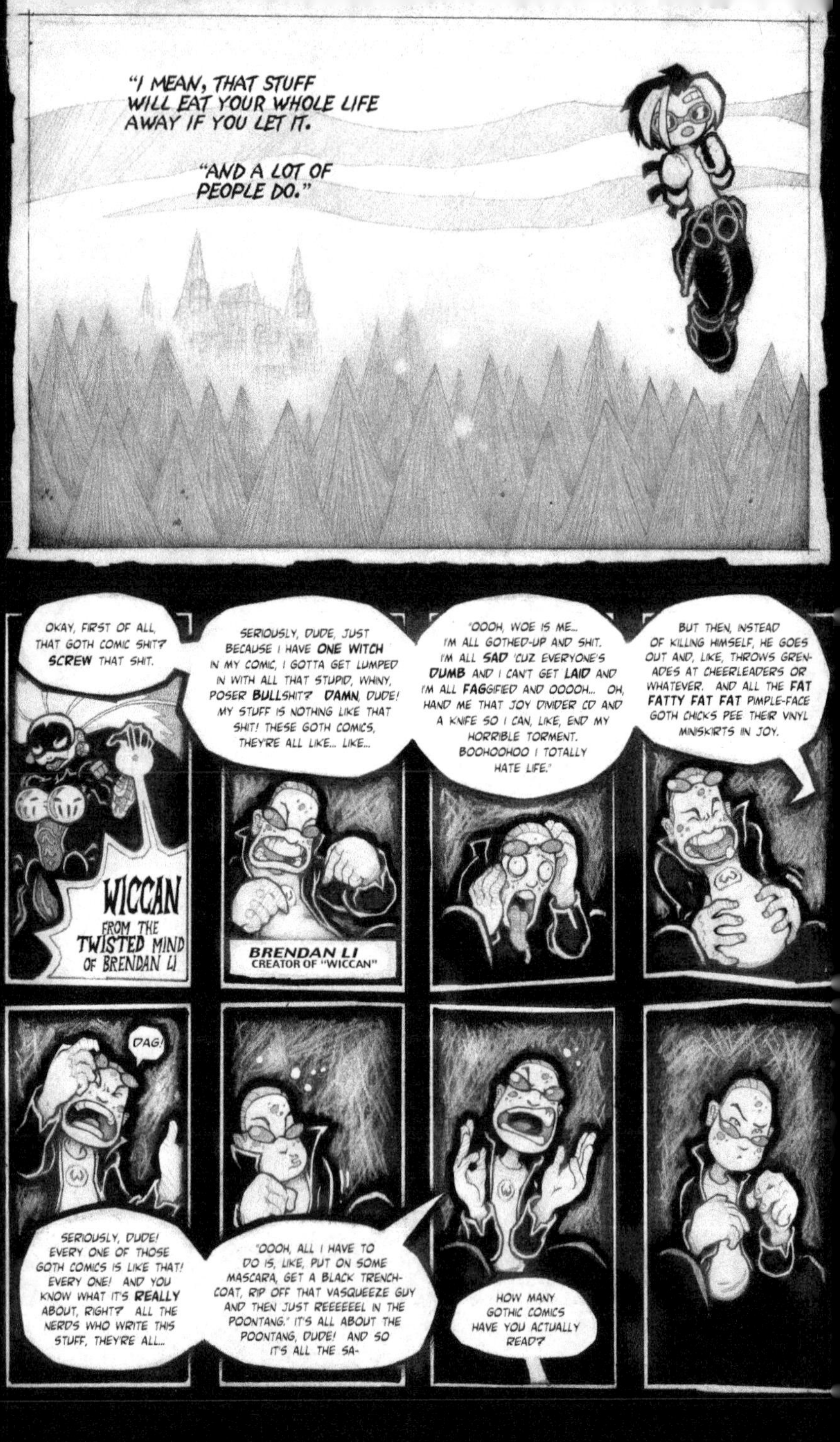

"I MEAN, THAT STUFF WILL EAT YOUR WHOLE LIFE AWAY IF YOU LET IT.
"AND A LOT OF PEOPLE DO."
OKAY, FIRST OF ALL, THAT GOTH COMIC SHIT? SCREW THAT SHIT.
WICCAN FROM THE TWISTED MIND OF BRENDAN LI
SERIOUSLY, DUDE, JUST BECAUSE I HAVE ONE WITCH IN MY COMIC, I GOTTA GET LUMPED IN WITH ALL THAT STUPID, WHINY, POSER BULLSHIT? DAMN, DUDE! MY STUFF IS NOTHING LIKE THAT SHIT! THESE GOTH COMICS, THEY'RE ALL LIKE... LIKE...
BRENDAN LI CREATOR OF "WICCAN"
"OOOH, WOE IS ME... I'M ALL GOTHED-UP AND SHIT. I'M ALL SAD 'CUZ EVERYONE'S DUMB AND I CAN'T GET LAID AND I'M ALL FAGGIFIED AND OOOOH... OH, HAND ME THAT JOY DIVIDER CD AND A KNIFE SO I CAN, LIKE, END MY HORRIBLE TORMENT. BOOHOOHOO I TOTALLY HATE LIFE."
BUT THEN, INSTEAD OF KILLING HIMSELF, HE GOES OUT AND, LIKE, THROWS GRENADES AT CHEERLEADERS OR WHATEVER. AND ALL THE FAT FATTY FAT FAT PIMPLE-FACE GOTH CHICKS PEE THEIR VINYL MINISKIRTS IN JOY.
DAG!
SERIOUSLY, DUDE! EVERY ONE OF THOSE GOTH COMICS IS LIKE THAT! EVERY ONE! AND YOU KNOW WHAT IT'S REALLY ABOUT, RIGHT? ALL THE NERDS WHO WRITE THIS STUFF, THEY'RE ALL...
"OOOH, ALL I HAVE TO DO IS, LIKE, PUT ON SOME MASCARA, GET A BLACK TRENCHCOAT, RIP OFF THAT VASQUEEZE GUY AND THEN JUST REEEEEEL IN THE POONTANG." IT'S ALL ABOUT THE POONTANG, DUDE! AND SO IT'S ALL THE SA-
HOW MANY GOTHIC COMICS HAVE YOU ACTUALLY READ?

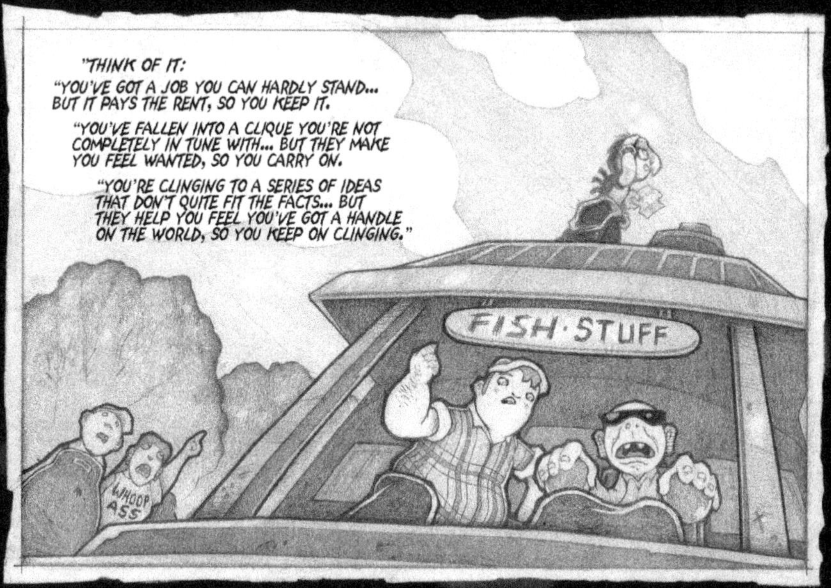
"THINK OF IT:
"YOU'VE GOT A JOB YOU CAN HARDLY STAND... BUT IT PAYS THE RENT, SO YOU KEEP IT.
"YOU'VE FALLEN INTO A CLIQUE YOU'RE NOT COMPLETELY IN TUNE WITH... BUT THEY MAKE YOU FEEL WANTED, SO YOU CARRY ON.
"YOU'RE CLINGING TO A SERIES OF IDEAS THAT DON'T QUITE FIT THE FACTS... BUT THEY HELP YOU FEEL YOU'VE GOT A HANDLE ON THE WORLD, SO YOU KEEP ON CLINGING."
FISH·STUFF
WHOOP ASS

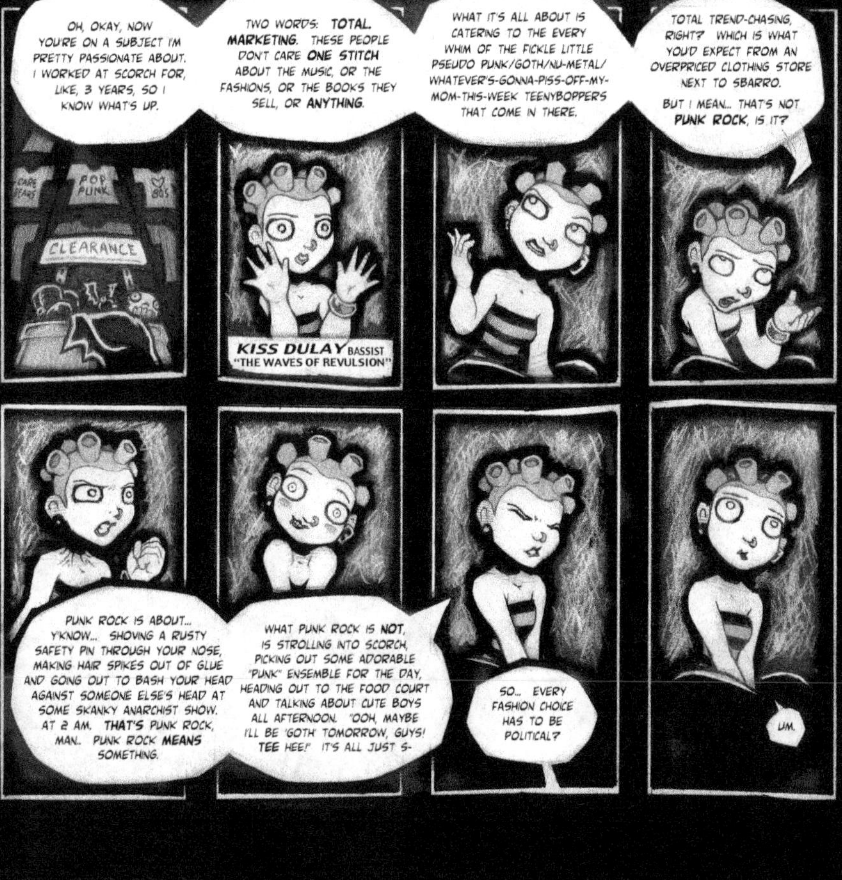
OH, OKAY, NOW YOU'RE ON A SUBJECT I'M PRETTY PASSIONATE ABOUT. I WORKED AT SCORCH FOR, LIKE, 3 YEARS, SO I KNOW WHAT'S UP.
POP PUNK
CLEARANCE
TWO WORDS: TOTAL. MARKETING. THESE PEOPLE DON'T CARE ONE STITCH ABOUT THE MUSIC, OR THE FASHIONS, OR THE BOOKS THEY SELL, OR ANYTHING.
KISS DULAY BASSIST "THE WAVES OF REVULSION"
WHAT IT'S ALL ABOUT IS CATERING TO THE EVERY WHIM OF THE FICKLE LITTLE PSEUDO PUNK/GOTH/NU-METAL/ WHATEVER'S-GONNA-PISS-OFF-MY-MOM-THIS-WEEK TEENYBOPPERS THAT COME IN THERE.
TOTAL TREND-CHASING, RIGHT? WHICH IS WHAT YOU'D EXPECT FROM AN OVERPRICED CLOTHING STORE NEXT TO SBARRO.
BUT I MEAN... THAT'S NOT PUNK ROCK, IS IT?
PUNK ROCK IS ABOUT... Y'KNOW... SHOVING A RUSTY SAFETY PIN THROUGH YOUR NOSE, MAKING HAIR SPIKES OUT OF GLUE AND GOING OUT TO BASH YOUR HEAD AGAINST SOMEONE ELSE'S HEAD AT SOME SKANKY ANARCHIST SHOW. AT 2 AM. THAT'S PUNK ROCK, MAN. PUNK ROCK MEANS SOMETHING.
WHAT PUNK ROCK IS NOT, IS STROLLING INTO SCORCH, PICKING OUT SOME ADORABLE "PUNK" ENSEMBLE FOR THE DAY, HEADING OUT TO THE FOOD COURT AND TALKING ABOUT CUTE BOYS ALL AFTERNOON. "OOH, MAYBE I'LL BE 'GOTH' TOMORROW, GUYS! TEE HEE!" IT'S ALL JUST S-
SO... EVERY FASHION CHOICE HAS TO BE POLITICAL?
UM.

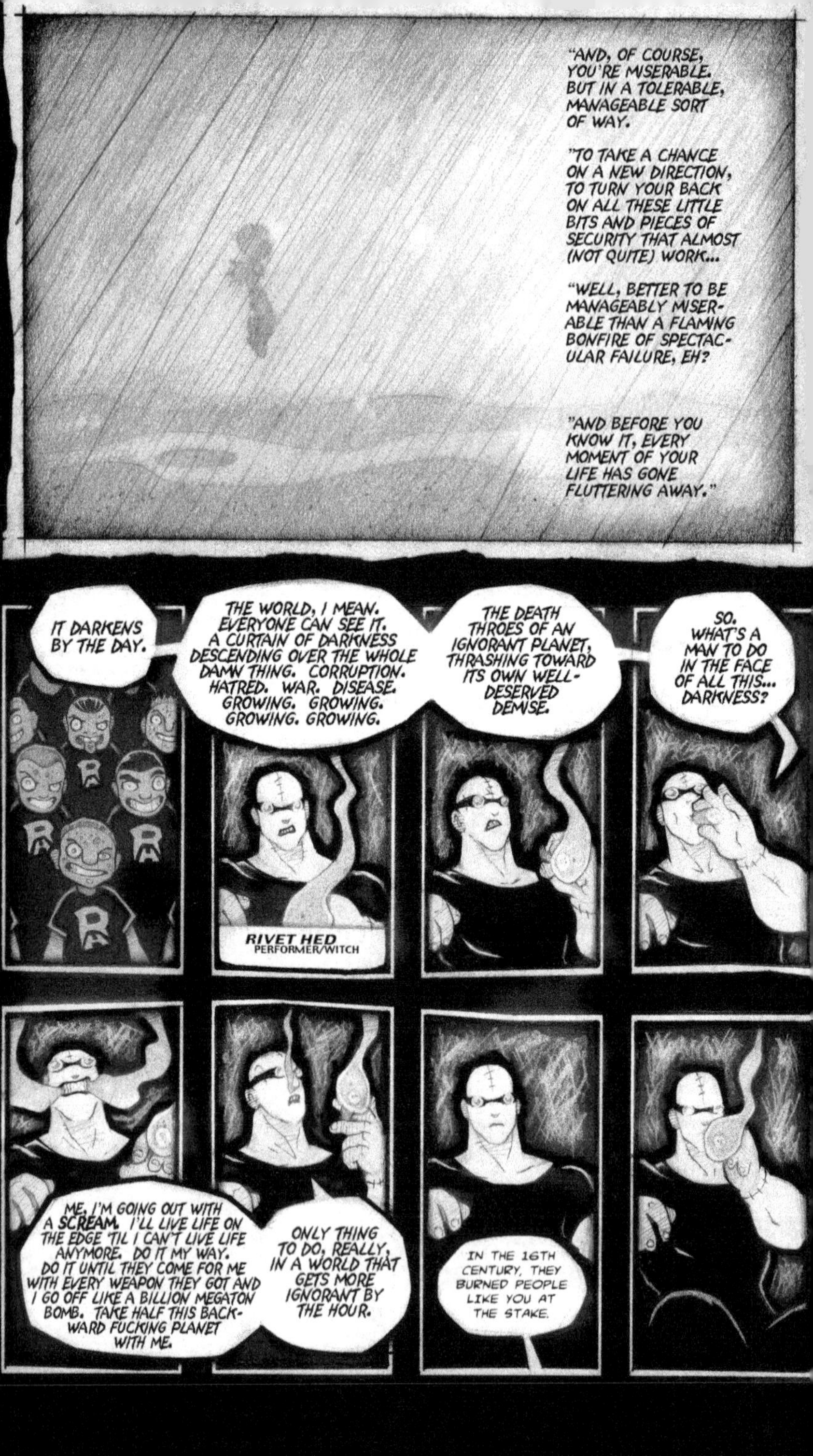
"AND, OF COURSE, YOU'RE MISERABLE. BUT IN A TOLERABLE, MANAGEABLE SORT OF WAY.
"TO TAKE A CHANCE ON A NEW DIRECTION, TO TURN YOUR BACK ON ALL THESE LITTLE BITS AND PIECES OF SECURITY THAT ALMOST (NOT QUITE) WORK...
"WELL, BETTER TO BE MANAGEABLY MISER-ABLE THAN A FLAMING BONFIRE OF SPECTAC-ULAR FAILURE, EH?
"AND BEFORE YOU KNOW IT, EVERY MOMENT OF YOUR LIFE HAS GONE FLUTTERING AWAY."
IT DARKENS BY THE DAY.
THE WORLD, I MEAN. EVERYONE CAN SEE IT. A CURTAIN OF DARKNESS DESCENDING OVER THE WHOLE DAMN THING. CORRUPTION. HATRED. WAR. DISEASE. GROWING. GROWING. GROWING. GROWING.
RIVET HED
PERFORMER/WITCH
THE DEATH THROES OF AN IGNORANT PLANET, THRASHING TOWARD ITS OWN WELL-DESERVED DEMISE.
SO. WHAT'S A MAN TO DO IN THE FACE OF ALL THIS... DARKNESS?
ME, I'M GOING OUT WITH A SCREAM. I'LL LIVE LIFE ON THE EDGE 'TIL I CAN'T LIVE LIFE ANYMORE. DO IT MY WAY. DO IT UNTIL THEY COME FOR ME WITH EVERY WEAPON THEY GOT AND I GO OFF LIKE A BILLION MEGATON BOMB. TAKE HALF THIS BACK-WARD FUCKING PLANET WITH ME.
ONLY THING TO DO, REALLY, IN A WORLD THAT GETS MORE IGNORANT BY THE HOUR.
IN THE 16TH CENTURY, THEY BURNED PEOPLE LIKE YOU AT THE STAKE.

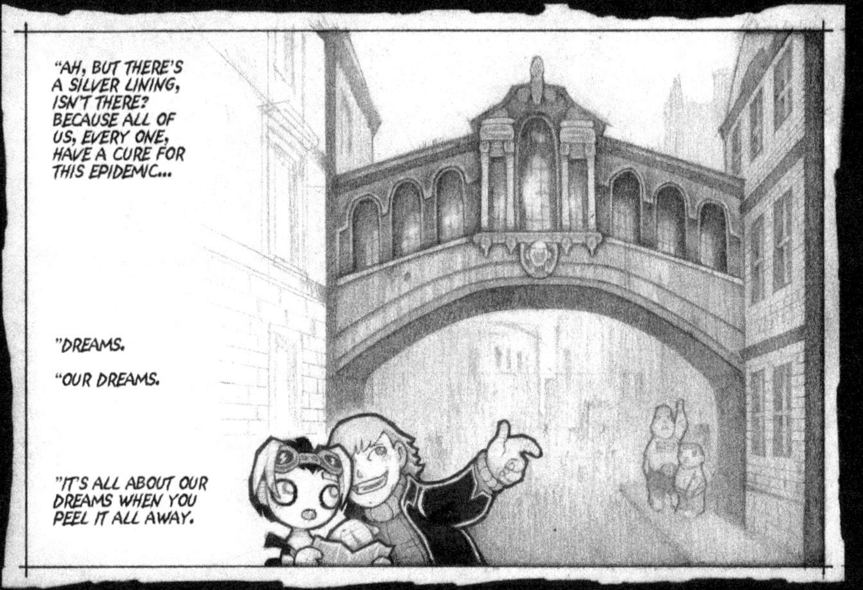
"AH, BUT THERE'S A SILVER LINING, ISN'T THERE? BECAUSE ALL OF US, EVERY ONE, HAVE A CURE FOR THIS EPIDEMIC...
"DREAMS.
"OUR DREAMS.
"IT'S ALL ABOUT OUR DREAMS WHEN YOU PEEL IT ALL AWAY.

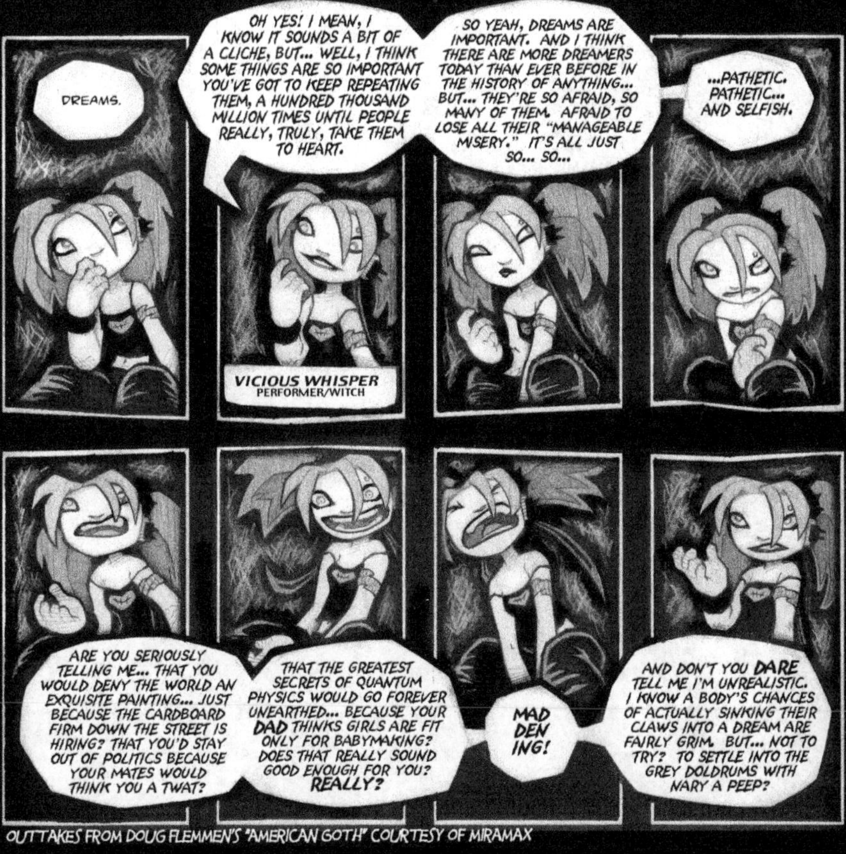
DREAMS.
OH YES! I MEAN, I KNOW IT SOUNDS A BIT OF A CLICHE, BUT... WELL, I THINK SOME THINGS ARE SO IMPORTANT YOU'VE GOT TO KEEP REPEATING THEM, A HUNDRED THOUSAND MILLION TIMES UNTIL PEOPLE REALLY, TRULY, TAKE THEM TO HEART.
VICIOUS WHISPER
PERFORMER/WITCH
SO YEAH, DREAMS ARE IMPORTANT. AND I THINK THERE ARE MORE DREAMERS TODAY THAN EVER BEFORE IN THE HISTORY OF ANYTHING... BUT... THEY'RE SO AFRAID, SO MANY OF THEM. AFRAID TO LOSE ALL THEIR "MANAGEABLE MISERY." IT'S ALL JUST SO... SO...
...PATHETIC. PATHETIC... AND SELFISH.
ARE YOU SERIOUSLY TELLING ME... THAT YOU WOULD DENY THE WORLD AN EXQUISITE PAINTING... JUST BECAUSE THE CARDBOARD FIRM DOWN THE STREET IS HIRING? THAT YOU'D STAY OUT OF POLITICS BECAUSE YOUR MATES WOULD THINK YOU A TWAT?
THAT THE GREATEST SECRETS OF QUANTUM PHYSICS WOULD GO FOREVER UNEARTHED... BECAUSE YOUR DAD THINKS GIRLS ARE FIT ONLY FOR BABYMAKING? DOES THAT REALLY SOUND GOOD ENOUGH FOR YOU? REALLY?
MAD DEN ING!
AND DON'T YOU DARE TELL ME I'M UNREALISTIC. I KNOW A BODY'S CHANCES OF ACTUALLY SINKING THEIR CLAWS INTO A DREAM ARE FAIRLY GRIM. BUT... NOT TO TRY? TO SETTLE INTO THE GREY DOLDRUMS WITH NARY A PEEP?

OUTTAKES FROM DOUG FLEMMEN'S "AMERICAN GOTH" COURTESY OF MIRAMAX

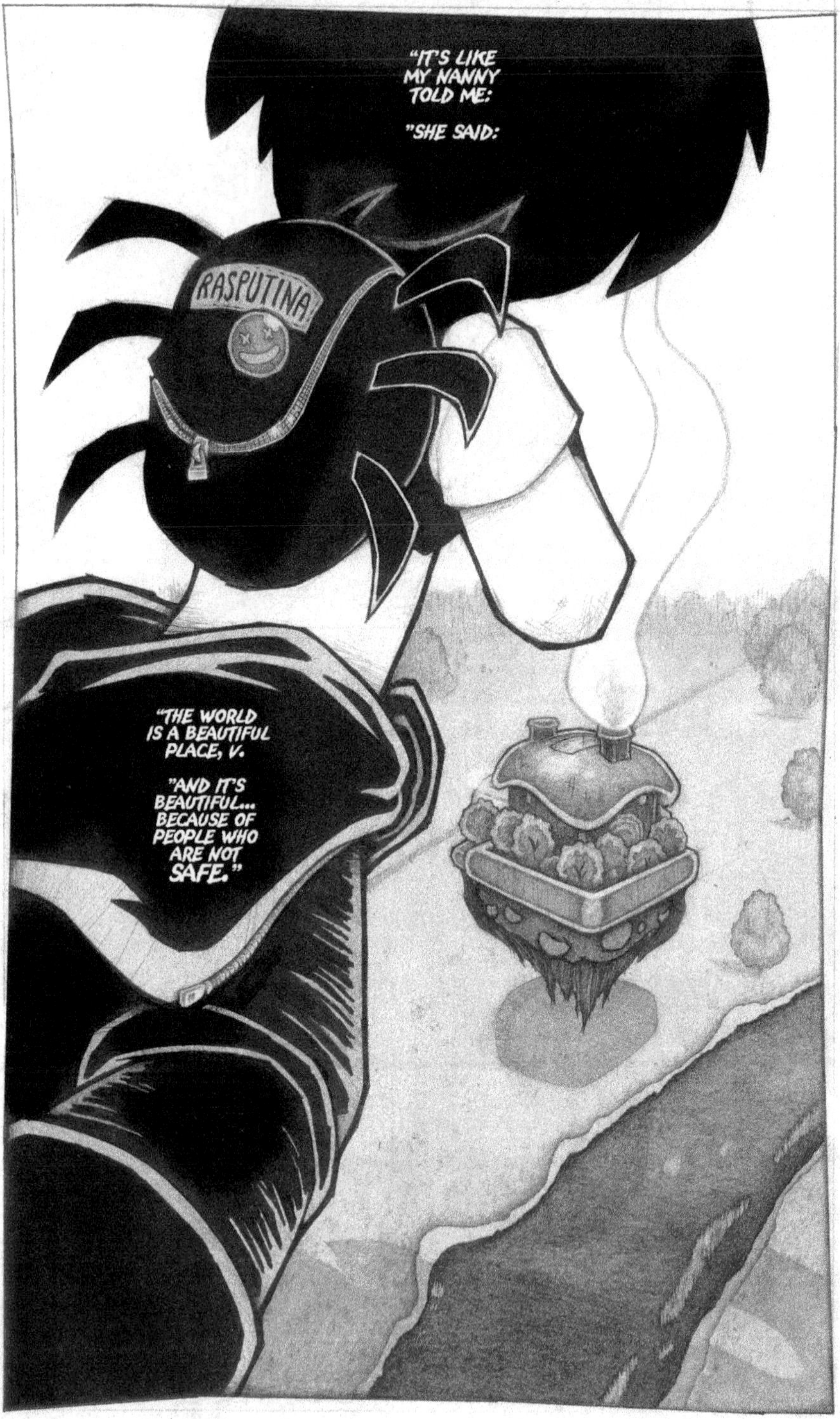
"IT'S LIKE MY NANNY TOLD ME:
"SHE SAID:
RASPUTINA
"THE WORLD IS A BEAUTIFUL PLACE, V.
"AND IT'S BEAUTIFUL... BECAUSE OF PEOPLE WHO ARE NOT SAFE."

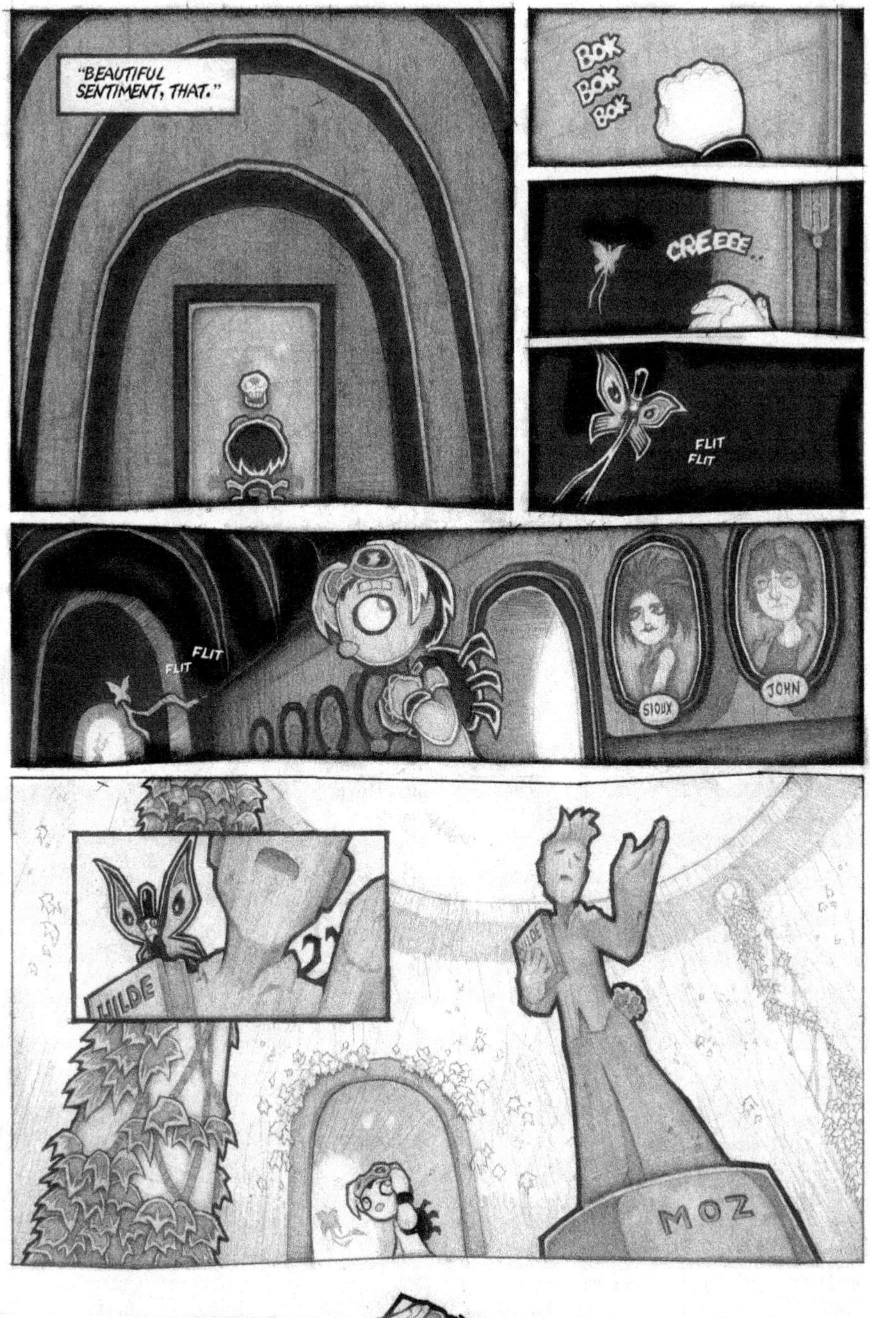
"BEAUTIFUL SENTIMENT, THAT."
BOK
BOK
BOK
CREEEE..
FLIT
FLIT
FLIT
FLIT
SIOUX
JOHN
WILDE
WILDE
MOZ

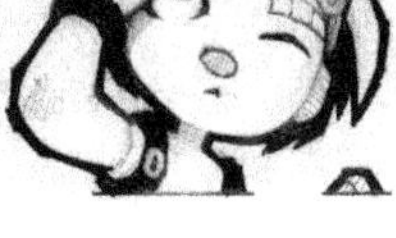

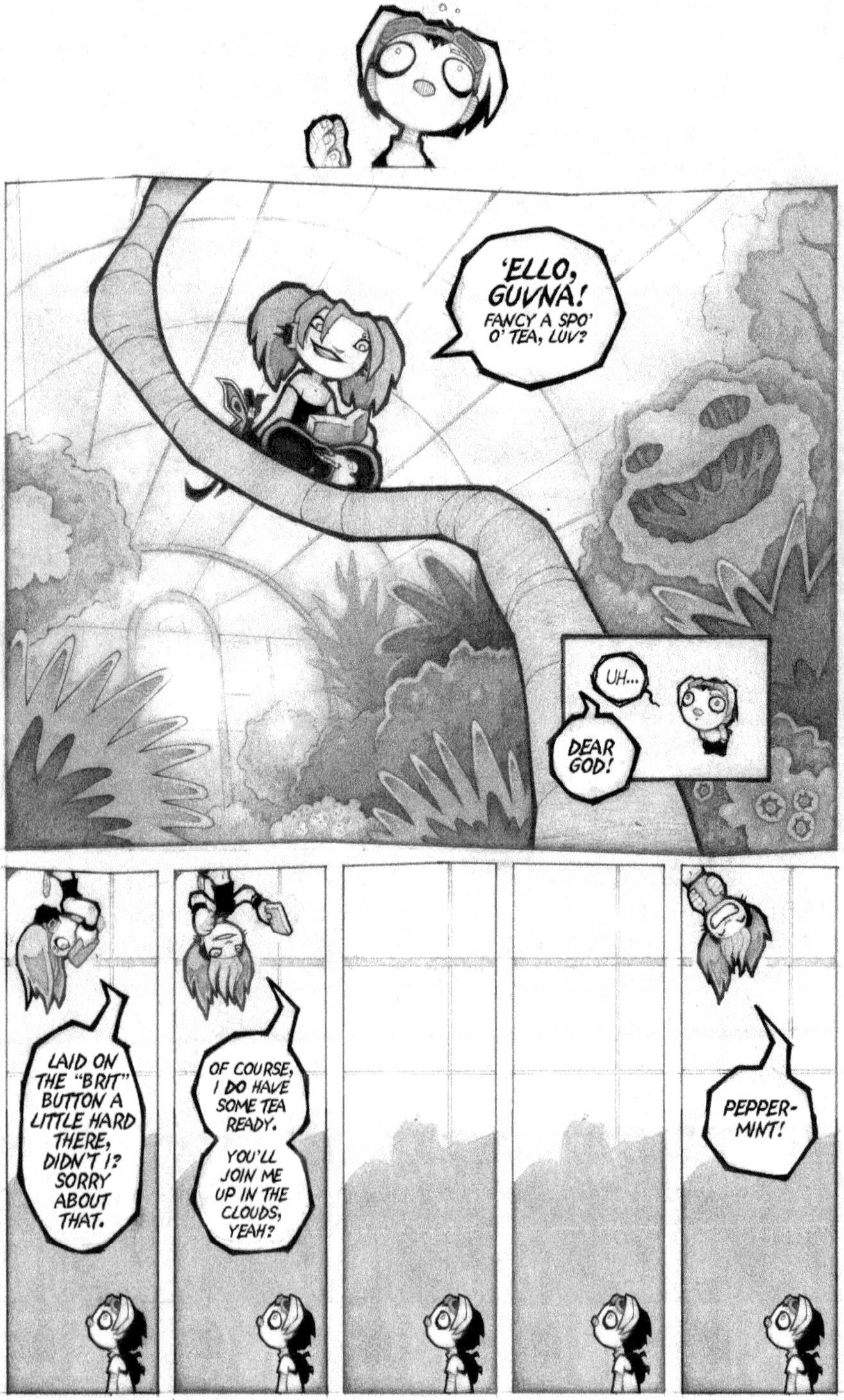
'ELLO, GUVNA! FANCY A SPO' O' TEA, LUV?
UH...
DEAR GOD!
LAID ON THE "BRIT" BUTTON A LITTLE HARD THERE, DIDN'T I? SORRY ABOUT THAT.
OF COURSE, I DO HAVE SOME TEA READY.
YOU'LL JOIN ME UP IN THE CLOUDS, YEAH?
PEPPER-MINT!

FROM FEARFUL THING: THE JOURNAL OF THE UNDERSIDE #5 (D.D. KELTON, ED.) DRAWED BY ME.

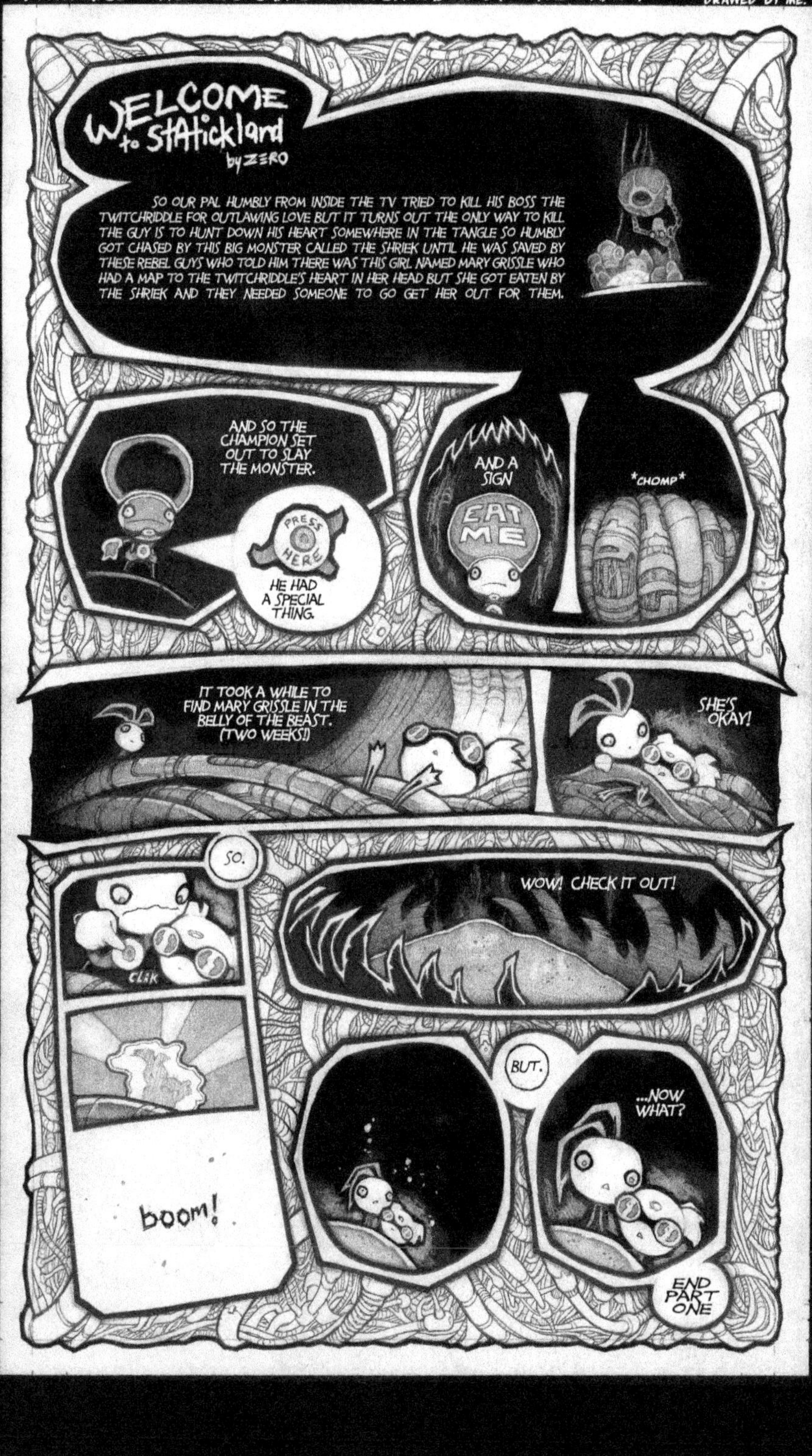
WELCOME to statickland
by ZERO
SO OUR PAL HUMBLY FROM INSIDE THE TV TRIED TO KILL HIS BOSS THE TWITCHRIDDLE FOR OUTLAWING LOVE BUT IT TURNS OUT THE ONLY WAY TO KILL THE GUY IS TO HUNT DOWN HIS HEART SOMEWHERE IN THE TANGLE SO HUMBLY GOT CHASED BY THIS BIG MONSTER CALLED THE SHRIEK UNTIL HE WAS SAVED BY THESE REBEL GUYS WHO TOLD HIM THERE WAS THIS GIRL NAMED MARY GRISSLE WHO HAD A MAP TO THE TWITCHRIDDLE'S HEART IN HER HEAD BUT SHE GOT EATEN BY THE SHRIEK AND THEY NEEDED SOMEONE TO GO GET HER OUT FOR THEM.
AND SO THE CHAMPION SET OUT TO SLAY THE MONSTER.
PRESS HERE
HE HAD A SPECIAL THING.
AND A SIGN
EAT ME
CHOMP
IT TOOK A WHILE TO FIND MARY GRISSLE IN THE BELLY OF THE BEAST. (TWO WEEKS!)
SHE'S OKAY!
SO.
CLIK
WOW! CHECK IT OUT!
boom!
BUT.
...NOW WHAT?
END PART ONE

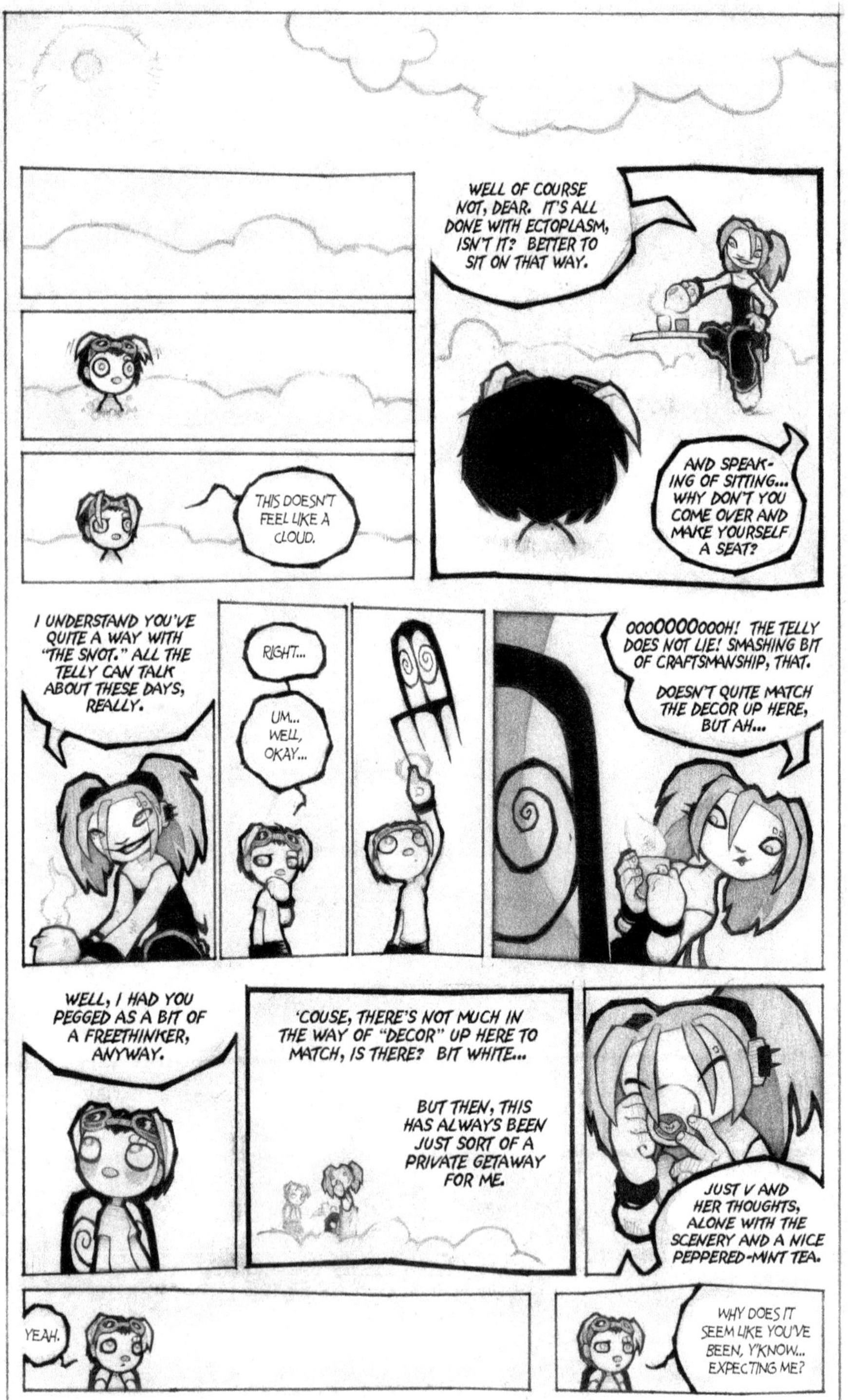

THIS DOESN'T FEEL LIKE A CLOUD.
WELL OF COURSE NOT, DEAR. IT'S ALL DONE WITH ECTOPLASM, ISN'T IT? BETTER TO SIT ON THAT WAY.
AND SPEAKING OF SITTING... WHY DON'T YOU COME OVER AND MAKE YOURSELF A SEAT?
I UNDERSTAND YOU'VE QUITE A WAY WITH "THE SNOT." ALL THE TELLY CAN TALK ABOUT THESE DAYS, REALLY.
RIGHT...
UM... WELL, OKAY...
OOOOOOOOOOH! THE TELLY DOES NOT LIE! SMASHING BIT OF CRAFTSMANSHIP, THAT.
DOESN'T QUITE MATCH THE DECOR UP HERE, BUT AH...
WELL, I HAD YOU PEGGED AS A BIT OF A FREETHINKER, ANYWAY.
'COUSE, THERE'S NOT MUCH IN THE WAY OF "DECOR" UP HERE TO MATCH, IS THERE? BIT WHITE...
BUT THEN, THIS HAS ALWAYS BEEN JUST SORT OF A PRIVATE GETAWAY FOR ME.
JUST V AND HER THOUGHTS, ALONE WITH THE SCENERY AND A NICE PEPPERED-MINT TEA.
YEAH.
WHY DOES IT SEEM LIKE YOU'VE BEEN, Y'KNOW... EXPECTING ME?

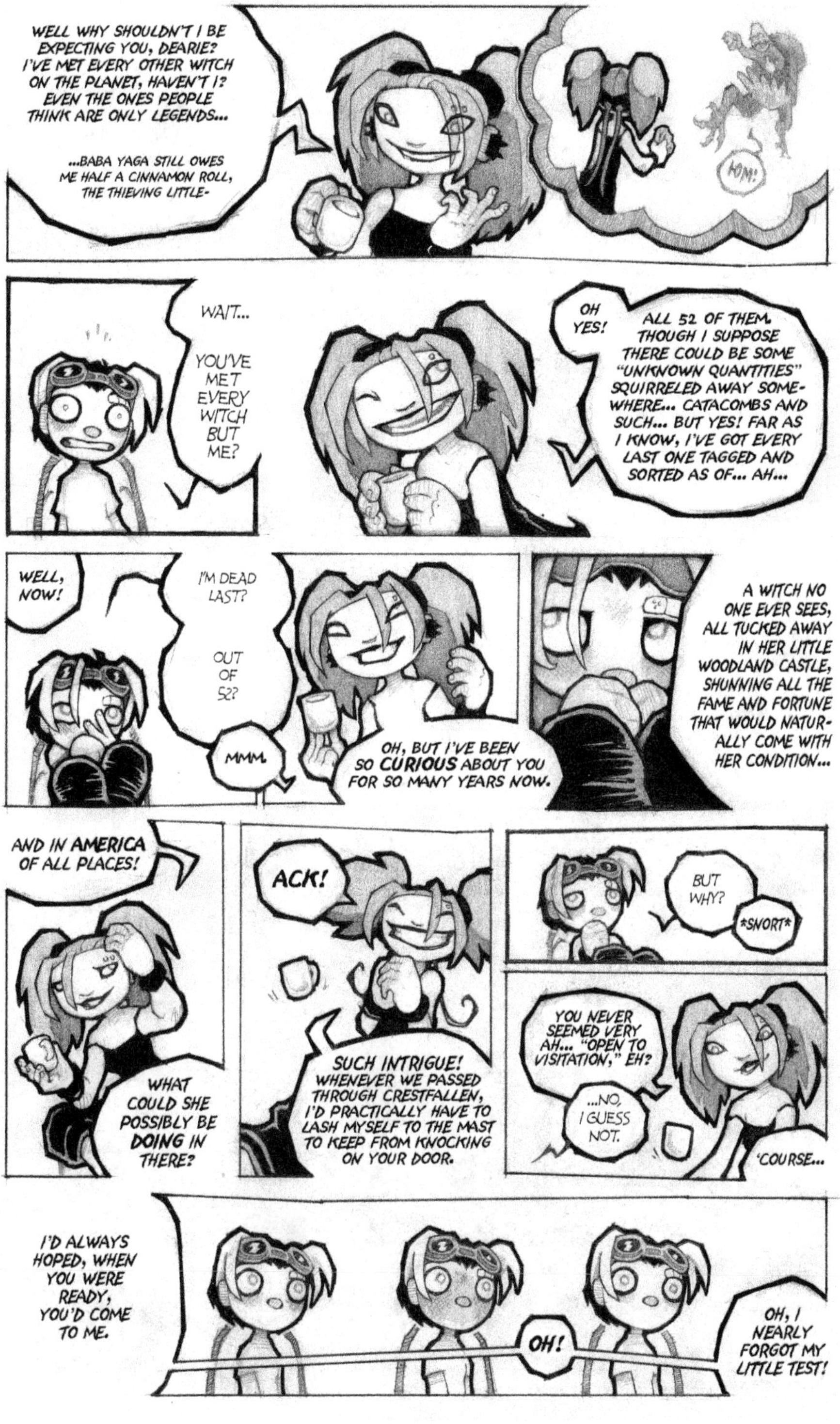
WELL WHY SHOULDN'T I BE EXPECTING YOU, DEARIE? I'VE MET EVERY OTHER WITCH ON THE PLANET, HAVEN'T I? EVEN THE ONES PEOPLE THINK ARE ONLY LEGENDS...
...BABA YAGA STILL OWES ME HALF A CINNAMON ROLL, THE THIEVING LITTLE-
HM!
WAIT...
YOU'VE MET EVERY WITCH BUT ME?
OH YES!
ALL 52 OF THEM. THOUGH I SUPPOSE THERE COULD BE SOME "UNKNOWN QUANTITIES" SQUIRRELED AWAY SOME-WHERE... CATACOMBS AND SUCH... BUT YES! FAR AS I KNOW, I'VE GOT EVERY LAST ONE TAGGED AND SORTED AS OF... AH...
WELL, NOW!
I'M DEAD LAST?
OUT OF 52?
MMM.
OH, BUT I'VE BEEN SO CURIOUS ABOUT YOU FOR SO MANY YEARS NOW.
A WITCH NO ONE EVER SEES, ALL TUCKED AWAY IN HER LITTLE WOODLAND CASTLE, SHUNNING ALL THE FAME AND FORTUNE THAT WOULD NATUR-ALLY COME WITH HER CONDITION...
AND IN AMERICA OF ALL PLACES!
WHAT COULD SHE POSSIBLY BE DOING IN THERE?
ACK!
SUCH INTRIGUE! WHENEVER WE PASSED THROUGH CRESTFALLEN, I'D PRACTICALLY HAVE TO LASH MYSELF TO THE MAST TO KEEP FROM KNOCKING ON YOUR DOOR.
BUT WHY?
SNORT
YOU NEVER SEEMED VERY AH... "OPEN TO VISITATION," EH?
...NO, I GUESS NOT.
'COURSE...
I'D ALWAYS HOPED, WHEN YOU WERE READY, YOU'D COME TO ME.
OH!
OH, I NEARLY FORGOT MY LITTLE TEST!

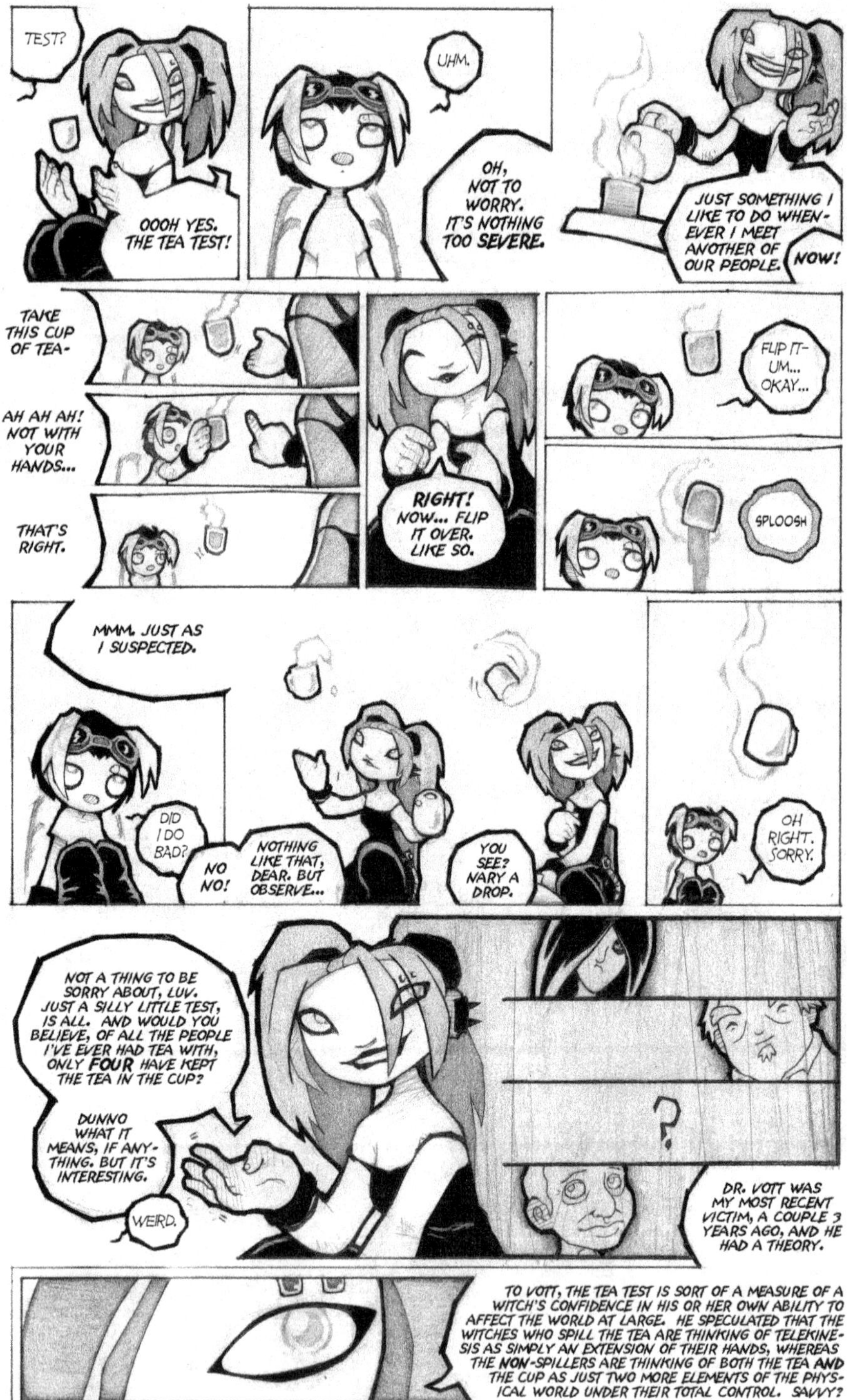

TEST?
OOOH YES. THE TEA TEST!
UHM.
OH, NOT TO WORRY. IT'S NOTHING TOO SEVERE.
JUST SOMETHING I LIKE TO DO WHEN-EVER I MEET ANOTHER OF OUR PEOPLE.
NOW!
TAKE THIS CUP OF TEA-
AH AH AH! NOT WITH YOUR HANDS...
THAT'S RIGHT.
RIGHT! NOW... FLIP IT OVER. LIKE SO.
FLIP IT-
UM... OKAY...
SPLOOSH
MMM. JUST AS I SUSPECTED.
DID I DO BAD?
NO NO!
NOTHING LIKE THAT, DEAR. BUT OBSERVE...
YOU SEE? NARY A DROP.
OH RIGHT. SORRY.
NOT A THING TO BE SORRY ABOUT, LUV. JUST A SILLY LITTLE TEST, IS ALL. AND WOULD YOU BELIEVE, OF ALL THE PEOPLE I'VE EVER HAD TEA WITH, ONLY FOUR HAVE KEPT THE TEA IN THE CUP?
DUNNO WHAT IT MEANS, IF ANY-THING. BUT IT'S INTERESTING.
WEIRD.
?
DR. VOTT WAS MY MOST RECENT VICTIM, A COUPLE 3 YEARS AGO, AND HE HAD A THEORY.
TO VOTT, THE TEA TEST IS SORT OF A MEASURE OF A WITCH'S CONFIDENCE IN HIS OR HER OWN ABILITY TO AFFECT THE WORLD AT LARGE. HE SPECULATED THAT THE WITCHES WHO SPILL THE TEA ARE THINKING OF TELEKINE-SIS AS SIMPLY AN EXTENSION OF THEIR HANDS, WHEREAS THE NON-SPILLERS ARE THINKING OF BOTH THE TEA AND THE CUP AS JUST TWO MORE ELEMENTS OF THE PHYS-ICAL WORLD UNDER THEIR TOTAL CONTROL. SAVVY?

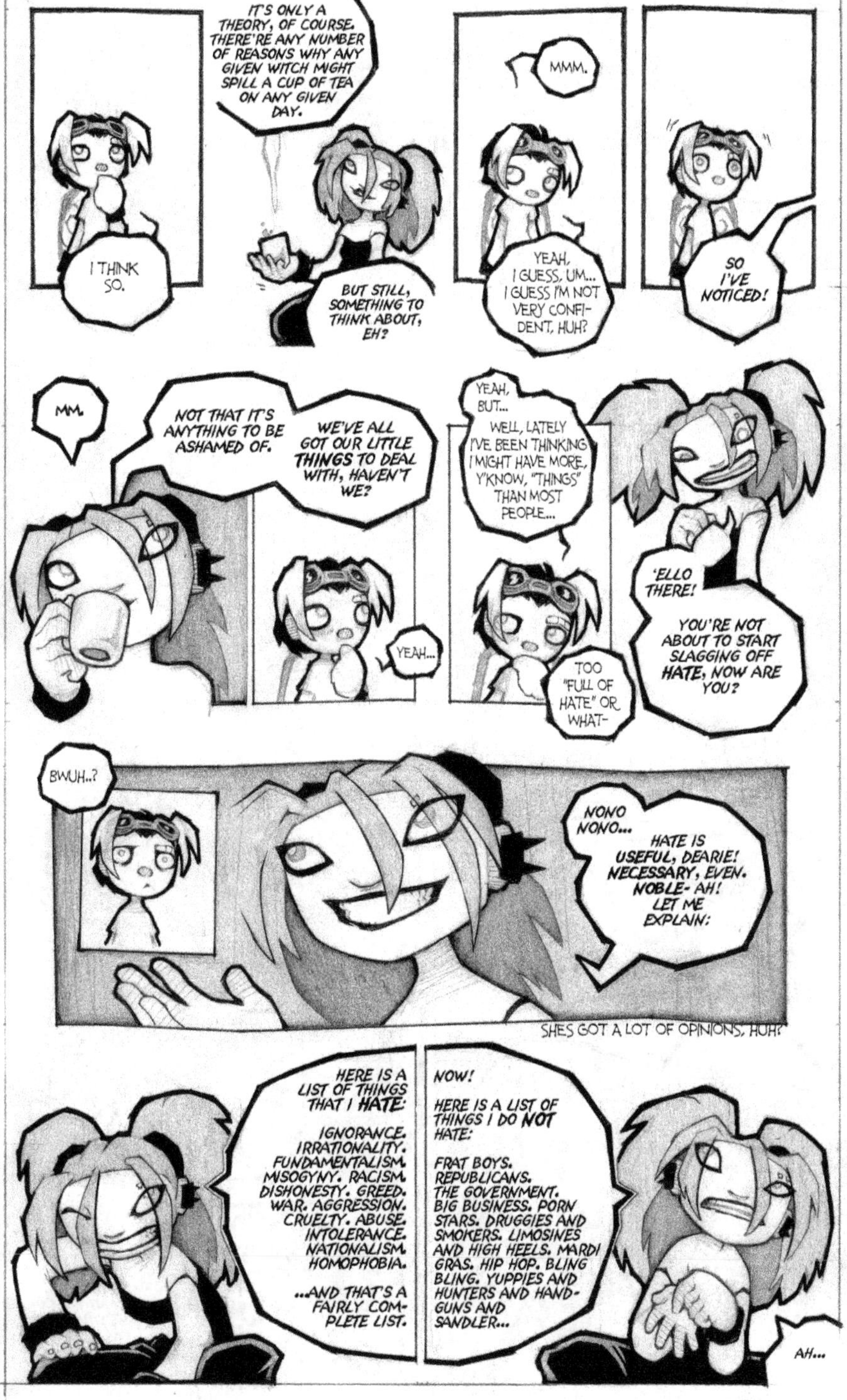
I THINK SO.
IT'S ONLY A THEORY, OF COURSE. THERE'RE ANY NUMBER OF REASONS WHY ANY GIVEN WITCH MIGHT SPILL A CUP OF TEA ON ANY GIVEN DAY.
BUT STILL, SOMETHING TO THINK ABOUT, EH?
MMM.
YEAH, I GUESS, UM... I GUESS I'M NOT VERY CONFI-DENT, HUH?
SO I'VE NOTICED!
MM.
NOT THAT IT'S ANYTHING TO BE ASHAMED OF.
WE'VE ALL GOT OUR LITTLE THINGS TO DEAL WITH, HAVEN'T WE?
YEAH...
YEAH, BUT... WELL, LATELY I'VE BEEN THINKING I MIGHT HAVE MORE, Y'KNOW, "THINGS" THAN MOST PEOPLE...
TOO "FULL OF HATE" OR WHAT-
'ELLO THERE!
YOU'RE NOT ABOUT TO START SLAGGING OFF HATE, NOW ARE YOU?
BWUH..?
NONO NONO... HATE IS USEFUL, DEARIE! NECESSARY, EVEN. NOBLE- AH! LET ME EXPLAIN:
SHES GOT A LOT OF OPINIONS, HUH?
HERE IS A LIST OF THINGS THAT I HATE:
IGNORANCE. IRRATIONALITY. FUNDAMENTALISM. MISOGYNY. RACISM. DISHONESTY. GREED. WAR. AGGRESSION. CRUELTY. ABUSE. INTOLERANCE. NATIONALISM. HOMOPHOBIA.
...AND THAT'S A FAIRLY COM-PLETE LIST.
NOW!
HERE IS A LIST OF THINGS I DO NOT HATE:
FRAT BOYS. REPUBLICANS. THE GOVERNMENT. BIG BUSINESS. PORN STARS. DRUGGIES AND SMOKERS. LIMOSINES AND HIGH HEELS. MARDI GRAS. HIP HOP. BLING BLING. YUPPIES AND HUNTERS AND HAND-GUNS AND SANDLER...
AH...

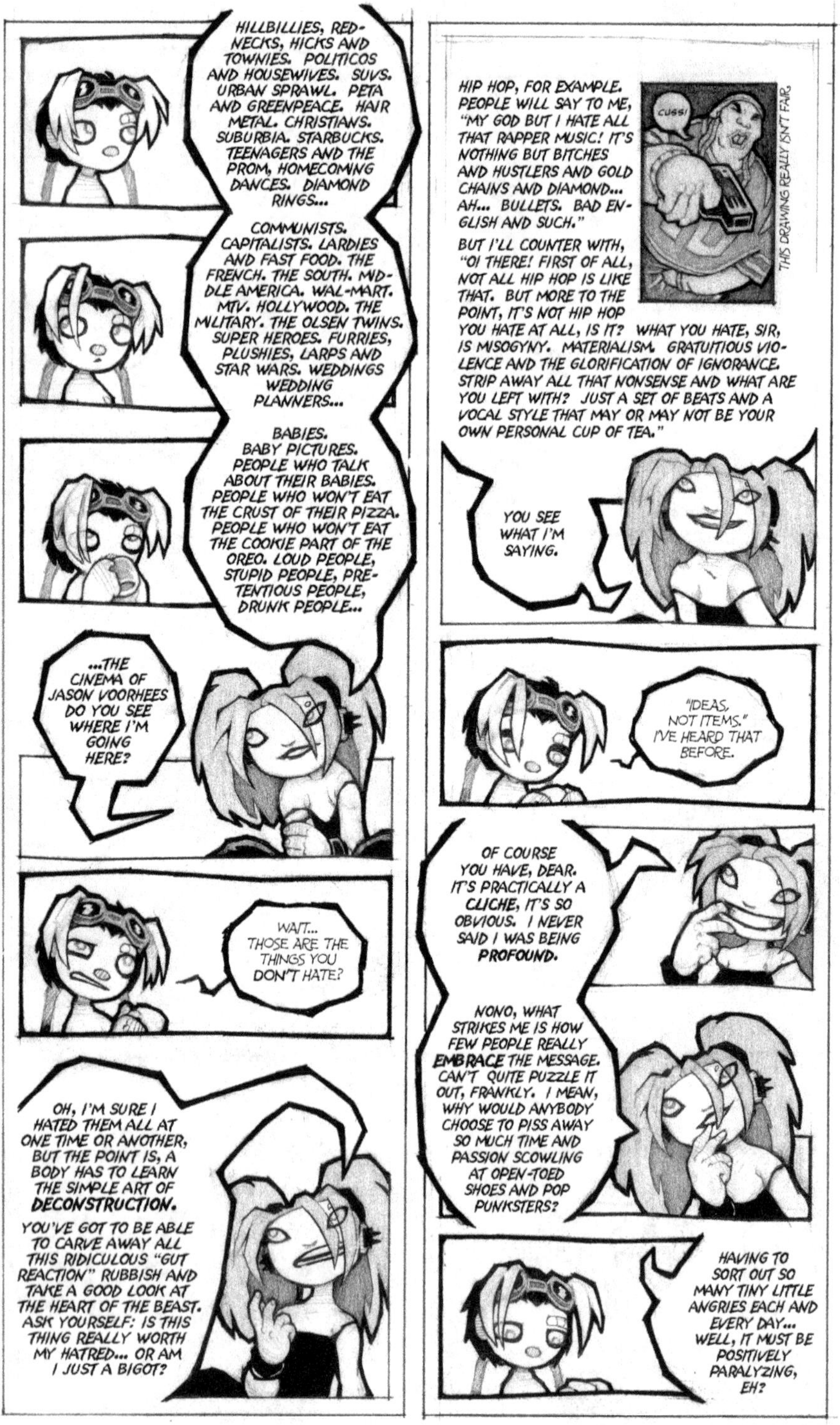
HILLBILLIES, RED-NECKS, HICKS AND TOWNIES. POLITICOS AND HOUSEWIVES. SUVS. URBAN SPRAWL. PETA AND GREENPEACE. HAIR METAL. CHRISTIANS. SUBURBIA. STARBUCKS. TEENAGERS AND THE PROM, HOMECOMING DANCES. DIAMOND RINGS...
COMMUNISTS. CAPITALISTS. LARDIES AND FAST FOOD. THE FRENCH. THE SOUTH. MID-DLE AMERICA. WAL-MART. MTV. HOLLYWOOD. THE MILITARY. THE OLSEN TWINS. SUPER HEROES. FURRIES, PLUSHIES, LARPS AND STAR WARS. WEDDINGS WEDDING PLANNERS...
BABIES. BABY PICTURES. PEOPLE WHO TALK ABOUT THEIR BABIES. PEOPLE WHO WON'T EAT THE CRUST OF THEIR PIZZA. PEOPLE WHO WON'T EAT THE COOKIE PART OF THE OREO. LOUD PEOPLE, STUPID PEOPLE, PRE-TENTIOUS PEOPLE, DRUNK PEOPLE...
...THE CINEMA OF JASON VOORHEES DO YOU SEE WHERE I'M GOING HERE?
WAIT... THOSE ARE THE THINGS YOU DON'T HATE?
OH, I'M SURE I HATED THEM ALL AT ONE TIME OR ANOTHER, BUT THE POINT IS, A BODY HAS TO LEARN THE SIMPLE ART OF DECONSTRUCTION.
YOU'VE GOT TO BE ABLE TO CARVE AWAY ALL THIS RIDICULOUS "GUT REACTION" RUBBISH AND TAKE A GOOD LOOK AT THE HEART OF THE BEAST. ASK YOURSELF: IS THIS THING REALLY WORTH MY HATRED... OR AM I JUST A BIGOT?
HIP HOP, FOR EXAMPLE. PEOPLE WILL SAY TO ME, "MY GOD BUT I HATE ALL THAT RAPPER MUSIC! IT'S NOTHING BUT BITCHES AND HUSTLERS AND GOLD CHAINS AND DIAMOND... AH... BULLETS. BAD EN-GLISH AND SUCH."
CUSS!
THIS DRAWING REALLY ISN'T FAIR.
BUT I'LL COUNTER WITH, "OI THERE! FIRST OF ALL, NOT ALL HIP HOP IS LIKE THAT. BUT MORE TO THE POINT, IT'S NOT HIP HOP YOU HATE AT ALL, IS IT? WHAT YOU HATE, SIR, IS MISOGYNY. MATERIALISM. GRATUITOUS VIO-LENCE AND THE GLORIFICATION OF IGNORANCE. STRIP AWAY ALL THAT NONSENSE AND WHAT ARE YOU LEFT WITH? JUST A SET OF BEATS AND A VOCAL STYLE THAT MAY OR MAY NOT BE YOUR OWN PERSONAL CUP OF TEA."
YOU SEE WHAT I'M SAYING.
"IDEAS, NOT ITEMS." I'VE HEARD THAT BEFORE.
OF COURSE YOU HAVE, DEAR. IT'S PRACTICALLY A CLICHE, IT'S SO OBVIOUS. I NEVER SAID I WAS BEING PROFOUND.
NONO, WHAT STRIKES ME IS HOW FEW PEOPLE REALLY EMBRACE THE MESSAGE. CAN'T QUITE PUZZLE IT OUT, FRANKLY. I MEAN, WHY WOULD ANYBODY CHOOSE TO PISS AWAY SO MUCH TIME AND PASSION SCOWLING AT OPEN-TOED SHOES AND POP PUNKSTERS?
HAVING TO SORT OUT SO MANY TINY LITTLE ANGRIES EACH AND EVERY DAY... WELL, IT MUST BE POSITIVELY PARALYZING, EH?

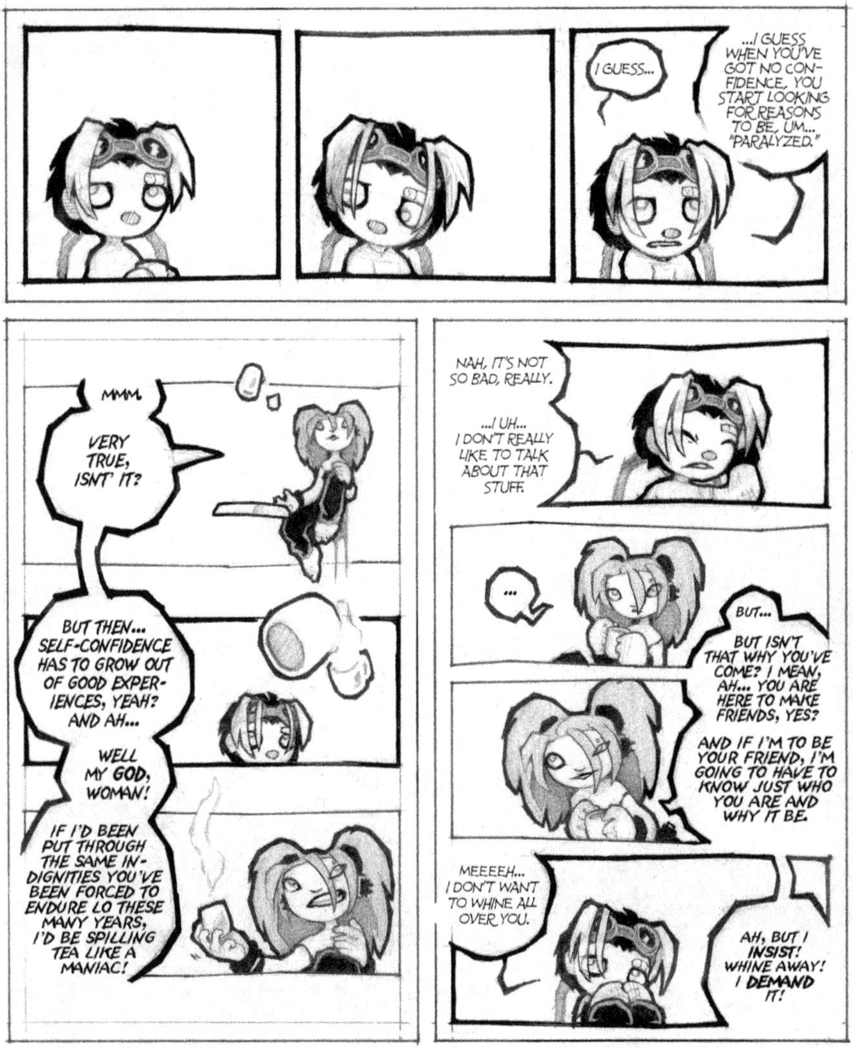
I GUESS...
...I GUESS WHEN YOU'VE GOT NO CON-FIDENCE, YOU START LOOKING FOR REASONS TO BE, UM... "PARALYZED."
MMM.
VERY TRUE, ISNT' IT?
BUT THEN... SELF-CONFIDENCE HAS TO GROW OUT OF GOOD EXPER-IENCES, YEAH? AND AH...
WELL MY GOD, WOMAN!
IF I'D BEEN PUT THROUGH THE SAME IN-DIGNITIES YOU'VE BEEN FORCED TO ENDURE LO THESE MANY YEARS, I'D BE SPILLING TEA LIKE A MANIAC!
NAH, IT'S NOT SO BAD, REALLY.
...I UH... I DON'T REALLY LIKE TO TALK ABOUT THAT STUFF.
...
BUT...
BUT ISN'T THAT WHY YOU'VE COME? I MEAN, AH... YOU ARE HERE TO MAKE FRIENDS, YES?
AND IF I'M TO BE YOUR FRIEND, I'M GOING TO HAVE TO KNOW JUST WHO YOU ARE AND WHY IT BE.
MEEEEEH... I DON'T WANT TO WHINE ALL OVER YOU.
AH, BUT I INSIST! WHINE AWAY! I DEMAND IT!

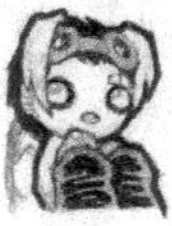

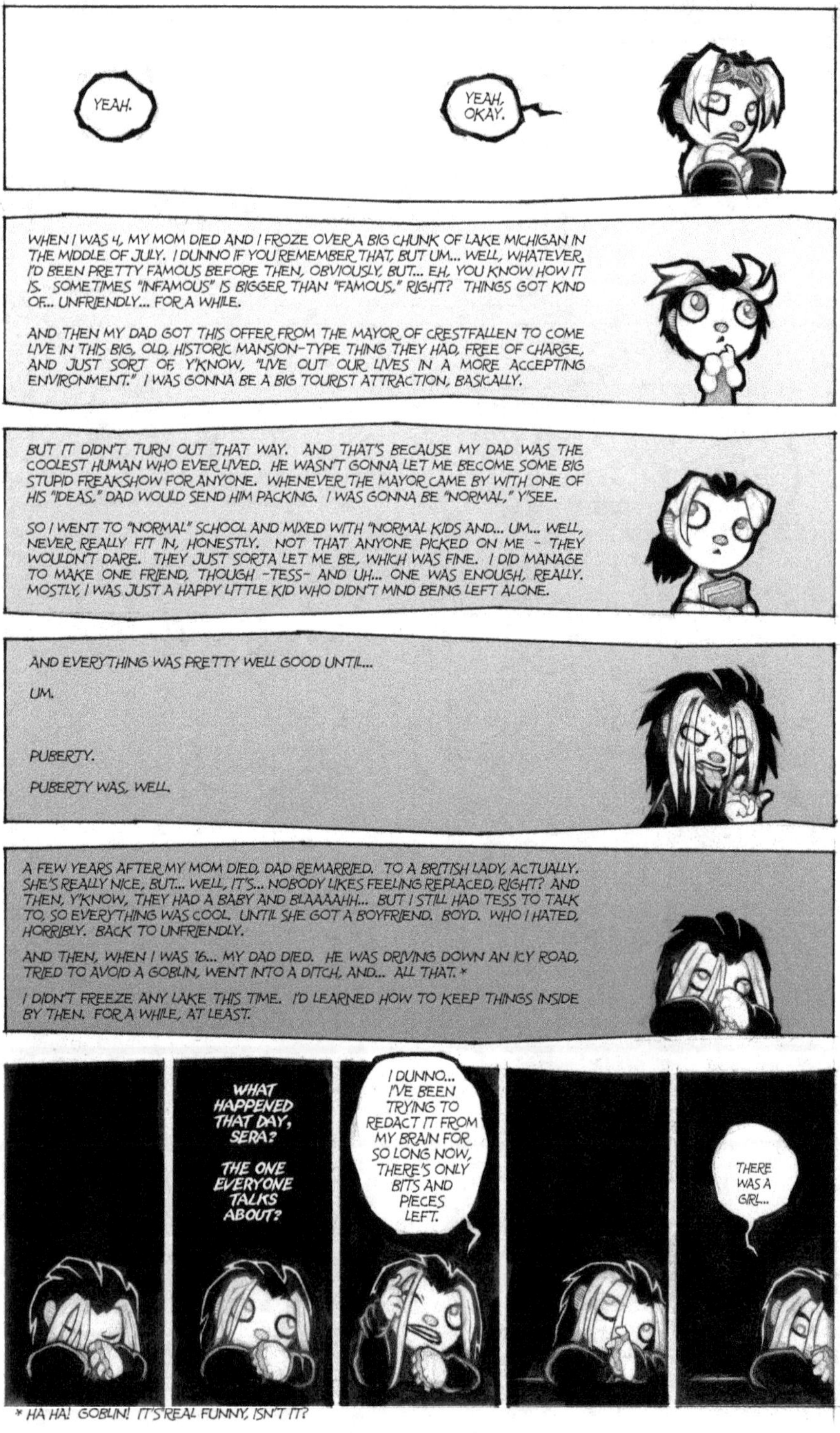
YEAH.
YEAH, OKAY.
WHEN I WAS 4, MY MOM DIED AND I FROZE OVER A BIG CHUNK OF LAKE MICHIGAN IN THE MIDDLE OF JULY. I DUNNO IF YOU REMEMBER THAT, BUT UM... WELL, WHATEVER. I'D BEEN PRETTY FAMOUS BEFORE THEN, OBVIOUSLY, BUT... EH, YOU KNOW HOW IT IS. SOMETIMES "INFAMOUS" IS BIGGER THAN "FAMOUS," RIGHT? THINGS GOT KIND OF... UNFRIENDLY... FOR A WHILE.
AND THEN MY DAD GOT THIS OFFER FROM THE MAYOR OF CRESTFALLEN TO COME LIVE IN THIS BIG, OLD, HISTORIC MANSION-TYPE THING THEY HAD, FREE OF CHARGE, AND JUST SORT OF, Y'KNOW, "LIVE OUT OUR LIVES IN A MORE ACCEPTING ENVIRONMENT." I WAS GONNA BE A BIG TOURIST ATTRACTION, BASICALLY.
BUT IT DIDN'T TURN OUT THAT WAY. AND THAT'S BECAUSE MY DAD WAS THE COOLEST HUMAN WHO EVER LIVED. HE WASN'T GONNA LET ME BECOME SOME BIG STUPID FREAKSHOW FOR ANYONE. WHENEVER THE MAYOR CAME BY WITH ONE OF HIS "IDEAS," DAD WOULD SEND HIM PACKING. I WAS GONNA BE "NORMAL," Y'SEE.
SO I WENT TO "NORMAL" SCHOOL AND MIXED WITH "NORMAL KIDS AND... UM... WELL, NEVER REALLY FIT IN, HONESTLY. NOT THAT ANYONE PICKED ON ME - THEY WOULDN'T DARE. THEY JUST SORTA LET ME BE, WHICH WAS FINE. I DID MANAGE TO MAKE ONE FRIEND, THOUGH -TESS- AND UH... ONE WAS ENOUGH, REALLY. MOSTLY, I WAS JUST A HAPPY LITTLE KID WHO DIDN'T MIND BEING LEFT ALONE.
AND EVERYTHING WAS PRETTY WELL GOOD UNTIL...
UM.
PUBERTY.
PUBERTY WAS, WELL.
A FEW YEARS AFTER MY MOM DIED, DAD REMARRIED. TO A BRITISH LADY, ACTUALLY. SHE'S REALLY NICE, BUT... WELL, IT'S... NOBODY LIKES FEELING REPLACED, RIGHT? AND THEN, Y'KNOW, THEY HAD A BABY AND BLAAAAHH... BUT I STILL HAD TESS TO TALK TO, SO EVERYTHING WAS COOL. UNTIL SHE GOT A BOYFRIEND. BOYD. WHO I HATED, HORRIBLY. BACK TO UNFRIENDLY.
AND THEN, WHEN I WAS 16... MY DAD DIED. HE WAS DRIVING DOWN AN ICY ROAD, TRIED TO AVOID A GOBLIN, WENT INTO A DITCH, AND... ALL THAT. *
I DIDN'T FREEZE ANY LAKE THIS TIME. I'D LEARNED HOW TO KEEP THINGS INSIDE BY THEN. FOR A WHILE, AT LEAST.
WHAT HAPPENED THAT DAY, SERA?
THE ONE EVERYONE TALKS ABOUT?
I DUNNO... I'VE BEEN TRYING TO REDACT IT FROM MY BRAIN FOR SO LONG NOW, THERE'S ONLY BITS AND PIECES LEFT.
THERE WAS A GIRL...

* HA HA! GOBLIN! IT'S REAL FUNNY, ISN'T IT?

BUS STOP
laughter
PUNK BEER
have a beer.
Maddy.

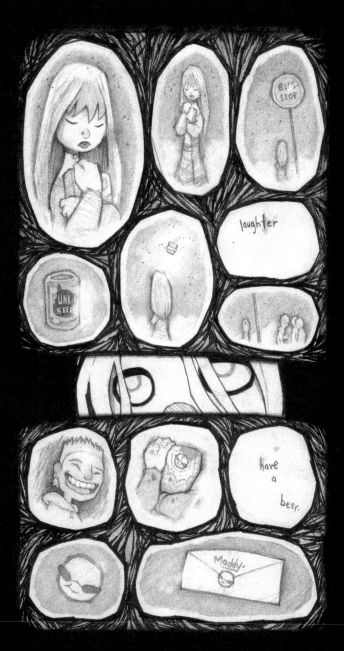

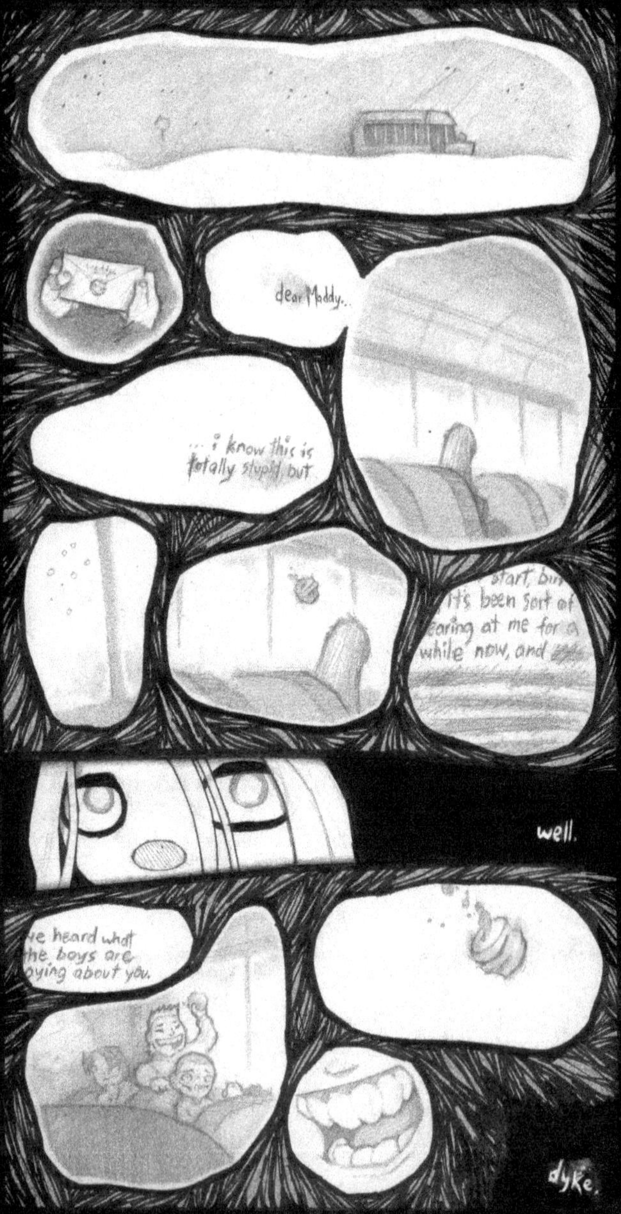
dear Maddy...
... i know this is totally stupid but
start, but
it's been sort of
earing at me for a
while now, and
well.
e heard what
the boys are
ying about you.
dyke.

lame.
but.. don't think you're
it hurts
please don't hate me.
"YOU
NEVER
DO
ANYTHING."
SCENE
MISSING

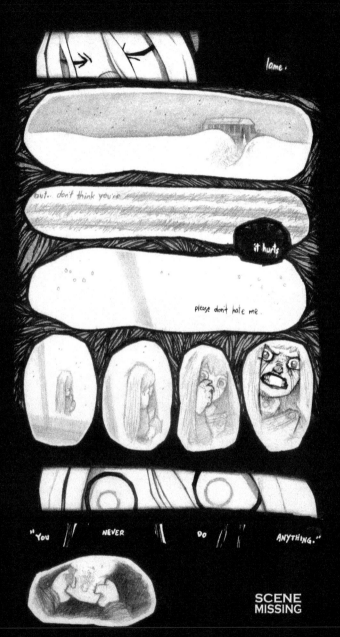

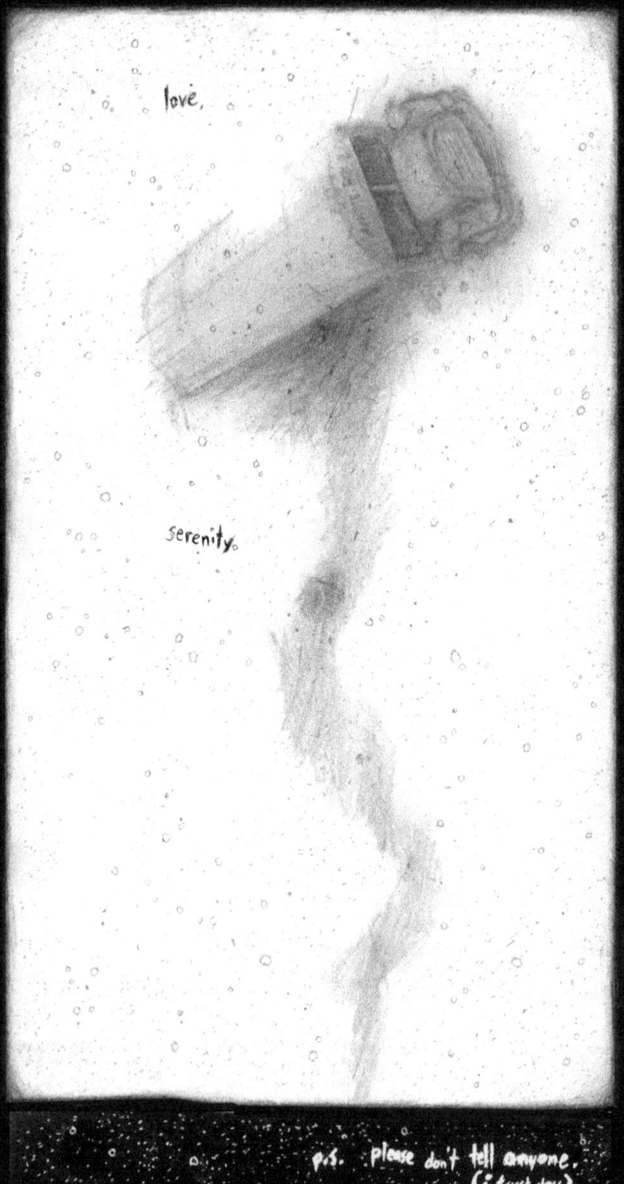
love,
serenity.
p.s. please don't tell anyone.
(i trust you)

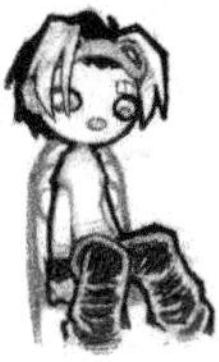

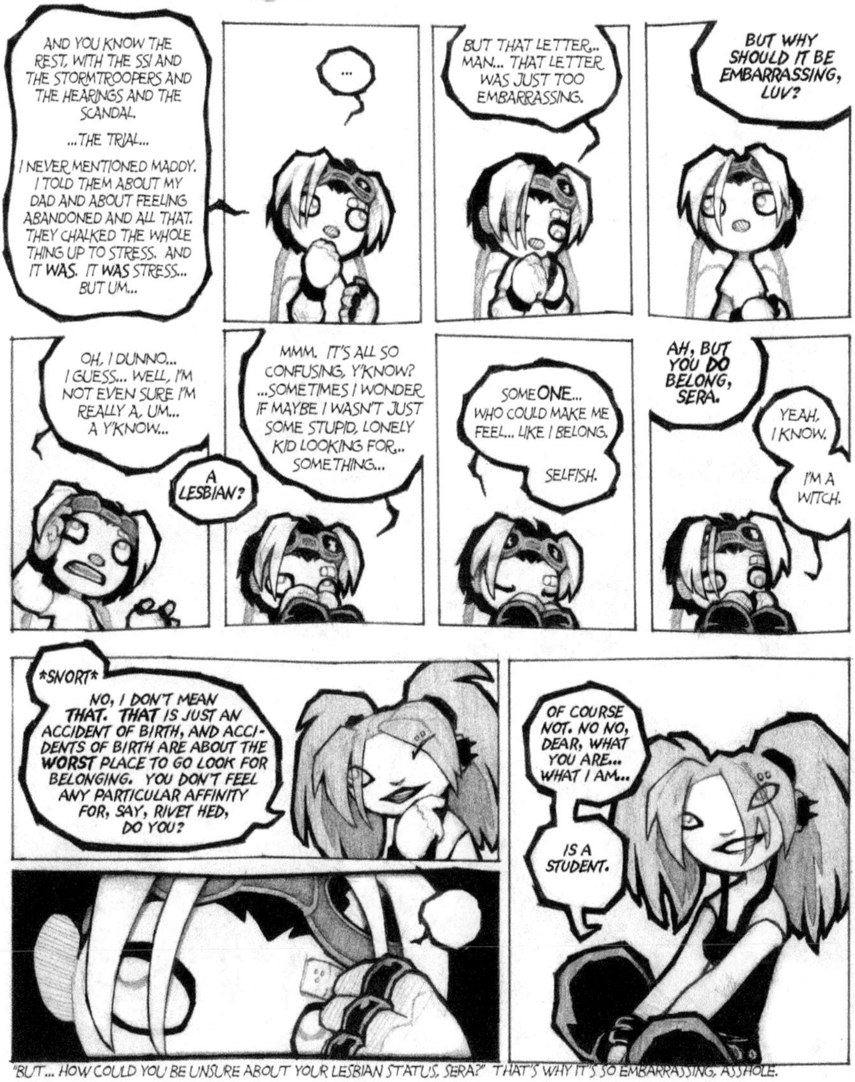

AND YOU KNOW THE REST, WITH THE SSI AND THE STORMTROOPERS AND THE HEARINGS AND THE SCANDAL.
...THE TRIAL...
I NEVER MENTIONED MADDY. I TOLD THEM ABOUT MY DAD AND ABOUT FEELING ABANDONED AND ALL THAT. THEY CHALKED THE WHOLE THING UP TO STRESS. AND IT WAS. IT WAS STRESS... BUT UM...
...
BUT THAT LETTER... MAN... THAT LETTER WAS JUST TOO EMBARRASSING.
BUT WHY SHOULD IT BE EMBARRASSING, LUV?
OH, I DUNNO... I GUESS... WELL, I'M NOT EVEN SURE I'M REALLY A, UM... A Y'KNOW...
A LESBIAN?
MMM. IT'S ALL SO CONFUSING, Y'KNOW? ...SOMETIMES I WONDER IF MAYBE I WASN'T JUST SOME STUPID, LONELY KID LOOKING FOR... SOMETHING...
SOMEONE... WHO COULD MAKE ME FEEL... LIKE I BELONG.
SELFISH.
AH, BUT YOU DO BELONG, SERA.
YEAH, I KNOW.
I'M A WITCH.
SNORT
NO, I DON'T MEAN THAT. THAT IS JUST AN ACCIDENT OF BIRTH, AND ACCIDENTS OF BIRTH ARE ABOUT THE WORST PLACE TO GO LOOK FOR BELONGING. YOU DON'T FEEL ANY PARTICULAR AFFINITY FOR, SAY, RIVET HED, DO YOU?
OF COURSE NOT. NO NO, DEAR, WHAT YOU ARE... WHAT I AM...
IS A STUDENT.

"BUT... HOW COULD YOU BE UNSURE ABOUT YOUR LESBIAN STATUS, SERA?" THAT'S WHY IT'S SO EMBARRASSING, ASSHOLE.

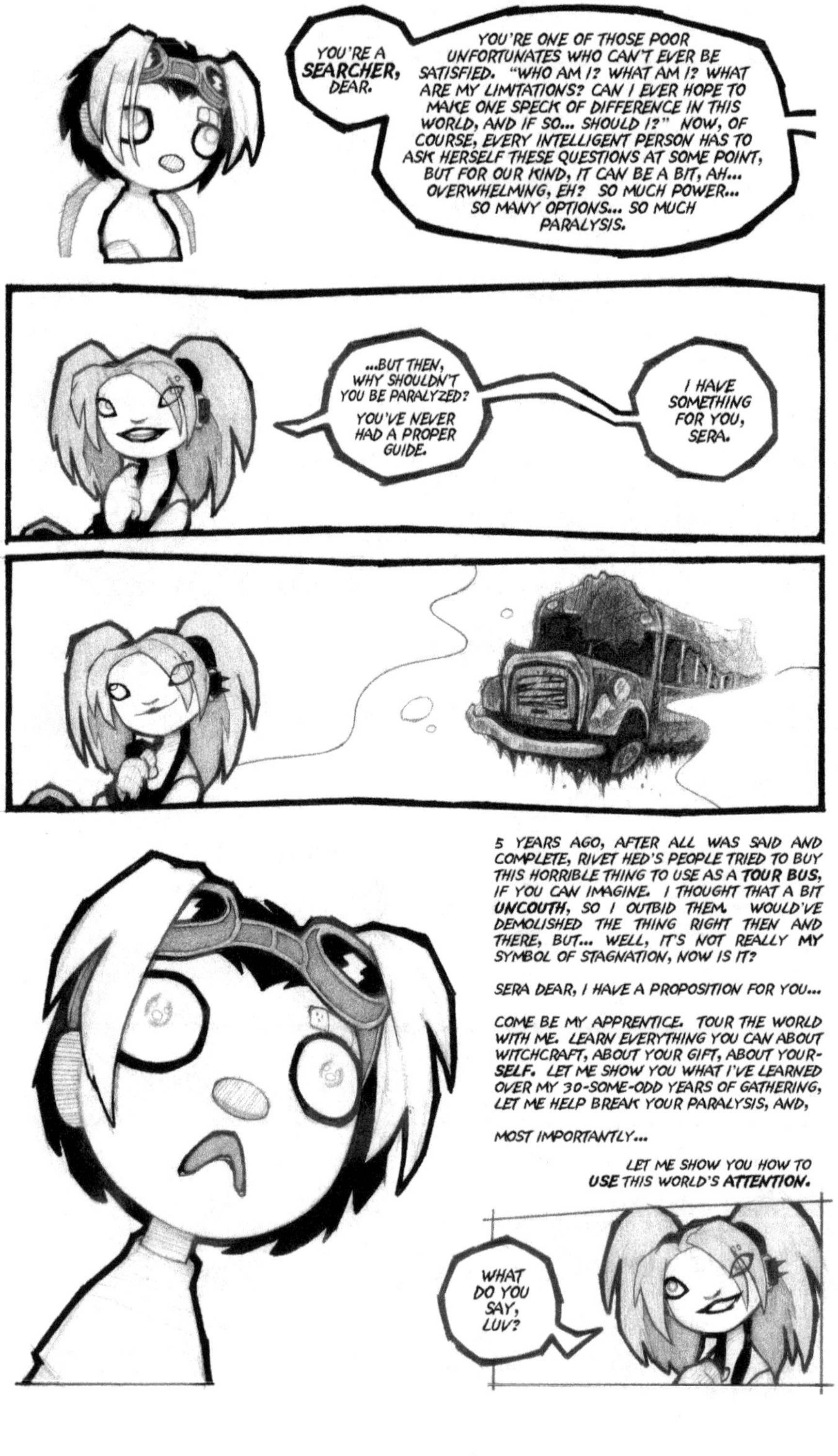
YOU'RE A SEARCHER, DEAR.
YOU'RE ONE OF THOSE POOR UNFORTUNATES WHO CAN'T EVER BE SATISFIED. "WHO AM I? WHAT AM I? WHAT ARE MY LIMITATIONS? CAN I EVER HOPE TO MAKE ONE SPECK OF DIFFERENCE IN THIS WORLD, AND IF SO... SHOULD I?" NOW, OF COURSE, EVERY INTELLIGENT PERSON HAS TO ASK HERSELF THESE QUESTIONS AT SOME POINT, BUT FOR OUR KIND, IT CAN BE A BIT, AH... OVERWHELMING, EH? SO MUCH POWER... SO MANY OPTIONS... SO MUCH PARALYSIS.
...BUT THEN, WHY SHOULDN'T YOU BE PARALYZED? YOU'VE NEVER HAD A PROPER GUIDE.
I HAVE SOMETHING FOR YOU, SERA.
5 YEARS AGO, AFTER ALL WAS SAID AND COMPLETE, RIVET HED'S PEOPLE TRIED TO BUY THIS HORRIBLE THING TO USE AS A TOUR BUS, IF YOU CAN IMAGINE. I THOUGHT THAT A BIT UNCOUTH, SO I OUTBID THEM. WOULD'VE DEMOLISHED THE THING RIGHT THEN AND THERE, BUT... WELL, IT'S NOT REALLY MY SYMBOL OF STAGNATION, NOW IS IT?
SERA DEAR, I HAVE A PROPOSITION FOR YOU...
COME BE MY APPRENTICE. TOUR THE WORLD WITH ME. LEARN EVERYTHING YOU CAN ABOUT WITCHCRAFT, ABOUT YOUR GIFT, ABOUT YOURSELF. LET ME SHOW YOU WHAT I'VE LEARNED OVER MY 30-SOME-ODD YEARS OF GATHERING, LET ME HELP BREAK YOUR PARALYSIS, AND,
MOST IMPORTANTLY...
LET ME SHOW YOU HOW TO USE THIS WORLD'S ATTENTION.
WHAT DO YOU SAY, LUV?

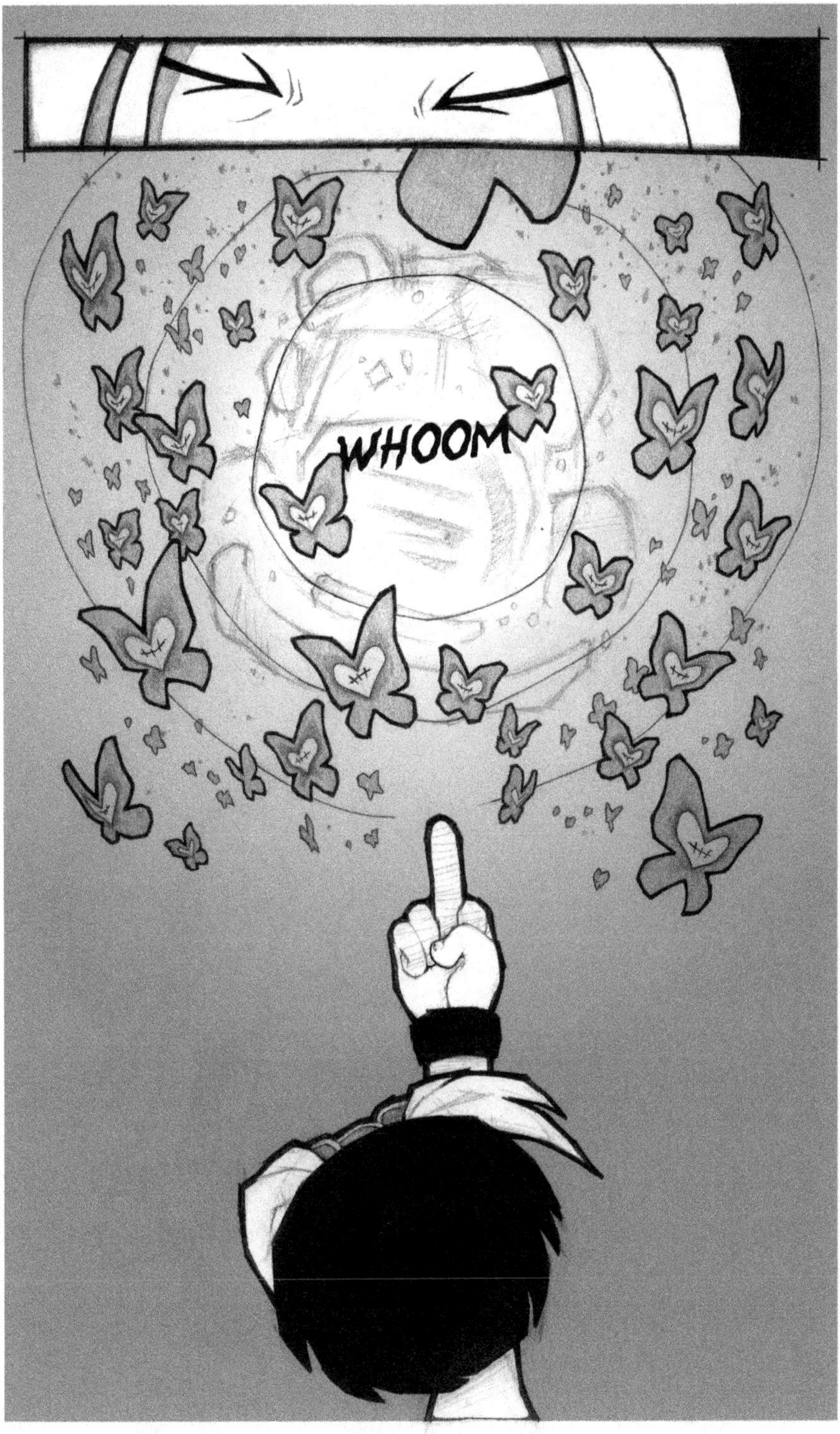
WHOOM

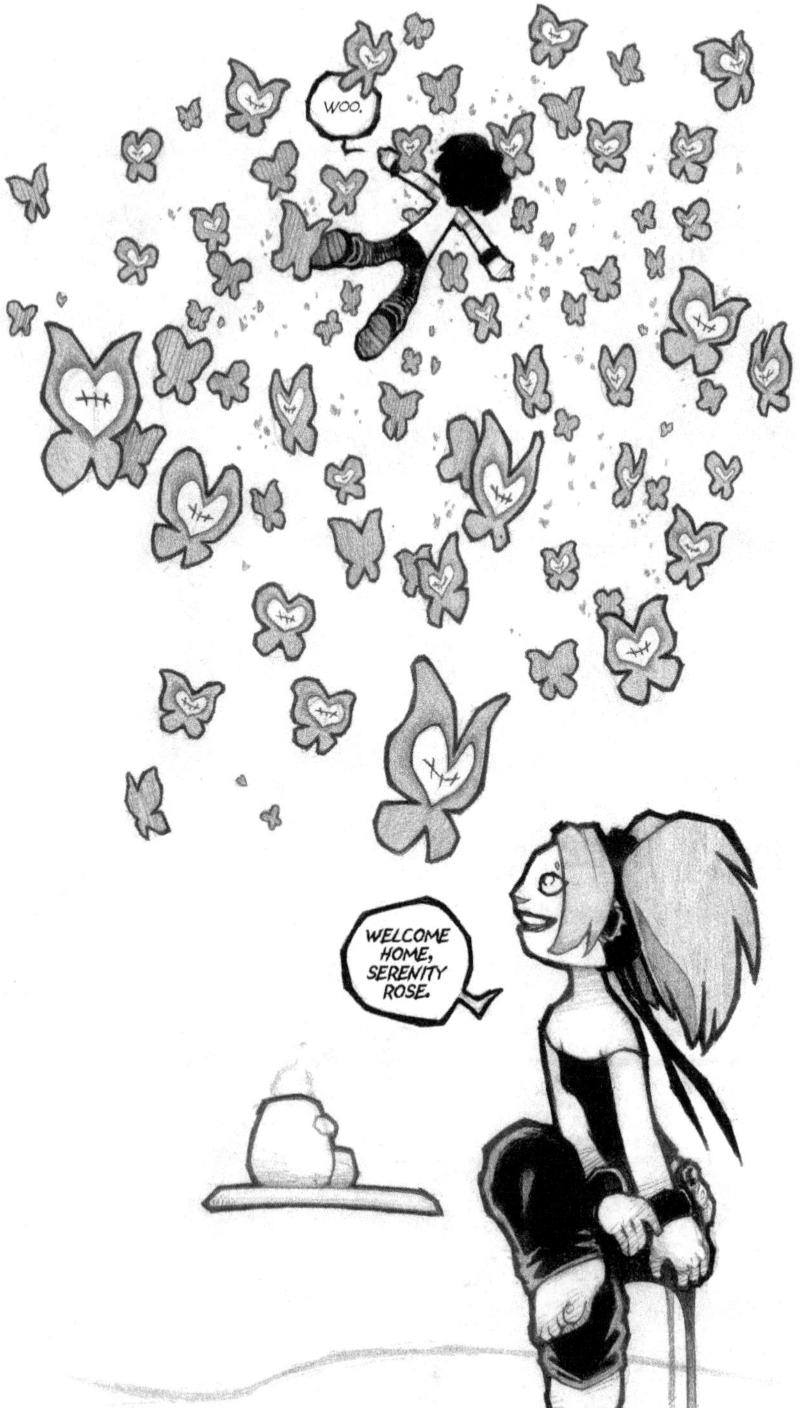
WOO.
WELCOME HOME, SERENITY ROSE.

"FREE COMIC DAY"
THINGEE, 2004

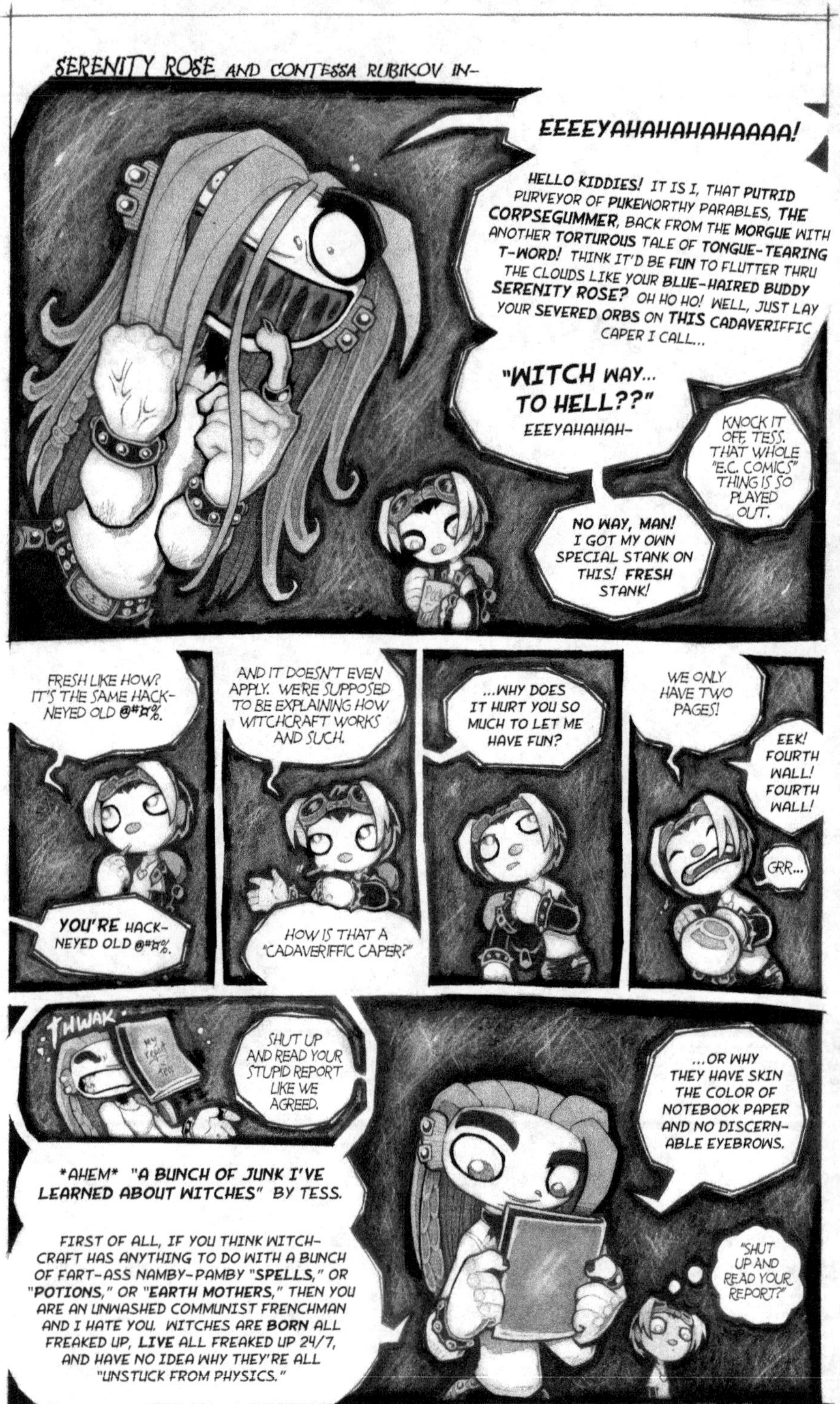
SERENITY ROSE AND CONTESSA RUBIKOV IN-
EEEEYAHAHAHAHAHAAAA!
HELLO KIDDIES! IT IS I, THAT PUTRID PURVEYOR OF PUKEWORTHY PARABLES, THE CORPSEGUMMER, BACK FROM THE MORGUE WITH ANOTHER TORTUROUS TALE OF TONGUE-TEARING T-WORD! THINK IT'D BE FUN TO FLUTTER THRU THE CLOUDS LIKE YOUR BLUE-HAIRED BUDDY SERENITY ROSE? OH HO HO! WELL, JUST LAY YOUR SEVERED ORBS ON THIS CADAVERIFFIC CAPER I CALL...
"WITCH WAY... TO HELL??" EEEYAHAHAH-
KNOCK IT OFF, TESS. THAT WHOLE "E.C. COMICS" THING IS SO PLAYED OUT.
NO WAY, MAN! I GOT MY OWN SPECIAL STANK ON THIS! FRESH STANK!
FRESH LIKE HOW? IT'S THE SAME HACK-NEYED OLD @#¤%.
YOU'RE HACK-NEYED OLD @#¤%.
AND IT DOESN'T EVEN APPLY. WE'RE SUPPOSED TO BE EXPLAINING HOW WITCHCRAFT WORKS AND SUCH.
HOW IS THAT A "CADAVERIFFIC CAPER?"
...WHY DOES IT HURT YOU SO MUCH TO LET ME HAVE FUN?
WE ONLY HAVE TWO PAGES!
EEK! FOURTH WALL! FOURTH WALL!
GRR...
THWAK
SHUT UP AND READ YOUR STUPID REPORT LIKE WE AGREED.
AHEM "A BUNCH OF JUNK I'VE LEARNED ABOUT WITCHES" BY TESS.
FIRST OF ALL, IF YOU THINK WITCH-CRAFT HAS ANYTHING TO DO WITH A BUNCH OF FART-ASS NAMBY-PAMBY "SPELLS," OR "POTIONS," OR "EARTH MOTHERS," THEN YOU ARE AN UNWASHED COMMUNIST FRENCHMAN AND I HATE YOU. WITCHES ARE BORN ALL FREAKED UP, LIVE ALL FREAKED UP 24/7, AND HAVE NO IDEA WHY THEY'RE ALL "UNSTUCK FROM PHYSICS."
...OR WHY THEY HAVE SKIN THE COLOR OF NOTEBOOK PAPER AND NO DISCERN-ABLE EYEBROWS.
"SHUT UP AND READ YOUR REPORT?"
REMEMBER, KIDS: IF YOU ADMIT SOMETHING IS HACKNEYED, THEN YOU'RE FREE TO HAVE FUN!

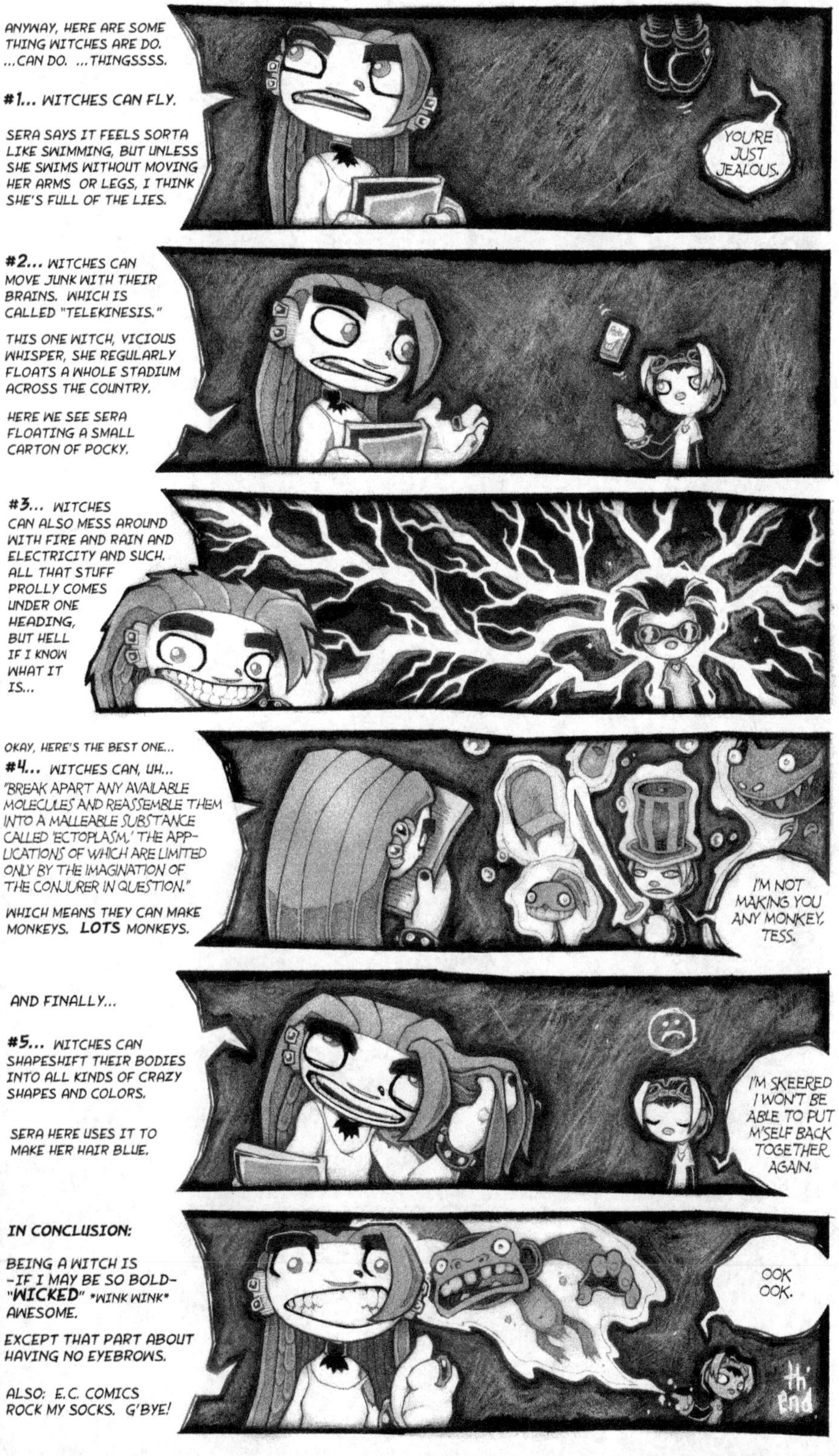
ANYWAY, HERE ARE SOME THING WITCHES ARE DO. ...CAN DO. ...THINGSSSS.
#1... WITCHES CAN FLY.
SERA SAYS IT FEELS SORTA LIKE SWIMMING, BUT UNLESS SHE SWIMS WITHOUT MOVING HER ARMS OR LEGS, I THINK SHE'S FULL OF THE LIES.
YOU'RE JUST JEALOUS.
#2... WITCHES CAN MOVE JUNK WITH THEIR BRAINS. WHICH IS CALLED "TELEKINESIS."
THIS ONE WITCH, VICIOUS WHISPER, SHE REGULARLY FLOATS A WHOLE STADIUM ACROSS THE COUNTRY.
HERE WE SEE SERA FLOATING A SMALL CARTON OF POCKY.
#3... WITCHES CAN ALSO MESS AROUND WITH FIRE AND RAIN AND ELECTRICITY AND SUCH. ALL THAT STUFF PROLLY COMES UNDER ONE HEADING, BUT HELL IF I KNOW WHAT IT IS...
OKAY, HERE'S THE BEST ONE...
#4... WITCHES CAN, UH... "BREAK APART ANY AVAILABLE MOLECULES AND REASSEMBLE THEM INTO A MALLEABLE SUBSTANCE CALLED 'ECTOPLASM,' THE APPLICATIONS OF WHICH ARE LIMITED ONLY BY THE IMAGINATION OF THE CONJURER IN QUESTION."
WHICH MEANS THEY CAN MAKE MONKEYS. LOTS MONKEYS.
I'M NOT MAKING YOU ANY MONKEY, TESS.
AND FINALLY...
#5... WITCHES CAN SHAPESHIFT THEIR BODIES INTO ALL KINDS OF CRAZY SHAPES AND COLORS.
SERA HERE USES IT TO MAKE HER HAIR BLUE.
I'M SKEERED I WON'T BE ABLE TO PUT M'SELF BACK TOGETHER AGAIN.
IN CONCLUSION:
BEING A WITCH IS -IF I MAY BE SO BOLD- "WICKED" *WINK WINK* AWESOME.
EXCEPT THAT PART ABOUT HAVING NO EYEBROWS.
ALSO: E.C. COMICS ROCK MY SOCKS. G'BYE!
OOK OOK.
th' End

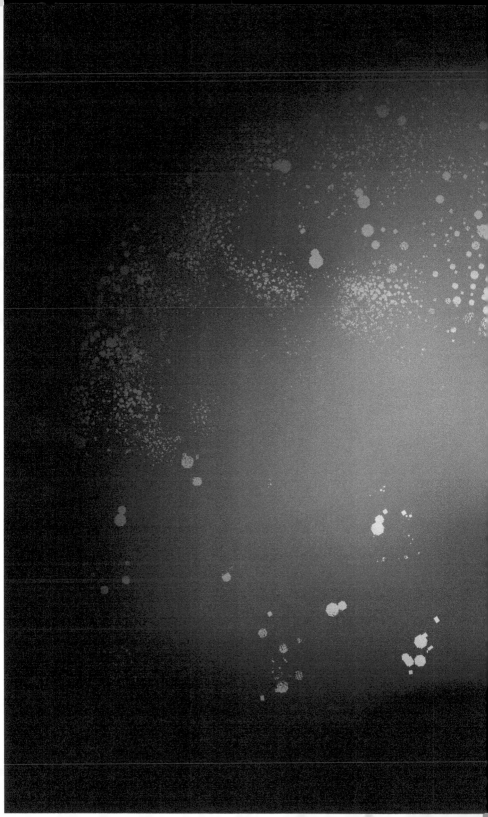

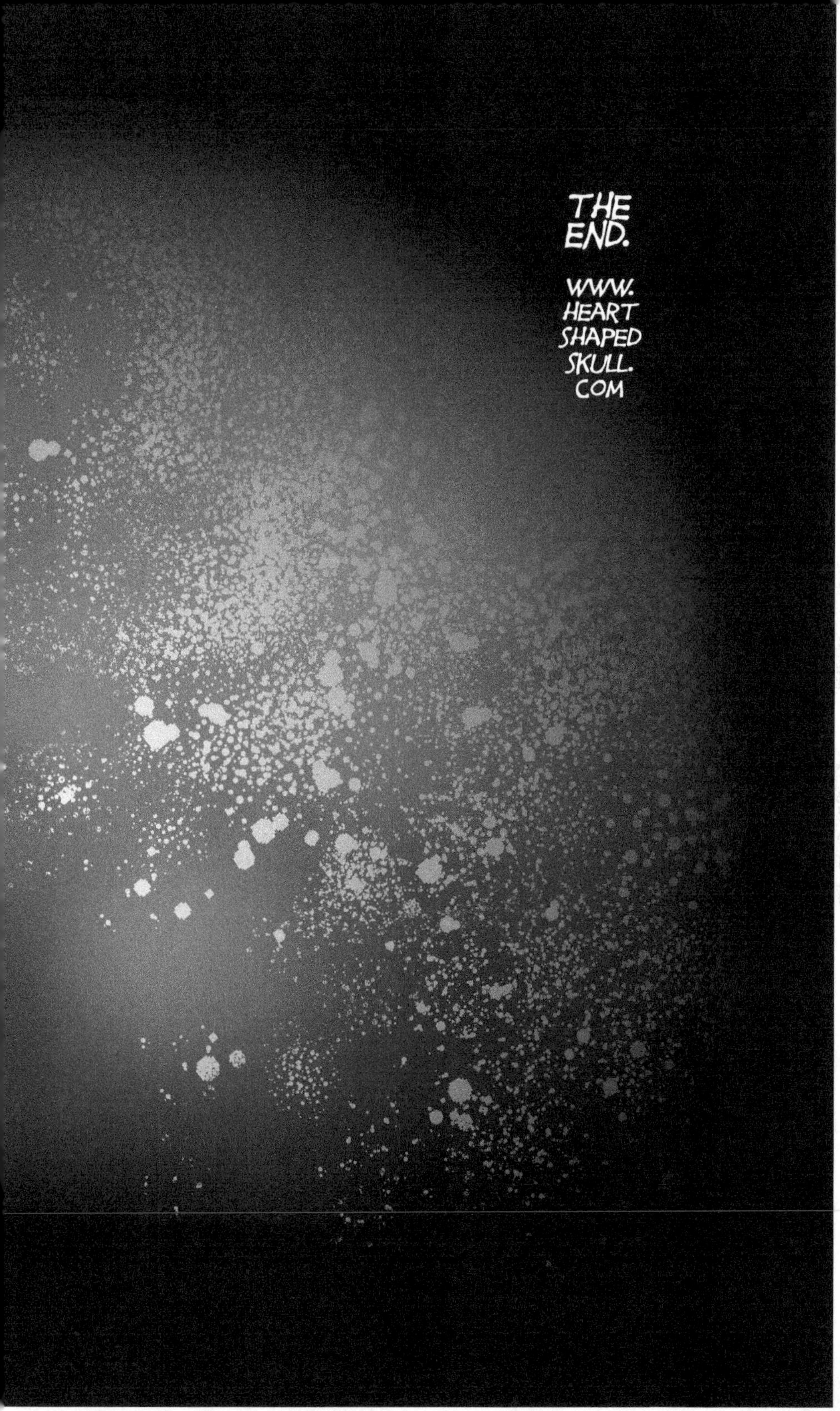
THE END.
WWW.HEARTSHAPEDSKULL.COM

GUEST ART BY FSC

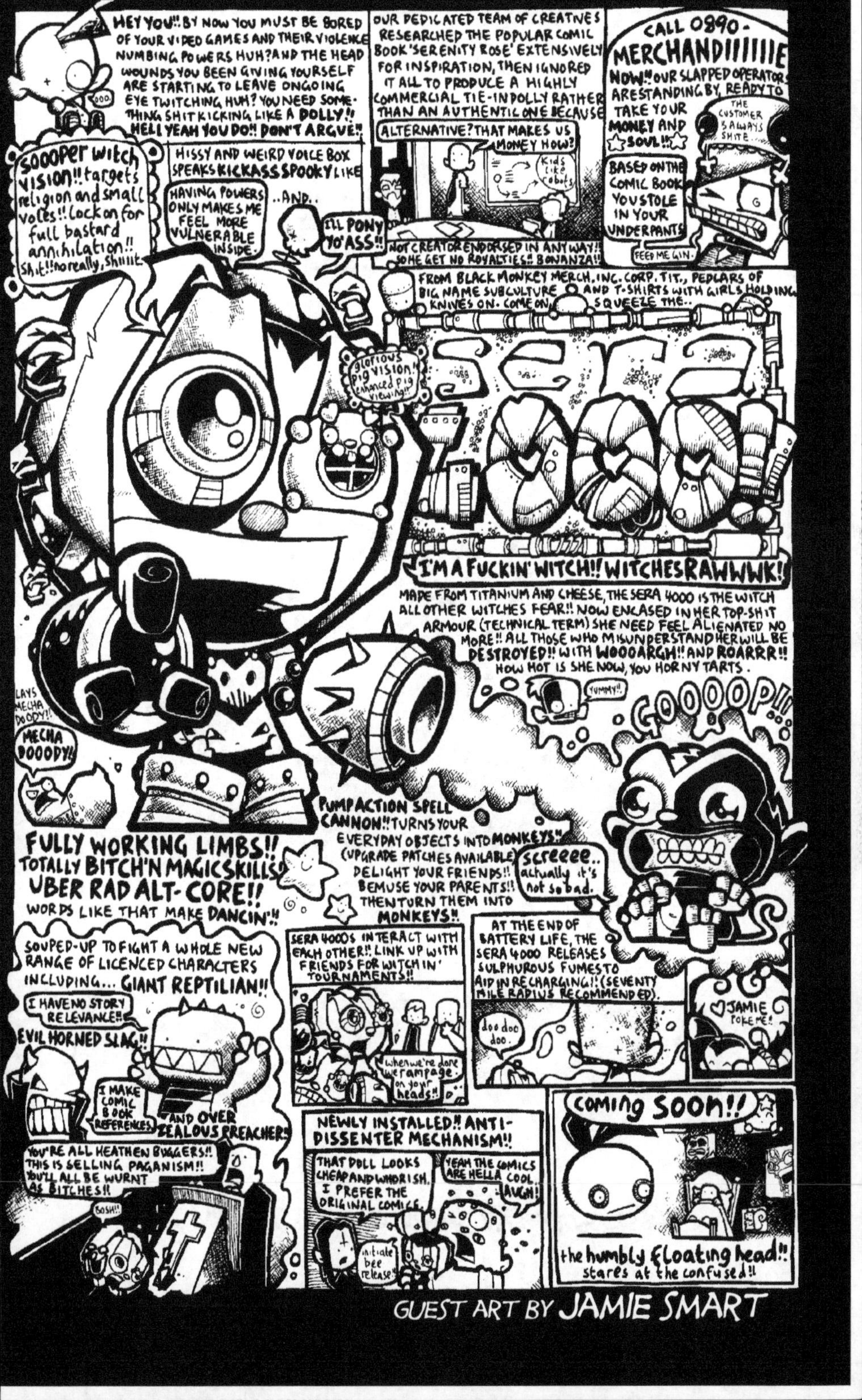
HEY YOU!! BY NOW YOU MUST BE BORED OF YOUR VIDEO GAMES AND THEIR VIOLENCE NUMBING POWERS HUH? AND THE HEAD WOUNDS YOU BEEN GIVING YOURSELF ARE STARTING TO LEAVE ONGOING EYE TWITCHING HUH? YOU NEED SOMETHING SHITKICKING LIKE A DOLLY!! HELL YEAH YOU DO!! DON'T ARGUE!!
OOO.
OUR DEDICATED TEAM OF CREATIVES RESEARCHED THE POPULAR COMIC BOOK 'SERENITY ROSE' EXTENSIVELY FOR INSPIRATION, THEN IGNORED IT ALL TO PRODUCE A HIGHLY COMMERCIAL TIE-IN DOLLY RATHER THAN AN AUTHENTIC ONE BECAUSE
ALTERNATIVE? THAT MAKES US MONEY HOW?
Kids like robots
NOT CREATOR ENDORSED IN ANY WAY!! SOME GET NO ROYALTIES!! BONANZA!!
CALL 0890-MERCHANDIIIIIIE NOW!! OUR SLAPPED OPERATORS ARE STANDING BY, READY TO TAKE YOUR MONEY AND SOUL!!
THE CUSTOMER IS ALWAYS SHITE
BASED ON THE COMIC BOOK YOU STOLE IN YOUR UNDERPANTS
FEED ME GIN.
sooooper witch vision!! targets religion and small voles!! Lock on for full bastard annihilation!! Shit!! no really, Shiiiit.
HISSY AND WEIRD VOICE BOX SPEAKS KICKASS SPOOKY LIKE
HAVING POWERS ONLY MAKES ME FEEL MORE VULNERABLE INSIDE.
..AND..
I'LL PONY YO'ASS!!
FROM BLACK MONKEY MERCH. INC. CORP. TIT., PEDLARS OF BIG NAME SUBCULTURE AND T-SHIRTS WITH GIRLS HOLDING KNIVES ON. COME ON, SQUEEZE THE..
sera 4000!
glorious pig vision! enhanced pig viewing!!
I'M A FUCKIN' WITCH!! WITCHES RAWWWK!
MADE FROM TITANIUM AND CHEESE, THE SERA 4000 IS THE WITCH ALL OTHER WITCHES FEAR!! NOW ENCASED IN HER TOP-SHIT ARMOUR (TECHNICAL TERM) SHE NEED FEEL ALIENATED NO MORE!! ALL THOSE WHO MISUNDERSTAND HER WILL BE DESTROYED!! WITH WOOOARGH!! AND ROARRR!! HOW HOT IS SHE NOW, YOU HORNY TARTS.
YUMMY!!
GOOOOP!!
LAYS MECHA DOODY!!
MECHA DOOODY!!
PUMPACTION SPELL CANNON!! TURNS YOUR EVERYDAY OBJECTS INTO MONKEYS!! (UPGRADE PATCHES AVAILABLE) DELIGHT YOUR FRIENDS!! BEMUSE YOUR PARENTS!! THEN TURN THEM INTO MONKEYS!!
screeee.. actually it's not so bad.
FULLY WORKING LIMBS!! TOTALLY BITCH'N MAGIC SKILLS! UBER RAD ALT-CORE!! WORDS LIKE THAT MAKE DANCIN'!!
SOUPED-UP TO FIGHT A WHOLE NEW RANGE OF LICENCED CHARACTERS INCLUDING... GIANT REPTILIAN!!
I HAVE NO STORY RELEVANCE!!
EVIL HORNED SLAG!!
I MAKE COMIC BOOK REFERENCES
AND OVER ZEALOUS PREACHERS!!
YOU'RE ALL HEATHEN BUGGERS!! THIS IS SELLING PAGANISM!! YOU'LL ALL BE BURNT AS BITCHES!!
BOSH!!
SERA 4000S INTERACT WITH EACH OTHER!! LINK UP WITH FRIENDS FOR WITCHIN' TOURNAMENTS!!
when we're done we rampage on your heads!!
AT THE END OF BATTERY LIFE, THE SERA 4000 RELEASES SULPHUROUS FUMES TO AID IN RECHARGING!! (SEVENTY MILE RADIUS RECOMMENDED).
doo doo doo.
JAMIE POKE ME!
NEWLY INSTALLED!! ANTI-DISSENTER MECHANISM!!
THAT DOLL LOOKS CHEAP AND WHORISH. I PREFER THE ORIGINAL COMICS.
YEAH THE COMICS ARE HELLA COOL. AUGH!
initiate bee release!
coming soon!!
the humbly floating head!! stares at the confused!!

GUEST ART BY JAMIE SMART

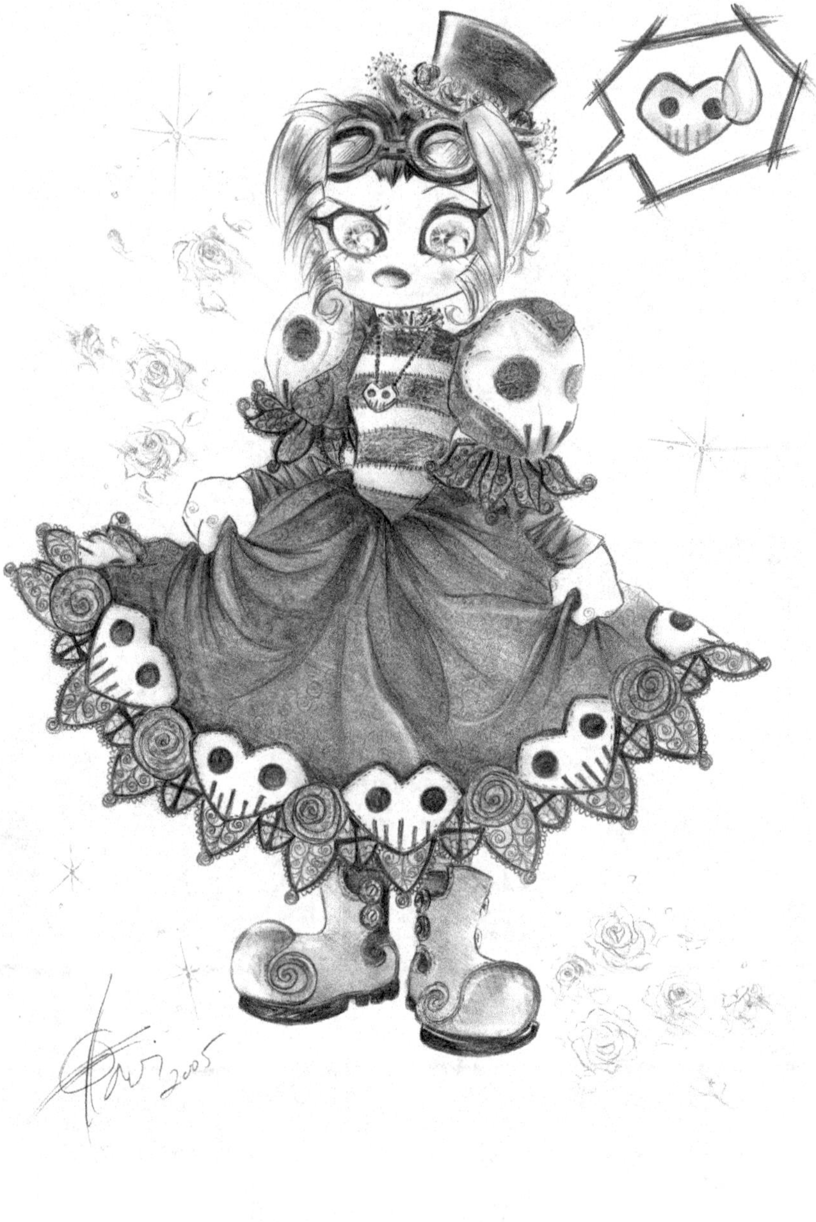

GUEST ART BY TAVISHA WOLFGARTH-SIMONS

GUEST ART BY TOMMY KOVAC

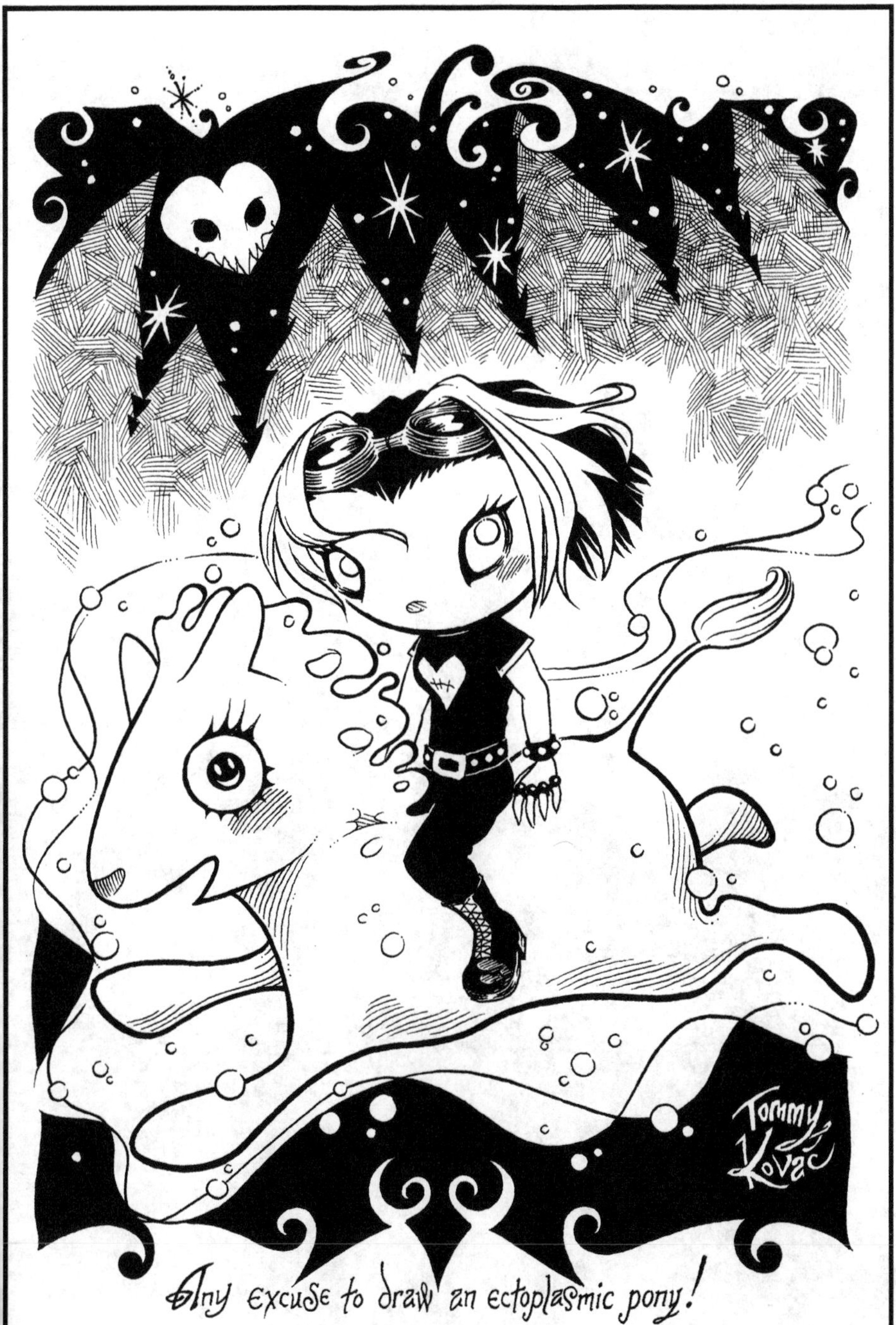
Tommy Kovac
Any excuse to draw an ectoplasmic pony!

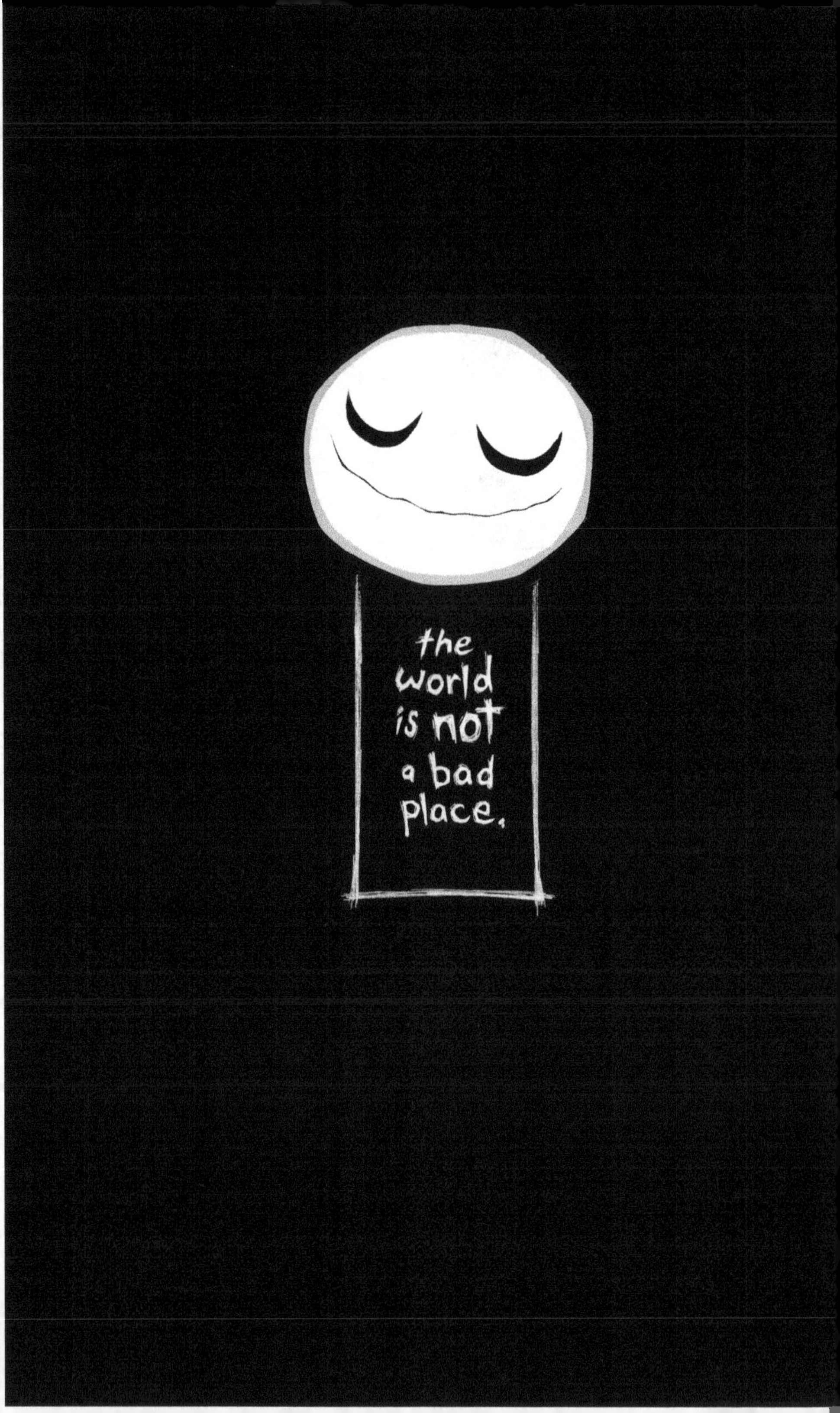
the world is not a bad place.